A TO Z
OF AFRICAN AMERICANS

AFRICAN AMERICANS
IN THE
PERFORMING ARTS

Revised Edition

Steven Otfinoski

Facts On File
An imprint of Infobase Publishing

≈

To Gregoire Mouning,
a fine actor and a good friend

≈

African Americans in the Performing Arts, Revised Edition

Copyright © 2010 by Steven Otfinoski

Facts On File, Inc.
132 West 31st Street
New York NY 10001

Library of Congress Cataloging-in-Publication Data
Otfinoski, Steven.
   African Americans in the performing arts / Steven Otfinoski.—Rev. ed.
     p. cm.—(A to Z of African Americans)
   Includes bibliographical references and index.
   ISBN 978-0-8160-7838-7
   1. African Americans in the performing arts—Biography—Dictionaries. I. Title.
   PN2286.O88 2009
   791.089'96073—dc22   2009012400

Facts On File books are available at special discounts when purchased in bulk quantities for businesses, associations, institutions, or sales promotions. Please call our Special Sales Department in New York at (212) 967-8800 or (800) 322-8755.

You can find Facts On File on the World Wide Web at http://www.factsonfile.com

Text design by Joan M. Toro
Composition by Hermitage Publishing Services
Cover printed by Sheridan Books, Ann Arbor, MI
Book printed and bound by Sheridan Books, Ann Arbor, MI
Date printed: March 2010
Printed in the United States of America

10 9 8 7 6 5 4 3 2 1

This book is printed on acid-free paper.

CONTENTS

LIST OF ENTRIES

INTRODUCTION

African Americans have been contributing to the performing arts in the United States almost from the moment they were first brought here as slaves. Music and dance and storytelling were a release from the suffering and deep loss they experienced. Participating in these art forms was a way to both keep their African traditions alive and forge new traditions in their adopted homeland. Music and dance remained the most liberating way for African Americans to express themselves creatively. Acting in theater, and later film, they were often forced to adopt stereotypical roles as bumblers (Bert Williams), exotics (Josephine Baker), and mammies (Hattie McDaniel). Through sheer talent and the power of personality, these, and many other gifted performers, managed to rise above the stereotypes, while later generations of performers broke through the race barrier to create characters expressing dignity, humor, and humanity.

It is difficult to condemn or even criticize the pioneering figures of the early 20th century. Even Stepin Fetchit, the prototype slow-walking, slow-talking, lazy black man in early Hollywood films, exhibited an individuality and comic persona that made him unique. Although he may have perpetuated a rank and offensive stereotype, he also opened the door for many black actors and actresses attempting to get into the movies.

Performing artists is a broad term, which in this work has been applied not only to actors but also to singers, musicians, comedians, dancers, choreographers, composers, and at least one classical musical conductor. Choreographers and composers have been included, however, only when they were performers as well as creators of performing works. That is why one will find Scott Joplin, Katherine Dunham, and Quincy Jones here, but not composer Ulysses Kay.

Choosing the people to include in such a work is always difficult. It is inevitable that a reader will be disappointed not to find a favorite performer or perhaps a number of them. In selecting the 192 individuals in this volume, several criteria were used. They included personal preference, historical importance, variety, and level of achievement. There are landmark figures who could not be left out—major artists such as Paul Robeson, Louis Armstrong, Bill Cosby, Diana Ross, Sidney Poitier, and Ella Fitzgerald. In addition to these cultural icons, there are many figures who are important in their field and have produced an impressive body of work. Then there are the minor figures who are included for variety, human interest, and historical importance: People such as the one-legged tap dancer Peg Leg Bates, the actress Gail Fisher, and the country singer Charley Pride.

The most difficult choices to make are from among the most contemporary performing artists. For instance, who among the many actors and singers, who are popular today, will have a lasting career? Included here are individuals who seem either to be in some way unique among their peers or who have already made a substantial contribution to their field. Only time will tell how accurate some of these judgments have been.

Being black has been important for many of these artists, and their blackness has infused their work. It is hard to find a black singer—whether popular or classical—who did not start out singing in a black church choir, more often than not with a parent as a pastor, choir director, or musician. Many of these people had to struggle against overwhelming odds—racism, poverty, abuse, drugs, and the temptations of a life of crime. Learning how they overcame these odds (though not all of them did) and not only survived but also succeeded in their chosen profession makes for inspiring reading.

Yet whether they came from the poorest urban ghetto or the privileged black middle class, many of these artists have used their gifts and celebrity to give back to the black community that produced them. Social activism is as much a part of their lives as their careers as performers. Actors such as Danny Glover and Alfre Woodard, singers such as Harry Belafonte and the late James Brown, and comedians such as Bill Cosby and Dick Greg-

ory have given their talents, time, and money to improving society both in the United States and abroad.

Some of these artists, particularly in earlier decades, have paid a price for their activism. Canada Lee, Paul Robeson, and Hazel Scott, to name a few, had their careers cut short or put on hold because of their social and political convictions.

Other artists were not overtly committed to political and social change but expressed and enriched the black experience through their own unique personality and gifts. Ethel Waters did so through her deep and abiding faith. Flip Wilson through his warm and human portrayals of ethnic characters.

Finally, the people in this book, while they often represent and express the hopes and dreams of the African-American community, should not be judged simply as reflections of the black experience. Each is an individual who has used his or her gifts to celebrate not only the black experience but also the human experience we all share. Artistic expression, in the final analysis, is universal and can be enjoyed and appreciated by all people and can empower all people, regardless of their ethnic origins.

A

Ailey, Alvin
(Alvin Ailey, Jr.)
(1931–1989) *modern dancer, choreographer, dance company director*

Alvin Ailey was one of the first choreographers to celebrate the African-American experience in the world of modern dance. Some people would go further and say Ailey was the first modern dancer and choreographer to appeal to a mass audience.

Alvin Ailey, Jr., was born on January 5, 1931, in Rogers, Texas, into a poor, single parent family. As a boy, he picked cotton alongside his mother, Lula Elizabeth Cooper, and moved with her to Los Angeles, California, when he was 11. His mother worked in an aircraft plant during World War II while Ailey attended black schools. He went to the University of California at Los Angeles (UCLA) to study literature, planning to teach. Ailey had no idea of becoming a dancer when his friend Carmen DeLavallade introduced him to dance instructor Lester Horton in 1949. He was entranced by Horton and his exciting ideas on modern dance. Soon after, Ailey left college to study with Horton and then join his dance company.

In 1953, Horton died, and Ailey took over his company. He also began to choreograph his own dances, four in 1954 alone. That year Ailey left the company and moved to New York. There he joined DeLavallade on Broadway, dancing in the musical *House of Flowers.*

Ailey developed an extremely athletic dance style. One critic described him as "a caged lion full of lashing power that he can contain or release at will." He stayed in New York where he studied under such great dancers as Martha Graham and Doris Humphrey. As a dancer he appeared in the film *Carmen Jones* (1954) and danced on and choreographed such television variety shows as *The Jack Benny Show, The Red Skelton Show,* and *The Today Show.*

In 1958, he formed the Alvin Ailey American Dance Theater (AAADT). In *Black Suite* (1958), one of the first dances he choreographed for his company, Ailey re-created incidents from his boyhood in Texas. The dance was set in a rundown bar populated by poor blacks whom he remembered. Two years later he examined another part of his youth—the Baptist church and its celebration of African-American faith—in *Revelations* (1960). The piece was set to the fervent sounds of spirituals and black gospel music. It became his most famous and popular work.

Ailey's energy and creativity soon made AAADT one of the most reputable modern dance companies in the United States. The group toured the nation and in 1962 was sent by the State Department on a tour of Australia and Southeast Asia.

Alvin Ailey was a pioneering choreographer who brought African-American themes into modern dance. *(AP Photo/Marty Reichenthal)*

In 1965, Ailey stopped dancing to devote himself to the development of his growing company. He began to showcase the work of other gifted African-American choreographers including KATHERINE DUNHAM and PEARL PRIMUS. He himself choreographed dances for other companies such as the American Ballet Theater, the Robert Joffrey Ballet, and the Paris Opera Ballet. Ailey sought out the best dancers in every ethnic and racial group, making his company one of the first in America to be completely multiracial. Other firsts followed. In 1970, AAADT became the first American dance troupe since World War II to tour the Soviet Union. In 1984, it became the first African-American troupe to perform at the Metropolitan Opera House, and in 1985, it was the first American dance troupe to tour Communist China.

Ailey was awarded the National Association for the Advancement of Colored People's (NAACP) Spingarn Medal in 1976, and in 1985, he became the first choreographer to be named distinguished professor by the City College of New York. He was a recipient of the Kennedy Center Honors for the Performing Arts in 1988 and died the following year of a blood disorder on December 1. JUDITH JAMISON, one of his leading dancers, managed the company after his death.

The Alvin Ailey American Dance Theater continues to be one of the premier modern dance companies in the world, a living legacy to the man who created it. As dance writer Allen Robertson put it, "His heartfelt celebration of black America became as popular as a musical comedy and as charged with energy as a rock concert."

Further Reading

Ailey, Alvin. *Revelations: The Autobiography of Alvin Ailey.* Secaucus, N.J.: Birch Lane Press, 1995.

Cruz, Barbara C. *Alvin Ailey: Celebrating African-American Culture in Dance.* Berkeley Heights, N.J.: Enslow Publishers, 2004.

Dunning, Jennifer. *Alvin Ailey: A Life in Dance.* Reading, Mass.: Addison-Wesley, 1996.

Further Viewing

Four by Ailey: An Evening with the Alvin Ailey American Dance Theater. Kultur Video, VHS, 1997.

Aldridge, Ira
("The African Roscius")
(ca. 1805–1867) *stage actor*

Ira Aldridge was the first major African-American actor in the Western world, but he had to find fame on the stages of Europe because of the racism that pervaded 19th-century America.

Little is known of Aldridge's early life; even the date and place of his birth are in question. He was probably born sometime between 1805 and 1807 in Senegal, Africa; New York City; or Bel Air, Maryland. Some sources claim his father, Daniel Aldridge, heir to Senegalese princes, was brought to the United States by a missionary and sent to Schenectady College in upstate New York.

Wherever he was born, Aldridge went on to attend the African Free School in New York City, where he first fell in love with the theater. He performed professionally at New York's African Theater, portraying such great Shakespearean characters as Hamlet and Romeo in all-black productions. Discouraged by the prejudice and ridicule African-American performers faced, he became determined to emigrate to Europe to pursue acting. Aldridge made the transatlantic voyage in 1825 and settled in Glasgow, Scotland. He studied voice and drama at the University of Glasgow and became a dresser for distinguished British actor Henry Wallack. Soon he was playing small roles in London productions, often as an African slave.

Aldridge's breakthrough role was Shakespeare's tragic hero Othello. He was probably the first black to play the jealous Moor; before that white actors played the part in blackface. He was so convincing as Othello that sometimes audience members would cry out and try to stop him as he murdered his innocent wife, Desdemona, in the play's climax. The London critics hailed Aldridge as "the African Roscius," after the great Roman actor who, like him, was equally adept at both tragic and comic roles. Aldridge also played other leading Shakespearean roles, including Richard II, Shylock in *The Merchant of Venice,* and, when he was older, King Lear.

Now wealthy and famous, Aldridge bought a house near London, married an Englishwoman, and became the first black to be knighted. He became friends with such celebrities as Frenchman Alexandre Dumas, the author of *The Three Musketeers,* who himself was black.

In 1852, Aldridge made his first tour of the European continent. He played before Frederick William IV of Prussia, Queen Victoria of England, and other heads of state. During an 1858 tour of Russia, he became friends with author Leo Tolstoy and his wife.

When his first wife died in 1864, Aldridge married a Swedish baroness. He was touring Russia and Poland in the summer of 1867 when an invitation arrived to perform in his native America. Before he could respond, he suddenly fell ill and died in Łódź, Poland. Ira Aldridge was buried in the Evangelical Cemetery in Łódź. His grave is cared for to this day by the Society of Polish Artists of Film and Theatre. A chair is dedicated to the memory of this pioneering African-American actor at the Shakespeare Memorial Theatre in Stratford-upon-Avon, England.

Further Reading

Lindfors, Bernth, ed. *Ira Aldridge: The African Roscius.* Reprint, Rochester, N.Y.: University of Rochester Press, 2007.

Marshall, Herbert. *Ira Aldridge: Negro Tragedian.* Washington, D.C.: Howard University Press, 1993.

Allen, Debbie

(1950–   ) *dancer, singer, actress, choreographer, director, television producer*

Few American performing artists have excelled in so many fields as Debbie Allen. One writer has compared her explosive talent and energy to "a stick of dynamite."

She was born on January 16, 1950, in Houston, Texas. Her father, Andrew Allen, was a dentist, and her mother, Vivian Ayers, was an artist and poet who was nominated for a Pulitzer Prize in 1953. Allen started dance lessons when she was three and was inspired to go on the stage after seeing ALVIN AILEY's ballet *Revelations.* After her parents separated, her mother took her to Mexico for a year to study at the Ballet Nacional de

Mexico. At age 14, Allen was admitted to the Houston Foundation for Ballet, where she was the only black dancer.

She graduated cum laude from Howard University in Washington, D.C., in 1971 and worked for a time as dance director at the Duke Ellington School of the Performing Arts. That same year she was hired as a dancer in the Broadway musical *Purlie*. Allen left the show after six weeks to become a principal dancer in George Faison's company, the Universal Dance Experience. In Faison's dance *Ti-Jean and His Brothers*, Allen portrayed a dancing firefly whose fire keeps going out. She returned to Broadway in 1973 to play a featured role in the musical *Raisin*, based on Lorraine Hansberry's play *A Raisin in the Sun*.

By 1975, she was beginning to find work in television. Her first assignment was acting in a Pampers disposable diaper commercial with her sister PHYLICIA RASHAD, who would go on to fame as BILL COSBY's wife on the 1980s sitcom *The*

Debbie Allen has shown the breadth of her talent in dance, theater, television, and film. *(Photofest)*

Cosby Show. In 1979, Allen played author Alex Haley's wife in the miniseries *Roots: The Next Generation.* She was a cheerleader in her first feature film, a basketball comedy entitled *The Fish That Saved Pittsburgh* (1979). During shooting, she met future husband Norm Nixon, a basketball player with the Los Angeles Clippers. They have three children.

Debbie Allen broke through to the big time in 1980. She earned glowing reviews and a Tony nomination as the fiery Anita in the Broadway revival of the musical *West Side Story*. She also played a bit part as a dance instructor in the movie *Fame*, about life at New York City's High School for the Performing Arts. She had only two lines in the film but made such an impression that when the TV network NBC adapted the film to a television series the next year, Allen was cast in it. She took the role of teacher Lydia Grant on the condition she would also be the show's choreographer. The producers agreed, and Allen became the hardest-working person on *Fame*, arriving at the studio every morning at six. At the end of its first season, *Fame* won five Emmys, one of them for Debbie Allen's choreography. NBC canceled the show after its second season, but it was quickly picked up by MGM and Metromedia and put into syndication. Allen became one of its producers and directors.

Full of confidence, Allen cowrote, directed, and played in her first one-hour television special *Dancin' in the Wings* in 1985. The following year she made a triumphant return to Broadway in the revival of the musical *Sweet Charity* and earned her second Tony nomination as best actress in a musical.

Fame went off the air in 1987. Since then, Allen has concentrated most of her energies on directing. She was the regular director of the sitcom *A Different World*, a spin-off from *The Cosby Show.* She has more recently directed episodes of the sitcoms *The Fresh Prince of Bel-Air* and *In the House* as well as several television movies. In 2001, she directed and starred in the PBS film *The Old*

Settler, which costarred her sister. The same year Allen received a Lifetime Achievement Award from the organization American Women in Radio and Television. In 2008, she directed her sister and JAMES EARL JONES in an all-black production of Tennessee Williams's *Cat on a Hot Tin Roof* on Broadway. Allen played the school principal in an updated film version of *Fame* (2009).

Further Reading

"Debbie Allen." *Current Biography Yearbook 1987.* New York: H. W. Wilson, 1988.

Shelton, Marla. "Allen, Debbie." The Museum of Broadcast Communications Web site. Available online. URL: http://www.museumtv/archives/etv/A/htmlA/allendebbie/allendebbie.htm. Downloaded on January 26, 2009.

Further Viewing

Fame: The Complete First Season (1982). MGM Home Video, DVD, 2005.

The Old Settler. PBS Home Video, VHS/DVD, 2001, 2005.

Anderson, Eddie "Rochester"

(1905–1977) *actor*

Perhaps no African-American actor has been as closely associated with a role over a longer period of time than Eddie Anderson was with Rochester, the wily valet and constant foil to comedian Jack Benny. It was a role he perfected over more than a quarter century on radio and television, and in movies.

Eddie Anderson was born on September 18, 1905, in Oakland, California. His father, Big Ed Anderson, was a minstrel performer and his mother, Ella May, a former circus tightrope walker. He supposedly got his trademark gravelly voice from straining his vocal cords while hawking newspapers as a youngster. Anderson's first job in show business was as a member of a theatrical chorus line. He later formed a song-and-dance

trio, Three Black Aces, with his brother Cornelius and a friend.

Until 1937, Anderson's biggest break in the business was playing Noah in the film adaptation of the all-black Broadway show *The Green Pastures* (1936). All that changed when Jack Benny hired him for a one-shot appearance on his popular radio show on Easter Sunday. Anderson played a Pullman porter, and his gravelly voice and comic timing made him an instant hit with the national radio audience. The one-shot appearance turned into a 28-year run. He was given the regular role of Rochester van Jones, Benny's personal valet.

Although the part contained the inevitable racial stereotyping of the time, Anderson made Rochester into a far more full-bodied and human character than the shuffling numskulls played by Willie Best, STEPIN FETCHIT, and other black male actors in Hollywood. Rochester was intelligent, clever, and showed far more common sense than his weak-willed boss. The Anderson-Benny team was so popular that Anderson appeared with the comedian in four Hollywood movies, including the western spoof *Buck Benny Rides Again* (1940). By then, Anderson was so closely identified with the character of Rochester that he incorporated the name into his own in all his billings and later officially changed his name to Eddie Rochester Anderson.

On his own, Anderson appeared in a number of other films, including a small role in *Gone With the Wind* (1939). In 1943, he starred in the all-black musical film *Cabin in the Sky.* As the protagonist Little Joe Jackson, Anderson had to choose between the devil's seductress, LENA HORNE, and faithful wife ETHEL WATERS. It was a test of Anderson's acting ability that he was able to hold his own with his two high-powered leading ladies.

When *The Jack Benny Show* came to television in 1950, Anderson's Rochester added physical comedy to his vocal dexterity. His rolling eyes and panicky tics became the trademarks of a master comic who could match Benny laugh for laugh.

The two were often referred to as "television's first interracial comedy team." After the show was canceled in 1965, Anderson effectively retired from show business. His last appearance in a film was in a small part in the all-star comedy extravaganza *It's a Mad Mad Mad Mad World* in 1963. He died on February 28, 1977, the most beloved African-American actor of television's golden age.

Further Reading

Anderson, Eddie. "Rochester." BlackPast.org. Available online. URL: http://www.blackpast-org/?q=aah/anderson-eddie-rochester 1905–1977. Downloaded on February 13, 2009.

Bogle, Donald. *Prime Time Blues: African Americans on Network Television*. New York: Farrar, Straus & Giroux, 2002, pp. 51–55.

Further Viewing

The Best of the Jack Benny Show, Vols. 1 and 2 (1950). Good Times Video, 2 DVDs, 2004.

Cabin in the Sky (1943). Warner Home Video, DVD, 2006.

Anderson, Marian

(1902–1993) *concert and opera singer*

Possessed with one of the most beautiful voices of the 20th century, Marian Anderson was a courageous pioneer both on the concert stage and in the arena of civil rights.

She was born on February 17, 1902, in Philadelphia, Pennsylvania, the oldest of four daughters of John and Anna Anderson. She first sang at age six in the local Baptist church where her father was an usher. When she was eight her father bought her a used piano, but he could not afford to pay for music lessons. The young girl taught herself to read music and to play the piano. She attended South Philadelphia High School where the principal was impressed by her rich contralto voice and helped find her a voice teacher. At 18, she gained an audition with the famous vocal teacher Giuseppe Boghetti. Boghetti was reluctant to take on a new student and found little remarkable in Anderson when she first sang for him. But when she began to sing the Negro spiritual "Deep River," tears came to his eyes, and he immediately found a place for her. When the funds saved by her church ran out after a year of lessons, Boghetti gave her free lessons for another year.

In 1925, a promoter convinced the young Anderson she was ready to give her first major concert. She appeared at New York's distinguished Town Hall in a concert that was a complete disaster. Few people came to hear her, and her nervousness caused her to sing less than her best. Anderson was devastated by the experience and may have given up on a singing career if not for her mother's encouragement.

In 1927, she competed with 300 other singers to win the Rosenwald Fellowship, which paid for her to study music in Europe. After studying in Germany, she sang all over Europe and in Salzburg, Austria, met the renowned conductor Arturo Toscanini. He told her that she had "a voice that comes once in a century."

In France on another European tour in 1935, she met the impresario Sol Hurok. He promised that he could arrange an American concert tour for her. Hurok's influence overcame the racial prejudice that had previously prevented Anderson from singing in American concert halls. The tour was a great success, and in 1936, she performed at the White House for President Franklin D. Roosevelt and First Lady Eleanor Roosevelt, who became a good friend.

When Anderson was scheduled to sing at Constitution Hall in 1939, the Daughters of the American Revolution (DAR), a women's organization that owned the building, said the dates she sought were unavailable. The racial prejudice behind this decision infuriated many Americans, including Eleanor Roosevelt. The first lady resigned from the DAR in protest and helped arrange for Anderson to sing on the steps of the Lincoln Memorial on Easter Sunday. The concert was a historic event that was heard live by 75,000 people and on radio by a listening audience of 2 million. The event made Marian Anderson not only one of the most celebrated singers in America but a symbol of African-American pride and achievement.

By 1941, Anderson was one of the highest paid concert singers in the country. Over the next quarter century, she sang all over the world and received countless awards and honorary degrees. In October 1954, she signed a contract to perform at the Metropolitan Opera in New York City. An editorial in the *New York Times* observed, "When there was 'discrimination' against Miss Anderson the real suffering was not hers but ours. It was we who were impoverished, not she."

On January 7, 1955, a month before her 58th birthday, Marian Anderson performed at the Met as Ulrica, the fortune-teller in Verdi's opera *A Masked Ball.* She was the first African American to sing solo at the Met and blazed the way for other black singers including LEONTYNE PRICE.

In 1957, Anderson was named a goodwill ambassador by the State Department and sent on a 12-nation tour that included India and the Far East. The following year President Dwight D. Eisenhower appointed her a delegate to the United Nations. On Easter Sunday 1965, exactly 26 years after her historic concert at the Lincoln Memorial, Marian Anderson sang in public for the last time at New York's Carnegie Hall. When the Kennedy Center for the Performing Arts in Washington began awarding special Lifetime Achievement Awards in the Performing Arts, Marian Anderson was the first recipient. She died April 8, 1993, in Portland, Oregon, at age 91.

Further Reading

Anderson, Marian. *My Lord, What a Morning: An Autobiography.* Champaign: University of Illinois Press, 2002.

Arsenault, Raymond. *The Sound of Freedom: Marian Anderson, The Lincoln Memorial and the Concert That Awakened America.* London: Bloomsbury Press, 2008.

Ferris, Jeri. *What I Had Was Singing: The Story of Marian Anderson.* Minneapolis, Minn.: Carolrhoda Books, 1994.

Freedman, Russell. *The Voice That Challenged a Nation: Marian Anderson and the Struggle for Equal Rights.* Boston, Mass.: Clarion Books, 2009 (YA).

Keiler, Allen. *Marian Anderson: A Singer's Journey.* New York: Scribners, 2000.

Further Listening

Spirituals. BMG/RCA Victor, CD, 1999.

Further Viewing

Marian Anderson: A Portrait in Music. Video Artists International, DVD, 2004.

Armstrong, Louis

(Daniel Louis Armstrong, "Satchmo," "Pops")
(1901–1971) *jazz trumpeter, singer, bandleader*

If jazz is America's greatest contribution to the world of music, then Louis Armstrong is undoubtedly the artist who most helped to shape this unique musical genre.

He was born Daniel Louis Armstrong in abject poverty in the Storyville district of New Orleans, Louisiana, birthplace of jazz, on August 4, 1901. His father Willie abandoned the family at about the time of his birth, and Louis was raised by his mother Mary-Ann, a woman to whom he attributed much of his success. His first experience with music was singing on street corners with a harmony quartet as a youth. One New Year's Eve, when he was 11 or 12 years old, he fired a pistol in the air to celebrate and was arrested by police and sent to the Colored Waifs' Home for two years. While at the home Armstrong learned to play cornet in the resident brass band. He fell in love with the instrument and on his return home decided to become a professional musician.

Not having the money to buy a cornet, Armstrong borrowed one whenever he could and played

Louis Armstrong was as well known for his inimitable singing as for his trumpet playing. *(Sipa via AP Images)*

local dates with small bands. The money he earned supplemented his income from his day job—delivering coal on a horse-drawn cart. But success as a musician was not long in coming. By 1917, the legendary cornetist and New Orleans bandleader Joseph "King" Oliver hired Armstrong for his band, and he became the young man's mentor. When Oliver left for Chicago in 1919, Armstrong, who was very much a shy, southern boy, remained in New Orleans. He played on riverboats on the Mississippi River with leading jazz bands.

Oliver summoned Armstrong to Chicago in 1922 to play second horn in his Creole Jazz Band. Their improvised duets were the talk of the town. Lillian Hardin, the band's pianist, befriended Armstrong and encouraged his ambitions. When they married in 1924, Lillian gave him the push he needed to leave Oliver and strike out on his own.

The couple moved to New York City where he played in Fletcher Henderson's band. Within a year Armstrong formed his own small ensemble, the Hot Five (later to become the Hot Seven). He began to record the musical numbers that would establish him as a leading jazz soloist. Today, such numbers as "Cornet Chop Suey" (1926), "Potato Head Blues" (1927), and "West End Blues" (1928) are considered classics of the form and among the greatest jazz recordings ever made.

In these and other recordings, Armstrong broke with the old style of jazz in which the different instruments fused together into one sound. He played a supple and graceful music that was a far cry from the jerky rhythms of early New Orleans jazz. Armstrong's music swung but was also extremely lyrical. "His sound carries the feeling and the meaning of jazz more than any other

musician's," notes jazz trumpeter WYNTON MAR-
SALIS. "It's warm, it's intelligent, it's spiritual, it's
tawdry, it's worldly, it's provincial. Anything you
want, he has it in his sound."

During this period, Armstrong made his other
great contribution to jazz. The story goes that during a recording session in 1926 he dropped the
sheet music of the song "Heebie Jeebies" and
improvised nonsense sounds for the lyrics. This
"scat singing," as it came to be called, was something new and later jazz singers adapted the style.
Armstrong, however, remained the supreme scat
singer. His rough-hewn voice was hardly appealing in a conventional way, but it exuded such a
warmth and personality that it was irresistible and
made him one of the most recognizable and
beloved singers of the 20th century.

Armstrong's inimitable voice also made him a
pop star. From 1926 to 1954, he had no fewer than
72 hit records on the pop charts. On stage he was
famous for his toothy smile, clownish expressions,
and his favorite prop, a big white handkerchief that
he would perpetually use to wipe his sweaty face.

Armstrong's talents as an all-around entertainer took him to Hollywood where he became
the first African American to appear regularly in
motion pictures. He was featured, often as himself, in more than 50 films. Some of the most
memorable ones were *Pennies from Heaven* (1936),
Cabin in the Sky (1943), and *High Society* (1956),
where he performed songs by Cole Porter with his
old friend, crooner Bing Crosby.

Despite all his success, Armstrong was not
immune to the racism in American society. For 35
years he had a white manager, the ruthless Joe
Glaser, who successfully ran his career but who
also took 50 percent of Armstrong's earnings.
Although realistic about racism, Armstrong never
let it dampen his enthusiasm for life and people,
regardless of their color. With his band, he traveled the world, playing in Africa, South America,
Europe, and elsewhere as an unofficial goodwill
ambassador for his country.

By the 1940s, Louis Armstrong and his music
were considered old-fashioned and unpopular
with a new generation of jazz musicians and fans.
It took another decade or so for his achievements
to be fully appreciated. He was criticized in the
1950s and 1960s for not taking a more active role
in the Civil Rights movement. Some black critics
even called him an Uncle Tom and branded his
stage performance an embarrassing example of
ethnic stereotyping. They forgot that Armstrong
belonged to an earlier generation and another
mindset. Activism for him was bringing people
together through his music, which he did better
than anyone.

Armstrong's popularity as an entertainer
reached its pinnacle in 1964, when his recording
of "Hello, Dolly!"—from the Broadway musical of
the same name—displaced the Beatles from the
top spot on the pop charts. At the Grammy
Awards in April 1965, Armstrong's record earned
him the award for best male vocal performance.

Nearly 70 years old, Armstrong was feeling his
age. He had suffered his first heart attack in 1959
and was in declining health. When he died in his
sleep on July 6, 1971, in New York City, his passing was mourned around the world. Many people
felt as if they had lost a close friend. Perhaps Armstrong himself best summed up his incredible
popularity: "People love me and my music and you
know I love them. The minute I walk on the
bandstand, they know they're going to get something good. I see to that."

In 1972, Louis Armstrong posthumously
received the Grammy Lifetime Achievement
Award and was inducted into the Rock and Roll
Hall of Fame in 1990 as an early influence on rock
music. His personal archives are preserved at
Queens College in New York City.

Further Reading

Armstrong, Louis. *Louis Armstrong, In His Own Words: Selected Writings.* New York: Oxford University Press, 1999.

Bergreen, Laurence. *Louis Armstrong*. New York: Broadway Books, 1997.

Giddins, Gary. *Satchmo: The Genius of Louis Armstrong*. Reprint, New York: Da Capo Press, 2001.

Further Listening

All Time Greatest Hits. MCA, CD, 1994.

The Best of Ella Fitzgerald & Louis Armstrong: 20th Century Masters. Verve, CD, 2007.

Ken Burns JAZZ Collection: Louis Armstrong. Sony/Columbia, CD, 2000.

Louis Armstrong: Greatest Performances of the '30s, '40s, '50s and '60s. Time-Life Records, CD, 2008.

B

Babyface
(Kenneth Brian Edmonds)
(1959–) *R & B singer; songwriter; record, film, and television producer*

No one so dominated rhythm and blues (R & B) music in the 1990s as writer, producer, and recording artist Kenny Edmonds, better known to the world as Babyface.

Kenneth Brian Edmonds was born on April 10, 1959, in Indianapolis, Indiana. His father Marvin died of lung cancer when he was in the eighth grade, leaving his mother Barbara, a processing plant manager, to raise six sons on her own. In school, Edmonds was an incurable romantic and painfully shy. He wrote his first love song to a girl named Rhonda whom he didn't have the courage to even talk to.

After high school, he joined several music groups such as Manchild, Tarnished Silver, and the Crowd Pleasers. In 1983, he joined the group the Deele and became close friends with drummer Antonio "L.A." Reid. Edmonds wrote three songs for the Deele's debut album. One song, "Street Beat," became a top-30 R & B single. Wanting to have control over the songs he wrote, Edmonds began producing them. With Reid he wrote half the songs for the next Deele album, *Material Thangz* (1986), and also produced it.

He got his nickname when another musician greeted him with "What's up, Babyface?" When the lead singer of the Deele introduced him later as "Babyface," the girls in the audience went wild. The name stuck.

Babyface and L.A. became a hot writing and producing team. In 1987 they had their first number-one R & B hit with "Rock Steady," sung by the Whispers. The next year they wrote and produced no less than eight number-one R & B singles, including "Girlfriend" for the Pebbles and "Every Little Step" for Bobby Brown.

Babyface's first effort at producing his own album, *Lovers,* was not successful. But his next album, *Tender Lover* (1989), sold 2 million copies and produced a handful of hit singles, including "Whip Appeal" and "It's No Crime." It was followed by the albums *A Closer Look* (1991) and *The Cool Is You* (1993), which won a Grammy Award for best R & B album. The same year he won the best R & B song award for "End of the Road," sung by Boyz II Men. This song remained number one for 13 weeks, breaking the record for weeks at number one set by Elvis Presley's "Heartbreak Hotel" back in 1956. Babyface entered the record books again two years later with "I'll Make Love to You," again performed by Boyz II Men, which stayed in the top spot for 14 weeks.

Having been married and divorced in the 1980s, Babyface met his second wife, Tracy McQuain, when she auditioned for the music video for "Whip Appeal." She got the part but had to drop out when she came down with chicken pox. Several months later Babyface ran into McQuain on the street and they began dating. They married in 1992 and have one son, Brandon. The couple divorced in 2007 but still have an amicable working partnership.

In 1994, Babyface ended his long collaboration with L.A., although they continue to be partners in their Atlanta-based label, LaFace. Having tied MICHAEL JACKSON's 12 Grammy nominations in one year and having been responsible for more than 30 number-one songs and a total of more than 110 top-40 singles, Babyface has gone on to conquer another medium—film. He produced the soundtrack for the film *Waiting to Exhale* (1996) and wrote the Oscar-nominated song "When You Believe" sung by WHITNEY HOUSTON and Mariah Carey in the Disney animated film *Prince of Egypt* (1998). His and his ex-wife's film production company, Edmonds Entertainment have release such films as *Soul Food* (1997) and *Josie and the Pussycats* (2001). They are executive producers of the Black Entertainment Television (BET) reality series *College Hill* (2004–   ).

Of Babyface's achievements, rock critic Ron Wynn has written, "His alternately innocent, hurt, and disillusioned vocals are the decade's equivalent of the soul/love songs of the '70s and '80s."

Babyface has been named Broadcast Music Incorporated (BMI) songwriter of the year six times and was twice named *Billboard* magazine's songwriter of the year.

Further Reading

"Babyface." *Current Biography Yearbook 1998.* New York: H. W. Wilson, 1998.
"Kenneth Edmonds." Wikipedia. Available online. URL: http://en-wikipedia.org/wiki/Kenneth_Edmonds. Downloaded on October 23, 2009.

Further Listening

Babyface: A Collection of His Greatest Hits. Sony/Epic, CD, 2000.
Playlist. Mercury, CD, 2007.

Badu, Erykah
(Erica Wright)
(1971–   )   *R & B singer, songwriter, actress*

Looking like an African princess in her huge turbans and possessing a voice that has been compared to BILLIE HOLIDAY's, Erykah Badu is one of the most intriguing of contemporary rhythm and blues (R & B) singers.

She was born Erica Wright on February 26, 1971, in Dallas, Texas. Her father, William Wright, left the family when she was a child, and she was raised by her mother Kolleen. Badu studied dance and drama at Booker T. Washington High School for the Performing and Visual Arts. After high school, she became a teacher and sang part time until landing a regular gig touring with rap and R & B groups. By now, she had taken the name Badu which means "to manifest the truth" in Arabic. She was the opening act for singer D'Angelo when she was discovered by producer Kenneth Marsenburg who signed her to Kedar Records in 1996.

Her debut album, *Baduizm* (1997), was almost completely self-written and created an immediate stir in the music world. Many reviewers saw it as a unique blending of traditional soul music with the new-style electronic R & B of the 1990s. Several tracks featured the hip-hop group the Roots and jazz bassist Ron Carter. *Baduizm* reached number one on the R & B charts and earned Badu a Grammy for best R & B album. The single "On and On" earned her a second Grammy for best female R & B vocal performance.

Pregnant with her second child by rapper Dre of the group Outkast, Badu joined the '97 Smokin' Grooves Tour and later made the unusual move of releasing a live disk, *Live,* as her second album. She took some time off to be with her new son, Seven, while making guest appearances on several records, including the Roots' Grammy-winning single, "You Got Me." Badu also began an acting career, playing a swamp queen in *Blues Brothers 2000* (1998). She had a more substantial role in *The Cider House Rules* (1999).

Her second album, *Mama's Gun* (2000), solidified Badu's reputation as a serious artist. Rock critic Steve Knopper called it "a gorgeous patchwork of soul, rock, reggae, and deeply personal lyrics." Recorded at the Tuff Gang studios of late reggae star Bob Marley in Jamaica, the album included the hit single "Bag Lady" and "In Love With You," a love duet sung with Marley's son, Stephen. Badu's album *Worldwide Underground* (2003) earned four Grammy nominations. *New Amerykah, Part One (4th World War)* was released in 2008 and is the first of a promised trilogy. Badu has had two more children, a daughter and a son, by rappers D.O.C. and Jay Electronica, the latter of whom she now lives with.

Further Reading

"Erykah Badu." All Music Guide Web site. Available online. URL: http://www.allmusic.com/cg/amg. dll?p=amg&sql=11.kifpxq9hldke. Downloaded on February 13, 2009.

McIver, Joel. *Erykah Badu: The First Lady of Neo Soul.* London: Sanctuary Publishing, 2002.

Further Listening

Baduizm. Universal Records, CD, 1997.

Mama's Gun. Motown, CD, 2000.

New Amerykah, Part One (4th World War). Motown, CD, 2008.

Further Viewing

The Cider House Rules (1999). Miramax Home Entertainment, VHS/DVD, 2001/2000.

Bailey, Pearl
(Pearl Mae Bailey)
(1918–1990) *singer, actress*

As well known for her sassy repartee as her winning way with a song, Pearl Bailey was one of the most beloved entertainers of her time.

She was born on March 29, 1918, in Newport News, Virginia, to Joseph James and Ella Mae Bai-

The beloved singer and actress Pearl Bailey strikes a characteristic pose. *(Photo courtesy of Showtime Archives, Toronto, and Pictorial Press)*

ley. Her father was a Pentecostal preacher, and she grew up singing and dancing to the spirited music of his church. The family moved to Washington, D.C., and then to Philadelphia when she was still a child. There she won an amateur singing contest and danced in the mining towns of Pennsylvania for $15 a week. At age 15, Bailey got her first job singing in a Washington nightclub.

By the mid-1930s, Bailey was a vocalist with songwriter Noble Sissle's band. She was already developing her unique singing style, sprinkling sly asides and dryly delivered ad libs through her songs, which she sang in a deep, husky voice. She went on to sing with other big bands in the early 1940s, most notably those of Cootie Williams, CAB CALLOWAY, and COUNT BASIE.

In 1946, Bailey made her Broadway debut in the Harold Arlen–Johnny Mercer musical *St. Louis Woman* and was hailed as a new theatrical star. The following year she made her film debut in *Variety Girl,* singing the hit song, "Tired." She married drummer Louis Bellson, her fourth husband, in 1952. Formerly with DUKE ELLINGTON's band, Bellson devoted himself to his wife's career, and the interracial marriage lasted 37 years until her death.

The year 1954 was the biggest yet for the still-rising star. Bailey starred on Broadway as Madame Fleur in another Harold Arlen musical, *House of Flowers,* and made a strong impression as a play-girl in *Carmen Jones,* the all-black film adaptation of George Bizet's opera *Carmen.* Other solid film roles followed in *That Certain Feeling* (1956) and *St. Louis Blues* (1958). In the latter she played NAT KING COLE's aunt, although she was only a year older than the singer.

Bailey continued to sing in cabarets and appeared regularly on television variety shows. She was a guest, along with dancer BILL ROBINSON, the first time comedian Milton Berle hosted the Texaco Star Theater in June 1948. In 1971, she hosted her own variety show on ABC TV from the Hollywood Palace, but it lasted only a few months.

Bailey returned to the Broadway stage after a 13-year absence as a replacement in the lead role of Dolly Levine in the smash musical *Hello, Dolly!* She played Dolly again in 1975 in an all-black Broadway revival and won the Tony Award for best actress in a musical. She loved the role, which she said gave her the chance to "sing, dance, say intelligent words on stage, love and be loved and deliver what God gave me—and I'm dressed up besides."

Love and God were central to Bailey's life and career. She was a voracious reader and wrote a string of best-selling books about her life and interests, filled with wit and inspiration. She announced her retirement at age 58 and devoted much of the rest of her life to humanitarian causes. In 1975, she was named a special goodwill ambassador to the United Nations, a post she held through three presidential administrations. Bailey tirelessly spoke out and raised money for the world's poor, AIDS research, child abuse, and literacy. In her 60s, she decided to get a college education and graduated from Georgetown University in Washington, D.C., with a degree in theology. In 1988, Bailey was awarded the Medal of Freedom by President Ronald Reagan. The Women's International Center presented her with their Living Legacy Award in 1989. She died on August 17, 1990 at age 72.

"I am not a liberated woman," Pearl Bailey once wrote about herself. "I am a woman who achieves. I can do about what a man can do, but I want to keep my right to blush."

Further Reading

Bailey, Pearl. *Between You and Me: A Heartfelt Memoir of Learning, Loving and Living.* New York: Doubleday, 1989.

Boyle, Donald. *Toms, Coons, Mulattoes Mammies & Bucks: An Interpretive History of Blacks in American Films.* New York: Continuum, 1997, pp. 183–190.

Brandt, Keith. *Pearl Bailey, with a Song in Her Heart.* Matawan, N.J.: Troll Communications, 1992.

Further Listening

The Very Best of Pearl Bailey. EMI, CD, 2007.

Further Viewing

Carmen Jones (1954). Fox/Lorber Home Video, VHS/DVD, 1994/2002.

Baker, Josephine

(Freda Josephine MacDonald, "The Black Venus")
(1906–1975) *dancer, singer, actress, social activist*

Ignored and unappreciated in her native America, Josephine Baker became a superstar in France in the 1920s and 1930s, embodying for Europeans the ideal of the exotic black woman.

She was born Freda Josephine MacDonald on June 3, 1906, in St. Louis, Missouri, to unwed parents, Louis Carson and Cary MacDonald. Her father played the drums in a band, and her mother was a washerwoman. Her mother later married Louis Baker, from whom Freda took her surname. She first worked as a maid in white homes at age eight. Baker ran away at 13, got married, and became a dancer in a traveling vaudeville show. She eventually ended up in New York where she auditioned for the all-black Broadway musical *Shuffle Along* (1921), but she was rejected for being too thin and too dark. Later she was hired and became the show's sensation as the comic girl in the chorus line.

In 1925, Baker went to Paris, France, to perform in the show *La Revue Nègre*. The show was a flop, but Baker created a sensation in the finale entitled "La Danse de Sauvage." She wildly danced the Charleston wearing nothing but a ring of feathers around her waist. The French found her exotic image fascinating, and she was quickly hired to perform at the legendary Parisian music hall, the Folies-Bergère. Her exotic costumes, exuberant dancing, and sense of humor soon made her a national obsession.

Baker became one of the highest-paid entertainers in France, and in the 1930s, she starred in a string of movies. She became known for her flamboyant off-stage life and kept such exotic pets as monkeys, snakes, a turkey, and a pig. Her favorite pet was a leopard named Chiquita that she walked on a leash through the streets of Paris.

Baker's fame in Europe, however, did not travel well across the Atlantic. When she appeared on Broadway in 1936 in the *Ziegfeld Follies*, she was a flop. Americans may have found her act too sophisticated and may also have resented a poor, black girl from St. Louis becoming a celebrity in Europe. Disappointed, Baker returned to France and immediately became a French citizen.

During World War II, she worked as an ambulance driver. When the Germans took over France, she gathered intelligence for the French Resistance. Baker also entertained French troops in Africa and the Middle East. For her patriotic efforts she was later awarded the Croix de Guerre and the Chevalier of the Legion d'Honneur.

She returned to the United States in 1951 and took a firm stand on civil rights. While touring, she refused to appear before segregated audiences or stay in segregated hotels. For this courageous stance, the National Association for the Advancement of Colored People (NAACP) named her most outstanding woman of the year. When she was refused service at New York's Stork Club because she was black, Baker got into a verbal fight with right-wing newspaper columnist Walter Winchell. Winchell labeled her a communist in his column, and she again became a subject of controversy.

In 1954, Baker and the second of her five husbands, French orchestra leader Jo Bouillon, adopted the first of a dozen children of different nationalities. For this reason, she called her country estate a World Village. Baker returned to the United States in the early 1960s and gave a benefit concert at New York's Carnegie Hall for civil rights groups. In 1963, she participated in the historic March on Washington led by Martin Luther King, Jr.

Baker's last years were sad ones. In 1969, she and her family were evicted from her chateau and it was auctioned off to pay her many debts. Princess Grace of Monaco generously gave her a villa to live in. She suffered two heart attacks and a stroke but nevertheless staged a comeback in 1973. Baker gave a triumphant concert at Carnegie Hall in early 1975, then returned to Paris for a gala to celebrate the 50th anniversary of her arrival in France. Four days later, on April 12, 1975, she died of a cerebral hemorrhage. Twenty thousand people attended her funeral in Paris. The following year Josephine Baker was named to the Black Filmmakers Hall of Fame.

Josephine Baker conquered a nation and a continent through the sheer force of her personality.

A made-for-television film about her life, *The Josephine Baker Story,* was shown on Home Box Office (HBO) in 1991 with actress Lynn Whitfield playing Baker.

Further Reading

Baker, Jean-Claude, with Chris Chase. *Josephine: The Hungry Heart.* Lanham, Md.: Cooper Square Press, 2001.

Haney, Lynn. *Naked at the Feast: A Biography of Josephine Baker.* London: Robson Books, 2003.

Rosette, Bennetta Jules, and Tyler Stovall. *Josephine Baker: Image and Icon.* St. Louis, Mo.: Reedy Press, 2006.

Further Listening

A Centenary Tribute: Songs from 1930–1953. Sepia Recordings, CD, 2006.

Further Viewing

The Josephine Baker Collection (Zou Zou/Princess Tam Tam, Siren of the Tropics). Kino Video, DVD box set, 2007.

The Josephine Baker Story (1991). HBO Home Video, VHS/DVD, 1999/2001.

Basie, Count

(William Basie)
(1904–1984) *jazz bandleader, pianist*

One of the greatest names in jazz, Count Basie is acknowledged as the bandleader who put the swing into "swing" music of the 1930s and 1940s.

He was born William Basie on August 21, 1904, in Red Bank, New Jersey. His father Harvey played the E-flat horn, and his mother Lillian played the piano. Basie's first instrument in the school band was the drums, but he became discouraged when another student played them better, and he took up the piano instead. The better drummer was Sonny Greer, who went on to play drums in DUKE ELLINGTON's band.

Basie's mother was his first piano teacher. He later took lessons in New York City from some of the greatest of the stride piano players, including James P. Johnson and FATS WALLER. Stride piano was an aggressive style of playing that emphasized rhythm. Basie's first professional job as a pianist was accompanying various performers on the vaudeville, or variety show, circuit. At age 20, he moved to Kansas City, Missouri. Three years later the group he was playing with there disbanded and for a time he played piano for silent movies. He eventually joined Benny Moten's Kansas City Orchestra. When Moten died suddenly during surgery, Basie organized the band members into a new unit, the Barons of Rhythm. They became one of Kansas City's top bands, developing a driving style built on rhythmic riffs, improvisation, and exciting solo turns.

The loose, easy sound of the Barons was first heard on local radio in 1936. A broadcast announcer, impressed by Basie's courtly style at the piano, dubbed him "Count." One broadcast caught the ear of journalist and record producer John Hammond. Hammond immediately set out to promote Basie and his band. Within a year, Basie's reputation as head of one of the swingingest bands in America was firmly established. He moved to New York City in late 1936 and enlarged his band to 12 musicians. They played at New York's Roseland Ballroom and then moved to the Famous Door nightclub in 1938. The previous year the band had signed with Decca Records and had their first hit record with "One O'Clock Jump" (1937), which became the band's signature song. Some of his other big hits of the 1940s were "All of Me" (1943), "Blue Skies" (1946), and the number-one novelty tune "Open the Door, Richard!" (1947). Among the more talented musicians who passed through Basie's band over the years were saxophonists Lester Young and Illinois Jacquet, drummer Jo Jones, and jazz singers BILLIE HOLIDAY, Joe Williams, and Jimmy Rushing.

While most big bands broke up in the late 1940s as the era drew to a close, Basie started a new 16-piece band in 1952. He never stopped playing, although in the 1950s he developed a smoother, more polished style. To capture the "Basie Sound" he hired a small group of talented arrangers that included Neal Hefti, Benny Carter, and QUINCY JONES. Basie's last big pop hit was "April in Paris" in 1956.

In the 1970s, Basie regularly performed as a pianist in all-star session jams, while continuing to tour with his big band. He also backed such great singers as Frank Sinatra and ELLA FITZGERALD in concert. A heart attack in 1976 temporarily sidelined Basie, but he was back a short time later conducting from a wheelchair. He won the Grammy's Trustee Award in 1981.

Count Basie died of pancreatic cancer at age 78 on April 26, 1984. He was one of the last of the great bandleaders of traditional swing jazz. The Count Basie Orchestra continues to tour and record today under the direction of Grover Mitchell. The orchestra won a Grammy Award in 1999 for best large jazz ensemble performance. "A band can really swing when it swings easy," Count Basie once said, "when it can play along like cutting butter."

Further Reading

Dance, Stanley. *The World of Count Basie.* New York: Da Capo Press, 1985.

Kliment, Bud. *Count Basie: Bandleader and Musician.* Black Americans of Achievement. Los Angeles: Melrose Square Publishing Co., 1994 (YA).

Murray, Albert, with Count Basie. *Good Morning Blues: The Autobiography of Count Basie.* Reprint, New York: Da Capo Press, 2002.

Further Listening

The Complete Atomic Basie. Blue Note, CD, 1994.

Count Basie's Finest Hour. Umvd, CD, 2002.

Further Viewing

Jazz Icons: Count Basie Live in '62. TDK DVD Video, DVD, 2006.

Bassett, Angela
(1958–   ) *actress*

A leading contemporary film actress, Angela Bassett has been adept at playing both real, historical women and fictional ones.

Born on August 16, 1958, in New York City, she was raised in St. Petersburg, Florida, by her mother Betty after her parents divorced. Bassett was a top student and the first black member of the National Honor Society at her high school.

She first decided to become an actor after seeing JAMES EARL JONES in a production of *Of Mice and Men* at the Kennedy Center for the Performing Arts during a high school class trip to Washington, D.C. "I couldn't move," she said in her interview recalling the experience, "and I remember thinking, 'My gosh, if I could make somebody feel the way I feel right now!'"

After graduating high school, she received a full scholarship to Yale University and went on to earn a master of fine arts (M.F.A.) degree in theater at the Yale School of Drama. Bassett moved to New York City in 1983 and auditioned for plays while working as a secretary in a skin-care salon and as a photo researcher at *U.S. News and World Report* magazine.

Later that same year she was invited to join the Negro Ensemble Company on tour and made her Broadway debut in August Wilson's black drama *Ma Rainey's Black Bottom* in 1984. Other stage roles followed, including parts in two Shakespeare productions in Hartford, Connecticut, and at the New York Shakespeare Festival. She returned to Broadway in another Wilson play, *Joe Turner's Come and Gone,* in 1988.

Bassett's film debut was a small role in the comedy thriller *F/X* (1986). Other minor roles followed in *Kindergarten Cop* (1990) and writer-director John Sayles's *City of Hope* (1991), an urban drama in which she played a college professor. She first gained wide critical notice as CUBA GOODING, JR.'s upwardly mobile divorced mother in *Boyz N the Hood* (1991), John Singleton's powerful film about life in the South Central section of Los Angeles. Then director Spike Lee cast her as Betty Shabazz, Malcolm X's wife, in his biographical film *Malcolm X* (1992). The same year Bassett played another famous woman, Katherine Jackson, mother of the Jackson Five in the television miniseries *The Jacksons: An American Dream*.

Bassett's big break came when she portrayed soul singer TINA TURNER in the biopic *What's Love Got to Do with It* (1993). The actress had never seen Turner perform before taking the role and prepared for the part by reading her autobiography several times, keeping to an arduous exercise schedule, and working on Turner's dance routines under the guidance of the singer herself. The hard work paid off in a dynamic performance that earned Bassett critical praise and an Academy Award nomination for best actress. The role also earned her both a Golden Globe Award and a National Association for the Advancement of Colored People (NAACP) Image Award for outstanding lead actress in a motion picture.

"When the real Tina Turner makes an appearance as herself at the end of the movie, it seems perfectly natural, as though she's been on screen throughout," wrote film critic Julie Salamon in praise of Bassett's performance.

Bassett went on to play more strong women in *Waiting to Exhale* (1995) and *How Stella Got Her Groove Back* (1998), both adapted from novels by Terry McMillan. She won two more Image Awards for her work in these films. In October 1997, she married African-American actor Courtney B. Vance.

Bassett starred in the film adaptation of the South African play *Boesman & Lena* (2000) and the heist thriller *The Score* (2001), in which her costars were Robert De Niro and Marlon Brando. The same year Bassett had the title role in the television movie *The Rosa Parks Story*, about the courageous black woman whose refusal to sit in the back of a segregated bus sparked the Montgomery, Alabama, bus boycott. She was particu-

larly close to the role of an actress returning home to Florida after 28 years in John Sayles's *Sunshine State* (2001), a film he wrote especially for her.

Good film roles have come harder to find for Bassett in recent years, and she has appeared more and more on series television. In 2005, she was a Central Intelligence Agency (CIA) director on four episodes of *Alias* (2001–06). During the 2008–09 season of the long-running medical series *ER* (1994–2009), its last on NBC, she appeared as Dr. Cate Banfield, chief of the ER. Courtney Vance, her real husband, played her TV husband on the series. The couple had their own medical miracle in 2006 when a twin son and daughter were born to them via a surrogate mother.

Further Reading

Bassett, Angela, and Courtney B. Vance. *Friends: A Love Story*. Buffalo, N.Y.: Kimoni, 2009.

Fitzgerald, Dawn. *Angela Bassett*. Black Americans of Achievement. New York: Chelsea House, 2001 (YA).

Further Viewing

Movies with Soul Collection (How Stella Got Her Groove Back/Waiting to Exhale/Soul Food). Fox Home Video, DVD box set, 2002.

The Rosa Parks Story (2000). Xenon, DVD, 2003.

What's Love Got to Do with It (1993). Walt Disney Video, VHS/DVD, 1997/1999.

Bates, Peg Leg
(Clayton Bates)
(1907–1998) *one-legged tap dancer*

A talented tap dancer who turned a handicap into an asset, Peg Leg Bates was an inspiration to millions.

He was born Clayton Bates on October 11, 1907, in Greenville, South Carolina, and grew up in the town of Fountain Inn. He began dancing on street corners at age five for spare change.

When he was 12, Bates lost his left leg in a cotton gin accident. His uncle whittled him a wooden leg and he learned to dance with it, tapping with his good leg while balancing on his peg leg.

Something of a novelty act, Bates performed in vaudeville shows in the 1920s and made it to Broadway in *Blackbirds of 1928*. His act was so amazing that he was immediately hired to appear at the Moulin Rouge, a legendary club in Paris, France, where he performed for 22 weeks. Over the years, he performed at clubs and theaters throughout the United States, including New York's Cotton Club, the Apollo Theater, and Radio City Music Hall. With the advent of television, Bates became a popular performer on variety shows and appeared more than 20 times on *The Ed Sullivan Show*.

Bates was not only a talented performer but also a good businessman. In 1951, he used his earnings to open a resort in Kerhonkson, New York. The Peg Leg Bates Country Club became the first resort in New York's Catskills to cater to black tourists. Over the years, Bates became a valuable and generous citizen of his adopted hometown. He was active in Kerhonkson civic organizations, sang weekly in the local Methodist Church choir, and helped create a senior citizens' center in neighboring Napanoch, New York, in the 1970s.

After his wife died in 1987, Bates sold his resort and retired from performing two years later. He continued, however, to perform for youth groups, the handicapped, and seniors into his 80s. In December 1998, he returned to Fountain Inn, South Carolina, for a celebration of his career. He was given the Order of the Palmetto, the highest honor in the state, and danced at a concert to raise money for a life-sized sculpture of himself to be placed at the entrance of City Hall. The next morning on his way to church, Peg Leg Bates collapsed and died of a heart attack. He was 91 years old.

"He was a courageous man who didn't give up," said local National Association for the Advance-ment of Colored People (NAACP) president Maude Brace. "He pursued his future, despite his handicap, and went on to encourage others to do what their dream was to do."

Further Reading

Barasch, Lynne. *Knockin' on Word: Starring Peg Leg Bates*. New York: Lee & Low Books, 2004 (children).

Frank, Rusty E. *Tap: The Great Tap Dance Stars and Their Stories, 1900–1955*. New York: Da Capo Press, 1995.

Belafonte, Harry
(Harold George Belafonte, Jr.)
(1927–) *folksinger, actor, social activist*

Catapulted to international stardom by the calypso craze in the mid-1950s, Harry Belafonte has remained a popular entertainer and social activist for more than half a century.

He was born Harold George Belafonte, Jr., in the Harlem section of New York City on March 1, 1927. His father, Harold Belafonte, Sr., was originally from Martinique, and his mother, Melvine Love, was Jamaican. He moved to Jamaica with his mother as a child, returning to New York five years later. The family was poor and Belafonte quit high school in 1944 to join the navy during World War II. When he was discharged two years later, he decided to try acting and studied at the New York Dramatic Workshop while working as a maintenance man. Some of his fellow acting students were Marlon Brando, Walter Matthau, and Tony Curtis. Belafonte began singing pop music in local clubs such as the Royal Roost in the late 1940s. He then became part owner of a restaurant in Greenwich Village and became interested in the folk music revival going on in Village clubs.

"I began to see my place in that world," he told writer Joe Smith in an interview. "I ain't no LEAD-BELLY, and I certain wasn't [Pete] Seeger, but I decided I would mold the material and carve out a unique place as a conduit of all this rich music." With a couple of musicians, Belafonte began working up a repertoire of old and new folk songs. A booking at the Village Vanguard led to a recording contract with RCA Records.

In 1953, Belafonte won a Tony Award for his performance in the Broadway revue *John Murray Anderson's Almanac* and appeared in his first movie, *Bright Road*. He played an earnest school principal in love with a teacher played by DOROTHY DANDRIDGE. The two would be teamed again in the black musical film *Carmen Jones* (1954), in which Belafonte played a soldier whose life and career is destroyed by his love for the reckless Carmen.

With the release of his album *Calypso* in 1956, based on the folk music of his mother's homeland, Belafonte became an international star. The exotic rhythms and melodies of "Jamaica Farewell" and "Banana Boat Song (Day-O)," both of which became huge hit singles, created a calypso craze that lasted through 1957. Much of the craze was due to Belafonte himself, with his handsome looks and husky voice.

"From the top of his head right down to that white shirt, he's the most beautiful man I ever set eyes on," said singer/actress DIAHANN CARROLL.

Hollywood took notice and cast Belafonte in several more movies. He was one of only a few African-American actors to play leading man roles in the 1950s. He was a West Indian revolutionary in *Island in the Sun* (1957) and a petty criminal involved in a doomed heist in *Odds Against Tomorrow* (1959). While a sensitive actor, Belafonte was not as effective on screen as in his live concerts, and after 1959, he didn't make another movie for 11 years. Perhaps his best screen role was the exuberant and wily backwoods preacher in the western *Buck and the Preacher* (1971), directed by his friend and costar SIDNEY POITIER.

Belafonte has fared better on television, where his intimate singing style has made him extremely popular. He became the first black man to win an Emmy Award in 1960 for his television special *Tonight with Belafonte*. He set off a storm of controversy in 1968 when he appeared on British singer Petula Clark's TV special, and she held his arm while they sang a duet. As innocent as it was, just the suggestion of interracial romance was enough to send television executives into a tizzy.

Racial intolerance and other social issues have been a central concern for Belafonte since the 1960s, and he has been one of the entertainment world's most prominent humanitarians. In 1987 he was appointed the United Nation Children's Fund (UNICEF) goodwill ambassador, and he helped organize the recording and video of "We Are the World," the proceeds of which have helped African famine-relief projects. He received the Leader for Peace Award from the Peace Corps in 1988 and was a recipient of the Kennedy Center Honors in 1989.

In 1994, Belafonte won the National Medal of Art. In 2001, he produced *The Long Road to Freedom: An Anthology of Black Music*. He had been working on this CD box set, which includes the work of dozens of African-American performers, since 1961. In 2006, Belafonte appeared in the film *Bobby*, about the events surrounding the assassination of Robert Kennedy in 1968. His daughter Shari Belafonte is an actress.

Further Reading

Fogelson, Genia. *Harry Belafonte*. Los Angeles: Holloway House, 2008.
"Harry Belafonte." The Internet Movie Database. Available online. URL: http://www.imdb.com/name/nm0000896/. Downloaded on February 13, 2009.

Further Listening

The Essential Harry Belafonte. RCA, 2 CDs, 2005.

Further Viewing

Buck and the Preacher (1971). Sony, VHS/DVD, 1998/2000.
An Evening with Harry Belafonte & Friends. Island, DVD, 2003.

Berry, Chuck
(Charles Edward Anderson Berry)
(1926–   ) *rock and R & B singer, guitarist, songwriter*

One of the authentic pioneers of rock 'n' roll and one of its most gifted songwriters, Chuck Berry remains one of his generation's few survivors.

He was born Charles Edward Anderson Berry on October 18, 1926, in St. Louis, Missouri, into a middle-class black family. He did not start playing the guitar until he was in his teens and then only as a hobby. A robbery put him in reform school for three years. When he got out in 1947 he got a job as an assembler at a car body plant. He later attended night school and became a hairdresser. Struggling to support a wife and two children, Berry got back into his music and formed a trio in 1953 that played blues at local clubs. Influenced by pioneer rhythm and blues (R & B) singer and bandleader LOUIS JORDAN, Berry started writing and singing his own humorous songs in a blues vein.

In 1955, he recorded two of his compositions, "Ida Red" and "Wee Wee Hours," on a borrowed tape machine and took them to Chicago. There he met the legendary blues singer MUDDY WATERS who was impressed by Berry's material and sent him to Chess Records for an audition. Leonard Chess, the label's owner, preferred the song "Ida Red" over Berry's own favorite "Wee Wee Hours." Chess thought the number, however, needed a bigger beat and a new title. He suggested "Maybelline." The driving beat and clever lyrics about a guy chasing his girl in his car were infectious. The combination of the blues and country licks on Berry's electrified guitar made "Maybelline" one of the first bona fide roll 'n' roll records and a smash hit.

Berry was one of the first African-American rockers to appeal to both white and black listeners. Part of this was due to his Midwestern accent, which did not sound particularly black. Another reason was the subject matter of his songs—rock 'n' roll, cute girls, school, and other teen themes. But there was also an inventiveness and freshness to the music and lyrics that put Berry far above most of the competition. Through the 1950s he had many hits, the biggest and best known including "Roll Over Beethoven" (1956), "Rock & Roll Music" (1957), "Sweet Little Sixteen" (1958), and "Johnny B. Goode" (1958). With his earnings Berry bought a new house and opened his own hometown nightclub, which he called Chuck Berry's Club Bandstand.

By 1960, his record sales were falling off, and two years later Berry was charged under the federal Mann Act with kidnapping an underage girl and transporting her across state lines for "immoral purposes." The girl in question was a 14-year-old Native American prostitute he picked up in New Mexico and brought to St. Louis to work as a hatcheck girl in his club. She had come with him willingly and only pressed charges after Berry had fired her for incompetence. The case against him was dubious at best, but after a drawn-out trial Berry was sentenced to two years in a federal penitentiary in Terre Haute, Indiana.

Prison turned Chuck Berry into a bitter, disillusioned man. When he was released in 1964 he picked up his career and returned to recording. He had several more hits with such classic tunes as "No Particular Place to Go," "You Never Can Tell," and "Promised Land," all released in 1964. Bands of the recent British Invasion—the Beatles, the Rolling Stones, and the Dave Clark Five among them—were playing and recording his songs and reviving his reputation, at least for a time. By the late 1960s, however, Berry was relegated to the oldies' circuit. He put most of his energies into Berry Park, a recreational park he was building 30 miles from St. Louis. Then in 1972 a live recording from a concert in England of a naughty little novelty he'd been singing for years called "My Ding-a-Ling" became a surprise hit. It zoomed up the charts giving Chuck Berry the first number-one hit of his career. In 1979, he won critical acclaim, if not large sales, with the album

Rockit, which *Rolling Stone* magazine called his best album in 15 years. That same year, he was arrested again, this time for tax evasion and returned to prison for a short term and many hours of community service.

Berry became notorious in the 1970s and 1980s for doing quickie, one-night stands during which he indifferently played his string of hits with pickup bands that he was openly contemptuous of. But there were still plenty of devoted fans, especially in the music business. One of his biggest fans was Keith Richards, lead guitarist of the Rolling Stones, whose inventive riffs owed much to Berry's pioneering guitar work. In 1987, Richards helped organize a celebratory all-star concert for Berry's 60th birthday, which was turned into a documentary by filmmaker Taylor Hackford entitled *Hail! Hail! Rock 'n' Roll.* The film affirmed Berry's place in the rock firmament but unfortunately also confirmed the flaws in his character as he railed against Richards and other musicians in rehearsal for the big concert.

Considering the difficulties he has endured in his troubled life, one must respect Berry for his courage, talent, and even his stubbornness. Now in his 80s, he remains one of the most uniquely gifted performers of American popular music.

Chuck Berry won Grammy's Lifetime Achievement Award in 1984 and was inducted into the Rock and Roll Hall of Fame in its initial year, 1986. *Rolling Stone* magazine in its 2004 list of the 100 Greatest Artists of All Time, ranked Berry number 5.

Further Reading

Berry, Chuck. *The Autobiography.* New York: Harmony Books, 1987.

DeWitt, Howard. *Chuck Berry: Rock 'n' Roll Music.* Ann Arbor, Mich.: Pierian Press, 1985.

Pegg, Bruce. *Brown Eyed Handsome Man: The Life and Hard Times of Chuck Berry.* New York: Routledge, 2005.

The Rock and Roll Hall of Fame Inductees. "Chuck Berry." The Rock and Roll Hall of Fame and Museum Web site. Available online. URL: http://www.rockhall.com/inductee/chuck-berry. Downloaded on January 26, 2009.

Further Listening

Anthology. Chess, 2 CDs, 2000.

Further Viewing

Hail! Hail! Rock 'n' Roll (1987). MCA Home Video/Image Entertainment, VHS, 1989/DVD box set, 2006.

Berry, Halle
(1968–   )   *actress*

The first African American to win an Academy Award for best actress, Halle Berry faced many personal struggles before reaching the pinnacle of success.

She was born on August 14, 1968, in Cleveland, Ohio, to a white mother and a black father. Her mother Judith named her after a favorite department store—Halle Brothers. When she was still a child, her father Jerome abandoned the family, and Berry's mother, a nurse, moved them to the white suburb of Bedford. There Halle proved herself to her white high-school classmates by achieving excellence at everything she put her hand to. Before she graduated, Berry was class president, editor of the school newspaper, and head cheerleader.

In 1986, she won the Miss Teen Ohio Pageant and went on to finish second in the Miss USA and third in the Miss World competitions. She left college and the study of broadcast journalism to pursue acting and modeling in Chicago. Berry moved to New York City in 1989 and almost immediately landed a leading role in the television situation comedy *Living Dolls.* The show folded quickly, but she went on to the prime-time soap opera *Knot's Landing* in 1991. A bigger break came that same year when director Spike Lee cast Berry as a crack addict and girlfriend of SAMUEL L.

JACKSON in his film *Jungle Fever.* To prepare for the role Berry toured a Washington, D.C., crack house with an undercover police officer and then did not shower for 10 days before shooting started.

Berry's film debut was auspicious, and she quickly appeared in more films. She was a stripper in the Bruce Willis action film *The Last Boy Scout* (1991) and EDDIE MURPHY's love interest in the romantic comedy *Boomerang* (1992). Her first major dramatic role in films came with *Losing Isaiah* (1995), where she again played a crack addict in the midst of a custody battle to win back her son from the white couple who adopted him.

In 1998, Berry was impressive in two offbeat roles. In *Why Do Fools Fall in Love* she was in another courtroom battle, this time as one of three wives vying for the estate of the late doo-wop singer FRANKIE LYMON. In *Bulworth,* an outrageous political satire, she was the girlfriend and would-be assassin of a U.S. senator, played by Warren Beatty, who put out a contract on himself.

By now, Berry finally had the clout in Hollywood to produce a dream project she had been trying to get done for years—a biopic of the African-American actress DOROTHY DANDRIDGE. *Introducing Dorothy Dandridge* (1999), starring Berry as the tortured movie star, was financed by the cable channel Home Box Office (HBO). The film was a critical and audience success, bringing HBO some of the best ratings in its history. Berry, who bears a striking resemblance to Dandridge, won the Emmy for outstanding lead actress in a miniseries or movie and the Golden Globe Award for best actress in a TV movie or miniseries. In March 2002, Berry became the first black actress to win the Academy Award for best actress, for her uncompromising portrayal of a widow of an executed felon in *Monster's Ball* (2001). In an emotional acceptance speech, Berry said, "This moment is for Dorothy Dandridge, Lena Horne, Diahann Carroll. It's for every nameless, faceless woman of color who now has a chance because this door tonight has been opened." Once named

Initially cast as an ingenue or sexpot in films, Halle Berry worked hard to establish herself as a serious dramatic actress. *(AP Photo/Dan Steinberg)*

one of the world's most beautiful people by *People* magazine, Halle was now hailed as one of the best dramatic actresses of her generation. Her recent roles include spy James Bond's partner in *Die Another Day* (2002), a psychiatrist in the supernatural thriller *Gothika* (2003), and the female protagonist in the television adaptation of Zora Neal Hurston's classic novel *Their Eyes Were Watching God* (2005). In *Frankie and Alice* (2009), Berry plays a woman with multiple personality disorder and stars opposite PHYLICIA RASHAD.

Berry's five-year marriage to Atlanta Braves outfielder David Justice ended in divorce in 1997. In February 2000, she was fined and put on probation for allegedly fleeing the scene of an auto accident she had caused. In 2001, Berry wed singer

Eric Benét. They divorced four years later. In 2008, Berry gave birth to a daughter, fathered by her partner, model Gabriel Aubry.

Further Reading

Blue, Rose, and Corrine J. Naden. *Halle Berry*. Black Americans of Achievement. New York: Chelsea House, 2001 (YA).

Farley, Christopher John. *Introducing Halle Berry*. New York: Pocket, 2002.

O'Brien Daniel. *Halle Berry*. Richmond, U.K.: Reynolds & Hearn, 2003.

Further Viewing

Bulworth (1998). 20th Century Fox Home Entertainment, VHS/DVD, 2001.

Introducing Dorothy Dandridge (1999). HBO Home Video, VHS/DVD, 2001.

Monster's Ball (2001). Lions Gate, DVD, 2002.

Blake, Eubie
(James Hubert Blake)
(1883–1983) *composer, pianist, singer*

Creator of one of the most popular all-black musicals in American theatrical history, Eubie Blake outlived all his contemporaries to bring his music to life for several generations of listeners.

He was born James Hubert Blake on February 7, 1883, in Baltimore, Maryland. He was playing his first instrument—the family pump organ—by the age of six and later took piano lessons from a neighbor. By age 15, Blake discovered ragtime music and, without his mother's knowledge, played ragtime piano in local brothels and bars. At 18, he made his professional debut in a medicine show in Pennsylvania.

Blake moved to New York City in 1905 where he tried and failed to get his first song, "Sounds of Africa," published. It would finally be published 14 years later as the "Charleston Rag." He returned to Baltimore and married Avis Lee, a classical pianist, in 1910. In 1915, while performing as a member of Joe Porter's Serenaders, Blake met fellow

Serenader Noble Sissle, and they soon became a songwriting team. Sissle wrote the words and Blake the music. After World War I, the two formed a vaudeville act, the Dixie Duo. Unlike other black vaudeville acts that copied white minstrel acts, the Dixie Duo wore no black face.

At a National Association for the Advancement of Colored People (NAACP) benefit in Philadelphia, Sissle and Blake met the more experienced songwriting team of Flourey E. Miller and Aubrey Lyles. The four men decided to write, direct, and star in a new all-black musical, a genre that had been popular more than a decade earlier. Their show, *Shuffle Along*, was based on a skit written by Miller and Lyles and featured songs by Sissle and Blake. It opened on May 23, 1921, in a dilapidated New York lecture hall. Despite the sparse sets and inexpensive costumes, the show's high spirits and sparkling score appealed to white theatergoers, and *Shuffle Along* became a smash success. The show's most popular song and Blake's best-known composition, *I'm Just Wild About Harry*, was almost cut from the show before its opening. The song was originally written as a waltz, and the performer who sang it felt white audiences would scoff at a waltz in a black show. To save the song, Blake changed it to an up-tempo one-step. More than 25 years later, the song was used in the reelection campaign of President Harry Truman.

Besides becoming the longest-running book musical produced, directed, written, and performed by blacks, *Shuffle Along* was the first black musical to contain serious romantic scenes between an African-American man and woman. It was also the first production in New York in which black patrons were allowed to sit in seats once reserved for "whites only."

After *Shuffle Along*, Sissle and Blake wrote songs for the white musical *Elsie* (1923) and another black musical, *Chocolate Dandies* (1924), which failed largely because it broke more racial stereotypes than *Shuffle Along*.

Sissle and Blake toured Europe in 1925 and contributed songs to a British musical revue. Their collaboration ended soon after they returned home. Through the 1930s, Blake wrote songs with other lyricists, most notably FATS WALLER's songwriting partner Andy Razaf. Their song "Memories of You" from the black musical *Blackbirds* (1930) has become a pop standard. Blake wrote a few more shows, including *Swing It* (1937) with lyricists Cecil Mack and Milton Reddie. He retired from show business in 1946.

In 1968, at the age of 86, Eubie Blake started the second phrase of his remarkable career. As the revival of ragtime music grew, Blake and Sissle were "rediscovered" by writers and critics as two of its few living practitioners. They made a record album, *The Eighty-Six Years of Eubie Blake* (1968), and were the subject of a book, *Reminiscing with Sissle and Blake* (1973). Sissle died in 1975. Blake went on to make a world tour, lecturing and playing his music on the piano. A musical revue based on his work called *Eubie!* played on Broadway in 1978.

The public celebrated Blake's longevity, which was all the more astonishing given his fondness for alcohol and cigarettes. (He smoked from his youth.) "I don't have any bad habits," he said in a 1979 interview. "They might be bad for other people, but they're all right for me."

Eubie Blake died five days after his 100th birthday on February 12, 1983. The following year his archives were given as a gift to the city of Baltimore, and the Eubie Blake National Jazz Institute and Cultural Center, where they are housed, was established. The organization's aim is "to showcase the works of renowned and aspiring artists with the focus on increasing public awareness of the contributions of African Americans in the Fine Arts."

Further Reading

"Everything Eubie." Eubie Blake National Jazz Institute and Cultural Center Web site. Available online. URL: http://www.eubieblake.org/everythingeubie.php. Downloaded on February 13, 2009.

Kimball, Robert, and William Bolcom. *Reminiscing with Noble Sissle and Eubie Blake*. Reprint, Lanham, Md.: Cooper Square Press, 2000.

Rose, Al. *Eubie Blake*. New York: Macmillan, 1983.

Further Listening

Memories of You: From Rare Piano Rolls (1990). Shout Factory, CD, 2003.

Tricky Fingers. Quicksilver Records, CD, 2003.

Blige, Mary J.
("The Queen of Hip-Hop Soul")
(1971–   ) *R & B singer, songwriter, actress*

One of the most prominent soul divas of the last decade and a half, with a voice having four-octave range, Mary J. Blige has deftly moved from hip hop to soul, to adult contemporary without missing a beat.

She was born on January 11, 1971, in the Bronx, New York. Her father, Thomas Blige, was a jazz musician, and her mother, Cora, a nurse. When Mary was four, her father left the family, and she moved with her mother and older sister, Latonya, to Yonkers, New York. Growing up in the projects was difficult, and Mary was sexually molested at age five by a family friend. She discovered her gift for singing at age seven but kept it hidden. "In the neighborhood I grew up in, if something good happened to you, you better not tell nobody," she said in an interview. "If you did something great, you had to pay for it!"

In her teens, Blige began writing gospel songs with her friends and sang in her church. Then, in 1988, she made in a mall booth a recording of an Anita Baker song; this changed her life. Her mother's then boyfriend brought the cassette to Uptown Records, and the label's CEO, Andre Harrell, was so impressed that he signed Blige to a recording contract the following year. For several years, Blige was confined to doing backup singing for other artists. Then, in 1992, Uptown released her debut album, *What's the 411?*, largely produced by SEAN COMBS. The title track, written by Blige, about her experiences as a telephone operator, became a number-one hit on the Billboard R & B charts. Her second album, *My Life* (1994), again produced by Combs, was mostly written by Blige and was largely autobiographical.

A gifted singer and songwriter, Mary J. Blige has used the raw material of her life to create memorable music. *(AP Photo/Paul Kramer)*

Producer and artist had a falling out, and Blige's next several albums, including the more adult-contemporary *Mary* (1999) and *No More Drama* (2001), which included "Family Affair," her first number-one pop single, were produced by others. She reunited with Combs on the highly anticipated *Love and Life* (2003), but it was a critical and commercial disappointment. The singer regained her momentum with the appropriately titled *The Breakthrough* (2005), which sold more than 6 million copies worldwide. Her most recent album, *Growing Pains* (2007), earned her a ninth Grammy for best contemporary R & B album.

A talented actress, Blige has appeared as a guest player on a number of television shows and starred in the Off-Broadway play *The Exonerated* in 2004.

She appeared in the film comedy *I Can Do Bad All by Myself* (2009), directed by Tyler Perry, and is scheduled to portray the late singer NINA SIMONE in a film due to be released in 2012.

After years of drug and alcohol abuse and living in a destructive relationship, Blige found peace and a renewed confidence in her relationship with record executive Martin Kendu Isaacs, whom she married in 2003. She is stepmother to Isaacs's two children. The couple lives in Saddle River, New Jersey.

"I had to learn to smell the roses, just enjoy and be happy," Blige has said about her up-and-down life. "I learned to not be afraid and to not be imprisoned by how serious I think life is. That's the balance."

Further Reading

Bailey, Diane. *Mary J. Blige.* New York: Rosen Classroom, 2009 (YA).
Brown, Terrell. *Mary J. Blige.* Hip-Hop. Broomall, Pa.: Mason Crest Publishers, 2007 (YA).
Louie, Rebecca. "Pain and Progress." *USA Weekend,* June 20–22, 2008, pp. 6,7.

Further Listening

My Life. MCA, CD, 1994.
Reflections—A Retrospective. Geffen Records, CD, 2006.

Further Viewing

An Intimate Evening with Mary J. Blige—Live from the House of Blues. Sanctuary Records, DVD, 2004.

Brandy
(Brandy Norwood)
(1979–   ) *R & B singer, actress*

One of the best-known pop divas of the 1990s, Brandy's acting career has been nearly as successful as her singing career.

She was born Brandy Norwood on February 11, 1979, in McComb, Mississippi, and raised in California. Her father was a minister and, like so many

African-American singers, she first sang in the church choir. Brandy decided she wanted to be a pop singer after hearing WHITNEY HOUSTON on the radio. Before that happened, she got an acting job on the short-lived television situation comedy *Thea* (1993), playing the daughter of a single mom.

The same year, Atlantic Records signed her to a recording contract. Her debut album, *Brandy* (1994), was an instant smash and produced the hit singles "Brokenhearted," "Baby," and "I Wanna Be Down." By year's end, she had her biggest hit to date with "Sittin' Up in My Room," from the soundtrack of the film *Waiting to Exhale* (1995), which starred Houston and ANGELA BASSETT. Another soundtrack hit was "Missing You," a collaboration with GLADYS KNIGHT, Chaka Khan, and Tamia from the movie *Set It Off* (1996).

In 1996, Brandy returned to television as the star of the United Paramount Network (UPN) sitcom *Moesha,* about black teenager Moesha Mitchell. It was, according to writer Donald Bogle, "one of the few programs that sensitively dramatized the experiences of an African American teenage girl." *Moesha* ran for six seasons and led to a spin-off series, *The Parkers* (1999), about Moesha's best friend and her mother.

Brandy's most endearing role to date was as Cinderella in an impressive multicultural television version of the Rodgers and Hammerstein musical, costarring Bernadette Peters, WHOOPI GOLDBERG, and Brandy's idol, Whitney Houston, who helped her get the part. *Cinderella* (1997) attracted 60 million viewers, including 70 percent of girls under the age of 18, a clear sign of Brandy's popularity with this segment of the population. She has also appeared in the movies *I Still Know What You Did Last Summer* (1998) and *Osmosis Jones* (2000).

Her much-anticipated second album, *Never Say Never,* was released in 1998. The next year she won a Grammy Award for her duet "The Boy Is Mine," sung with Monica. Her next two albums, *Full Moon* (2002) and *Afrodisiac* (2004), sold poorly, although the latter was well received by

critics. Her latest album, *Human* (2008), has sold far better, but its songs were criticized by some reviewers for being too imitative of other singers.

Brandy supposedly married record producer Robert Smith in the summer of 2001 but did not publicly announce the marriage until February 2002. The following June she gave birth to her first child, Sy'rai. The marriage was later exposed as a ruse. Brandy was engaged to L.A. Clipper basketball player Quentin Richardson in 2005, but they have since split.

Brandy sees her career as rising above others' expectations of her. "I didn't think my record company believed in me at first," she said in one interview. "I didn't think the people on *Moesha* believed in me. I feel like my whole career has been a proving ground."

Further Reading

Daniels, Karu F. *Brandy: An Intimate Look.* Kansas City, Mo.: Andrews McMeel Publishing, 1999.

Golden, Anna Louise. *Brandy: Sittin' on Top of the World.* New York: St. Martin's Paperbacks, 1999.

Newman, Matthew. *Brandy.* Galaxy of Superstars. New York: Chelsea House, 2000 (YA).

Further Listening

Afrodisiac. Atlantic, CD, 2004.
Brandy. Atlantic, CD, 1994.
Never Say Never. Atlantic, CD, 1998.

Further Viewing

Brandy—The Videos (1999). Atlantic, DVD, 2000.
Rodgers and Hammerstein's Cinderella (1997). Walt Disney Video, VHS/DVD, 1998/2003.

Braugher, Andre
(1962–   ) *actor*

A star of one of the most acclaimed dramatic television shows of the 1990s, Andre Braugher has been called by critic John Leonard "the best actor on series television."

He was born on July 1, 1962, on the West Side of Chicago, Illinois, the youngest of four children. His father Floyd was a heavy equipment operator and his mother Sally a postal worker. They struggled to send him to a Catholic preparatory school and then to Stanford University in California where Braugher started out as a pre-med student. He later switched to theater and graduated in 1984. He went on to earn a master of fine arts degree from the Juilliard School in New York four years later.

Braugher got his first break in television in 1989 when he was cast as a cop on the long-running crime show *Kojak*. His character was a compulsive womanizer, which Braugher loathed. *Kojak* ended its run in 1990, and Braugher was cast as another cop in the NBC crime show *Homicide: Life on the Street* in 1993. He was part of a gifted ensemble of actors that included African Americans Yaphet Kotto and Clark Johnson. Braugher's character, detective Frank Pembleton, was a complex man—intense, hot-tempered, but also thoughtful and compassionate. His wife on the series was played by his real wife, Ami Brabson, whom he married in 1991.

Filmed on location in Baltimore, Maryland, *Homicide* was a huge critical success but had difficulty finding its audience. It was nearly canceled by the network several times. The show lasted six seasons, however, and earned Braugher an Emmy Award for outstanding leading actor in a drama in 1998. The previous year he had won an Obie (Off-Broadway) award for his vibrant portrayal in the title role in Shakespeare's *Henry V*. As *Homicide* wound down, Braugher made several films, playing an angel opposite Nicholas Cage in *City of Angels* (1998) and another cop in *A Better Way to Die* (2000). He made an impressive directorial debut in one of three short works, collectively called *Love Song* (2000), on cable television's Showtime channel.

In the fall of 2000, Braugher returned to prime-time television as Dr. Ben Gideon, a teaching doctor at a Boston hospital in the highly touted series *Gideon's Crossing*. Every bit as complex a character as Frank Pembleton, Gideon's specialty was hopeless cases, which he treated in highly unorthodox ways. Unfortunately, the critically acclaimed series received low ratings and was canceled after only one season. He has since played recurring characters on the dramatic series *Hack* (2002–03) and *Thief* (2006–07). Braugher had a leading role in *The Mist* (2007), a horror film based on a Stephen King novel, and he appears in a 10-part dramatic series, *Men of a Certain Age*, also starring Ray Romano.

"I've been very fortunate to come along at a time when opportunities for African-American actors are mushrooming, they're burgeoning; they're everywhere," Braugher has said in an interview. "So I'm going to take advantage of it while I can. And then do the same for my kids, as my parents did for me."

Further Reading
The Andre Braugher Web site. Available online. URL: http://www.geocities.com/TelevisionCity/Set/9266/intro.html. Downloaded on February 13, 2009.

Kalat, David P. *Homicide: Life on the Street: The Unofficial Companion*. Los Angeles: Renaissance Books, 1998.

Further Viewing
Homicide: Life on the Street: Seasons 1–4 (1993). A & E Home Video, DVD box set, 2004.

Homicide: The Movie (2000). Trimark Home Entertainment, VHS/DVD, 2001.

The Mist (2007). Genius Products, DVD, 2008.

Broadus, Calvin   See Snoop Dogg.

Brown, James
(James Joe Brown, Jr., "The Godfather of Soul", "Soul Brother Number One", "Mr. Dynamite")
(1928–2006) *R & B singer, bandleader, musician, songwriter*

Often called the "hardest-working man in show business," James Brown made the hard work pay

James Brown, the Godfather of Soul, had a musical career that spanned five decades. *(AP Photo/Eugene Hoshiko)*

off in a career that spanned five decades, more than 100 hit single records, and some of the greatest live performances in the history of popular music.

He was born James Joe Brown, Jr., in a shack near Barnwell, South Carolina, on May 3, 1933, and raised in Augusta, Georgia, by his father after he divorced James's mother, Susie. Father Joe Brown worked in a furniture store. Little James's first musical instrument was a three-legged pump organ that his father brought home one day during his lunch break. As a boy, he worked on street corners shining shoes and dancing for pennies. He also did other things on the street, such as shoplifting and breaking into cars. At age 15, this lat-

ter activity landed him in prison for an eight-to-16-year stretch.

Prison was a training ground for Brown. He formed his first musical group, whose only instruments were a washtub bass and pocket combs played as harmonicas. His musical talents earned him a parole in just three years. Once on the outside, Brown played semi-pro baseball and tried boxing for a time. But a leg injury ended his athletic career, and he turned back to music for a living. He formed the vocal group the Famous Flames and was soon playing backup for such top rhythm and blues (R & B) artists as Little Willie John and Etta James.

In 1955, Brown's group signed with King Records of Cincinnati, and after much pleading he was allowed to cut his first disk, the self-penned "Please Please Please." This record introduced Brown's explosive, gutbucket singing style that would one day make him famous. But that day hadn't come yet. While "Please Please Please" was a big R & B hit, his next 10 releases were too derivative of other black singers of the day and went nowhere.

By the early 1960s, however, the James Brown Show with his 40-member band and singers had become a staple on the black concert circuit. With his wild wailing, athletic gyrations, and hysterical dramatics, Brown was a whole show in himself. When he asked King to release a live recording of his performance at the Apollo Theater in New York, the label refused. Brown financed and produced the album himself and *Live at the Apollo, Vol. 1*, became a best-seller in 1963, remaining on the *Billboard* charts for 66 weeks. Eventually Brown would form his own production company and be one of the first African-American performers to have total control over his career.

One of the most popular R & B entertainers among black audiences, Brown in 1963 was almost unknown to white listeners. All that changed in 1964–65 when he revolutionized the sound of R & B with a trio of groundbreaking recordings—"Out of Sight," "Papa's Got a Brand New Bag," and "I Got You (I Feel Good)." Brown's "new bag" was funk, which broke down the melody in R & B music into rhythmic, infectious riffs. "Suddenly instead of the vamp being the tag or the end of the song, with 'Papa's Got a Brand New Bag,' the vamp became the song itself, the whole song," said Brown's former road manager Alan Leeds. "What James and [arranger] Nat Jones did was throw away the traditional song structure . . . in order to focus on the rhythms."

Along with inventing funk, Brown tapped into the black pride movement of the late 1960s with such African-American anthems as "Say It Loud—I'm Black and I'm Proud" (1968) and the cautionary "Don't Be a Drop-Out" (1966), which encouraged black youth to stay in school.

"I tell them to get an education," he said in an interview. "And I don't talk down to them. I come from the ghetto and I still have my shoeshine box in my hand." But his music had made him a millionaire, and he gave generously to the black community and the urban poor of every color.

By the late 1970s, Brown's career was beginning to flag. Personal problems exacerbated his public ones. His three radio stations failed, the Internal Revenue Service (IRS) was hounding him for millions in back taxes, his second wife Deirdre walked out on him, and his oldest son died in an auto accident. For nearly a decade he dropped out of the limelight. Then in the mid-1980s, the Godfather of Soul experienced a comeback. In 1986, "Living in America" from the soundtrack of the movie *Rocky IV* became his first top-10 hit in more than a decade. A new album, *Gravity* (1986), was well received, and he was among the first group of artists inducted into the Rock and Roll Hall of Fame that same year.

But personal problems continued to plague the man known as Mr. Dynamite. On December 15, 1988, he was sentenced to six years in prison after police pursued him in an interstate car chase during which he was allegedly intoxicated. He was released in February 1991. In May 2003, Brown was pardoned by South Carolina officials for his past crimes in the state. James Brown died of heart failure at age 73 on December 25, 2006, while hospitalized for pneumonia.

Further Reading

Brown, James. *I Feel Good: A Memoir of a Life of Soul.* New York: New American Library, 2005.

Rose, Cynthia. *Living in America: The Soul Saga of James Brown.* London: Serpent's Tail, 1990.

Vincent, Rickey. *Funk: The Music, the People, and the Rhythm of the One.* New York: St. Martin's Press, 1996.

Further Listening

Foundations of Funk: A Brand New Bag: 1964–1969.
    A & M, 2 CDs, 1996.
Live at the Apollo, Vol. 2. Polydor, 2 CDs, 2001.
20 All-Time Greatest Hits. Mercury, CD, 1991.

Further Viewing

I Got the Feelin': James Brown in the 60s (2008). Shout
    Factory, DVD box set, 2008.

Browne, Roscoe Lee
(1925–2007) *actor*

One of the most erudite and intelligent black
actors of his generation, Roscoe Lee Browne found
success on the stage, screen, and television.

He was born on May 2, 1925, in Woodbury,
New Jersey, and studied at Lincoln University in
Pennsylvania, Middlebury College in Vermont,
and Columbia University in New York City. In college he was an outstanding track star and won the
1951 world championship in the 800-meter run.

He returned to Lincoln to teach French and
literature but left teaching to pursue an acting
career. Browne had the good fortune to join the
New York Shakespeare Festival Theater in its
inaugural season in 1956. Over the next seven
years, he played a wide range of classical roles in
Shakespeare's plays and other works. During this
time, he made an impressive directorial debut
with *A Hand Is on the Gate,* a "celebration of the
African-American experience in poetry and
song." Browne created the work and starred in it
along with such rising black actors as JAMES EARL
JONES and CICELY TYSON. The production later
moved to Broadway.

His first film role was in the drug drama *The
Connection* (1961). For a time Browne specialized
in playing corrupt, guilt-ridden middle-class blacks
in such films as *Uptight* (1968) and *The Liberation
of L. B. Jones* (1970). "His characters were cynical,
lost, sterile [uncle] toms, products of a decadent

black bourgeoisie," writes film historian Donald
Bogle. "Perhaps his were the most realistic toms
ever presented in American films."

But Browne was too gifted an actor to be type-
cast. He was equally memorable as a dandy in *The
Comedians* (1967), a wily CIA agent in *Topaz* (1969)
directed by Alfred Hitchcock, and a sensitive cook
in *The Cowboys* (1972) starring John Wayne. More
recently, he was the narrator in the Oscar-nominated film *Babe* (1995) about a barnyard pig, and its
sequel, *Babe: Pig in the City* (1998). He played Polo-
nius, the king's adviser, in the Campbell Scott version of Shakespeare's *Hamlet* (2000).

On stage, Browne appeared in four plays by
West Indian Nobel laureate Derek Wolcott,
including *Dream on Monkey Mountain,* for which
he won the Los Angeles Drama Critics Award for
best actor. In 1992, he was nominated for a Tony
Award for his role in black playwright August
Wilson's *Two Trains Running.*

Television viewers will remember Browne as
the haughty butler Saunders on the last season of
the television comedy series *Soap* in 1980–81. He
also played opposite Tony Curtis as a smooth con
man on the series *McCoy* in the mid-1970s. A
guest shot on *The Cosby Show* during the 1985–86
season earned him an Emmy Award.

Roscoe Lee Browne was also a published author
of short stories and poetry. He died of cancer at
age 81 on April 11, 2007.

Further Reading

Bogle, Donald. *Toms, Coons, Mulattoes, Mammies &
    Bucks: An Interpretive History of Blacks in American
    Films.* New York: Continuum, 1997, pp. 206–207.
"Roscoe Lee Browne, 81, Actor of Stage and Screen,
    Dies." *New York Times,* April 12, 2007, Obituaries,
    p. C15.

Further Viewing

The Cowboys (1972). Warner Home Video, VHS/DVD,
    1997/2007.
Hamlet (2000). Lions Gate, DVD, 2001.

Burleigh, Henry T.
(Henry Thacker Burleigh)
(1866–1949) *concert singer, arranger, composer*

Henry T. Burleigh has probably done more to preserve and promote the rich heritage of Negro spirituals than any other American.

He was born Henry Thacker Burleigh on December 2, 1866, in Erie, Pennsylvania, the grandson of slaves. Listening to his maternal grandfather Hamilton Waters sing plantation songs as he went about his job as the town crier and lamplighter was Burleigh's first introduction to the music he would devote much of his life to. His mother, Elizabeth, had a college education and knew French and Greek, but because of her race she was forced to work as a domestic in white people's homes. As a youth, Burleigh worked as a doorman at one of the homes where his mother was employed just so he could listen to the classical music at their parties. He had a fine baritone and sang regularly with black church choirs and choral ensembles.

In 1892, at age 26, Burleigh won a scholarship to study at the National Conservatory of Music in New York City. There he studied composition with the great Czech composer Antonín Dvořák, who was a visiting director at the conservatory. Meeting Dvořák was a turning point in Burleigh's life. Dvořák, who loved all kinds of folk music, was fascinated by the Negro spirituals that Burleigh sang for him. He ended up incorporating one of them, "Swing Low, Sweet Chariot," in the first movement of his masterwork, *Symphony No. 9, From the New World*. For his part, Dvořák encouraged Burleigh to put his people's spirituals down on paper and publish them. In 1916, he began to do just that, arranging popular spirituals for performance in concert halls by trained singers. The first spiritual Burleigh arranged was "Deep River." It became one of his most celebrated arrangements and was popularized by such great African-American singers as MARIAN ANDERSON and PAUL ROBESON.

Burleigh himself took these spirituals into churches and concert halls throughout the United States and later Europe. During this time, he sang as a baritone soloist at St. George's Episcopal Church and Temple Emmanuel, both in New York City. In 1946, he celebrated his 50th year at St. George's.

In addition to the more than 100 spirituals and folk songs he arranged, Burleigh wrote between 200 and 300 original songs and choral and chamber works. His compositions were influenced by Dvořák's nationalistic style. Among his best-known songs are "The Prayer," "Ethiopia Saluting the Colors," and the song cycle "Who's Dat Yonder."

Burleigh was a charter member of the American Society of Composers, Authors, and Publishers (ASCAP), founded in 1914, and was the recipient of the National Association for the Advancement of Colored People's (NAACP) Spingarn Medal in 1917. He was the third African American to receive this distinguished award.

Henry Burleigh died of heart failure on September 12, 1949.

"In Negro spirituals my race has pure gold," Burleigh once wrote. "In them we show a spiritual security as old as the ages. . . . America's only original and distinctive style of music is destined to be appreciated more and more." It is appreciated today, thanks to him.

Further Reading
Burleigh, Henry T. *The Spirituals of Harry T. Burleigh.* North Hills, Colo.: Alfred Publishing, 2007.
Jones, Randye L. "H. T. Burleigh (1866–1949)." Afrocentric Voices in "Classical" Music Web site. Available online. URL: http://www.afrovoices.com/burleigh.html. Downloaded on February 13, 2009.

Further Listening
Burleigh: Deep River. Albany Records, CD, 1999.
Spirituals in Zion: A Spiritual Heritage for the Soul. Albany Records, CD, 2003.

Burrel, Stanley Kirk   See M. C. HAMMER.

C

Calloway, Cab
(Cabell Calloway III)
(1907–1994) *jazz bandleader, singer, actor*

Cab Calloway was a consummate performer and one of jazz's most distinctive and popular personalities. His wild stage antics and novelty songs strongly influenced rhythm and blues (R & B) and rock 'n' roll.

He was born on Christmas Day, 1907, in Rochester, New York, the second of six children. The family moved to Baltimore, Maryland, when he was six. His father, Cabell, was a lawyer and sold real estate. Calloway's older sister Blanche preceded him in show business and was a respected jazz singer until her retirement in the mid-1930s.

Calloway's early ambition was to be a lawyer, but he soon dropped out of school to pursue a career on the stage. He first performed professionally in the musical show *Plantation Days* at Chicago's Loop Theater. In 1929, he was vocalist and master of ceremonies for the band the Alabamians, but he didn't find success until he led another band, the Missourians, the following year. He changed the band's name to Cab Calloway and His Orchestra and began recording.

In 1931, the band recorded the down-and-dirty "Minnie the Moocher," which became their first hit and signature song. Calloway danced and sang while the band played, often upstaging them with his antics. His gyrating performance of "Minnie" was so popular that in 1932 he "starred" in a Betty Boop cartoon named for the song. A ghost that moved with Calloway's long strut pursued the animated Betty through a dark cave while singing "Minnie." The following year, Calloway sang his hit "St. James Infirmary" in another Betty Boop cartoon, "Snow White," which some historians call one of the most surreal animated films ever made.

Bandleader Cab Calloway often upstaged his excellent jazz band with his own outlandish stage antics. *(Photo courtesy of Showtime Archives, Toronto, and Colin Escott)*

Back in the live world, Calloway and his band replaced DUKE ELLINGTON at New York's legendary Cotton Club. Strutting around the stage in his flashy zoot suit and singing his nonsensical choruses of "Hi De Ho," Calloway was one of the most popular entertainers of the 1930s and 1940s. His band at various times included such jazz greats as trumpeters DIZZY GILLESPIE and Jonah Jones and drummer Cozy Cole. Calloway was among the most generous of the big bandleaders. He always paid his musicians top salaries and gave them plenty of artistic freedom.

Calloway reluctantly disbanded his orchestra in 1948 and later acted in a number of films including *St. Louis Blues* (1958) and *The Cincinnati Kid* (1965). In the 1950s, he starred on Broadway and in London as the extravagant character Sportin' Life in the revival of George Gershwin's folk opera *Porgy and Bess*. He always claimed that Gershwin had modeled the character after him. He later costarred with PEARL BAILEY in the all-black Broadway revival of *Hello Dolly!* (1975).

A popular entertainer for more than five decades, Cab Calloway died on October 18, 1994, at age 87.

Further Reading

Calloway, Cab, with Bryant Rollins. *Of Minnie the Moocher and Me.* New York: Crowell, 1976.

Jazz Profiles. "Cab Calloway: 'A Hi De Ho Centennial.'" NPR Web site. Available online. URL: http//www.npr.org/templates/story/story.php?storyId=17408368. Downloaded on February 3, 2009.

Further Listening

Are You Hep to the Jive? (1935). Sbme Special Mkts, CD, 2008.

Further Viewing

Cab Calloway Swinging at His Best. Passport Video, DVD, 2005.

Cambridge, Godfrey
(1933–1976) *comedian, actor*

Godfrey Cambridge was of the brightest members of the new generation of African-American comics to emerge in the early 1960s, but his career was tragically cut short by his early death at age 43.

He was born on February 26, 1933, in New York City. His parents, Alexander and Sarah Cambridge, were immigrants from British New Guinea who settled in Nova Scotia, Canada, and later moved to the United States. Cambridge was a top student and leader in high school. He was described in the class yearbook as "Unforgettable Godfrey Wonder Boy Cambridge." He attended Hofstra College in New York, where for the first time he found himself the victim of racism and dropped out. After attending City College of New York for a while, he left to pursue a career in acting. While making the rounds of play auditions, he supported himself with a variety of jobs including taxi driver, bouncer at a club, hospital ambulance driver, and judo instructor.

By the late 1950s, Cambridge was acting in Off-Broadway plays and portrayed a hoodlum in his first film, *The Last Angry Man* (1959). Other stage roles followed, including that of the ultimate "Uncle Tom" in OSSIE DAVIS's satirical play *Purlie Victorious* (1962), for which he was nominated for a Tony Award. It was as a stand-up comedian, however, that Cambridge finally won national recognition. He, along with DICK GREGORY, BILL COSBY, and RICHARD PRYOR, represented a new kind of young black comedian, whose sophisticated humor appealed to both black and white audiences. While Gregory was a satirist of race and politics and Cosby dealt with nonracial humor, Cambridge was comfortable with both kinds of material. As he told one audience, "If I would do just racial material, I would go out of my cotton picking mind." A taped appearance on *The Jack Paar Show* in 1964 led to many television appearances and a recording contract with Epic Records. His first comedy album, *Ready or Not, Here's Godfrey Cambridge* (1964), became a best seller.

By the late 1960s, Cambridge's film career began to take off, and he appeared in such offbeat comedies as *The President's Analyst* (1967), where he played a CIA agent, and *Bye Bye Braverman* (1968), which found him in the unlikely role of a Jewish cab driver. Cambridge had the lead role in black filmmaker Melvin van Peebles's *Watermelon Man* (1970), playing a white insurance man (in whiteface!) who wakes up one morning to find himself black. The same year he played black detective Grave Digger Jones in the memorable comedy mystery *Cotton Comes to Harlem,* adapted from a Chester Himes novel and directed by Ossie Davis. He also appeared in the horror comedy *Beware! The Blob!* (1972) and *Friday Foster* (1975), a blaxploitation movie starring PAM GRIER.

In 1976, Cambridge was given one of the most challenging roles of his career, playing Ugandan dictator Idi Amin Dada in the ABC made-for-television movie *Victory at Entebbe.* During filming, Cambridge, who had been overweight for years, suffered a fatal heart attack on the set on November 29.

Further Reading

Bogle, Donald. *Toms, Coons, Mulattoes, Mammies & Bucks: An Interpretive History of Blacks in American Films.* New York: Continuum, 1997, pp. 234–235.

"Godfrey Cambridge." *Current Biography Yearbook 1969.* New York: H. W. Wilson, 1970.

Further Viewing

Cotton Comes to Harlem (1970). MGM Home Entertainment, VHS/DVD, 2001.

Watermelon Man (1970). Sony, DVD, 2004.

Carroll, Diahann
(Carol Diann Johnson)
(1935–) *actress, singer*

One of the most successful and talented African-American female performers of the 1950s and 1960s, Diahann Carroll was the first actress to star as a contemporary black woman in a television series.

Carol Diann Johnson was born on July 17, 1935, in the Bronx, New York. Her father, John Johnson, worked, among other jobs, as a subway conductor and a printer. Her mother, Mabel, was a nurse. Carroll's singing career began at age six in the Tiny Tots choir at the Abyssinian Baptist Church in Harlem. As a youngster she appeared on Arthur Godfrey's television show *Talent Scouts* and won. Her prize was appearing on Godfrey's radio show for three weeks. At age 10 she entered New York's High School of Music and Art on a scholarship from the Metropolitan Opera. While a student majoring in sociology at New York University, she earned extra money by modeling and singing in nightclubs and on television.

Carroll's career in show business took off in 1954 when she made her screen and Broadway debut. She had a small role as a bar girl in the movie *Carmen Jones,* an all-black retelling of Bizet's famous opera, and took Broadway by storm as the ingenue in *House of Flowers,* a musical written by Truman Capote and composer Harold Arlen. Her beguiling delivery of the song "A Sleepin' Bee" helped earned her a Tony nomination as best supporting actress in a musical. During the production she met casting director Monte Kay. Their interracial marriage in 1956 did not please her family.

Carroll's classic beauty and pristine voice made her a celebrity in the late 1950s. She recorded her first solo album and made several more films, including *Porgy and Bess* (1959) and *Paris Blues* (1961) with Paul Newman and SIDNEY POITIER. Recently divorced, Carroll began a nine-year relationship with Poitier that she referred to years later in her autobiography as "self-destructive."

She reached the peak of her career in 1962 when she starred on Broadway in the musical *No Strings,* a show written especially for her by composer Richard Rodgers. She won a Tony Award for her performance, and the original cast album won the Grammy for best original cast show album.

Carroll had made some 60 appearances on television variety shows and had been nominated for an Emmy Award, when in 1968 she starred in the landmark television situation comedy *Julia* on NBC. It was the first TV series to star an African-American woman since *Beulah* went off the air 15 years earlier. Carroll played Julia Baker, a nurse and single mother whose husband was killed in Vietnam. Never before had the American television audience seen an intelligent, middle-class black woman as the leading character in a dramatic series. *Julia* was the seventh-highest-rated series in its first season and ran until 1971, when Carroll decided not to renew her contract. Three years later she was nominated for an Academy Award as best actress in the movie *Claudine* (1974) in which she played a working-class welfare mother.

Her star faded temporarily after that, but she experienced a comeback in 1984 when she appeared in a recurring role on the popular TV drama *Dynasty*. As singer Dominique Deveraux, half sister of the show's star, Blake Carrington, she proved she was still ravishing at age 49. In 1995 Carroll made a triumphant return to the stage as the fading silent screen star Norma Desmond in the Canadian production of the Andrew Lloyd Webber musical *Sunset Boulevard*. Two years later she released her first album in 19 years, *The Time of My Life*, and launched her own fashion line of women's apparel. She has continued to work in television. She played Aunt Ruthie in two episodes of the dramatic series *Soul Food* and the mother of Dr. Preston Burke in the medical series *Grey's Anatomy* during the 2006–07 season.

Carroll's personal life has had its share of ups and downs. She has been married four times. Her second husband, Freddie Glausman, physically abused her. Her fourth husband was singer Vic Damone, whom she divorced in 1996. Carroll was diagnosed with breast cancer in 1998 and has made a full recovery.

Further Reading
Bogle, Donald. *Prime Time Blues: African Americans on Network Television*. New York: Farrar, Straus & Giroux, 2002, pp. 140–156, 262–263.
Carroll, Diahann. *The Legs Are the Last to Go: Aging, Acting, Marrying, and Other Things I Learned the Hard Way*. New York: Amistad, 2008.

Further Listening
The Magic of Diahann Carroll. DRG, CD, 2005.
No Strings (1962) Angel, CD, 1993.

Further Viewing
Claudine (1974). Fox Home Video, DVD, 2003.

Carter, Nell
(Nell Hardy)
(1948–2003) *actress, singer*

Nell Carter was one of the rare performers who parlayed Broadway stardom into a successful acting career in films and television.

She was born Nell Hardy on September 13, 1948, in Birmingham, Alabama. The fifth of nine children, she moved to New York City at age 19 to pursue stage acting. She made her stage debut in a play called *Soon* that costarred two other future Broadway stars, Peter Allen and Barry Bostwick, as well as soon-to-be film star Richard Gere. It would be eight years, however, before Carter became a national celebrity for her role in the Broadway revue, *Ain't Misbehavin'*, based on the songs of FATS WALLER. Carter's sassy, powerhouse delivery of her numbers made her a standout in a top-notch African-American cast that included Ken Page and Andre DeShields. She won the Tony Award for best actress in a musical, the Theater World Award, and the Drama Desk Award. When the show was reprised on television in 1982, Carter won an Emmy Award for outstanding individual achievement.

The previous year she starred in the television situation comedy *Gimme a Break!* as a feisty housekeeper working for a widowed white police officer and his three daughters. The show ran on NBC for six years and earned her two Emmy nominations. However, many people in the black community criticized the show and Carter for perpetuating the black stereotype of the good-hearted maid. "I'm called Mammy and everything else," Carter responded in an interview. "Why can't anyone say, 'Look, there's a black gal that's got her own show!'"

Carter went on to star in several other sitcoms, including *Hangin' with Mr. Cooper*, in which she played a school principal. None of these shows were as successful as *Gimme a Break!* Carter was featured in many television specials, usually as a singer. She also appeared in several movies including *The Grass Harp* with Jack Lemmon and Walter Matthau, and *The Proprietor* (both 1996).

A big woman with energy to spare, Carter faced many difficulties in her private life. Two marriages ended in divorce, a brother died of AIDS, and she fought a long battle against alcohol and drug addiction. In 1992, she nearly died during brain surgery for a double aneurysm. "They tell me I wouldn't survive," Carter later said, "but I had to live for my children." She died suddenly on January 23, 2003, of heart disease at her Beverly Hills home. She was 54 years old.

Further Reading

"Nell Carter." The Internet Movie Database. Available online. URL: http//imdb.com/name/nm0141846/. Downloaded on February 3, 2009.

"Nell Carter: Biography." TV.com. Available online. URL: http://www.TV.com/nell-carter/person/14725/biography.html. Downloaded on February 3, 2009.

Further Listening

Ain't Misbehavin' (1978). RCA Victor Broadway, 2 CDs, 1990.

Further Viewing

Gimme a Break!—Season 1 (1981). Universal, DVD box set, 2006.

Chapman, Tracy
(1964–   ) *folksinger, songwriter, guitarist*

An unlikely pop star for the 1980s and 1990s, Tracy Chapman has brought the social and personal concerns of American folk music to a new generation of listeners.

She was born on March 20, 1964, in Cleveland, Ohio. Her parents divorced when she was four, and she and her older sister were raised by their mother, an amateur guitarist. A gifted child, she composed her first song at age eight and started playing the guitar a few years later. Although the family was poor, Chapman attended a private boarding school in Connecticut on a scholarship. Her dedication to her music was evident to her classmates. The prediction in the yearbook under her picture said that she would marry her guitar and live happily ever after. After graduation, she attended Tufts University, outside Boston, Massachusetts, where she studied anthropology and sang her songs on the streets of Harvard Square.

A classmate introduced her to an agent who got her an audition with Elektra Records. Elektra was impressed by Chapman's talent but felt her sparse style and acoustic guitar would be difficult to market. In 1988, they released an album, titled simply *Tracy Chapman*. To everyone's surprise, including Chapman's, her songs of poverty, depression, and dreams struck a chord with contemporary listeners. The album became a phenomenon and eventually sold 10 million copies worldwide. "Fast Car," a song about two young people's desperate attempt to escape ghetto life, became a top-10 hit. Another cut, "Talkin' 'Bout a Revolution," made the top 50.

Chapman was nominated for six Grammy Awards that year and was expected to sweep the awards. But the conservative Grammy community was not ready for her sharp social criticism, and she lost in the categories of best song and record of the year to "Don't Worry, Be Happy" by BOBBY MCFERRIN. She did win Grammys for best new artist, best pop vocal performance by a female for "Fast Car," and best contemporary folk music album.

Chapman's next album, *Crossroads* (1989), was critically acclaimed but not as well received by the public. The title song was an intriguing twist on the old African-American folk tale about selling one's soul to the devil at the crossroads. *New Beginnings* (1995), her fourth album, contained the song "Give Me One Reason," which became her biggest hit single to date and won her a fourth Grammy, for best song.

Chapman's commitment to social change does not end with her songs. She has performed in such live concerts as London's Freedomfest, honoring Nelson Mandela, and Amnesty International's Human Rights Tour. Her fifth album, *Telling Stories*, was released in 2000. Reviewing her 2008 album *Our Bright Future*, a *Billboard* critic wrote: "Twenty years after her self-titled debut, Tracy Chapman remains true to her musical calling: soul-rich folk melodies around a voice of honesty and nuance that nails ambivalence like no other."

Further Reading

"About Tracy Chapman." Available online. URL: http://www.about-tracy-chapman.net/. Downloaded on February 12, 2009.

The Official Tracy Chapman Web site. Available online. URL: http://www.tracychapman.com. Downloaded on February 3, 2009.

Further Listening

Our Bright Future. Atlantic, CD, 2008.

Tracy Chapman. Elektra Entertainment, CD, 1988.

Charles, Ray

(Ray Charles Robinson)
(1930–2004) *singer, pianist, bandleader, songwriter*

By blending gospel music and rhythm and blues (R & B), Ray Charles, more than any other performer, could lay claim to inventing soul music.

As writer Peter Guralnick puts it, if JAMES BROWN is the Godfather of Soul then Ray Charles is nothing less than soul's grandfather.

Ray Charles Robinson was born on September 23, 1930, in Albany, Georgia. His family moved to Greenville, Florida, while he was still an infant. He developed glaucoma at an early age and became completely blind by age seven. Robinson attended St. Augustine's School for the Deaf and Blind in Orlando, where he studied classical piano and clarinet in imitation of one of his idols, bandleader and clarinetist Artie Shaw.

Robinson's father, Bailey, a handyman, died two years later. Robinson's mother, Reather, passed away when he was 15. He left school at 15 and got a job playing with a country and western band in Jacksonville, Florida.

Wanting a fresh start, Robinson had a friend find him the farthermost point from Florida on a United States map. It was Seattle, Washington, and he moved there in 1948. In Seattle, Robinson formed a trio of piano, bass, and guitar. The group played jazzy, cocktail music, modeling themselves after the then-popular NAT KING COLE trio. During this time, Robinson dropped his last name to avoid confusion with the boxer Sugar Ray Robinson.

Finding little success with his first recordings, Charles disbanded the trio and moved to Los Angeles. There he signed with the pioneer R & B label Atlantic in 1952, but he remained a kind of bluesy Nat King Cole imitator and his records did not sell. When he moved to New Orleans the following year, Charles finally began to develop his own musical identity—one that drew on gospel music and an earthier kind of blues. His recording of "I've Got a Woman" (1955), made in an Atlanta, Georgia, radio station, was his breakthrough disk. The song's hard-driving gospel sound wedded to rhythm and blues was something new in popular music, and it became a national hit on the R & B charts.

Charles began a string of R & B hits for Atlantic that included such classic recordings as "This

A prime creator of soul music, Ray Charles enjoyed popularity that eventually transcended every musical genre. *(AP Photo)*

Little Girl of Mine," "Drown in My Own Tears," and "Hallelujah I Love Her So." In 1959, his self-penned "What'd I Say" featured his backup girl group the Raelettes in a call-and-respond that came straight from black church music. The song became Charles's first million-seller and one of the most performed R & B songs of the decade.

In 1960, Charles signed with the ABC-Paramount label and soon had his first number-one pop hit with the classic Hoagy Carmichael song "Georgia on My Mind." It was one of the proudest moments in the singer's life when years later his soulful rendition became the official state song of Georgia.

Charles's big band was one of the most exciting in the nation and, with him on piano, had a top-10 instrumental hit with "One Mint Julep" (1961). Later that year, he reached number one again with the infectious rocker "Hit the Road Jack." Then Charles made a bold and, some thought, foolhardy move: he released an album of country and western songs. Charles's instincts were right, and his soulful voice and arrangements brought new life and vitality to the country classics on *Modern Sounds in Country and Western Music* (1962). It became one of the biggest-selling albums of the decade and the track "I Can't Stop Loving You" was the number-two record of the year.

Through the mid-1960s, everything Charles touched seemed to turn to gold. He hit the charts with everything from country and western ("Take These Chains From My Heart," "Crying Time") to jazz ("Smack Dab in the Middle"), to R & B ("Let's Go Get Stoned"). But there were personal problems, too. In 1965, he was arrested for heroin possession, and it was learned that he had been taking drugs since the age of 16. Charles entered a sanitarium in California and eventually kicked his heroin habit.

By the late 1960s, most of his albums were middle-of-the-road efforts and they included many covers of popular songs by the Beatles and others. Charles's music had lost its cutting edge. He spent a good part of the 1970s touring around the world and developing his own record company and music publishing firm.

In the 1980s, Ray Charles had become a national treasure whose popularity crossed all lines of race, age, and musical taste. Anything the "genius of soul" sang became special, including his memorable rendition of "America the Beautiful." In 1986 he was a recipient of the Kennedy Center Honors in the Performing Arts and was inducted into the Rock and Roll Hall of Fame. In 1987, he received Grammy's Lifetime Achievement Award. He won a total of 12 Grammys.

Much has been said and written about Ray Charles's "genius," but the singer took all such talk in his stride. "Whatever people say about me or call me, that's their business," he told one interviewer. "I don't get hung up on it. It's the highest compliment, and I'm not trying to be cute, but I didn't create the fuss, so all I really have to do is continue what I'm doing for as long as God keeps breath in my body." Ray Charles died at age 73 of complications of liver disease on June 10, 2004. *Ray,* a biopic directed by Taylor Hackford with JAMIE FOXX as Charles, was released the same year.

Further Reading

Charles, Ray, and David Ritz. *Brother Ray: Ray Charles' Own Story.* New York: Da Capo Press, 2004.

Duggelby, John. *Uh Huh!: The Story of Ray Charles.* Greensboro, N.C.: Morgan Reynolds Publishing, 2005.

Lydon, Michael. *Ray Charles: Man and Music.* New York: Routledge, 2004.

Further Listening

The Birth of Soul: The Complete Atlantic Rhythm and Blues Recordings 1952–1959. Atlantic, CD box set, 1991.

Genius Loves Company. Concord Records, CD, 2004.

Ray Charles: Ultimate Hits Collection. Rhino, 2 CDs, 1999.

Further Viewing

Ray (2004). Universal, DVD, 2005.

Ray Charles: In Concert (1999). Image Entertainment, DVD, 2001.

Cheadle, Don
(Donald Frank Cheadle)
(1964–   ) *actor, film producer, social activist*

Perhaps not as well known as some of his contemporaries, Don Cheadle is nonetheless one of the busiest and most respected black actors in Hollywood and has played a wide range of roles with conviction and skill.

He was born Donald Frank Cheadle on November 29, 1964, in Kansas City, Missouri. His father, Donald, is a clinical psychologist, and his mother, Betty, a bank manager and psychology teacher. Drawn to acting as a child, Cheadle played a rat in a fifth-grade production of *Charlotte's Web.* "I read up on rats and got into their psychology," he said in an interview. Cheadle graduated from East High School in Denver, Colorado, and went on to earn a bachelor of arts from the California Institute of Arts, majoring in fine arts.

His first professional work on stage was as a stand-up comedian. In 1982, he was cast as a student in the television series *Fame.* He made his film debut in the comedy *Moving Violations*

(1985), in which he delivered two lines. Cheadle's first substantial role was as a soldier in Vietnam in *Hamburger Hill* (1987). He continued to play small parts in films until he gained major notice as DENZEL WASHINGTON's out-of-control pal in the detective mystery *Devil in a Blue Dress* (1995). The role earned him a best supporting actor award from the Los Angeles film critics. Better roles followed, and Cheadle quickly gained a reputation as an "actor's actor" who could enliven any part through drive and personality. He played a cowboy porno star in *Boogie Nights* (1997); an inept, comical ex-con in *Out of Sight* (1998); a prison teacher in *A Lesson before Dying* (1999); and a dedicated Drug Enforcement Agency (DEA) agent in *Traffic* (2000). *Out of Sight* and *Traffic* were directed by Stephen Soderbergh, who has cast Cheadle in three other films. "Don gives you this energy, that's totally explosive, and if you're not ready for it, he'll blow you off the screen," Soderbergh has said.

Cheadle moved into star roles with his powerful portrayal of a real-life hotel manager devoted to saving the lives of people targeted during a genocidal civil war in Africa in *Hotel Rwanda* (2004). The role earned him an Academy Award nomination for best actor. His involvement in the film made Cheadle an impassioned advocate for international intervention in Darfur and other African nations where civil war has led to widespread genocide. Besides raising money for these causes and testifying before congressional committees, Cheadle coauthored a book on the subject in 2007. That same year, he was awarded the Black Entertainment Television (BET) Humanitarian Award.

More recent roles include the detective in the Oscar-winning film *Crash* (2004), real-life radio talk show host Ralph "Petey" Greene in *Talk to Me* (2007), and the title character in the controversial *Traitor* (2008). Cheadle also produced all three movies.

Don Cheadle lives with actress Brigid Coulter and their two daughters, Iamni and Ayana.

He is a champion poker player and plays the saxophone. Averaging four films a year, Cheadle is one of the hardest-working actors in Hollywood. Thanks to recent starring roles, he is no longer, as writer David Hochman called him in 2003, "the most famous actor most people never heard of."

Further Reading

Cheadle, Don, and John Prendergast. *Not on Our Watch: The Mission to End Genocide in Darfur and Beyond.* New York: Hyperion, 2007.

"Don Cheadle." The Internet Movie Database. Available online. URL: http://www.imdb.com/name/nm0000332/. Downloaded on December 9, 2008.

Hochman, David. "You Know Him, the D.E.A. Agent? The Cowboy Porn Star?" *New York Times*, June 8, 2003, Arts & Leisure, p. 13.

Further Viewing

Crash (2005). Lions Gate, DVD, 2005.

Hotel Rwanda (2005). MGM Home Entertainment, DVD, 2005.

A Lesson before Dying (1999). HBO Home Video, DVD, 2000.

Traitor (2008). Anchor Bay, DVD, 2008.

Checker, Chubby

(Ernest Evans)
(1941–) *rock singer*

One of the biggest hit makers of the pre-Beatles 1960s, Chubby Checker will always be associated with the twist, the dance he made an international craze.

He was born Ernest Evans in Spring Valley, South Carolina, on October 3, 1941. His father was a construction worker who moved the family to Philadelphia when Ernest was 10. He started singing in the local Baptist church and attended South Philadelphia High, the alma mater of two other 1960s teen idols, Fabian and Frankie

Avalon. Evans sang in a doo-wop group called the Quentrells and earned the nickname "Fat Ernie" for his portly size.

After graduation, he went to work in a poultry shop, where he entertained fellow workers and customers by doing impressions of famous singers while he plucked chickens. His boss sensed talent here and brought Evans to his friend Kal Mann, who owned Cameo-Parkway Records. Mann's friend Dick Clark, who hosted television's *American Bandstand,* was looking for someone to make a novelty record for his annual Christmas card, and Mann suggested Evans. While Evans was working on his impression of singer FATS DOMINO, Clark's wife entered the studio and christened him Chubby Checker, because he looked and sang like a young Fats Domino. The name stuck.

Soon after, Mann had Checker record his first single for the label, a novelty song called "The Class." The record scraped the top 40, but several follow-up novelties flopped. Then Mann gave Checker "The Twist" to record. The song had already been a modest hit for rhythm and blues (R & B) singer Hank Ballard, who also wrote it. The Checker version was a carbon copy of the original, so much so that when Ballard first heard the song on the radio he thought it was him singing.

Chubby Checker's version roared up the charts to number one in September 1960. Ballard had never clarified how the twist was actually danced, and Checker's label had to make up the movements. "Just pretend you're wiping your bottom with a towel as you get out of the shower and putting out a cigarette with both feet," Chubby told a national audience on Clark's Saturday night program.

Checker had another number-one hit with "The Pony" in early 1961 and then struck with "Let's Twist Again" that summer. The dance was starting to fade among teens, but that fall it caught on with the high society crowd that danced at the Peppermint Lounge in midtown

New York. Cameo Parkway reissued the single, and it climbed again to the number-one position in early 1962. The only other record to achieve this distinction was Bing Crosby's recording of "White Christmas."

Checker continued to mine the rich twist vein with such hits as "Slow Twistin'" and "Twistin' U.S.A." A passable singer with little charisma, he made some of his most appealing records from folk material—"Twenty Miles," "Loddy Lo," based on a Bahamian folk song, and "Hey, Bobble Needle."

By the mid 1960s, his music was losing ground to newer, fresher sounds in rock. A couple of comebacks in the early 1970s and 1980s fizzled. Checker finally returned to the record charts in 1988 with his first top-40 song in 23 years. It was (what else?) "The Twist (Yo, Twist)" backed up by the contemporary rock group Fat Boys.

In 2001, on the eve of his 60th birthday, Chubby Checker took out a full-page ad in *Billboard* magazine in which he demanded a statue of himself in the courtyard of the Rock and Roll Hall of Fame and Museum in Cleveland, Ohio. Many believe Checker's anger comes from his failure so far to be even nominated for recognition there. "The Twist" was ranked number one on *Billboard*'s 2008 list of the most popular singles since 1958.

Further Reading

"Chubby Checker Online." The Official Chubby Checker Web site. Available online. URL: http//www.chubbychecker.com. Downloaded on February 3, 2009.

Dawson, Jim. *The Twist.* Boston: Faber & Faber, 1995.

Further Listening

Chubby Checker's Greatest Hits (1972). K-Tel, CD, 1993.

Further Viewing

Twist (1993). Home Vision Entertainment, DVD, 2002.

Cole, Nat King
(Nathaniel Adams Coles)
(1919–1965) *pop singer, jazz pianist, songwriter, actor*

One of the premier popular singers of the 1950s and 1960s, Nat King Cole was perhaps the first African-American vocalist to successfully reach a large white audience.

He was born Nathaniel Adams Coles on March 17, 1919, in Montgomery, Alabama. His father, Edward Coles, was a minister, and his first musical experience was playing organ in his father's church. The family moved to Chicago, Illinois, where Coles formed his first band, the Royal Dukes, while still in high school. In 1936, he joined the touring company of the hit all-black musical revue *Shuffle Along* as a pianist. When the show ended its run in Los Angeles, California, Coles made a precarious living for several years as a pianist in local bars and clubs. One club owner dubbed him "King" in 1937. He formed a trio with bassist Wesley Prince and guitarist Oscar Moore in 1939 and dropped the *s* from his last name. The group was supposed to be a quartet but the drummer failed to show up on the opening night of the group's debut.

The Nat King Cole Trio specialized in jazzy cocktail music and found it difficult to compete with the big bands then popular. Gradually the trio found an audience, however, due in large part to Cole's inventive piano playing and smooth singing. Few of his later pop fans realized that in the 1940s Cole was one of the best jazz pianists and a key figure in the transition from the swing music of the 1930s to the modern jazz of the late 1940s. He was one of the first pianists to master the method of hitting chords in short, rhythmic bursts called "comping."

The trio's intricate interplay amazed no less a jazz master than COUNT BASIE, who remarked, "These cats used to read each others minds—it was unbelievable."

The trio signed with Capitol Records in 1942 and in 1944 had their first hit record, Cole's original song "Straighten Up and Fly Right." Two years later they recorded Mel Tormé's "The Christmas Song," which would become a holiday standard. The same year the Nat King Cole Trio became the first black musical group to have their own radio program, which was broadcast weekly for more than a year.

In December 1947, Cole made his first solo recording, "Nature Boy," in New York backed by a string orchestra. Released in early 1948, it shot to number one on the pop charts within a week and established Cole as a major ballad singer. Later that year he married singer Marie Ellington. Cole's creamy, silken tenor and clear articulation made him as popular with white listeners as black ones. He left the trio in 1950 and concentrated on singing after that, abandoning both jazz and the piano, something that jazz critics never forgave him for.

Few pop singers have been so beloved by the public as Nat King Cole. *(Photo courtesy of Showtime Archives, Toronto, and Pictorial Press)*

Cole turned out one hit song after another, most of them ballads. Among his biggest hits were "Mona Lisa" (1950), "Too Young" (1951), "Unforgettable" (1952), and "A Blossom Fell" (1954). In 1956, Cole was given his own television variety show on NBC. *The Nat King Cole Show* was the first major TV series to be hosted by an African American. Many southern stations refused to carry a show starring a Negro, and most sponsors shied away from the program. Top white and black performers supported the show by appearing for scale wages, but that was not enough to save it; it went off the air in December 1957.

In his own quiet way, Cole stood up courageously against racial prejudice. He refused to perform before segregated audiences in the South, and during a concert in Birmingham, Alabama, in 1956, he was brutally assaulted by white racists.

In the 1950s, he appeared as himself in a number of Hollywood films including *The Blue Gardenia* (1953) and *Istanbul* (1957). His big attempt at a dramatic role was playing composer W. C. HANDY in the biopic *St. Louis Blues* (1958). The highly fictionalized film was a disappointment, and Cole's acting was weak and unconvincing.

Cole had only a few big hit records in the late 1950s, but he returned to the top of the charts in the early 1960s with such hits as "Ramblin' Rose" (1962), "Those Lazy-Hazy Crazy Days of Summer" (1963), and the sweetly wistful "That Sunday, That Summer" (1963). His last top-40 song was "I Don't Want to See Tomorrow" (1964), whose title was grimly prophetic. That same year, Cole, a longtime smoker, was diagnosed with lung cancer. He died February 15, 1965, in Santa Monica, California, at age 45.

Nat King Cole had a remarkable 104 charting records. The last of them was perhaps his strangest. His daughter Natalie Cole, who followed in her father's footsteps and became a rhythm and blues (R & B) singer, recorded a duet with her father by dubbing his voice onto a new version of "Unforgettable" in 1991. Cole's two brothers, Ike and Freddy, were also jazz musicians.

Nat King Cole was posthumously awarded Grammy's Lifetime Achievement Award in 1990. He was honored with a U.S. postage stamp in 1994 as part of the Legends of American Music Series. In 2000, he was inducted into the Rock and Roll Hall of Fame as an early influence.

Further Reading

Cole, Maria, with Louie Robinson. *Nat King Cole: An Intimate Biography.* New York: William Morrow, 1971.

Epstein, Daniel Mark. *Nat King Cole.* Holliston, Mass.: Northeastern, 2000.

Gourse, Leslie. *Unforgettable.* Lanham, Md.: Cooper Square Press, 2000.

Ruuth, Marianne. *Nat King Cole.* Black American Series. Los Angeles: Holloway House, 1992.

Simpkins, Daphne. *Nat King Cole: An Unforgettable Life of Music.* Montgomery, Ala.: June Bug Books, 2001 (YA).

Further Listening

The Best of the Nat King Cole Trio: The Vocal Classics, Vol. 1 (1942–46), Vol. 2 (1947–1950). Blue Note, 2 CDs, 1995, 1996.

Nat King Cole Trio: Instrumental Classics. Blue Note, CD, 1992.

The Very Best of Nat King Cole. Capitol, CD, 2006.

Further Viewing

The Incomparable Nat King Cole, Vols. 1 & 2 (1956). White Star, DVD, 2002.

Coltrane, John
("Trane")
(1926–1967) *jazz saxophonist, composer, bandleader*

Considered by many to be one of the true visionaries of jazz, John Coltrane moved from style to style over his two-decade career but never lost the lyricism and honesty that made his music unique.

He was born on September 23, 1926, in Hamlet, North Carolina. After high school he moved to Philadelphia, Pennsylvania, and enlisted in the navy, where he played alto saxophone in a military band. After service, he played in several bands during the early postwar years. During this time he switched to the tenor sax and found the perfect "voice" for his talents.

In 1948, Coltrane joined DIZZY GILLESPIE's big band and then played in Gillespie's sextet through 1951. He returned to Philadelphia and went to school to study music. He joined MILES DAVIS's famous quintet in 1955. During this time he became addicted to alcohol and heroin and quit Davis's group to kick his habit. He later returned to the group but also began pursuing a solo career.

Coltrane first recorded for Atlantic Records in 1959 and soon reached his full maturity as a musician, composer, and bandleader. His first and greatest quartet included McCoy Tyner on piano, Jimmy Garrison on bass, and Elvin Jones on drums. "His colleagues," wrote jazz critic Nat Hentoff in 1964, "have become so sensitized to him and to each other that they move through Coltrane's moods with a unity of feeling and a subtle interplay of complementary ideas which make this one of the most organically fused combos in . . . jazz."

Besides an innate lyricism, Coltrane's music was marked by a deep spirituality. *A Love Supreme* (1964), a four-part devotional suite, became one of the decade's best-selling jazz albums. Jazz musician WYNTON MARSALIS claims that all Coltrane's music is characterized by "the lyrical shout of the preacher in the heat and full fury of attempting to transform the congregation."

By the mid-1960s, Coltrane's music was moving into the uncharted territory of free jazz that disregarded traditional forms, rhythms, and tonalities. This experimental music has since grown in stature, but it appealed to few listeners at the time.

Although he strove to be a saint in his music and personal life, Coltrane's misspent youth caught up with him and he died of cancer July 17, 1967, at age 40. A church in San Francisco is named in his honor. It is the only church in the United States dedicated to a jazz musician. In 1995, he was honored on a U.S. postage stamp along with nine other jazz musicians.

Once asked about the nature of his music, John Coltrane replied, "I don't know what I'm looking for, something that hasn't been played before. I don't know what it is, I know I'll have that feeling when I get it."

Further Reading

Nisenson, Eric. *Ascension: John Coltrane and His Quest.* New York: Da Capo Press, 1995.

Porter, Lewis. *John Coltrane: His Life and Music.* Ann Arbor: University of Michigan Press, 2000.

Ratliff, Ben. *Coltrane: The Story of a Sound.* New York: Picador, 2008.

Thomas, J. C. *Chasin' the Trane: The Music and Mystique of John Coltrane.* New York: Da Capo Press, 1988.

Weatherford, Carole Boston. *Before John Was a Jazz Giant: A Song of John Coltrane.* New York: Henry Holt, 2008 (children).

Further Listening

A Love Supreme (1964). Impulse Records, CD, 2003.

The Very Best of John Coltrane. Atlantic, CD, 2000.

Further Viewing

Jazz Icons: John Coltrane Live in '60, '61 & '65. Jazz Icons, DVD, 2007.

Combs, Sean "Puffy"

("Puff Daddy," "P Diddy")
(1969–   ) *record, film, and television producer; arranger; rap singer; actor*

Hip-hop's most successful entrepreneur, Sean "Puffy" Combs launched the careers of a number of top recording artists before making his own stellar debut as a rapper.

Sean Combs has found success in every endeavor—from record producer to rap singer to business entrepreneur. *(AP Photo/Chris Pizzello)*

He was born on November 4, 1969, in New York City. His father died when he was three and his mother Janice, a former kindergarten teacher, raised him. He earned the nickname "Puffy" as a child because he would huff and puff when he lost his temper. Combs attended a Catholic boys' high school before going to Howard University in Washington, D.C., to major in business management. He left Howard in 1990 during his junior year to take an internship at Uptown Records in New York. Within a year, he was vice president of artists and repertory and helped guide the career of the queen of hip-hop, MARY J. BLIGE.

In 1993, Combs formed his own label, Bad Boy, with the help of Arista Records. In three years, Combs's label sold more than 12 million albums, introducing such performers as Faith, Mase, and Christopher ("The Notorious B.I.G.") Wallace, who became his best friend. As a producer, Combs used creative sampling, taking bits and piece of other people's hit records, mostly from the 1980s, to make commercial hip-hop that appealed to a mass listening audience.

In 1997, Combs and Wallace flew to Los Angeles to attend the Soul Train Awards. After the party following the awards ceremony, Wallace and Combs were sitting in a car when an unknown assailant shot Wallace to death. The experience almost drove Combs to leave the record business. Instead he was inspired to make a record about Wallace's death and how it had changed him. *No Way Out* (1996), Combs's debut album, was released under the name "Puff Daddy." The album contained the song "I'll Be Missing You," a tribute to Wallace, that sampled the Police's 1980s hit "Every Breath You Take" and featured the late rapper's wife, Faith Evans. "I'll Be Missing You" became a number-one hit in 16 countries and won Combs the American Society of Composers, Authors, and Producers (ASCAP) songwriter of the year award. In 2009, he was executive producer of a biopic *Notorious*, about Wallace's life.

Combs's reputation as the producer with the golden touch has brought him such divergent clients as ARETHA FRANKLIN, Mariah Carey, and Boyz II Men. His business skills seem to know no bounds. He opened a Caribbean and soul food restaurant, Justin's, named for his son, in Manhattan. He also started his own clothing line and is developing a movie company, Bad Boy Films. Combs's charity foundation, Daddy's Home Social Programs, helps underprivileged inner city children. In his first major acting role, Combs played a condemned prisoner in the movie *Monster's Ball* (2001) opposite HALLE BERRY. He was interviewed for the television rap music documentary *Street Dreams* (2002). In 2004, Combs made his Broadway debut in a leading role in a revival of the Lorraine Hansberry play *A Raisin in the Sun.* His costars were AUDRA McDONALD and PHYLICIA RASHAD. He reprised the role in a 2008 television version of the production.

Not all the publicity Combs gets, however, is positive. In 1999, while at a Manhattan nightclub with former girlfriend and singer Jennifer Lopez, Combs was implicated in a shooting that left three people injured. His protégé, rapper Jamal Barrow, aka Shyne, was sentenced to 10 years in prison for the shooting in June 2001.

In recent years, Combs has been polishing his image. He ran in the 2003 New York City Marathon, raising $2 million for children's charities. He led the Citizen Change's "Vote or Die!" campaign in 2004 to get young people and minorities to the polls to vote. Among his numerous television production credits is the reality series *I Want to Work for Diddy* (2008).

Further Reading

Bowman, Elizabeth Atkins. *Sean 'Puffy' Combs.* Black Americans of Achievement. New York: Chelsea House, 2003.

Cable, Andrew. *A Family Affair: The Unauthorized Sean "Puffy" Combs Story.* New York: Ballantine Books, 1998.

Ro, Ronin. *Bad Boy: The Influence of Sean "Puffy" Combs on the Music Industry.* New York: Atria, 2001.

Further Listening

No Way Out. Bad Boy Entertainment, CD, 1997.
Press Play. Bad Boy Entertainment, CD, 2006.

Further Viewing

Fade to Black (2004). Paramount, DVD, 2005.
A Raisin in the Sun. Sony, DVD, 2008.

Cooke, Sam
(Samuel Cook, Dale Cook)
(1931–1964) *R & B singer, songwriter, record producer*

A singer with a voice unmatched for its purity of tone, Sam Cooke, more than almost any other recording artist, was responsible for the soul music explosion of the 1960s and 1970s. Cooke had not yet reached the heights of his career when he was tragically killed under circumstances that remain mysterious to this day.

He was born Samuel Cook on January 22, 1931, in Clarksdale, Mississippi, the son of Reverend Charles Cook, a Baptist minister, and his wife, Annie May. The family moved to Chicago a short time later and by age six Sam was singing in the choir of his father's church. At 15, he was a member of the Highway QC's, a gospel group. Cook's dynamic voice, with its unique ability to bend a note, quickly made him a great success in the gospel world. In 1950, at age 20, he replaced the legendary R. H. Harris in the premier gospel group, the Soul Stirrers. For nearly six years Cook toured the country with the Soul Stirrers, gaining more fervent fans wherever he sang.

By 1956, Cook decided to forsake the gospel market for the more lucrative field of pop music. He recorded his first pop song, "Lovable," under the name Dale Cook, so as not to dismay his gospel fans. The record sold poorly and Specialty Records, which produced his gospel records, dropped him. Cook went to Keen Records, a small label in Los Angeles, and recorded the deceptively simple ballad "You Send Me" (1957), a song he wrote himself. It sold 2.5 million copies, went to number one on the pop charts, and made Sam Cooke, who recently added an *e* to his name, an overnight pop star. Over the next two years, he had a string of catchy hits on Keen, including "Everybody Likes to Cha Cha Cha," "Only Sixteen," and "Wonderful World."

Perhaps the first black teen idol, Cooke signed with RCA Records in 1960 and soon had a smash hit with the classic "Chain Gang." While the catchy song was definitely pop, a number of his later RCA records would be in a more mature, blues vein, drawing as well on his gospel roots. They include "Sad Mood" (1960), "Having a Party" (1962), and "Bring It on Home to Me" (1962), which had a gospel call and response featuring Cooke's friend and protégé, LOU RAWLS.

Cooke wrote many of his best songs, including "Twistin' the Night Away" (1962), "Another Saturday Night" (1963), and the achingly beautiful, understated civil rights anthem, "A Change Is Gonna Come" (1965), which appeared a month after his death.

Cooke was one of the first black entertainers to have complete control over his career. He had his own publishing company, Kags Music, and his own record company, Sar/Derby Records, which he founded in 1960. Sar became a showcase for other black artists making the crossover from gospel to rhythm and blues (R & B) and included such future stars as Bobby Womack, Billy Preston, Mel Carter, Johnnie Taylor, as well as Rawls.

Sam Cooke was at the top of his game when one misstep ended it all. On the evening of December 11, 1964, Cooke, a notorious womanizer, picked up a Hispanic woman and brought her to the Hacienda Motel in Los Angeles. The woman claimed that Cooke tried to rape her, and she fled with his clothes to a phone booth where she called police. Meanwhile, an enraged Cooke stormed into the motel office and was shot three times by the motel manager, a black woman. He died shortly after. All charges against the two women were dropped, and the killing was declared to be in self-defense. In an exhaustive study of the events, Cooke biographer Daniel Wolff makes a convincing case in Cooke's defense. According to his evidence, the apparent "victim" was actually a prostitute who probably stole Cooke's wallet along with his clothes while he was in the bathroom. The motel manager also knew her and may have been part of a scam operation.

As scandalous as his early death was, Sam Cooke's memory lived on. More than 40 years later, the legacy of his music looms larger than ever.

Further Reading

Guralnick, Peter. *Dream Boogie: The Triumph of Sam Cooke.* San Francisco, Calif.: Back Bay Books, 2006.

Wolff, Daniel, with S. R. Crain, Clifton White, and G. David Tenebaum. *You Send Me: The Life and Times of Sam Cooke.* New York: William Morrow, 1996.

Further Listening

The Man Who Invented Soul. RCA, CD box set, 2000.
Portrait of a Legend, 1951–1964. AbKCo, CD, 2003.

Further Viewing

Sam Cooke—Legend. AbKCo, DVD, 2003.

Cosby, Bill
(William Henry Cosby, Jr.)
(1937–) *comedian, actor, film and television producer*

The preeminent television star of the 1980s, Bill Cosby has had an impact on contemporary American culture that few other African Americans have had. He has used his celebrity to entertain, to educate, and to improve life for all Americans.

He was born William Henry Cosby, Jr., on July 12, 1937, in Germantown, a poor section of Philadelphia, Pennsylvania. He quit high school in 10th grade to join the navy, following in the footsteps of his father, who was a navy mess steward. While in the navy, Cosby earned his high school equivalency and went on to attend Temple University in Philadelphia after his discharge. A naturally funny storyteller and quipster in college, Cosby left Temple before graduating to try to become a standup comic. Success wasn't long in coming. His nonracial humor was clean, imaginative, and very funny. In 1963, he made the first of 22 best-selling comedy albums, *Bill Cosby Is a Very Funny Fellow . . . Right!* Five of his albums would win Grammy Awards. About the same time he made his national television debut on *The Tonight Show* and later became the first African American to regularly guest-host that late-night talk show.

Television producer Leonard Sheldon cast the appealing young comic in the action adventure series *I Spy* in 1965. The show's sponsors and network, NBC, insisted that Cosby, who had never acted before, be replaced. Sheldon threatened to quit if he was dropped, and the network relented. Cosby proved to be up to the job and won an Emmy Award as best actor in a dramatic series for the three years the show was on the air. He became the first black performer to star in a prime-time dramatic series.

A year after *I Spy* ended, Cosby returned to television as a high-school basketball coach in *The Bill Cosby Show,* which he also helped produce. The show ran only two seasons. His third series, *The New Bill Cosby Show,* a comedy and variety show, lasted just one season in 1972. The same year he had far greater success with an animated Saturday morning show, *Fat Albert and the Cosby Kids.* The characters were based on childhood friends who were already a staple of his comedy act. The show was a hit with young viewers and was praised by educators for teaching kids good values. Cosby's deep interest in education led him to return to college and earn a doctoral degree in education at the University of Massachusetts at Amherst.

His fourth effort in prime-time television, *Cos* (1976), was another flop. Cosby was more successful in a series of light comedy films, in which he costarred with SIDNEY POITIER. They included *Uptown Saturday Night* (1974) and *A Piece of the Action* (1977). Few of his later films hold up as well as these.

A sharp critic of the lack of values and the prevalent violence on American television, Cosby got his chance to present an alternative in 1984 with *The Cosby Show.* Cosby took this sitcom about an upper-middle-class black family seriously. He hired black writers and black directors to make it as authentic as possible and even hired Dr. Alvin Poussaint, a leading black child psychologist, as an adviser for the show. Cosby played Dr. Cliff Huxtable, a married man with five children. PHYLICIA RASHAD costarred as his lawyer wife. Some people criticized the show for not being overtly black and dealing with black problems. Yet most viewers found *The Cosby Show* to be intelligent, funny, and relevant without being preachy. "I want to show a family like the kind I know," Cosby said. "Children who are almost a pain in the neck, and parents who aren't far behind."

Although race was not central to the Huxtables' lives, it was not ignored either. Cosby brought in such great African-American performers for guest shots as jazzman DIZZY GILLESPIE, singer LENA HORNE, and modern dancer and choreographer JUDITH JAMISON. The artwork of African-American artist Varnette Honeywood hung on the walls of the Huxtable home and they frequently listened to rhythm and blues (R & B) and jazz.

The Cosby Show was one of television's most popular programs. It was the number-one show on TV for three years and ran for eight seasons. Cosby himself seemed to be everywhere on television in the 1980s. He appeared in commercials for Jell-O, Coca-Cola, Eastman Kodak, and other products. By then one of the wealthiest men in show business, Cosby gave generously to many causes including African-American colleges, the National Association for the Advancement of Colored People (NAACP), and the National Sickle-Cell Foundation.

He returned to prime time in 1996 in *Cosby,* in which he played retiree Hilton Lucas with Phylicia Rashad once again playing his wife. The show ran for four seasons.

Cosby is also the best-selling author of a number of books, mostly about his own experiences. They include *Fatherhood* (1986), *Love and Marriage* (1989), and *Cosbyology* (2002).

In 1997, Cosby's only son, Ennis, was murdered in Southern California during an attempted robbery. Cosby and his wife Camille established the Hello Friend/Ennis William Cosby Foundation in his honor to promote education and understanding.

Cosby returned to television in 1998 to host *Kids Say the Darnest Things,* which ran for two seasons. In 1999, Nickelodeon ran an animated series, *Little Bill,* based on his series of *Little Bill* children's books. In recent years, Cosby has been an outspoken critic of black parents who do not provide responsible role models for their children. His message has been sharply criticized by some in the black community. This has led Cosby to tone down his rhetoric, but he continues to speak publicly around the country, urging blacks to empower themselves and their children for success. In 2009, Cosby was the recipient of the Kennedy Center's Mark Twain Prize for American humor.

Further Reading

Cosby, Bill. *Cosbyology: Essays and Observations from the Doctor of Comedy.* New York: Hyperion, 2002.

Cosby, Bill, and Alvin F. Poussaint. *Come On People: On the Path from Victims to Victors.* Nashville, Tenn.: Thomas Nelson, 2007.

Herbert, Solomon J., and George H. Hill. *Bill Cosby.* Black Americans of Achievement. New York: Chelsea House, 1992 (YA).

Schuman, Michael A. *Bill Cosby: Actor and Comedian.* People to Know. Berkeley Heights, N.J.: Enslow Publishers, 1995 (YA).

Smith, Ronald L. *Cosby: The Life of a Comedy Legend.* Amherst, N.Y.: Prometheus Books, 1997.

Further Listening

The Best of Bill Cosby (1969). Rhino, CD, 2005.

Further Viewing

Bill Cosby, Himself (1983). Fox Home Video, DVD, 2004.

The Cosby Show—Season 1 (1984). Urban Works, DVD box set, 2005.

A Piece of the Action/Uptown Saturday Night (1974). Warner Home Video, DVD, 2006.

D

Dandridge, Dorothy
(1923–1965) *actress, singer, dancer*

The first African American to receive an Academy Award nomination as best actress, Dorothy Dandridge never achieved the success in films that her talents deserved, and she ended her life as a sad and tragic figure.

She was born on November 9, 1923, in Cleveland, Ohio. Her father, Cyril Dandridge, was a minister, and her mother, Ruby, was an actress who transferred her ambitions to her daughters. At age four, Dandridge was performing with her older sister Vivian in a vaudeville act called "The Wonder Children." At age 15, Dandridge formed a singing group with Vivian and friend Etta Jones; they called themselves the Dandridge Sisters. A year earlier, Dandridge made her screen debut as the exuberant leader of a big production number in the Marx Brothers film *A Day at the Races* (1937).

She sang at New York's legendary Cotton Club at age 16 and met HAROLD NICHOLAS, half of the dancing Nicholas Brothers. The couple married in 1942 and had a daughter who was mentally retarded. The marriage ended seven years later.

After playing small roles, often as an exotic jungle woman, in a string of B movies, Dandridge landed her first starring role in the black drama *Bright Road* (1953). She played a grade-school teacher struggling to get through to a problem student. Dandridge received excellent reviews, but she was turned down when she auditioned for the leading role in the musical *Carmen Jones* (1954). The film's director, Otto Preminger, thought she was too sophisticated to play the low-life heroine. Dandridge was determined, however, and came back to Preminger's office in garish makeup and low-cut, cheap clothes, talking in a southern accent. She got the part.

Her animal magnetism as Carmen was galvanizing and earned her an Oscar nomination as best actress. (She lost to Grace Kelly.) *Carmen Jones*, however, made Dandridge a full-fledged star, and she became the first African American to be featured on the cover of *Life* magazine.

Although a star, Dandridge received few film offers. White America apparently was not ready to accept a black leading lady as a sex symbol. She did not appear in another film for three years. In *Island in the Sun* (1957), set in the West Indies, Dandridge played an island girl involved with a white man, the first interracial love affair depicted in a major Hollywood film. Frustrated with the kinds of stereotyped roles offered her, Dandridge made two films in Europe, but both were disappointing. The melancholy mood of the characters she now played seemed to be ripped from the pages of her own life as an actress trapped by race in limited roles.

Dandridge was found dead in her apartment on September 8, 1965, from an overdose of antidepressant pills. Whether it was an accident or suicide has never been fully determined. She was not quite 42.

Dorothy Dandridge's career may have turned out very differently if she had risen to stardom in the 1960s or 1970s, or if she had been born white. As she once said, "If I were white, I could capture the world."

In 1999, actress HALLE BERRY portrayed Dandridge in a biopic *Introducing Dorothy Dandridge* on the cable network Home Box Office (HBO).

Further Reading

Bogle, Donald. *Dorothy Dandridge: A Biography.* New York: Berkley Trade, 1999.

Dandridge, Dorothy, and Earl Conrad. *Everything and Nothing: The Dorothy Dandridge Tragedy.* New York: Harperperennial Library, 2000.

Mills, Earl. *Dorothy Dandridge.* Los Angeles: Holloway House, 1999.

Further Viewing

Carmen Jones (1954). Fox/Lorber Home Video, VHS/DVD, 1994/2002.

Introducing Dorothy Dandridge (1999). HBO Home Video, VHS/DVD, 2001.

Song of Tears—The Dorothy Dandridge Story. Biografilm, DVD, 2008.

Actress Dorothy Dandridge never achieved the stardom she should have had in her short and tragic career. *(Photofest)*

She finally found another part worthy of her talents in the film version of George Gershwin's folk opera *Porgy and Bess* (1959), again directed by Otto Preminger. Dandridge played the vivacious Bess opposite SIDNEY POITIER as the crippled Porgy. Poitier was the bigger star, but the movie belonged to Dandridge, whose colorful personality again stole the show. The role earned her a Foreign Press Golden Globe nomination as best actress in a musical.

Again, she found herself offered inferior roles in inferior films. She appeared in only two more films, both disappointments. Dandridge continued to sing in clubs and appear in television shows, but she was washed up in Hollywood. She divorced her abusive second husband, restaurateur Jack Denison, and lost all her money in a shady oil investment scheme. To make matters worse, she became hopelessly addicted to alcohol and sleeping pills.

Davis, Miles

(Miles Dewey Davis, Jr.)
(1926–1991) *jazz trumpeter, composer, bandleader*

Jazz's most restless innovator, Miles Davis took jazz into new and unknown territory over four decades, revitalizing the music by blending it with everything from African rhythms to rock.

He was born Miles Dewey Davis, Jr., in Alton, Illinois, on May 25, 1926, and grew up in East St. Louis, where his family moved when he was still an infant. The Davis family was considerably well-to-do: His father, Miles Davis, Sr., was a dentist and owned a ranch. Davis started playing the trumpet as a boy and was a precocious musician. He was good enough to sit in with such seasoned professionals as Coleman Hawkins and CHARLIE PARKER at local clubs while he was still in high school.

Davis attended the prestigious Juilliard School of Music in New York after graduating from high school but soon dropped out to become a full-time jazz musician. He toured with Parker's combo and other jazz groups, until he formed his own combo in 1949. Although he previously played the complex bebop jazz pioneered by Parker and DIZZY GILLESPIE, Davis created his own music, called cool jazz, that had a freer, more improvisatory sound. Cool jazz was as intense as bebop but was a quieter, more controlled music. The style may have reached its peak with Davis's *Kind of Blue* (1959), a groundbreaking album that also pointed the way to free or modal jazz. Free jazz broke with traditional harmonies and long melodic lines. *Kind of Blue* was extremely influential and has since become the best-selling jazz album of all time.

But Davis soon moved on to other styles. An experience in 1959 changed him profoundly. He was escorting a woman friend to a cab outside a New York jazz club when white police officers grabbed and beat him. The experience turned Davis more political and militant, both in his life and in his music. He founded a new quartet in the mid 1960s and began to experiment with elements of rock and funk, the new music pioneered by rhythm and blues (R & B) singer JAMES BROWN. This "fusion jazz," as it came to be called, brought new energy and excitement to the form, although some jazz purists abhorred it. Davis's fusion style was exemplified in the classic album *Bitches Brew* (1969), which also included electronic music. It won a Grammy Award for jazz performance, large group, the following year.

Through all these changes, Davis surrounded himself with great musicians who inspired him as much as he inspired them. Many of them went on to create their own styles and groups, including JOHN COLTRANE, Herbie Hancock, and Chick Corea.

In the 1970s, Davis tried to extend jazz still further into disco and heavy funk. His efforts to reach a new generation, dressed as a character out of a blaxploitation movie, largely failed. Then in 1975, he underwent a personal crisis, became mysteriously ill, and dropped out of view for several years. He reemerged in 1980 and entered a new phase of creativity built on many elements of his former styles, including minimalism and lyricism. His album *Decoy* (1984) was voted the best jazz album of the year in *Down Beat* magazine. Throughout the decade he continued to try new things. He brought elements of R & B and even hip-hop into his music and created music videos to capture a new generation of listeners.

Davis continued to compose and play despite the cancer that finally took his life on September 29, 1991. A complex and contrary man, who could be both sensitive and callous to the people around him, he was married three times. His third wife was actress CICELY TYSON, whom he credited with helping him recover from his long illness. Miles Davis, as writer Ben Ratliff has observed, "contributed new templates for making jazz, whereas most of his peers were content to inscribe established ones."

Further Reading

Carr, Ian. *Miles Davis: The Definitive Biography*. New York: Da Capo Press, 2006.

Davis, Miles, with Quincy Troupe. *Miles: The Autobiography*. New York: Touchstone Books, 1990.

Kahn, Ashley. *Kind of Blue: The Making of The Miles Davis Masterpiece*. New York: Da Capo Press, 2007.

Maher, Paul, Jr., and Michael K. Dorr, eds. *Miles on Miles. Interviews and Encounters with Miles Davis*. Chicago: Lawrence Hill Books, 2008.

Further Listening

*The Complete Columbia Recordings: Miles Davis & John
   Coltrane* (1955). Sony, CD box set, 2004.
The Essential Miles Davis. Sony/Legacy, 2 CDs, 2001.

Further Viewing

Miles Davis—Live in Paris. Warner Home Video, VHS/
   DVD, 1990/2001.
The Miles Davis Story. Sony, DVD, 2002.

Davis, Ossie
(Raiford Charmas Davis)
(1917–2005) *actor, writer, director*

For more than five decades, Ossie Davis was a
respected and gifted figure in African-American
theater and film, using his many talents to raise
the social consciousness of all Americans.

He was born Raiford Charmas Davis on
December 18, 1917, in Cogdell, Georgia, the oldest of five children. His father, Kince Charles
Davis, was a railroad engineer who later moved
the family to Waycross, Georgia. Davis's mother,
Laura, called him R.C., his first two initials, which
neighbors misheard as "Ossie," the name he soon
became known by.

Davis attended Howard University in Washington, D.C., and after graduating moved to New
York City to pursue a writing career. While working at his craft, he held a number of jobs including
stock clerk, janitor, and handcart pusher in New
York City's garment district. He served in the
army during World War II, then returned to New
York to pursue acting. He won the lead in the
Broadway play *Jeb* in 1945, where his costar was
RUBY DEE. They married three years later, becoming the most dynamic African-American couple
in show business.

Davis continued to get leading roles on stage
and made his film debut in the racial drama *No
Way Out* (1950). His and his wife's social activism
landed them in trouble during the anticommunist
movement of the early 1950s, and they were black-

listed in films and television. After a performance
of the play *The Cherry Orchard*, Davis and Dee
hid for hours in a costume hamper to shake off
government agents who had been following
them.

The blacklist ended in the late 1950s, and
Davis's career received a boost when he appeared
on Broadway in *Purlie Victorious* (1961), his own
satirical play about southern plantation life. He
later adapted it to the screen as *Gone Are the Days*
(1964) and still later as a hit Broadway musical,
Purlie! (1970).

Through the 1960s, Davis appeared in such
diverse films as *The Cardinal* (1963), *The Hill*
(1965), and *The Scalphunters* (1968). He continued to be active in the Civil Rights movement and
emceed the historic 1963 March on Washington
led by Dr. Martin Luther King, Jr. Later Davis
delivered moving eulogies at the funerals of King
in 1968 and black civil rights leader Malcolm X in
1965.

In 1970, Davis directed his first film, *Cotton
Comes to Harlem*, a black detective mystery filled
with ethnic humor and a host of talented African-
American actors. He went on to direct a handful
of other films including *Black Girl* (1972) and
Gordon's War (1973), about a black Vietnam veteran who goes to war against drug pushers in his
native Harlem. He also directed two films set in
Africa—*Kongi's Harvest* (1976), based on a novel
by African writer Wole Soyinka, and *Countdown
at Kusini* (1976), the first American movie filmed
entirely in Africa by a black company.

Davis gave one of his most memorable performances as da Mayor, an outspoken old drunk in
Spike Lee's *Do the Right Thing* (1989). He appeared
in three other Lee films—*Jungle Fever* (1991),
Malcolm X (1994), in which he reenacted his
eulogy at Malcolm's funeral, and *Get on the Bus*
(1996). Davis had a regular role on the sitcom
Evening Shade (1990–94) and costarred with his
wife in the made-for-television movie of Stephen
King's novel *The Stand* (1994). In 1996, he won a
National Association for the Advancement of

Colored People (NAACP) Image Award for his work in the TV series *Promised Land.*

Davis was also the recipient, with his wife, of the Image Hall of Fame Award in 1989 for outstanding artistic achievement and was awarded the U.S. National Medal for the Arts in 1995. In 1998, Ossie Davis and Ruby Dee celebrated their 50th wedding anniversary with the publication of their joint autobiography. He also wrote a historical novel, *Just Like Martin,* about the Civil Rights movement, for young readers. In 2004, Davis and Dee were recipients of the Kennedy Center Honors. Ossie Davis died at age 87 on February 4, 2005.

Further Reading

Bogle, Donald. *Prime Time Blues: African Americans on Network Television.* New York: Farrar, Straus and Giroux, 2002, pp. 353–354.

Davis, Ossie. *Just Like Martin.* New York: Puffin Books, 1995.

———. *Life Lit by Some Large Vision: Selected Speeches and Writings.* New York: Atria, 2006.

Davis, Ossie, and Ruby Dee. *With Ossie and Ruby: In This Life Together.* New York: Harper Paperbacks, 2000.

Further Viewing

Do the Right Thing (1989). Universal Studios Home Video, VHS/DVD, 2000/1998.

The Stand (1994). Republic Home Video, 2 DVDs, 2002.

Davis, Sammy, Jr.

("Mr. Entertainment")
(1925–1990) *singer, dancer, comedian, actor*

A show business legend, Sammy Davis, Jr., was versatility personified, and he exhibited an indomitable spirit throughout his life that may have been his greatest legacy.

He was born in New York City on December 8, 1925, into a show business family. His parents, Sammy Davis, Sr., and Elvera Sanchez Davis, were dancers in Will Mastin's "Holiday in Dixieland" vaudeville act. Little Sammy entered the act at age three. When his parents divorced, Davis stayed with his dad and Mastin, whom he called Uncle Will. The act was scaled back to the Will Mastin Trio during the Great Depression. To avoid trouble with child labor laws, Mastin billed young Sammy as "Silent Sam the Dancing Midget." A natural entertainer, Davis made his film debut in the all-black short *Rufus Jones for President* in which he sat on ETHEL WATERS's lap while she sang him a lullaby.

Davis began to add impressions, comedy, and instrument playing to the lively song-and-dance act, and soon he was getting top billing. He entered the army in 1943 during World War II and experienced the racism of being a black soldier in a largely white army. He returned to the

A performer par excellence, Sammy Davis, Jr., truly lived up to his title, "Mr. Entertainment." *(Photo courtesy of Showtime Archives, Toronto)*

trio in 1945. By then, the group was the opening act at big-name nightclubs for such stars as Jack Benny, Bob Hope, and Frank Sinatra, who became Davis's good friend.

In 1946, Davis signed a recording contract with Capitol Records but had little success until he signed with Decca in 1954. His debut album with the label, *Starring Sammy Davis, Jr.*, went to number one on the charts, and the following year his single of "Something's Gotta Give" became a top-10 hit. In between these dual successes, Davis was in a serious car accident that nearly took his life. He lost his left eye and was hospitalized for months. While recuperating, he converted to Judaism and found the faith and courage to continue his career.

In 1956, Davis made his Broadway debut in the musical *Mr. Wonderful* and starred in his first Hollywood feature film, *The Benny Goodman Story*. Always loyal to his family, he found roles in *Mr. Wonderful* for both his father and Uncle Will. He appeared frequently on television variety and dramatic shows. In 1959, he found perhaps his best screen role as the colorful Sportin' Life in the film adaptation of the Gershwin musical *Porgy and Bess* (1959).

The 1960s proved to be Davis's golden decade as an entertainer. He became the only African-American member of Frank Sinatra's notorious Rat Pack, which also included singer Dean Martin, actor Peter Lawford, and comic Joey Bishop. Together they appeared in a legendary Las Vegas show and a series of mostly forgettable movies, beginning with the heist film *Ocean's Eleven* (1960).

Davis was thrown into the whirlwind of controversy when he divorced his first wife, dancer Loray White, in 1960 and married Swedish actress Mai Britt. The interracial marriage made him the target of death threats from white racists. But Davis survived the controversy and triumphed on Broadway in his second musical, *Golden Boy* (1964), as the ambitious boxer Joe Wellington. The next year he published the first of three auto-

biographies, *Yes I Can* (1965), one of the best-written and most candid of celebrity autobiographies. It became a best seller and earned him the National Association for the Advancement of Colored People's (NAACP) Spingarn Medal.

As the 1960s ended, Davis's career began to decline. A Kennedy Democrat for years, he switched his allegiance in 1968 and supported Republican president Richard Nixon. The nightclub scene, Davis's best venue, was starting to disappear, and the few movies he made were disappointing. One unqualified success at the time was his first number-one record, "The Candy Man" (1972), a song from the children's movie *Willy Wonka and the Chocolate Factory*. In 1974, however, the years of high living with the Rat Pack caught up with him and he was hospitalized with alcohol-related liver and kidney problems.

Davis bounced back in the stage show *Sammy on Broadway* and a syndicated 90-minute television variety show called *Sammy and Company* (1975–77). Davis's popularity faded again in the 1980s, but he continued to perform tirelessly. He went to Lebanon to entertain U.S. troops in 1983, and in 1988, he toured with his old pal Frank Sinatra and singer-actress Liza Minnelli, although he was in poor health. Among a new generation of Davis admirers was dancer and actor GREGORY HINES who convinced Davis to join him and a group of legendary tap dancers in the movie *Tap* (1989). It was one of the last performances Davis gave before dying of lung cancer on May 16, 1990, at age 64. Like Sinatra, Martin, and other great entertainers, Sammy Davis, Jr., retains a special place in the history of show business.

Further Reading

Birkbeck, Matt. *Deconstructing Sammy: Music Money, Madness, and the Mob*. New York: Harper Paperbacks, 2009.

Davis, Sammy, Jr., Jane Boyar, and Burt Boyar. *Sammy: The Autobiography of Sammy Davis, Jr.* New York: Farrar, Straus & Giroux, 2000.

Davis, Tracey, with Dolores A. Barclay. *Sammy Davis, Jr.: My Father.* Los Angeles: General Publishing Group, 1996.

Further Listening

The Definitive Collection: Sammy Davis, Jr. Hip-O. Records, CD, 2006.

That's All! Recorded Live at the Sands Hotel in Las Vegas (1967). Rhino, 2 CDs, 2001.

Further Viewing

Ocean's Eleven (1960). Warner Home Video, VHS/ DVD, 1995/2007.

Sammy Davis Jr.—One Cool Cat (2004). White Star, DVD, 2005.

Tap (1989). Sony, DVD, 2006.

Dee, Ruby

(Ruby Ann Wallace)
(1924–) *actress*

A gifted actress, Ruby Dee was too often relegated to playing quietly suffering helpmates opposite strong males, a stereotype she broke out of later in her long and distinguished career.

She was born Ruby Ann Wallace on October 27, 1924, in Cleveland, Ohio. Her mother, Gladys, abandoned her father and their four children to live with a traveling preacher, and Ruby's father, Edward, a waiter on the Pennsylvania Railroad, remarried. His second wife, Emma, was a schoolteacher and social activist who served as an important role model for Ruby.

She attended Hunter College in New York and was soon acting on stage as a member of the American Negro Theater. She married Frankie Dee, a promoter for a distillery, but the marriage soon ended. Ruby Dee met her second husband, OSSIE DAVIS, in the Broadway production of *Jeb* in 1945. He was the male lead in the play, and she was the understudy for the female lead, whom she soon replaced.

Dee made her film debut with Davis in *No Way Out* (1950) and the same year played baseball player Jackie Robinson's wife in *The Jackie Robinson Story.* She was the good, uncomplaining wife again to SIDNEY POITIER in *Edge of the City* (1956) and to NAT KING COLE, as W. C. HANDY, in *St. Louis Blues* (1958). She was cast in this kind of role so often that one critic dubbed her "the Negro June Allyson," after a contemporary white film star who played similar "good girl" parts.

She convincingly played a more assertive wife opposite Poitier in the film version of the black drama *A Raisin in the Sun* (1961). Another strong black woman role came her way in the western *Buck and the Preacher* (1972), which costarred HARRY BELAFONTE, a lifelong friend and fellow activist.

As late as 1980, Dee told an interviewer that she and Davis made 90 percent of their income from poetry readings at colleges. "We aren't allowed to practice our craft," she said. "Sometimes the projects we are offered are so ridiculous that we wouldn't play them."

One place Dee found good roles was on television. She was acclaimed for her performances in the television adaptations of Maya Angelou's *I Know Why the Caged Bird Sings* (1969) and James Baldwin's *Go Tell It on the Mountain* (1984). She won an Emmy Award for outstanding supporting actress in a miniseries or special for her performance in the TV movie *Decoration Day* (1990).

She joined her husband in more than 30 stage, screen, theatrical, and radio productions, including the TV movies *Lincoln,* and *The Stand,* based on the Stephen King novel, as well as the Spike Lee films *Do the Right Thing* (1989) and *Jungle Fever* (1991). In 1980, Dee and Davis hosted *Ossie and Ruby,* their own half-hour talk show on the Public Broadcasting Series (PBS), on which they presented the work of black artists.

In 1989, the two were jointly inducted into the National Association for the Advancement of Colored People's (NAACP) Image Award Hall of Fame.

They published their combined autobiography *With Ossie and Ruby: In This Life Together* in 1998.

Since the death of her husband in 2005, Dee has continued to remain active. In 2007, at age 83, she was nominated for an Academy Award for best supporting actress for her role in *American Gangster* (2006). She was the second-oldest nominee in that category to date. The same year, she also won a Grammy for best spoken word album with her late husband for *With Ossie and Ruby: In This Life Together,* based on their autobiography.

Further Reading

Bogle, Donald. *Toms, Coons, Mulattoes, Mammies & Bucks: An Interpretive History of Blacks in American Films.* New York, Continuum, 1997, pp. 181, 182, 184, 185, 197–199.

Davis, Ossie, and Ruby Dee. *With Ossie and Ruby: In This Life Together.* New York: Harper Paperbacks, 2000.

Dee, Ruby. *My One Good Nerve.* New York: John Wiley and Sons, 1998.

Further Viewing

Decoration Day (1990). Hallmark Home Entertainment, VHS/DVD, 1999/2002.

A Raisin in the Sun (1961). Sony, VHS/DVD, 1998/2000.

Diddley, Bo
(Otha Ellas Bates McDaniel)
(1928–2008) *rock and R & B singer, guitarist, songwriter*

One of the undisputed founding fathers of rock 'n' roll, Bo Diddley created a unique, propulsive guitar beat that has been one of the most imitated sounds in rock.

He was born Otha Ellas Bates on December 30, 1928, in Magnolia, Mississippi. As a child, he was adopted by his mother's cousin Gussie McDaniel and took her last name. Ellas moved to Chicago with the McDaniel family when he was seven. His first instrument was not a guitar but the violin. He studied it for seven years, taking lessons from the musical director of the Ebenezer Baptist Church. "But you don't find any black people playing violins, and that kind of worried me a bit," he recalled years later in an interview. He soon took up guitar and harmonica and played on street corners for quarters with his lifelong friend, Jerome Green, who played the maracas. A poor student, he was something of a loner and liked to stand up and fight for smaller students, which earned him the nickname Bo Diddley, who was a mean-tempered slave in southern folklore.

Diddley quit vocational high school and with Green formed a music group called the Langley Avenue Jives Cats before being drafted into the army during World War II. When discharged, the two began playing in local Chicago clubs. To make ends meet, Diddley fought as a semiprofessional boxer. With his hard-earned winnings, he bought an electric guitar and developed a relentless, syncopated bass line rhythm that would become his musical signature.

After being rejected by VeeJay Records, Bo and his group tried out at Chess Records, the other big rhythm and blues (R & B) label in Chicago. Leonard Chess liked his song "Uncle John" but wanted to change the title because it sounded too backwoods country. Diddley gave the nursery rhyme rocker his own name, and it became a number-one R & B hit along with its flip side, the slower, bluesier "I'm a Man." Neither song made it on the pop charts.

Through the 1950s and early 1960s, Diddley had none of the pop success of other African-American rock pioneers such as CHUCK BERRY and LITTLE RICHARD. His sound was too raw for white listeners, although he was a big draw in live rock concerts. Dressed in black with a Stetson hat, and at times playing his rectangular guitar with his teeth, Diddley was an exciting performer. Young Elvis Presley saw him perform at the Apollo Theater in 1955 and adapted his wild gyrations in his own act. It was Bo Diddley that inspired New

York disc jockey Alan Freed to first use the phrase "rock 'n' roll" to describe his unique rhythmic beat. Bo himself has referred to his beat as "that freight train sound."

Through the 1950s and 1960s, that sound was imitated on hit records by countless artists from Buddy Holly to the Rolling Stones. Diddley got no credit or royalties from these songs. As he ruefully said once, "You can't copyright a beat." But the songs he wrote and recorded through 1962 have become rock classics. They include "Who Do You Love?" "Mona," "Road Runner," and "You Can't Judge a Book by Its Cover" (written by Willie Dixon). None of these were huge hits, but in 1959, quite by accident, Bo Diddley had his first and only top-20 hit single, "Say Man." The record was actually a dissing session between Bo and Jerome Green that was overheard and recorded by the engineer during a break in a recording session. Rock critic Robert Palmer called "Say Man" the first rap track.

Diddley had his last charting record in 1967 and was all but forgotten when he appeared in the rock documentary *Let the Good Times Roll* (1973) and was rediscovered by a new generation of rock fans. He began to appear again on television and in 1979 went on tour with the rock band the Clash. Diddley continued to tour through the 1980s and even made a TV commercial for sports shoes with athlete Bo Jackson in 1989.

In 1987, Bo Diddley was among the first rock musicians inducted into the Rock and Rock Hall of Fame. His last album, *A Man Amongst Men* (1996), was nominated for a Grammy. His place in history secure, Bo Diddley remained a little bitter about the years of neglect. "Maybe one day when I'm dead," he once said, "they'll [the public] wake up and realize they lost me." Bo Diddley died of heart failure at age 79 on June 2, 2008, at his home in Archer, Florida.

Further Reading

Rock and Roll Hall of Fame Inductees. "Bo Diddley." Rock and Roll Hall of Fame Web site. Available online. URL: http://www.rockhall.com/inductee/bo-diddley/. Downloaded on February 13, 2009.

White, George R. *Bo Diddley: Living Legend.* London: Sanctuary Publishing, 1998.

Further Listening

The Definitive Collection: Bo Diddley. Geffen Records, CD, 2007.

Further Viewing

Rock 'n' Roll All Star Jam. ABC Records UK, DVD, 2009.

Domino, Fats

(Antoine Domino)

(1928–) *rock and R & B singer, pianist, songwriter*

Of the founding fathers of rock 'n' roll, none had greater success nor sold more records, with the exception of Elvis Presley, than Fats Domino. While other rockers struck a rebel stance in their lives and music, Domino just sat back and delivered an easy, down-home brand of New Orleans rhythm and blues (R & B) that made him an idol to millions.

He was born Antoine Domino on February 28, 1928, in New Orleans, Louisiana, the youngest of nine children. His father, Antoine, Sr., worked at a local racetrack and played violin in his spare time. The young Domino's brother-in-law, Harrison Verrett, 20 years his senior, played guitar and banjo in a Dixieland band and helped him master the piano. Verrett would write the names of the notes on the piano keys for Domino. By age 10, he was playing boogie-woogie piano in public and in 1946, at age 18, Domino was hired for $3 a week to play with a band at the Hideaway Club. Bandleader Billy Diamond first called the 220-pound pianist "Fats," and he soon became a local favorite. Domino married his wife Rosemary in 1948 and had eight children, each one given a name beginning with the letter "A."

One fateful night in late 1949, bandleader and record producer Dave Bartholomew and Imperial Record owner Lew Chudd heard Domino play at the Hideaway Club. They quickly signed him to a recording contract, and a short time later he entered a studio and recorded "The Fat Man," a song he wrote about himself. It became a million seller on the R & B charts. For the next five years, Domino had a string of hit R & B records, but it wasn't until "Ain't That a Shame" in 1955 that he had his first hit on the new *Billboard* pop charts. The song, which made the top 10, was even a bigger hit that same year for teen idol Pat Boone. For Domino, it was the start of an incredible string of hit records that would continue into the early 1960s.

As easy and natural as most of Domino's classic records sound, a lot of hard work went into them. Domino, who never learned to write music, would sing and play his musical ideas into a tape recorder and then work them out with Bartholomew. Bartholomew, a perfectionist in the recording studio, would embellish his tight arrangements with catchy instrumental hooks that, when combined with Domino's warm, inviting vocals, were irresistible. Among the long string of 1950s classics they produced together are "I'm in Love Again" (1956), "Blue Monday" (1957), "I'm Walkin'" (1957), "Whole Lotta Loving" (1958), "I Want to Walk You Home" (1959), and "Be My Guest" (1959). Bartholomew thought the song "Blueberry Hill" (1956) was "no good" and urged Domino not to release it. But the singer did anyway, and it sold 2 million copies and became his biggest pop hit.

The beautiful "Walking to New Orleans" (1960) was the first Domino record backed by a string section. Despite this innovation, Domino's music stayed remarkably unchanged over the years, almost completely untouched by shifting musical tastes. Domino could seemingly take any song, from an old standard like "My Blue Heaven" to a Hank Williams country and western classic like "Jambalaya," and put his inimitable stamp on it.

The "Fat Man" appeared in four rock movies in the 1950s, including *Shake, Rattle, and Rock* and *The Girl Can't Help It* (both 1956), which contains his definitive performance of "Blue Monday," one of his favorite songs.

By 1962, however, the hits started to dry up, and the following year Domino left Imperial and signed with ABC-Paramount. His fortunes did not improve, and over the next 10 years he recorded on a number of labels. His last charting single was "Lady Madonna" (1968), a song written by Beatle Paul McCartney as a kind of tribute to Domino and his keyboard style.

Fats Domino remained a big draw as a live performer into the early 1990s and still tours occasionally. He was one of the first artists inducted into the Rock and Roll Hall of Fame in 1986 and received Grammy's Lifetime Achievement Award in 1987.

Domino's home in New Orleans's Lower Ninth Ward was flooded when Hurricane Katrina struck the city in 2005. He had to be rescued by a Coast Guard helicopter. "We've lost everything," Domino later said, but his home has since been rebuilt. At age 78, he recorded a new album, *Alive and Kickin'* (2006), and donated the proceeds to local indigent musicians. New Orleans mayor Ray Nagin declared January 12, 2007, "Fats Domino Day" in New Orleans.

"That unique vocal delivery, timeless songs, and priceless recordings are true gems in the history of popular music," rock star Elton John has said. "Mix those with his legendary stage performances and you have an artist to be cherished."

Further Reading

Coleman, Rick. *Blue Monday: Fats Domino and the Lost Dawn of Rock 'n' Roll.* New York: Da Capo Press, 2007.

Rock and Roll Hall of Fame Inductees. "Fats Domino." Rock and Roll Hall of Fame Web site. Available online. URL: http://www.rockhall.com/inductee/fats-domino. Downloaded on February 13, 2009.

Further Listening

Greatest Hits: Walking to New Orleans. Capitol, CD, 2007.

Further Viewing

The Legends of New Orleans—The Music of Fats Domino. Shout Factory, DVD, 2003.

Dr. Dre

(Andre Young)
(1965–   ) *rap singer, songwriter, record producer*

One of the pioneers of gangsta rap and the leading architect of contemporary rap, Dr. Dre's influence as a producer well exceeds his achievements as a rap artist.

He was born Andre Young on February 18, 1965, in Compton, California, where he was raised in a housing project by his mother and grandmother. He grew up with the street gangs he would later sing about and got interested in hip-hop while still in high school. As "Dr. Dre," Young began performing at local clubs and house parties around South Central Los Angeles with a group called World Class Wreckin' Crew. In 1986 he met Ice Cube, and the two formed a songwriting partnership. They sold some songs to Ruthless Records, owned by former drug pusher Ernie "Eazy-E" Wright. The three, along with Lorenzo "M.C. Ren" Patterson, formed the group Niggaz With Attitude (NWA). Their second album, *Straight Outta Compton* (1988), was so hard-core in its language and subject matter that it received no air play on radio stations. Nonetheless, word of mouth made it a double platinum hit, selling 2 million copies. One track so incensed the Federal Bureau of Investigation (FBI) that it sent a letter of warning to the label.

Ice Cube left the group within a year, and Dre left in 1992 over money problems. Dre formed a new label, Death Row Records, with partner Suge Knight. His first solo album, *The Chronic* (1997), featured his innovative adaptation of the funk sound made popular by George Clinton's group Funkadelic in the 1970s. Dre's sound, loose but with a tight beat, revolutionized hip-hop and shifted the emphasis from the words to the music.

Dre's collaboration with Snoop Dogg, then known as Snoop Doggy Dogg, led to the production of Snoop's first smash album, *Doggystyle* (1993). Dre produced other hit albums for his group Blackstreet and his half brother Warren G.

In 1996 Dre declared gangsta rap dead and formed a new label called appropriately, Aftermath. The label's first release, *Dr. Dre Presents . . . The Aftermath* sold poorly but produced the hit single "Been There Done That." In 1999 he released two albums, *Dr. Dre 2001* and *2001 Instrumental.* Dre's long-awaited third studio album, *DeTox,* is scheduled to be released in late 2009. He has claimed it will be his "final album." In 2008, his commercial line of headphones, called "Beats," went into production.

As a producer, Dre continues to exert a great influence on rap and hip-hop, with his own music and with that with other artists, such as white rapper Eminem, with whom he shared a 2010 Best Rap Grammy. "All I want to do is sit in the studio with that person [new talent] for a year and try to create another masterpiece," he has said.

Further Reading

Borgmeyer, John, and Holly Lang. *Dr. Dre: A Biography.* Westport, Conn.: Greenwood Press, 2006.

Kenyatta, Kelly. *You Forget About Dre: The Unauthorized Biography of Dr. Dre and Eminem—From N.W.A. to Slim Shady, a Tale of Gangsta Rap, Violence, and Hit Records.* Phoenix, Ariz.: Amber Books, 2001.

Ro, Ronnin. *Dr. Dre: The Biography.* New York: Da Capo Press, 2007.

Further Listening

The Chronic. Death Row Records, CD, 2001. Digitally remastered.

Dr. Dre 2001. Interscope Records, CD, 1999.

Further Viewing

The Up in Smoke Tour (2000). Eagle Rock Entertainment, VHS/DVD, 2002.

Dunham, Katherine

(1910–2006) *choreographer, modern dancer, dance company director, scholar, teacher*

Considered by many to be the first great African-American choreographer, Katherine Dunham transformed the vibrant dances of the West Indies and Africa into an integral part of modern American dance.

She was born of interracial parents on June 22, 1910, in Chicago, Illinois. Her black father, Albert

Katherine Dunham brings to life one of the rhythmic Caribbean dances she created for her famous dance company. *(Photofest)*

Millard, was a tailor and an aspiring jazz guitarist. Her mother, Fanny June Dunham, was of French-Canadian and American Indian descent and was an assistant school principal. Dunham's mother died when she was four, and her father remarried and moved the family to Joliet, Illinois, where he ran a dry-cleaning business. At nine, Dunham staged her first dance revue with neighborhood children to raise money for charity.

When Dunham reached her teens, her father began to molest her, and she moved out and later joined her older brother at the University of Chicago, where she paid her way by giving dance lessons. Dunham majored in anthropology, the study of human cultures, but looked for a way to combine the subject with her interest in dance. She did field research in the Caribbean, studying the folk and ceremonial dances of the local peoples. This became the subject of her master's thesis.

While still a student, Dunham formed the first black concert dance group with two friends. Calling themselves the Ballet Nègre, they first danced at Chicago's Beaux Arts Balls in 1931. She later founded a dance company called the Negro Dance Group and performed at the 1934 Chicago World's Fair.

In 1936, Dunham received a fellowship to study dance in the West Indies for two years. She studied the dances of Jamaica and Haiti. She was particularly drawn to Haiti and its Vodun religion (often known as Voodoo), which was part African and part Christian. She later wrote three books about her experiences.

Adapting the techniques of the Afro-Caribbean dances, Dunham stressed the movement of hands and other body parts separate from the rest of the body in her choreography. By the late 1930s, she was creating exciting dances for her company, now called the Katherine Dunham Dance Company. At the same time she was staging dances for such theatrical productions as Eugene O'Neill's play *The Emperor Jones* and the labor musical *Pins and Needles.* In 1940, Dunham choreographed the black Broadway musical *Cabin in the Sky* and also played the leading role of the seductive Georgia Brown.

In 1941, Dunham married Canadian-American John Pratt, a stage and costume designer. He designed all her subsequent dances and shows. In the early 1940s, Dunham and her troupe went to Hollywood and appeared in the all-black musical film *Stormy Weather* and the film version of *Cabin in the Sky* (both 1943). The part Dunham played on Broadway was played by LENA HORNE in the film. Other film work followed, and in 1945, she opened the Dunham School of Dance, a unique learning center that combined dance with the study of anthropology and other disciplines. Among some of her most famous students were actor Marlon Brando and singer EARTHA KITT, who danced with her company when she was 16. Through the 1950s, Dunham divided her time between teaching and touring with her troupe in Europe and South America.

In 1963, she became the first African-American choreographer to work at the Metropolitan Opera in New York, choreographing Verdi's opera *Aida,* which is set in ancient Egypt. She traveled to Africa in 1965 and served as a cultural adviser to the president of Senegal and organized the first World Festival of Negro Arts.

Then in her 50s, Dunham retired from performing and took a teaching position at Southern Illinois University. Eventually she developed a cultural arts program for urban youth in neighboring East St. Louis. One of her last professional jobs was directing and choreographing the acclaimed revival of SCOTT JOPLIN's folk opera *Treemonisha* in 1972.

Having been inspired by Haiti and its dance, she continued, while in her 80s, to support the democratic administration of Haitian president Jean-Bertrand Aristide. An indomitable spirit, on stage and off, Katherine Dunham was a recipient of the Kennedy Center Honors in 1983. She died at age 96 on May 21, 2006, in New York City.

Further Reading

Aschenbrenner, Joyce. *Katherine Dunham: Dancing a Life.* Champaign: University of Illinois Press, 2002.

Clark, Veve A., and Sara E. Johnson, eds. *Kaiso!: Writings by and about Katherine Dunham.* Madison: University of Wisconsin Press, 2006.

Dunham, Katherine. *A Touch of Innocence: Memories of Childhood.* Chicago: University of Chicago Press, 1994.

O'Connor, Barbara. *Katherine Dunham: Pioneer of Black Dance.* New York: Carolrhoda Books, 2000 (YA).

Further Viewing

Stormy Weather (1943). CBS/Fox Home Video, VHS, 1991.

Dutton, Charles S.
("Roc Dutton")
(1951–   )   *actor, director*

Few actors have overcome so much to achieve success as Charles S. Dutton, who, through talent and determination, went from a life behind bars to life in front of the bright lights of Broadway.

He was born on January 30, 1951, in Baltimore, Maryland, and at an early age got into trouble on the streets. Dutton landed in reform school when he was 12, and at 17 he got into a street fight and knifed another young black man in self-defense. The man died, and Dutton was sentenced to five years in prison for manslaughter. He was released in 18 months, but was rearrested for possession of a deadly weapon. While spending time in solitary confinement, Dutton read his first play, *Days of Absence,* by the African-American author Douglas Turner Ward. He saw acting as one way to express his feelings, and later he and other inmates put on the play in the prison. The group regularly produced plays in the prison, including those of Shakespeare.

Released in 1976, Dutton attended Towson State University in Maryland where he studied drama. Drawn to acting, but uncertain of his future, he was encouraged by one of his professors to apply to Yale University's School of Drama. He was accepted in the fall of 1980 and became friends with the school's director, Lloyd Richards. When Richards was casting actors for a Broadway production of *Ma Rainey's Black Bottom*, black playwright August Wilson's first major play, he remembered Dutton. Richards cast him as a tortured jazz musician who senselessly stabs another musician to death in the play's closing moments. Dutton's performance was hailed by critics as electrifying, and he was nominated for a Tony Award. He went on to play major roles in two other plays by Wilson on Broadway—*Joe Turner's Come and Gone* and *The Piano Lesson*. His stage success soon earned him supporting roles in such action movies as *No Mercy* (1986), *Q & A* (1990), and *Alien 3* (1992). In *Rudy* (1993), he had one of his best film roles as a kindly janitor at Notre Dame University.

Dutton's most popular role to date was as the star of the Fox TV sitcom *Roc*, which premiered in 1994. In the series, he played Roc Emerson, a Baltimore garbage collector struggling to make a life for himself and his family. Roc was actually Dutton's nickname as a youth. In Roc "he created a man who seemed all heart, all fundamental decency," noted writer Donald Bogle, "a character with everyday dreams and longings that many middle-class families could identify with." The show had more substance than most of the black sitcoms of the 1990s and was extremely popular with African Americans. When *Roc* was canceled in 1997, the Congressional Black Caucus petitioned Fox to keep it in production.

Dutton has since appeared in such diverse films as the thriller *Nick of Time* (1995), Robert Altman's black comedy *Cookie's Fortune* (1999), and the supernatural thriller, *Gothika* (2003) opposite HALLE BERRY.

More recently, Dutton has been seen frequently on television. He was nominated for Emmy Awards for outstanding guest actor in 2002 and 2003 for roles on *The Practice* and *Without a Trace*. He also appeared opposite DANNY GLOVER in the film *Honeydripper* (2007), set in an Alabama blues club in 1950. In the spring of 2009, he played Willy Loman in an all-black production of Arthur Miller's *Death of a Salesman* at the Yale Repertory the in New Haven, Connecticut.

Dutton directed the miniseries *The Corner* (2000), about life on the streets of his native East Baltimore, for Home Box Office (HBO). He is currently developing new movies for HBO as a director and actor.

Further Reading

Bogle, Donald. *Prime Time Blues: African Americans on Network Television*. New York: Farrar, Straus & Giroux, 2002, pp. 411–413.

"Charles Dutton." The Internet Movie Database. Available online. URL: http://imdb.com/name/nm0001165/. Downloaded on February 4, 2009.

Further Viewing

The Piano Lesson (1995). Hallmark Home Entertainment, VHS/DVD, 1999/2002.

Rudy (1994). Sony, DVD, 2008.

E

Edmonds, Kenneth Brian   See BABYFACE.

Ellington, Duke
(Edward Kennedy Ellington)
(1899–1974) *jazz composer, bandleader, pianist*

One of the greatest figures in the history of jazz, as both a composer and a bandleader, Duke Ellington, more than any other individual, made jazz as artistically respectable as any other kind of music.

He was born Edward Kennedy Ellington on April 29, 1899, in Washington, D.C. His father, James Edward Ellington, was a blueprint maker in the Department of the Navy who moonlighted as a butler at the White House. Edward was extremely close to his mother, Daisy, who told him from an early age that he could do anything he wanted to do. He began piano lessons at age seven and composed his first composition, "Soda Fountain Rag," when he was 16. While still in high school, Ellington won a scholarship to the Pratt Institute of Fine Arts in Brooklyn, New York, but turned it down to pursue a career in music. He earned the nickname "Duke" because of his aristocratic bearing and the elegant clothes he wore.

A skilled artist, Ellington supported himself by painting signs by day while he played piano with his own small band at night. After a failed attempt to make it performing in New York City, he returned to Washington and joined the Washingtonians, a jazz band. The group eventually went to New York and set up residency at the Hollywood Club in Times Square.

Then as the leader of the Washingtonians, Ellington made his first recordings, "I'm Going to Hang Around My Sugar" and "Trombone Blues," in 1924. The group became known for its "jungle music," characterized by muted, growling trumpets. In December 1927, the then-named Duke Ellington Band moved uptown to the Cotton Club in Harlem. During their three-year stay there, the group gained national attention, thanks to CBS Radio's live broadcasts of their performances. Always looking for new venues for his music, Ellington took the band downtown nightly to play in the George Gershwin musical *Show Girl* (1929) on Broadway.

After leaving the Cotton Club in 1931, Ellington took his band on tour. At one time, they played 28 dates in 28 days in Europe. During the 1930s, Ellington produced some of his most popular and enduring songs, including "Sophisticated Lady," "Mood Indigo," "Solitude," and the more upbeat "It Don't Mean a Thing If It Ain't Got

Duke Ellington conducts one of the orchestral pieces that made him jazz's greatest composer. *(Photo courtesy of Showtime Archives, Toronto)*

That Swing." Ellington's band was one of the era's top swing bands, but it never reached the popularity of white bands led by the Dorsey Brothers, Artie Shaw, and Benny Goodman, who, much to Ellington's chagrin, was dubbed "the King of Swing."

Next, Ellington was ready to abandon swing and move his music in a new direction. Composer and arranger Billy Strayhorn, whom he hired in 1939, helped him achieve this goal. Strayhorn became Ellington's closest creative collaborator until his death in 1967. He wrote the classic "Take the A Train," which became Ellington's theme song. Together they created jazz music far more complex and subtle than anything that preceded it. They turned out delightful jazz adaptations of such classical music as Tchaikovsky's *Nutcracker Suite* and long, ambitious tone poems and concert pieces such as *Black, Brown, and Beige* that distilled the history of the "American Negro" into 50 minutes. This work was first performed at New York's Carnegie Hall in 1943. Each year for the next seven years, Ellington produced a new concert piece that he and his band premiered at Carnegie Hall.

By 1950, the big band era was over, but Ellington kept his band intact longer that almost any other bandleader. His fame, however, was eclipsed by the newer sounds of postwar bebop jazz. Then in 1956, Duke Ellington and his band were rediscovered after playing his "Diminuendo and Crescendo in Blue" at the Newport Jazz Festival in Newport, Rhode Island. Hailed as a living legend of jazz, Ellington continued to break new musical ground, turning out some of the finest and most sublime music of his career, such as the exotic *Far East Suite* (1966), written after a State Department tour of Southeast Asia, and a pageant of black history entitled *My People*. He also wrote musical scores for motion pictures, the best known of which is probably his score for the Otto Preminger film *Anatomy of a Murder* (1959). In the final decade of his life, Ellington wrote long religious pieces, which he called sacred concerts. They were played in churches and expressed his deep religious convictions.

Ellington won Grammy's Lifetime Achievement Award in 1966 and its Trustee Award two years later. He celebrated his 70th birthday in 1969 as the guest of President Richard Nixon at the White House, where his father worked so many years. When Duke Ellington died of cancer on May 24, 1974, he left behind a vast catalog of great music, much of which is still being assessed today. The Duke Ellington Band continued to perform for years under the direction of his son Mercer Ellington, the result of a brief marriage to Edna Thompson. His granddaughter Mercedes is a dancer.

A man of profound feeling and infinite variety, Duke Ellington ranks among the greatest of 20th-century American composers.

Further Reading

Bradbury, David. *Duke Ellington (Life & Times)*. Dulles, Va.: Haus Publishers, 2005.
Ellington, Duke. *Music Is My Mistress*. New York: Da Capo Press, 1973.

Hasse, John Edward. *Beyond Category: The Life and Genius of Duke Ellington.* New York: Da Capo Press, 1995.

Lawrence, A. H. *Duke Ellington and His World.* New York: Routledge, 2001.

Pinkney, Andrea, and Brian Pinkney, illustrator. *Duke Ellington: The Piano Prince and His Orchestra.* New York: Hyperion Books, 2006 (children).

Further Listening

The Centennial Edition—Highlights from 1927–1973. RCA, CD box set, 2000.

Greatest Hits. Collectables, CD, 2005.

Three Suites (1960). SBME Special Markets, CD, 2008.

Further Viewing

Duke Ellington's Sacred Concerts (1998). Image Entertainment, VHS/DVD, 2000.

A Duke Named Ellington. Council for Positive Images, Inc., DVD, 2007.

Jazz Icons: Duke Ellington Live in '58. Jazz Icons, DVD, 2007.

F

Fetchit, Stepin
(Lincoln Theodore Monroe Andrew Perry)
(ca. 1902–1985) *actor*

One of the first successful African-American movie actors, Stepin Fetchit opened the doors for many black actors who followed him, although the "coon" characters he helped create kept black performers in stereotypical roles for decades.

He was born Lincoln Theodore Monroe Andrew Perry, so he claimed, on May 30, 1902, in Key West, Florida, although other sources give his date of birth as 1896 or 1898. Perry was named by his patriotic parents for four U.S. presidents and attended Catholic boarding school. He considered entering the religious life but found performing held a greater appeal. Perry formed a minstrel act with comic Ed Lee and they billed themselves as "Step 'n' Fetchit: Two Dancing Fools from Dixie." In the early 1920s, the act broke up, Perry went solo and changed his name to Stepin Fetchit.

A talent scout from Fox Pictures caught his act, and Stepin Fetchit was soon signed to a film contract. One of his early roles was as Pilot Joe in the first film version of the Broadway musical *Show Boat* (1929). Through the mid-1930s, Fetchit appeared in dozen of films, perfecting the character of a slow-witted, slow-moving, tongue-twisted, and often unintelligible black servant or handyman. It was a racial stereotype that confirmed white beliefs that African Americans were lazy, shiftless, and stupid. Stereotypes aside, Fetchit was a master comic actor and became a full-fledged movie star and a wealthy man.

Among his best and most typical films are four he made with comedian Will Rogers—*David Harum* (1934), *Judge Priest* (1934), *Steamboat 'Round the Bend* (1935), and *The Country Chairman* (1935). *Priest* and *Steamboat* were directed by legendary filmmaker John Ford.

Fetchit called his stereotypical character a "lazy man with a soul," but by the late 1930s many African Americans were finding his performances denigrating and embarrassing. Under attack from civil rights groups, Fetchit retired from Hollywood films, but he continued acting in all-black independent movies through the 1940s.

In his heyday, Fetchit made millions but spent all of it on a lavish lifestyle that included, so it is reported, six houses, 16 servants, and a pink Cadillac with his name emblazoned on the side in neon lights. He declared bankruptcy in 1947, the same year he played the leading role in the independent black film *Miracle in Harlem*.

Stepin Fetchit made a brief comeback in Hollywood films in the early 1950s, but audiences no longer found his act very funny. He reemerged in 1970 to sue CBS TV for $3 million for defamation of character when it showed clips from his films as part of a critical documentary on how Hollywood

68

stereotyped blacks. In his defense, he claimed, "I made the Negro a first-class citizen all over the world."

Fetchit appeared in two more films, one of which, *Amazing Grace* (1974), featured other classic black actors such as BUTTERFLY MCQUEEN and MOMS MABLEY. When he died on November 19, 1985, Stepin Fetchit was all but forgotten. Little appreciated today, Stepin Fetchit knew the bounds in which he could act in a racist movie industry and remained within them. He was elected into The Black Filmmaker's Hall of Fame in 1978.

Further Reading

Bogle, Donald. *Toms, Coons, Mulattoes, Mammies & Bucks: An Interpretive History of Blacks in American Films.* New York: Continuum, 1997, pp. 38–44.

Watkins, Mel. *Stepin Fetchit: The Life & Times of Lincoln Perry.* New York: Vintage, 2006.

Further Viewing

Judge Priest (1934). Real Enterprises, DVD, 2007.

Fishburne, Laurence
(Larry Fishburne)
(1961–   ) *actor*

Although he started acting at age 10, it took Laurence Fishburne years to be recognized as one of Hollywood's finest African-American actors.

He was born on July 30, 1961, in Augusta, Georgia, but was raised in Brooklyn, New York. His father, Laurence Fishburne II, was a corrections officer and his mother a schoolteacher. He took to acting early and was a regular on the TV soap opera *One Life to Live* when he was 10. He remained on the program until he was 13. At age 12 Fishburne made his film debut in *Cornbread, Earl and Me* (1975), about a black basketball player mistakenly killed by the police.

Fishburne's first adult role was as a member of the PT boat crew that took Martin Sheen deep into the jungles of Vietnam in *Apocalypse Now* (1979), directed by Francis Ford Coppola. Only 16, Fishburne lied about his age to get the part and found making the picture a life-altering experience. He had major roles in two more Coppola films—*Rumble Fish* (1983) and *The Cotton Club* (1984). For the rest of the decade he played strong supporting roles in such films as *The Color Purple* (1984) and *Gardens of Stone* (1986) and had the leading role of a student activist in Spike Lee's *School Daze* (1987). He also appeared in some forgettable pictures including *Death Wish II* (1982) and *A Nightmare on Elm Street III* (1987). In 1986 Fishburne became a regular on the Saturday morning TV series *Pee-Wee's Playhouse*, playing the character Cowboy Curtis.

Critical attention largely bypassed him, however, and producers saw his looks as more fitting a villain than a leading man. "People saw my face and went 'Oooh,'" Fishburne has said. It was as the villainous henchman of vice boss Christopher Walken in *King of New York* (1990) that he first gained critical notice. But his big breakthrough came the following year when he played a young father struggling to make a life for himself and his son in South Central Los Angeles in John Singleton's *Boyz N the Hood* (1991). Fishburne's portrayal of a socially committed, decent, yet embittered black man was powerful. It was perhaps the most full-bodied characterization of a mature contemporary black man seen up to that time in a mainstream movie. As if sensing the shift in the direction of his career, Fishburne billed himself for the first time not as "Larry" but "Laurence."

In 1992, he conquered Broadway on his first time out, winning a Tony Award as best actor in a play for his role in August Wilson's *Two Trains Running*. The same year he got his first leading role in a film as a loner undercover narcotics agent in *Deep Cover* (1992). Fishburne won an Emmy Award in 1993 for a guest appearance on an episode of the dramatic series *Tribeca*, produced by Robert De Niro. His biggest acting challenge to date was playing Ike Turner in the biopic *What's Love Got to Do with It* (1993), about the life of soul singer Tina Turner. Ike, Tina's husband, manipulated and abused the singer for years, but in Fishburne's gifted hands, he became a complex character, full of charm and even humor. "He saved Ike," said ANGELA BASSETT who played Tina Turner in the film. "He brought out Ike's dignity." Both Bassett and Fishburne were nominated for Academy Awards for best actress and actor for their riveting performances.

Since then, Fishburne has played a gallery of memorable and diverse characters, including a chess-playing street hustler in *Searching for Bobby Fischer* (1993); Shakespeare's tragic black hero in *Othello* (1995), a role he was destined to play, and a spelling bee coach in *Akeelah and the Bee* in 2006.

He played Morpheus in the science-fiction blockbuster *The Matrix* (1999) and reprised the role in two sequels. Fishburne is also the author of a play, *Riff Raff*. He adapted it into a film, *Once in the Life* (2000), which he also directed, produced, and starred in. In December 2008, Fishburne replaced William Petersen as the head of a police forensic team on the hit CBS crime series *CSI* (1998–   ). It is his first regular role in a television series.

Further Reading

Fishburne, Laurence. *Riff Raff*. New York: Dramatists Play Service, 1997.

"Laurence Fishburne." The Internet Movie Database. Available online. URL: http://www.imdb.com/name/nm0000401/. Downloaded on February 4, 2009.

Further Viewing

Boyz N the Hood (1991). Sony, VHS/2 DVDs, 1995/2003.

Othello (1995). Turner Home Entertainment, DVD, 2000.

What's Love Got to Do with It (1993). Walt Disney Video, VHS/DVD, 1997/1999.

Fisher, Gail
(1935–2000) *actress*

The first African-American actress to win an Emmy for her continuing work on a dramatic television series, Gail Fisher was never able to repeat her initial success and eventually came to a sad end.

She was born on August 18, 1935, in Orange, New Jersey. Named Miss Black New Jersey in her teens, she won a scholarship to the American Academy of Dramatic Arts in New York City. Later she found work in the New York theater and became a member of the distinguished Lincoln Center Repertory Company. She was RUBY DEE's understudy in the Broadway play *Purlie Victorious* and was in a touring company of Lorraine Hansberry's *A Raisin in the Sun*. In 1961, portraying a dental patient, Fisher became the first black female to speak lines in a national television commercial.

In 1968, she was cast as Peggy Fair, secretary to private detective Joe Mannix in the hit CBS series *Mannix*. The network didn't want to hire an African American on the show, but star Mike Connors and producer Bruce Geller insisted on Fisher playing the part.

As Peggy Fair, Fisher was more than a prop on the set. She played a meaningful role in many episodes. In one episode, she was shot protecting her boss and, while recuperating in the hospital, fell in love with an African premier with an incurable disease. Peggy Fair became a role model for African-American women at a time when there were very few blacks on network television. In 1969, Fisher won a National Association for the Advancement of Colored People (NAACP) Image Award and an Emmy for best supporting actress in a dramatic series in the 1969–70 season.

When *Mannix* went off the air in 1975, Fisher found few acting opportunities in television. She made guest appearances on such series as *Medical Center* and *Love, American Style*, but found no steady work. She became addicted to drugs and was arrested for cocaine possession in 1978. Fisher entered a rehab center but struggled with addiction for most of the rest of her life. Her last role on television was as a secretary in the TV film *Donor* in 1990.

Gail Fisher died of lung cancer on December 2, 2000. In a bizarre twist of fate, her brother Clifton, a businessman, died the same day of heart failure.

"I think she opened new ground for a lot of people and allowed African-American actresses to be seen in a different light," said her costar and friend Mike Connors at the time of her death.

Further Reading

Bogle, Donald. *Prime Time Blues: African Americans on Network Television.* New York: Farrar, Straus & Giroux, 2002, pp. 137–139.
"Gail Fisher: The Girl from Mannix." *Ebony* (October 1969): 140–144.

Further Viewing

Mannix: The Second Season. Paramount Home Video, DVD box set, 2009.

Fitzgerald, Ella
("The First Lady of Song," "The First Lady of Jazz")
(ca. 1917–1996) *jazz and pop singer, songwriter*

In a career that stretched over six decades, Ella Fitzgerald was hailed as the greatest of jazz singers and one of the finest pop singers of the 20th century.

She was born, according to her birth certificate, on April 25, 1917, in Newport News, Virginia, although most sources give her birth year as 1918. Her childhood was marred by poverty, and her father, William Fitzgerald, abandoned the family when she was a child. Fitzgerald moved with her mother, Temperance, to Yonkers, New York, where she performed as a dancer with a friend at local clubs. When her mother died sud-

Ella Fitzgerald's crystal clear tones and unparalleled scat singing earned her the title "First Lady of Jazz." *(Photo courtesy of Showtime Archives, Toronto)*

denly in 1932, Fitzgerald moved in with an aunt in Harlem. Two years later she sang professionally for the first time in an amateur contest at the Apollo Theater and brought home the first prize. Bandleader CHICK WEBB heard her sing and immediately hired her for his legendary band that played the Savoy Ballroom in Harlem. Fitzgerald made her first recording with Webb's band in 1935. In 1938, at age 21, she had her first hit with the novelty song "A-Tisket, A-Tasket." Her honey-toned, girlish voice was soon being heard all over the nation on radio and records.

When Webb died in 1939, Fitzgerald became the nominal leader of his band for the next three years. She was labeled on recordings as "Ella Fitzgerald and Her Famous Orchestra." After that, she went solo and amazed the jazz world in 1945 with her vocal scat-singing on the hit song "Flying Home." Fitzgerald's voice flew up and down the scale, inventively imitating the jazz instruments backing her singing. Although LOUIS ARMSTRONG preceded her as a scat singer, Fitzgerald took the style to a new level of excellence and creativity that has never been surpassed.

"I started doing a do-do-do-do-doodley-do and this man said I was scat singing," she told writer Joe Smith. "I never called it jazz or bop. . . . I didn't pay much attention to what people were calling it. That's what's so funny."

Her "normal" voice, unlike that of her great rival BILLIE HOLIDAY, was always crystal clear, bright in tone, and without a trace of black dialect. She may have lacked the dramatic weight of Holiday's voice but nevertheless had, as one writer called it, "a voice of profound reassurance and hope."

In 1947, while singing with DIZZY GILLESPIE's band, Fitzgerald married the band's bassist, Ray Brown. They were divorced five years later. Through the late 1940s and early 1950s, Fitzgerald experimented with the bebop music championed by Gillespie and CHARLIE PARKER, proving she could match their frantic pace note for note with her amazing voice. During this time she also recorded with such black vocal groups as the Ink Spots and the Delta Rhythm Boys as well as LOUIS ARMSTRONG and LOUIS JORDAN.

Her career entered a new phase in 1955 when Norman Granz of Verve Records became her manager. He convinced her to record a series of "Songbook" albums, each devoted to a great pop composer. The first album was *The Cole Porter Songbook* and it was followed by songbooks devoted to Irving Berlin, the Gershwins, Rodgers and Hart, DUKE ELLINGTON, and others. "It was like beginning all over again," she later recalled. "People who never heard me suddenly heard songs which surprised them because they didn't think I could sing them." These classic albums brought serious attention to these individual composers for the first time and greatly extended Fitzgerald's appeal beyond the world of jazz. When lyricist Ira Gershwin heard her *Gershwin Songbook* he commented, "I never knew how good our songs were until I heard Ella Fitzgerald sing them." Fitzgerald was herself a songwriter and penned such standards as "You Showed Me the Way" and "Oh, But I Do."

Her newfound fame made her a bigger star than ever and she gave memorable performances at the Hollywood Bowl in 1957 and at Carnegie Hall with Duke Ellington in 1958. She toured Europe several times with jazz pianist OSCAR PETERSON and his trio.

Fitzgerald took a rare misstep in her career in the 1960s when she tried to keep up with the times and recorded everything from Beatles songs to country and western. She regained her momentum in the early 1970s when she returned to singing jazz on Granz's new label, Pablo. In later years, her diabetes caused serious circulatory and eye problems. Yet she continued to perform regularly into her mid-70s. One of her later major appearances was at the Kool Jazz Festival at Carnegie Hall in 1985.

In 1993, Fitzgerald's legs were amputated below the knees. She died on June 15, 1996, and the world mourned the passing of one of the great voices in popular music history.

Ella Fitzgerald won 13 Grammy Awards, including one for Lifetime Achievement in 1967. The jazz magazine *Down Beat* named her top female vocalist in their yearly poll more than 20 times. In 1979, she was the recipient of the Kennedy Center Honors for a lifetime in the performing arts. As her obituary in the *New York Times* put it, she "brought a classic sense of musical proportion and balance to everything she touched."

Further Reading

Gourse, Leslie, ed. *The Ella Fitzgerald Companion: Seven Decades of Commentary.* New York: Schirmer Books, 2000.

Nicholson, Stuart. *Ella Fitzgerald: A Biography of the First Lady of Jazz.* New York: Routledge, 2004.

Stone, Tanya Lee. *Up Close: Ella Fitzgerald.* New York: Viking Juvenile, 2008 (children).

Further Listening

Best of Ella Fitzgerald and Louis Armstrong. Uni/Verve, CD, 1997.

The Best of the Songbooks. Uni/Verve, CD, 1993.

Gold. Verve, CD, 2007.

Further Viewing

Ella Fitzgerald: Something to Live For. WinStar Home Video, VHS/DVD, 1999/2000.

Jazz Icons: Ella Fitzgerald Live in '57 and '63. TDK DVD Video, DVD, 2006.

Foxx, Jamie

(Eric Marlon Bishop)

(1967–   ) *actor, R & B singer, comedian*

The third African-American to win an Oscar for best actor, Jamie Foxx has succeeded on television, in the movies, and has more recently begun a career as a singer. He was born Eric Marlon Bishop on December 13, 1967, in Terrell, Texas. His parents divorced when he was still an infant, and Eric was formally adopted by his maternal grandparents, Mark and Estelle Tolley. As a boy, Eric sang in the church choir and was a Boy Scout. He played quarterback on his high school football team and, after graduating, attended the U.S. International University in San Diego, California, on a music scholarship. He left college without graduating in 1988.

One day in 1989, a girlfriend challenged Bishop to do stand-up comedy at the Comedy Club in Los Angeles. He accepted the challenge, changing his last name to Foxx in honor of the comic REDD FOXX. and his first name to Jamie because it could be that of a man or woman. Foxx noticed that women comics received preference on open-mike nights. Jamie Foxx became a hit on the comedy club circuit, which led to an offer in 1991 to become a regular cast member on Fox TV's hit comedy revue show *In Living Color.* Foxx stayed with the show until it went off the air in 1994. Two years later, he lauded his own sitcom, *The Jamie Foxx Show,* which ran until 2002. By then his film career had taken off with a solid dramatic role as a football quarterback who finally gets his chance for the big time in *Any Given Sunday* (1999), directed by Oliver Stone.

In 2003, director Taylor Hackford chose Foxx to play the great R & B singer and musician RAY CHARLES in his biopic *Ray.* Foxx, who had impersonated Charles in comedy sketches on *In Living Color,* delved deeply into the role. He lost more than 30 pounds to play the younger Charles and endured prosthetic eyelids that allowed him to experience the blindness that Charles lived with most of his life. The hard work paid off. Foxx's performance as both actor and singer was a marvel. It earned him an Academy Award and a Golden Globe Award for best actor. He was also nominated for an Academy Award in the supporting actor category for the role of a cabbie who spends a night driving a hit man (Tom Cruise) on his errands in the thriller *Collateral* (2004). Foxx became the first African-American actor to be nominated for two Oscars in the same year.

The Oscar has been seen as the kiss of death for some of its winners, and Foxx seemed to flounder after his triumph. *Jarhead* (2005), in which he played a staff sergeant stationed in Iraq, and *Miami Vice* (2006), a big-screen remake of the popular 1980s television crime series, both flopped at the box office. Foxx's next role as the ambitious manager of a female singing trio in the movie version of the Broadway musical *Dreamgirls* (2006) put him on solid ground again. He was also effective in the thriller *The Kingdom* (2007), in which he led a crew of counterterrorist FBI agents. In 2009, he played a former classical music prodigy who is now homeless, in *The Soloist.*

Praised for his singing in *Ray,* Foxx's long anticipated album *Unpredictable* came out in 2005, featuring duets with such top recording artists as MARY J. BLIGE. Foxx made a splash in the music world the previous year appearing on Kanye West's hit single "Gold Digger." His third album, *Intuition,* was released in 2008.

Presently single, Foxx has a daughter from a previous relationship. In 2010, Foxx won a first Grammy award in the Best R&B Performance by a Duo or Group category for "Blame It."

Further Reading

The Official Web site of Jamie Foxx. Available online. URL: http://www.jamiefoxx.com/index2.cfm. Downloaded on December 9, 2008.

Orr, Tamra. *Jamie Foxx.* Hockessin, Del.: Mitchell Lane Publishers, 2006 (YA).

Todd, Anne M. *Jamie Foxx: Entertainer.* New York: Chelsea House, 2008 (YA).

Further Listening

Unpredictable. J-Records, CD, 2005.

Further Viewing

Any Given Sunday (1999). Warner Home Video, DVD, 2000.

The Jamie Foxx Film Collection. Universal, DVD box set, includes *Ray, Jarhead, Miami Vice,* and *The Kingdom,* 2008.

Foxx, Redd

(John Elroy Sanford)
(1922–1991) *comedian, actor*

The first black comic to be a best-selling recording artist, Redd Foxx became a superstar when he gave up his racy nightclub act for a successful television series.

He was born John Elroy Sanford on December 9, 1922, in St. Louis, Missouri. His father was an electrician and his mother a domestic. His parents divorced when John was in his teens, and he followed his mother to Chicago. He quit high school after a year and formed a washtub band with two friends. His stage name came from his ruddy complexion and his admiration for baseball player Jimmie Foxx.

Few successful entertainers have "paid their dues" as long as Redd Foxx did. The washtub band disbanded in New York during World War II, and Foxx lived a skid row existence for some time. He was arrested for stealing a bottle of milk and sent to jail on Rikers Island. When he got out, he worked at a series of jobs including that of short-order cook and dishwasher. One of his coworkers washing dishes was Malcolm Little, who years later would become the civil rights leader Malcolm X.

Foxx teamed up with comic Slappy White in 1947, but he periodically took other jobs to make ends meet. His first real break came in 1955. While appearing solo at Los Angeles' Club Oasis, he was spotted by a representative from Dooto Records who caught his risqué act and asked him if he'd like to make a record. He was paid $25 to make *Laff of the Party,* which contained off-color jokes and stories. Over the next 15 years Foxx made more than 50 "party" albums, most of them too risqué to be played on radio or even sold openly in white-owned record stores. But the records did well in black communities, and he eventually sold more than 10 million copies.

In 1959, Foxx was booked into New York's Basin St. East. Afraid a middle-class white audience would be offended by his material, he did a "clean" act and bombed. Show business friends in the audience called for him to do his regular act. When he did, he was a sensation. The date led to appearances on television and eventually an invitation to perform in Las Vegas.

OSSIE DAVIS cast Foxx in his comedy-mystery *Cotton Comes to Harlem* (1970), the first feature film the comic appeared in. He was very funny as a junkman and caught the eye of producers Bud Yorkin and Norman Lear, who were looking for someone to cast in a new television situation comedy. Foxx got the part and played junk dealer Fred Sanford in *Sanford and Son,* which premiered on NBC in January 1972. Foxx's ethnic but clean humor appealed to both whites and blacks, and *Sanford and Son* became the network's most popular prime-time series for four seasons. A superstar at last, Redd Foxx let success go to his head. He became demanding and difficult to work with, although he was generous to a fault with his friends and colleagues.

Sanford and Son, probably the most successful black sitcom in television history, finally ended its run in 1977. That fall, Foxx starred in his own variety show on ABC, *The Redd Foxx Show,* which lasted only four months. An attempt to revive Fred Sanford without his son, in a sitcom called *Sanford,* also failed. Meanwhile Foxx's private problems rivaled his professional ones. His second marriage to singer Betty Jean Harris ended in divorce, and the Internal Revenue Service (IRS) hounded him for about $3 million in back taxes. He declared bankruptcy in the early 1980s.

As a new generation of black comics emerged, Foxx's fortunes rose again. EDDIE MURPHY, who expressed his debt to Foxx and his liberating humor, gave him a role in his black gangster film *Harlem Nights* (1989). In 1991, Foxx starred in a new sitcom, *The Royal Family,* which costarred DELLA REESE. On October 11, 1991, during a rehearsal for the show, Redd Foxx suffered a major heart attack and was rushed to a hospital, where he died.

As irascible as his memorable character of Fred Sanford, Redd Foxx was an influence on many of the black comedians who came after him. No less a talent than BILL COSBY has called him "the comedic father of us all."

Further Reading

Foxx, Redd. *The Redd Foxx Encyclopedia of Black Humor.* Pasadena, Calif.: W. Ritchie Press, 1977.

Johnson, Michael Dalton. *Talking Trash with Redd Foxx.* Del Mar, Calif.: Emery Dalton Books, 1995.

The Official Site of Redd Foxx. "Biography." Redd Foxx Web site. Available online. URL: http://www.reddfoxx.com/biography.html. Downloaded on February 13, 2009.

Further Viewing

On Location with Redd Foxx (1978). Standing Room Only, DVD, 2006.

Sanford and Son: The First Season. Sony, 2 DVDs, 2002.

Franklin, Aretha
("Lady Soul," "Queen of Soul")
(1942–) *R & B singer*

The greatest female African-American soul singer of the 1960s and 1970s, Aretha Franklin remains today the personification of soul music for millions of listeners.

She was born on March 25, 1942, in Memphis, Tennessee, and grew up in Buffalo, New York, and Detroit, Michigan. Her father was the Rev. Clarence L. Franklin, one of the most famous black ministers in the United States and pastor of Detroit's New Bethel Baptist Church. Aretha grew up listening to and modeling herself after such great gospel singers as Clara Ward and MAHALIA JACKSON. Jackson was a surrogate mother to Aretha, who own mother, Barbara, died when she was 10.

By age 14, Franklin was an experienced gospel singer herself and toured the Midwest. But she soon learned life was not as simple as in a gospel hymn. She had two children out of wedlock by the time she was 17. At age 18, Franklin followed the example of SAM COOKE and other top gospel singers and decided to break into the secular world of pop music. She moved to New York City, where John Hammond of Columbia Records quickly signed her to a recording contract. Usually an astute evaluator of musical talent, Hammond seriously misjudged Franklin's gifts. He felt her fiery, gospel style of singing was too raw for the commercial music market and recast her as a pop singer of show tunes and standards. After six frustrating years in which she only had one top-40 hit record, Franklin left Columbia and signed with Atlantic Records.

Atlantic was one of the premier labels of rhythm and blues (R & B) music and nurtured Franklin's gift for soul music. Her first Atlantic recording date in January 1967 took place at Fame Studios in Muscle Shoals, Alabama. The first session in the studio produced "I Never Loved a Man (The Way I Love You)." The song revealed all the gutsy power of Franklin's gospel-trained voice. It went to number nine on the pop charts, and the album of the same name became the first of many best-selling albums. Franklin's second single was "Respect," a song written and previously recorded by Otis Redding. Aretha turned this male lament into a dynamic cry for female liberation, using a gospel call-and-response-style shout, backed by her two sisters, Carolyn and Erma. It was her first number-one hit and became *the* song of the summer of 1967, an anthem of independence and radical politics for both women and young African Americans.

For the next seven years, Aretha Franklin produced a string of hits, including such soul classics as "Baby I Love You," "A Natural Woman (You Make Me Feel Like)" (both 1968), "Chain of Fools," and "Think" (both 1969). She could take others songs, such as Ben E. King's "Spanish Harlem" and Simon and Garfunkle's "Bridge over Troubled Water" (both 1971), and make them her own. Franklin won the Grammy for best R & B female vocal performance every year from 1968 to 1975—an unprecedented feat. She had 14 top-10 hits in that period, finishing with her biggest seller to date, "Until You Come Back to Me (That's What I'm Gonna Do)" (1974), written by STEVIE WONDER.

Then disco music pushed the "Queen of Soul" from her throne, and Franklin's career hit a dry spell. New releases on Atlantic lacked the spark and originality of her earlier recordings, and she finally left the label in the late 1970s. Franklin moved to Los Angeles to study acting. There she met and wed actor Glynn Turman (the couple divorced in 1984), and she landed a role as a waitress in the comedy/musical *The Blues Brothers* (1980). Her star turn in that film jump-started Franklin's career again. She signed with Arista Records and returned to the charts with the album

Jump to It (1983). She updated her sound with the song "Freeway of Love" (1985) from the album *Who's Zooming Who?*, and it became her second-biggest-selling single. By mid-1986, Franklin had a total of 24 gold records and 14 Grammy Awards. That same year, she hosted her first TV special, *Aretha!* In 1987, she hit number one again with "I Knew You Were Waiting (For Me)," a duet with George Michael, and became the first woman inducted into the Rock and Roll Hall of Fame. She received Grammy's Living Legend Award in 1991 and its Lifetime Achievement Award in 1994.

Franklin won her 18th standard Grammy for the song "Wonderful," from the album *So Damn Happy* (2003). In 2007, she released *Jewels in the Crown: All-Star Duets with the Queen*, which included duets with WHITNEY HOUSTON, MARY J. BLIGE, and Gloria Estefan. Franklin sang "My Country, Tis of Thee" at the inauguration of President Barack Obama on January 20, 2009.

Further Reading

Bego, Mark. *Aretha Franklin: The Queen of Soul.* New York: Da Capo Press, 2001.

Dobkin, Matt. *I Never Loved a Man the Way I Love You: Aretha Franklin, Respect, and the Making of a Soul Music Masterpiece.* New York: St. Martin's Griffin, 2008.

Franklin, Aretha, and David Ritz. *Aretha: From These Roots.* New York: Villard Books, 1999.

Further Listening

30 Greatest Hits. Atlantic, CD, 1986.

Further Viewing

Aretha Franklin: Live at Park West (1985). Image Entertainment, DVD, 1999.

Freeman, Morgan

(1937–   ) *actor*

Possibly the most distinguished African-American actor working in films today, Morgan Freeman has brought strength and conviction to every role he's played, from a murderous pimp to the president of the United States.

He was born in Memphis, Tennessee, on June 1, 1937. His father, Morgan Porterfield Morgan, was a barber. The family later moved to Chicago, then his mother, Mayne Edna, left her husband and took him and his sister to Greenwood, Mississippi. Freeman got involved in theater at school and, while in seventh grade, won a state competition for acting. When he graduated from high school, he enlisted in the air force. He later studied drama at Los Angeles City College and tried to find film work in Hollywood. He was unsuccessful and moved to New York City to pursue theater acting.

Freeman got his first break acting on the daytime soap opera *Another World* and later became a regular on the PBS children's series *The Electric Company*. This most serious of dramatic actors made his Broadway debut as a hoofer in the all-black production of *Hello Dolly!* (1968) starring PEARL BAILEY. He spent most of the next decade honing his craft on stage, garnering a Tony Award nomination for his portrayal of a gang member in the Broadway drama *The Mighty Gents* in 1978. He later won Obie (Off-Broadway) Awards for his work in Shakespeare's *Coriolanus* (1979), Bertolt Brecht's *Mother Courage* (1980), and *The Gospel at Colonus* (1983).

In 1980, at age 43, Freeman made his Hollywood screen debut in *Brubaker*, playing a death row inmate. In the independent film *Death of a Prophet* (1981) he was a revolutionary leader based on Malcolm X. But despite other good supporting roles, it was another six years before audiences and critics alike took notice of his talent in the low-budget film *Street Smart* (1987). Freeman played a pimp named Fast Black, a chilling portrayal that film historian Donald Bogle has called "one of the most powerful film performances of the decade." It earned him his first Academy Award nomination for best supporting actor and won him the New York Film Critics Circle's best supporting actor award.

One of the finest black actors in film today, Morgan Freeman did not get his first major film role until he was 49. *(AP Photo/Chris Pizzello)*

Freeman went on to play a series of memorable roles that solidified his reputation as a leading character actor. In *Driving Miss Daisy* (1989) he played the southern chauffeur Hoke Colburn, who strikes up an unlikely friendship with his elderly female white patron. The part earned him a second Oscar nomination, for best actor. The same year he appeared in *Glory* as Sergeant John Rawlins, a Union soldier in an all-black Civil War regiment, which he calls his favorite role. His first starring role was as the controversial, real-life high school principal Joe Clark in *Lean on Me* (1989).

Through the 1990s, Freeman alternated between leading roles and strong supporting ones.

He was Kevin Costner's Moorish sidekick in *Robin Hood, Prince of Thieves* (1991) and Clint Eastwood's outlaw partner in the Oscar-winning western *Unforgiven* (1992). In *The Shawshank Redemption* (1994), based on a Stephen King story, he played a thoughtful convict and earned his third Oscar nomination, for best actor. Freeman was a general in *Outbreak* (1995), the president in the end-of-the-world film *Deep Impact* (1998), and a lovelorn hit man in the dark comedy *Nurse Betty* (2000). Twice he has portrayed writer James Patterson's popular sleuth Alex Cross, first in *Kiss the Girls* (1997) and then *Along Came a Spider* (2001). In 1993 Freeman made his directorial debut in the South African drama *Bopha!*

Morgan Freeman reunited with Eastwood in the boxing drama *Million Dollar Baby* (2004). His portrayal of ex-boxer and trainer's aide Eddie Scrap-Iron Dupris earned him an Academy Award for best supporting actor. Freeman played Batman's aide Lucius Fox in *Batman Begins* (2005) and *The Dark Knight* (2008). He returned to Broadway in April 2008 in a revival of the Clifford Odets's play *The Country Girl*. Freeman was a 2008 recipient of the Kennedy Center Honors. He stars as Nelson Mandela in Clint Eastwood's *Invictus* (2009).

Further Reading

Bogle, Donald. *Toms, Coons, Mulattoes, Mammies & Bucks: An Interpretive History of Blacks in American Films.* New York: Continuum, 1997, pp. 308, 309–311, 312, 314–317.

DeAngelis, Gina. *Morgan Freeman.* Black Americans of Achievement. New York: Chelsea House, 1999 (YA).

Tracy, Kathleen. *Morgan Freeman: A Biography.* Melbourne, Australia: Barricade Books, 2006.

Further Viewing

Driving Miss Daisy (1990). Warner Home Video, VHS/DVD, 2001/2003.

Million Dollar Baby (2004). Warner Home Video, 2 DVDs, 2005.

The Shawshank Redemption (1994). Castle Rock, 2 DVDs, 2004.

Street Smart (1987). MGM Home Entertainment, VHS/DVD, 1989/2003.

G

Gaye, Marvin
(Marvin Pentz Gay II)
(1939–1984) *R & B singer, songwriter, record producer*

One of the most gifted and successful African-American singers of the 1960s, Marvin Gaye brought soul music into a new era of social concern and sexual frankness in the 1970s and early 1980s.

He was born Marvin Pentz Gay II, on April 2, 1939, in Washington, D.C. His father, Marvin Gay, Sr., was a Pentecostal minister who abused him emotionally as a child. His mother, Alberta, was a former sharecropper. He first sang in his father's church at age three and later played the organ and piano for services. After high school, Gaye, who later added the *e* to his last name, served briefly in the air force and in 1958 formed a doo-wop group, the Marquees, in Washington. The Marquees impressed Harvey Fuqua, leader of the famous doo-wop group the Moonglows. He hired the Marquees as the new Moonglows and took them on tour.

After three years as a Moonglow, Gaye ended up in Detroit where he met Berry Gordy, owner of Motown Records, at a party. Gaye sang for Gordy, and he was impressed enough to hire the young singer. Gaye started at Motown as a session drummer and played drums on such early Motown hits as "Please Mr. Postman" by the Marvelettes. In 1961, he married Gordy's sister Anna, who was 17 years his senior.

Now a member of the family, Gaye got his chance to sing and made an album of standard pop songs that was poorly received. Although he preferred to sing romantic ballads in the style of NAT KING COLE, he reluctantly tried rhythm and blues (R & B) music. His fourth single, "A Stubborn Kind of Fellow" (1962), was a modest hit and marked the beginning of one of the most remarkable string of hit records by a male artist in the 1960s. His sixth single, "Pride and Joy" (1963), became the first of several number-one hits on the R & B charts. Gaye's smoldering, insinuating tenor, usually backed by a female chorus, made him Motown's most successful male singer and a sex symbol to millions of young African-American women. Classic songs like "Can I Get a Witness" (1963), "Baby Don't You Do It" (1964), and "How Sweet It Is to Be Loved by You" (1965) would be covered by such divergent white artists as the Rolling Stones, the Band, and James Taylor.

Through the 1960s and into the 1970s, Gaye teamed up for duets with nearly every Motown female artist including Mary Wells, Kim Weston, and DIANA ROSS. But his favorite partner, and the one he made the most memorable music with, was Tammi Terrell. Together they had a total of 11 hit songs, including the top-10 hits "Your Precious Love," "If I Could Build My Whole World Around

You," "Ain't Nothing Like the Real Thing," and "You're All I Need to Get By." In 1967, during a live performance at a college in Virginia, Terrell collapsed in Gaye's arms. Her death from a brain tumor three years later deeply affected him.

Gaye continued to have great success as a single act, particularly with his hard-driving version of "I Heard It Through the Grapevine" (1968), his first number-one pop hit. But by 1970, he was frustrated with the assembly line production at Motown and was ready to produce his own records. Gordy reluctantly agreed to give him total creative control, but when he heard

One of Motown's biggest hit makers of the 1960s, Marvin Gaye took soul music into new territory in the 1970s. *(AP Photo)*

Gaye's album *What's Going On* (1971), he urged him not to release it. "They all thought it was garbage," recalled Gaye's friend Elgie Stover. "Marvin had to bet his life to get them to release it." When it was released, *What's Going On* became the biggest critical success of Gaye's career. The songs, a number of them written by the singer, dealt with serious issues, such as racism, the Vietnam War, and the environment, that had rarely if ever been the subjects of Motown or R & B records. The title track, "Inner City Blues (Make Me Wanna Holler)," and "Mercy Mercy Me (The Ecology)" all became top-10 hits. With *What's Going On*, R & B grew up, so to speak, while retaining its melodic and rhythmic appeal. Gaye also set an example for other black artists, such as Motown's STEVIE WONDER, to take control of their careers.

In *Let's Get It On* (1973) Gaye did for erotic love what he had previously done for social issues. While the album's love songs were more explicit than anything he had sung before, there was a sensitivity and a kind of spirituality to the music and lyrics that are sadly missing from the work of most contemporary R & B artists.

Gaye's personal life, however, was not as fulfilling as his music. His marriage to Anna Gordy fell apart, and the couple divorced in 1975. A second marriage to dancer Janis Hunter, 17 years his junior, also failed. Gaye relied on drugs to lift him out of his dark moods and became addicted to cocaine. By the late 1970s, he was in a creative slump and selling few records. When the Internal Revenue Service (IRS) came after him for back taxes, he fled to Europe, where he remained for three years in self-imposed exile. When he returned to the United States in 1981, he ended his long relationship with Motown and signed with Columbia Records. His first Columbia release, the album *Midnight Love* (1982), returned to the subject of erotic love and was a creative and commercial triumph. The track "Sexual Healing" went to number three on the pop charts and earned Gaye his first Grammy Awards—for best

R & B male performance and best R & B instrumental performance.

The comeback, however, was short-lived. Gaye's personal demons turned what should have been a celebratory tour into a nightmare. His drug addiction was worse than ever, and he moved in with his parents in the Crenshaw section of Los Angeles. Gaye's long, unresolved relationship with his father came to a head on April Fools' Day, 1984. After a violent argument, Marvin Gay, Sr., shot his son with a gun that Gaye had given him for protection. Gaye died an hour later, one day before his 45th birthday. At his trial, Gaye's father was acquitted on the defense that a brain tumor had caused his violent behavior. Many people believe that Gaye wanted to die and provoked his father into shooting him.

Marvin Gaye was posthumously inducted into the Rock and Roll Hall of Fame in 1987. He won Grammy's Lifetime Achievement Award in 1996. A biopic *Sexual Healing* is scheduled for 2011, with Jesse L. Martin playing Gaye. His daughter Nona Gaye was a recording artist in the 1990s. She had an acting role in the film *Ali* (2001), starring WILL SMITH.

Further Reading

Davis, Sharon. *Marvin Gaye: I Heard It Through the Grapevine*. Edinburgh, Scotland: Mainstream Publishing, 2003.

Dyson, Michael Eric. *Mercy, Mercy Me: The Art, Loves and Dreams of Marvin Gaye*. New York: Basic Civitas Books, 2005.

Ritz, David. *Divided Soul: The Life of Marvin Gaye*. New York: Da Capo Press, 2003.

Turner, Steve. *Trouble Man: The Life and Death of Marvin Gaye*. Hopewell, N.J.: Ecco Press, 2000.

Further Listening

The Very Best of Marvin Gaye. Universal UK, 2 CDs, 2001.

Further Viewing

Real Thing: In Performance 1964–1981. Hip-O Records, DVD, 2006.

Gillespie, Dizzy
(John Birks Gillespie)
(1917–1993) *jazz trumpeter, bandleader, composer*

One of the founding fathers of bebop jazz, Dizzy Gillespie was a major force in jazz for more than half a century as a musician, composer, and bandleader.

He was born John Birks Gillespie on October 21, 1917, in Cheraw, South Carolina. When Gillespie was 10 years old, his father, John, a brickmason and amateur musician, died but his talents lived on in his son. Gillespie showed an aptitude for music at an early age and won a scholarship to the Laurinburg Institute, a music school in North Carolina. His mother, Lottie, moved to Philadelphia soon after and he joined her there after completing his studies in 1935. Gillespie later moved to New York City where he replaced his idol, trumpeter Roy Eldridge, in Teddy Hill's jazz band. In 1939, at age 21, he joined CAB CALLOWAY's band, but Gillespie's wild antics and showmanship, which earned him his nickname, "Dizzy," did not please Calloway, who fired him two years later.

Gillespie joined forces with gifted saxophonist CHARLIE PARKER, whom he had met earlier in Kansas City, Missouri, and the two began experimenting with a new kind of jazz that was daring, modern, and too fast to dance to. Gillespie and Parker formed a quartet in 1945, and their first recording, "Salt Peanuts" on Decca Records, is considered the first "bebop" record. It was soon followed by such classics as "Hot House" and "Groovin' High."

Parker was often perceived as the more creative genius, but it was Gillespie who was the theoretician and composer. He kept the music alive and growing long after Parker burned out on the alcohol and drugs that eventually killed him. As one writer put it, "If Charlie Parker was the soul of bebop, Gillespie was its heart and public face."

Few jazz artists were as beloved and recognizable to the public as Dizzy Gillespie. With his trademark beret, puffed cheeks known as "Gillespie's Pouches," and his distinctively up-turned trumpet, he was, along with LOUIS ARMSTRONG, one of jazz's most exuberant ambassadors.

The bent trumpet came about when a dancer accidentally stepped on Gillespie's instrument during a party in 1954. When he played it later he was happily surprised to find he could hear himself much better over the other instruments. After that, he had all his trumpets made that way.

Gillespie pioneered the small jazz combo, but he never lost his love of big bands. With tremendous success, he adapted the bebop sound to the bands of Woody Herman and Earl Hines among others. By the mid-1940s he formed his own big band, which he kept together in one form or another for 20 years. His landmark Carnegie Hall concert in New York, just before his 30th birthday, showcased his big band and small combo playing bebop.

As he grew older, Gillespie's musical interests ranged far beyond bebop. Like DUKE ELLINGTON, he was extremely prolific in his composing and playing. He produced albums of everything from Afro-Cuban and bossa nova music to Negro spirituals and ambitious jazz compositions such as *Africana* and *A Night in Tunisia*.

His creative scat-singing was in a league with Armstrong and ELLA FITZGERALD, and his legendary sense of humor produced such gems as "Swing Low, Sweet Cadillac." All the on-stage antics led many listeners to misjudge him as a clown and entertainer though he was actually a serious and thoughtful musician and intellectual.

In 1956, Gillespie took his band on an international tour, the first jazz band to be sponsored abroad by the State Department. He was elected to the *Down Beat* Hall of Fame in 1960 and was a recipient of the Kennedy Center Honors in 1990. Those puffed-out cheeks finally fell silent on January 6, 1993, when Dizzy Gillespie died of cancer.

Further Reading

Gentry, Tony. *Dizzy Gillespie*. Black Americans of Achievement. New York: Chelsea House, 1991 (YA).

Gillespie, Dizzy. *Dizzy: To Be or Not to Bop: Memoirs of Dizzy Gillespie with Al Fraser*. Minneapolis: University of Minnesota Press, 2009.

Gourse, Leslie. *Dizzy Gillespie and the Birth of Bebop*. New York: Atheneum, 1995.

Maggin, Donald L. *Dizzy: The Life and Times of John Birks Gillespie*. New York: Harper Paperbacks, 2006.

Shipton, Alyn. *Groovin' High: The Life of Dizzy Gillespie*. New York: Oxford University Press, 2001.

Further Listening

Dizzy Gillespie: Ken Burns JAZZ Collection. Verve, CD, 2000.

A Night in Tunisia: The Very Best of Dizzy Gillespie. RCA, CD, 2006.

Further Viewing

Jazz Icons: Dizzy Gillespie Live in '58 and '70. TDK DVD Video, DVD, 2006.

Glover, Danny
(1947–   ) *actor, social activist*

Danny Glover is one of the most talented, reliable, and bankable of "the middle generation" of African-American movie actors. An actor with a strong social conscience, he has played a wide range of roles with both strength and sensitivity.

He was born in San Francisco, California, on July 22, 1947. His parents, James and Carrie Glover, both worked for the U.S. Postal Service and were political activists in the National Association for the Advancement of Colored People (NAACP) and the postal service. Glover himself participated in the student activist movement during the 1960s and studied economics at San Francisco State University. After graduation, he worked as an economic planner for the city. It was only in his mid-20s that Glover became seriously interested in acting. He became part of the American Conservatory Theater's Black Actors' Workshop and was about 30 when he got his first professional jobs on stage and television. In the late 1970s, he appeared on such dramatic TV series as *Lou Grant, Hill Street Blues,* and *Palmerston, USA.* His film debut was in a small role in the Clint Eastwood movie *Escape from Alcatraz* (1979).

In 1980, Glover made an auspicious Off-Broadway debut in New York when he starred in the two-character play *The Blood Knot* by South African playwright Athol Fugard. He gave another riveting performance in Fugard's *Master Harold and the Boys* (1982), which earned him a Theatre World Award. Filmmaker Robert Benton was so impressed by his performance, that he cast Glover in his new film *Places in the Heart* (1984). He won rave reviews as a sharecropper who comes to the aid of farmer Sally Field. The following year Glover had leading roles in three box office hits. In the rousing western *Silverado* he played a black cowboy. In *Witness* he was a cop gone bad, and in *The Color Purple* he was Whoopi Goldberg's abusive husband. But it was the action-adventure film *Lethal Weapon* (1987) that made Danny Glover a full-fledged movie star. This time he was a good cop and family man partnered with the wild and unpredictable Mel Gibson. The two made a great team, and the film was so successful that they were reunited in three sequels, the most recent released in 1998.

The success and money Glover has made on the *Lethal Weapon* films have allowed him to devote more time and effort to the many social causes he believes in so strongly. "He's up to his eyeballs in devoting time to community services and just causes," Mel Gibson has said. "He keeps going whether or not the public knows about it."

He has also used his money and clout to pursue more personal projects. He was executive producer and star of *To Sleep with Anger* (1990), directed by African-American filmmaker Charles Burnett.

Glover played an old southern friend who brings nothing but trouble to a middle-class black family living in Los Angeles. It is one of his best performances to date.

He has had other good roles in *Grand Canyon* (1991), *Bopha!* (1993), a South African drama directed by actor MORGAN FREEMAN, and *Beloved* (1998), the screen adaptation of a Toni Morrison novel. On television, Glover has starred in the miniseries *Mandela* (1987), Alex Haley's *Queen* (1993), and *The Saint of Fort Washington* (1993).

Glover made headlines in 1999 when he filed a complaint with the New York City Taxi and Limousine Commission claiming that city cab drivers have repeatedly refused to pick him up because he is black. "It happens to countless people every single day," Glover told the press. "The fact that I am a celebrity, the fact that I am visible, allows me to draw attention to the issue." A full investigation into the situation resulted from his complaint.

Danny Glover has been the recipient of five NAACP Image Awards and has been nominated for four Emmy Awards, most recently for the TV movie, *Freedom Song* (2000). In 2005, Glover played MEKHI PHIFER's estranged father in several episodes of the medical TV series *ER.* He was a detective in the horror movie *Saw* (2004) and played the owner of a blues club in 1950s Alabama in *Honeydripper* (2007), directed by John Sayles. Glover is currently planning to produce and direct a film about Haitian revolutionary leader Toussaint Louverture to star WESLEY SNIPES, ANGELA BASSETT, and DON CHEADLE.

Further Reading

Blakely, Gloria. *Danny Glover.* Black Americans of Achievement. New York: Chelsea House, 2001 (YA).

Boyle, Donald. *Toms, Coons, Mulattoes, Mummies & Bucks: An Interpretive History of Blacks in American Films.* New York: Continuum, 1997, pp. 274–276.

"Danny Glover." The Internet Movie Database. Available online. URL: http://www.imdb.com/name/nm0000418/. Downloaded on February 4, 2009.

Further Viewing
Beloved (1998). Walt Disney Video, VHS/DVD, 1999.
Honeydripper (2007). Universal, DVD, 2008.

Glover, Savion

(1973–   ) *tap dancer, choreographer*

Called by GREGORY HINES "perhaps the best tap dancer that ever lived," Savion Glover has reinvented tap dancing for a new generation of dancers and dance lovers through his innovative choreography.

He was born on November 19, 1973, in Newark, New Jersey, into a family of achievers. His great-grandfather, Dick Lundy, was a shortstop and manager in the Negro Baseball Leagues. His grandfather, Bill Lewis, was a pianist and vocalist in a big band, and his grandmother, Anna Lundy Lewis, was minister of music at a Newark church where WHITNEY HOUSTON once sang. His mother, Yvette, a singer and actress, gave him his unusual first name—a variation on the word "savior."

Glover first showed signs of his unusual dancing talent at age two, beating out rhythms on the walls and doors of his house with pots. At seven he became the youngest recipient of a scholarship at the Newark City School for the Arts. He later took tap lessons at the Broadway Dance Center in New York City. Tap interested him more than any other kind of dance because it involved the whole foot.

At age 11, Glover made his Broadway debut as the lead in the musical *The Tap Dance Kid* (1984). Three years later he appeared back on Broadway in the musical revue *Black and Blue* (1987) and became one of the youngest men ever nominated for a Tony Award for his performance. In 1989 Glover made his film debut in *Tap,* playing opposite his mentor Gregory Hines and show business legend SAMMY DAVIS, JR., in his last film appearance.

Glover returned to Broadway opposite Hines in the musical *Jelly's Last Jam* (1992), based on the life of jazz composer and pianist JELLY ROLL MORTON. His performance earned him a Drama Desk Award for best actor, and he toured for a year in the show with Hines's brother Maurice. In 1996, at age 23, Glover became the youngest recipient of a National Education Arts (NEA) grant. That same year he brought his funky style of tap to Broadway in the show *Bring in 'Da Noise, Bring in 'Da Funk*. Conceived, choreographed, and performed by Glover, the dance show won him a Tony for best choreography as well as a Drama Desk Award. Glover starred as a modern-day minstrel dancer in filmmaker Spike Lee's controversial movie *Bamboozled* (2000). In 2007, Glover performed in the JOHN COLTRANE tribute *If Trane Wuz Here* with saxophonist Matana Roberts. He later performed in "Classical Savion," a tap program set to classical music played by a string group, in 2009.

When he is not appearing on television (he did five years on the PBS children's show *Sesame Street*) or developing new dance steps, Glover is teaching tap to young people. "I feel it's one of my responsibilities to keep the dance alive," he said in an interview, "to keep it out there, to keep the style."

Further Reading
Glover, Savion, Bruce Weber, and Gregory Hines. *Savion: My Life in Tap*. New York: HarperCollins, 2000.
Hasda, Judy L. *Savion Glover: Entertainer*. Black American of Achievement. New York: Chelsea House, 2006 (YA).

Further Viewing
Bamboozled (2000). New Line Platinum Series, VHS/DVD, 2001.
Tap (1989). Sony, DVD, 2006.

Goldberg, Whoopi
(Caryn Johnson)
(1955–   ) *actress, comedian*

The second African-American actress to win an Academy Award, Whoopi Goldberg has proved her worth as both a leading comic and a serious actress on stage and screen.

She was born Caryn Johnson on November 13, 1955, in the Chelsea section of New York City where she was raised by her mother. A natural performer, by age eight she was acting at the Helena Rubinstein Children's Theater. Johnson dreamed of winning an Academy Award and recited her own acceptance speeches to her family. Dyslexia, however, made learning difficult for her, and she dropped out of high school to become part of the 1960s hippie generation. She married, divorced, and, after appearing in the chorus of several Broadway musicals, including *Hair*, moved to California in 1974, where she adopted her stage name. "Goldberg's a part of my family somewhere and that's all I can say about it," she once explained.

Goldberg became a founding member of the San Diego Repertory Company and worked on stage with that group for six years. She worked another two years with an improvisational theater company and then developed her own one-woman show, *The Spook Show.* Her talent for creating offbeat characters made the show a success, and she toured with it across the United States and Europe. Film and stage director Mike Nichols saw her perform at the Dance Theater Workshop in New York in 1983, and he was so impressed with her talent that he offered to direct her in a one-woman show on Broadway. Within a year, the show, *Whoopi Goldberg,* opened and was a hit with both critics and audiences.

Based on Goldberg's stage success, though she had never appeared in a film before, film director Steven Spielberg decided to cast her as the lead in his adaptation of Alice Walker's novel *The Color Purple* (1985). Goldberg played Celie, an unedu-

One of the most frequently miscast actresses in Hollywood, Whoopi Goldberg finally won an Oscar for her role in *Ghost* in 1990. *(Photofest)*

cated and much-abused rural southern black woman. She received an Academy Award nomination for best actress. The film received a total of 11 nominations but won no awards.

Goldberg was now a full-fledged movie star, and Hollywood quickly capitalized on her stardom. She was cast in a string of action-adventure films in which she played offbeat, goofy heroines. Such poorly made movies as *Jumpin' Jack Flash, Burglar* (both 1987) and *The Telephone* (1988) wasted Goldberg's talents. African-American audiences particularly found little to like in these films because they depicted Goldberg as an oddball with no identity as a black woman.

She fared better in *Clara's Heart* (1988), a drama in which she played a caring Jamaican maid to a white family in Baltimore. Yet it was not until *Ghost* (1990), a little movie that turned into a monster hit, that Goldberg found a role that audiences fully responded to. She played Oda Mae Brown, a fake medium who is as surprised as anyone when she finally communicates with the dead spirit of Sam, a murdered man. Through Oda Mae's efforts, Sam is reunited with his girlfriend. Goldberg's medium was at times outrageous but always grounded in reality. The role earned her another Oscar nomination, this time for best supporting actress, and she won. Goldberg became only the second African-American actress, after HATTIE MCDANIEL back in 1939, to win an Academy Award and only the fifth black performer to win.

Goldberg next stretched her dramatic muscles in *The Long Walk Home* (1990), playing a domestic who walks miles to her job during the 1955 Montgomery, Alabama, bus boycott. But her biggest success was in the comedy *Sister Act* (1992) in which she played a lounge singer who hides out from gangsters in a convent, disguised as a nun. The part was originally to be played by actress/singer Bette Midler. *Sister Act* was so successful that it spawned a sequel—*Sister Act 2: Back in the Habit* (1994).

Since then, Goldberg has generally found solid roles. She portrayed Myrlie Evers, widow of assassinated black civil rights leader Medgar Evers, in *Ghosts of Mississippi* (1995), and she was a playful companion to ANGELA BASSETT in *How Stella Got Her Groove Back* (1998), adapted from a Terry McMillan novel.

A champion of social causes, Goldberg is cofounder of Comic Relief, an annual fundraising event to help the homeless in 1992. She was the first woman to host the Academy Awards ceremonies alone in 1994. She returned as host in 1996, 1999, and 2002. She had her own TV sitcom, *Whoopi*, that ran briefly from 2003 to 2004. Goldberg played black abolitionists Harriet Tubman and Sojourner Truth in the TV miniseries *Freedom: A History of Us* (2003). She is also the coauthor of several children's books, including the *Sugar Plum Ballerinas* series

(2008–   ). In 2007, Goldberg became a cohost of the Emmy Award–winning talk show *The View.*

Further Reading

Caper, William. *Whoopi Goldberg: Comedian and Movie Star.* Berkeley Heights, N.J.: Enslow Publishers, 1999 (YA).

Goldberg, Whoopi. *Book.* New York: Time Warner Paperbacks, 2004.

Parish, James Robert. *Whoopi Goldberg: Her Journey from Poverty to Mega-Stardom.* Bridgewater, N.J.: Replica Books, 2002.

Further Viewing

The Color Purple (1985). Warner Home Video, DVD, 2007.

Ghost (1990). Paramount Home Video, Special Collector's Edition DVD, 2009.

Whoopi: Back to Broadway—The 20th Anniversary Show. HBO Video, 2 DVDs, 2005.

Gooding, Cuba, Jr.
(1968–   ) *actor*

One of only a handful of African-American actors to have won an Academy Award, Cuba Gooding, Jr., is one of the busiest black film actors of his generation.

He was born in the Bronx, New York, on January 2, 1968, into a musical family. His father, Cuba Gooding, Sr., was lead singer with the 1970s soul group the Main Ingredient, and his mother, Shirley, was a backup singer in the 1960s for rhythm and blues (R & B) singer JACKIE WILSON.

Life was going well for the Goodings when they moved to Los Angeles in the 1970s. Then Cuba Gooding, Sr., left his family, taking most of his earnings with him. His son turned to religion for solace and became a born-again Christian at age 13. He was ambitious as well as devout and became class president at three different high schools he attended.

In 1984, Gooding got his first taste of the spotlight when he was one of the break-dancers on stage with singer LIONEL RICHIE during the grand finale of the Los Angeles Summer Olympics. A role in a high school production brought the notice of a friend's father, who became his agent, and one of his first professional jobs was a television commercial for Burger King.

Gooding played a walk-on role in his first film, *Coming to America* (1990), starring EDDIE MURPHY. He had his first big break when he was cast in John Singleton's debut film *Boyz N the Hood* (1991), a powerful portrait of the lives of urban black youth. Gooding played Tre Styles, a decent young man who comes to live with his father, played by LAURENCE FISHBURNE, in South Central Los Angeles.

Unfortunately, such good parts were hard to come by for young black actors at the time, and Gooding soon found himself appearing in such inferior films as *Gladiator* (1992), *Hitz* (1993), and *Lightning Jack* (1994), in which he played a mute sidekick to Australian actor Paul Hogan. He fared better in supporting roles in *A Few Good Men* (1995) and then in *Losing Isaiah* (1996), where he played opposite HALLE BERRY.

Gooding desperately wanted the role of flamboyant football player Rod Tidwell in the comedy *Jerry Maguire* (1996), but when he auditioned, the film's producers thought he was too short to be convincing as a football player. Gooding persisted, however, and finally director Cameron Crowe gave him the part. His delightful performance was one of the film's highlights. His repeated line, "Show me the money," became a national catchphrase for a time, and Gooding went on to win the Academy Award for best supporting actor. Since then, Gooding has appeared in a variety of films, including the comedy *As Good as It Gets* (1997); *What Dreams May Come* (1998), opposite Robin Williams; *Instinct* (1999), opposite Anthony Hopkins; and *The Fighting Temptations* (2003), with BEYONCÉ KNOWLES. Perhaps his best role since *Jerry McGuire* has been that of the real-life mentally challenged title character in *Radio* (2003), who became the inspiration for a South Carolina high school football team.

Gooding is married to his high school sweetheart Sara Kopfer, a schoolteacher. They have two sons. His younger brother Omar is also an actor. "How rich and famous you are doesn't matter," Gooding has said. "It all comes down to what you appreciate about life."

Further Reading

"Cuba Gooding Jr." The Internet Movie Database. Available online. URL:http://www.imdb.com/name/nm0000421/. Downloaded on February 13, 2009.

Edelson, Paula. *Cuba Gooding, Jr.* Black Americans of Achievement. New York: Chelsea House, 2000 (YA).

Further Viewing

Jerry Maguire (1996). Sony, DVD, 1997.
Radio (2003). Sony, DVD, 2004.

Gossett, Louis, Jr.
(1936–) *actor*

Only the third African-American actor to win an Academy Award, Louis Gossett, Jr., has been a powerful and impressive presence in a wide range of stage and screen roles for half a century.

He was born in Brooklyn, New York, on May 27, 1936. His father, Louis Gossett, Sr., was a porter and his mother, Helen, a maid. Gossett's first ambition was to be a pro basketball player, but a leg injury sidelined him and he turned his interest to acting. At age 17, he got the leading role in the Broadway play *Take a Giant Step* (1953), playing a troubled youth, and won the Donaldson Award for best newcomer of the year.

Gossett went to New York University on a basketball scholarship but decided to stay with acting even after receiving an invitation to try out for the New York Knicks. For a short time between acting jobs he sang with the doo-wop group the Revileers. In 1959, he was cast in a small role in the Broadway play *A Raisin in the Sun* and made his big screen debut reprising the part in the film adaptation two years later. But stardom would elude him for another 15 years as he played small roles on television and was increasingly impressive in offbeat parts in such films as *The Landlord* (1970), *The Skin Game* (1971), and *Travels with My Aunt* (1972). He was also excellent as Isak Poole, a blacksmith in Revolutionary War times, in the short-lived historical adventure television series *The Young Rebels* (1970–71).

Then, in 1977, Gossett was cast in a key role in the television miniseries *Roots,* based on Alex Haley's book about his ancestors. His portrayal of Fiddler, a slave musician whose dream of buying his freedom is finally dashed by a crafty master, was hailed by critics. It earned him an Emmy Award for outstanding actor for a single performance in a drama or comedy series. Unfortunately, there were few roles for a mature black actor at that time, and Gossett had little to do when cast as the mentor of an alien boy in the TV series *The Powers of Matthew Star* (1982–83). Then he appeared in *An Officer and a Gentleman* (1982), the film that made him a bankable star. The part of Drill Sergeant Foley originally was to be played by a white actor, but Gossett was so persistent and impressive in the auditions that he finally won the part. Although Richard Gere and Debra Winger were the nominal stars, Gossett stole the picture. His Sergeant Foley was a formidable figure who under a crusty exterior had a compassionate heart. He won the Academy Award for the best supporting actor and joined the select company of HATTIE MCDANIEL and SIDNEY POITIER as only the third African-American actor to win an Oscar.

Again, Gossett found plenty of film work, but not many good roles. He appeared in such exploitative films as *Jaws 3-D* (1983) and *The Principal* (1987), and he was unrecognizable under pounds of makeup as an alien creature in the sci-fi film *Enemy Mine* (1984). He fared better as another tough armed forces figure in the commercial hit *Iron Eagle* (1986) and its two sequels. On television, Gossett found more challenging parts playing historical figures in such television movies as *Sadat* (1983) and *Don't Look Back: The Leroy "Satchel" Paige Story* (1981). He was excellent as an old black man fighting racism in the TV adaptation of Ernest Gaines's novel *A Gathering of Old Men* (1987). Gossett played an amateur detective and anthropology professor in the short-lived TV series *Gideon Oliver* (1989). He returned to Broadway after 38 years in 2002, in a revival of the musical *Chicago.*

A complex man with a turbulent personal life and three failed marriages, Louis Gossett has found few roles worthy of his talents since the 1980s. His cousin Robert Gossett is also a film actor.

Further Reading

Bogle, Donald. *Toms, Coons, Mulattoes, Mammies & Bucks: An Interpretive History of Blacks in American Films.* New York: Continuum, 1997, pp. 270–272.

"Louis Gossett Jr." The Internet Movie Database. Available online. URL: http://www.imdb.com/name/nm0001283/. Downloaded on February 2, 2009.

Further Viewing

An Officer and a Gentleman (1982). Paramount Home Video, Special Collector's Edition, DVD, 2007.

Roots (1977). Warner Home Video, 30th Anniversary Edition DVD box set, 2007.

Gough, Eleanora Fagan   See HOLIDAY, BILLIE.

Green, Al
(Albert Leornes Green)
(1946–   ) *R & B singer, songwriter*

The most successful soul singer of the 1970s, Al Green later made the transition from entertainer to minister and from pop to gospel music without missing a beat.

He was born Albert Leornes Green on April 13, 1946, in Forrest City, Arkansas to sharecroppers Robert and Cora Green. At age eight, Green was inspired to become a singer after hearing a SAM COOKE record. Still a youngster, he formed a gospel group with his four brothers. The Greene Brothers, as they called themselves, sang for six years, during which time the family moved to Grand Rapids, Michigan. While in high school he formed a rhythm and blues (R & B) group called Al Green and the Creations and played in the Midwest and South for three years. He later reformed the group as Al Green and the Soul Mates. In 1967, their record "Back Up Train" just missed the top 40. Green did not have enough good material to capitalize on his success, and he later admitted "I wasn't ready for a hit."

By 1969, he was back in small clubs singing solo when by chance he met trumpeter and bandleader Willie Mitchell in a club in Midland, Texas. Mitchell was also the vice president of Hi Records of Memphis, Tennessee, and signed Green to a recording contract.

Green's laid-back vocal delivery that slid easily into a high, sensuous falsetto was perfectly matched by Mitchell's floating, ultra-cool arrangements as played by the Hi rhythm section. Their first hit was "I Can't Get Next to You," a new version of a song by the Motown group The Temptations, which went to number one on the R & B charts in early 1971. Five gold singles followed in quick succession—"Tired of Being Alone," "Let's Stay Together," "Look What You Done for Me," "I'm Still in Love with You," and "You Ought to Be with Me." By now, Green was known as the premier stylist of soul and was named Rock 'n' Pop Star of 1972 by *Rolling Stone* magazine.

But fame had its downside. On October 25, 1974, Green's ex-girlfriend Mary Woodson broke into his apartment while he was taking a shower. In a fit of anger, she tossed boiling grits at him and then took her own life. Green was hospitalized with second-degree burns for weeks and made a decision he had been thinking about for some time. After recovering, he became an ordained minister of the Full Gospel Tabernacle Church and bought his own church in Memphis. He continued to record commercial soul music, while meeting his pastoral duties for several years. Then at a concert in Cincinnati, Ohio, in 1979 he fell off the stage and was nearly killed when he hit a steel instrument case. Back in the hospital, Green saw the accident as a sign from heaven. "I was moving towards God," he said, "but I wasn't moving fast enough."

When he recovered he stopped singing pop music and devoted himself entirely to gospel. In 1980, Green's first of many gospel albums, *The Lord Will Make a Way*, appeared. Two years later he performed on Broadway opposite singer PATTI LABELLE in the gospel-inspired musical *Your Arms Too Short to Box with God*. Although nominated several times as a pop star, Green never won a Grammy Award. Since turning to gospel he has won six, including a Grammy in 1984 for best soul gospel performance by a duo or group for his duet "Sailin' on the Sea of Your Love" with gospel singer Shirley Caesar.

More recently, Reverend Al Green has returned to singing soul music along with gospel. At the inaugural concert for the Rock and Roll Hall of Fame and Museum, he gave a stirring performance of his idol Sam Cooke's "A Change Is Gonna Come." In 1988, Green returned to the pop charts for the first time in 10 years with "Put a Little Love in Your Heart," a duet sung with singer Annie Lennox. In 2003, Green produced the secular album *I Can't Stop*, his first collaboration with Willie Mitchell since 1985. His most recent album, *Lay it Down* (2008), has been called by the *New York Times*, a "faithful evocation of the vintage Al Green sound." Al Green was inducted into the Rock and Roll Hall of Fame in 1995 and received a Grammy Lifetime Achievement Award in 2002.

Further Reading

Chinen, Nate. "Al Green Pays Tribute to the Old Al Green." *New York Times,* May 25, 2008, Arts & Leisure, p. 15.

Green, Al, with Davin Seay. *Take Me to the River: An Autobiography.* Chicago, Ill.: Chicago Review Press, 2009.

The Official Website of Al Green. Available online. URL: http//www.algreenmusic.com/. Downloaded on February 5, 2009.

Further Listening

Definitive Greatest Hits. Capitol, CD, 2007.

Further Viewing

Al Green: Everything's Gonna Be Alright: Live in Anaheim (1991). Xenon, DVD, 2004.

Gregory, Dick

(Richard Claxton Gregory)
(1932–) *comedian, social activist*

The sharpest satirist among the black comics of the 1960s, Dick Gregory abandoned comedy to become one of America's most unrelenting social critics.

Richard Claxton Gregory was born in poverty in St. Louis, Missouri, on October 12, 1932. In high school he was already a social activist, leading a protest march against segregation in schools. In 1951, Gregory entered Southern Illinois University on a track scholarship. A champion middle-distance runner, he was named the school's outstanding athlete in 1953. He left school that year and did a stint in the army. There he first honed his comedy skills in military shows. After being discharged, Gregory returned briefly to Southern Illinois, but the racism and the pressure of sports caused him to leave without getting his degree. He came to the conclusion that the university "didn't want me to study, they wanted me to run."

For the next four years, he lived in Chicago and tried to make it as a stand-up comic. Like BILL COSBY and GODFREY CAMBRIDGE, Gregory was a new kind of African-American comedian who refused to play the stereotyped black clown. He wanted respect as well as laughs from his audience. Unlike Cosby, who dealt primarily with the ups and downs of everyday life, Gregory drew his jokes from the news of the day, particularly race relations. He played mostly in black clubs where the pay was low and there was little chance to gain widespread recognition. He held down a day job in the post office to make ends meet.

Then in 1961, Gregory played Chicago's Playboy Club for what was supposed to be a one-night stand. His wry, topical humor was a hit with the white audience, and the one-night stand stretched into a six-week engagement. Gregory's career was off and running. He was written about in *Time* magazine and began appearing on *The Tonight Show* and other television programs.

After only a brief time in the limelight, however, Gregory began to abandon it for social causes. He participated in demonstrations and marches for civil rights and against the war in Vietnam. He spoke out on such issues as world hunger and drug abuse. He chartered a plane to bring seven tons of food to poor communities in Mississippi when local governments refused to distribute federal food surpluses in reaction to black voter registration drives.

Gregory also wrote books—some funny and others serious. *Write Me In* (1968) dealt with his write-in presidential candidacy on the Freedom and Peace Party ticket. He received a surprising 1.5 million votes and, ironically, may have tilted the election in favor of Republican candidate Richard Nixon, who won the presidency. In another book, *Code Name Zorro: The Murder of Martin Luther King, Jr.* (1978), Gregory argued that a conspiracy involving the Federal Bureau of Investigation (FBI) was responsible for the assassination of the civil rights leader.

As an activist, Gregory knew how to make a point. When Iran held more than 50 U.S. citizens hostage in 1979, he traveled there to meet with the Iranian leader Ayatollah Khomeini and went on a fast until the hostages were released. When he returned to America unsuccessful, he weighed only 97 pounds.

Gregory's interest in fasting, however, is more than a form of political protest. He is a committed vegetarian and in 1984 founded Health Enterprises, Inc., which sold weight-loss products through his Slim-Safe Bahamian Diet. Gregory claims he started the business partly to help African Americans, many of whom are plagued by poor nutrition and low life expectancy. Unfortunately, Gregory fell out with his business partners, which brought huge losses and led him to be evicted from his home in 1992. The same year he led a "Campaign for Human Dignity" to combat street crime in the black neighborhoods of his native St. Louis.

In 1996, legions of Gregory fans were pleased when after 30 years he returned to performing in his one-man stage show, *Dick Gregory Live!* He appeared as himself in the Ken Burns documentary *Mark Twain* (2002) on the Public Broadcasting Service (PBS). Gregory and his wife Lillian have 10 children.

Further Reading

Gregory, Dick, and Robert Lipsyte. *Nigger: An Autobiography*. New York: Pocket Books, 1995.

Gregory, Dick, and Sheila P. Moses. *Callus on My Soul: A Memoir*. New York: Kensington, 2003.

Headlam, Bruce. "For Him, the Political Has Always Been Comical." *New York Times*, March 14, 2009, C1, C7.

Further Listening

In Living Black and White (1961). Collector's Choice, CD, 2008.

Live at the Village Gate. Collectable Records, CD, 1997.

Grier, Pam

(Pamela Suzette Grier)
(1949–) *actress*

The first successful African-American female action hero in films, Pam Grier returned to stardom two decades after her initial success in one of the most impressive comebacks of the 1990s.

She was born Pamela Suzette Grier on May 26, 1949, in Winston-Salem, North Carolina, of black, Asian, white, and American Indian ancestry. Her father, Clarence, was a mechanic for the U.S. Air Force, and she spent most of her childhood living on various air bases in Europe. The family returned stateside when Grier was 14 and settled in Denver, Colorado. She attended Metropolitan State College in Denver and entered the Miss Universe Beauty Pageant to earn income for school. She was second runner-up in the contest and soon had an agent interested in taking her to Hollywood to pursue an acting career. Grier at first was against the move, but her mother encouraged her to give show business a try.

After being rejected in many auditions, the only film role she landed was as an extra in the sleazy *Beyond the Valley of the Dolls* (1970). She took a job as a switchboard operator at American International Pictures, a B-movie studio. She would listen in on phone conversations to find out what films were being cast and finally won a role in a women's prison drama entitled *The Big Doll House* (1971) and produced by Roger Corman. She appeared in two sequels, *The Big Bird Cage* and *Women in Cages*, both released in 1972.

More cheap, exploitative films followed until she was cast in the lead of *Coffy* (1973), the first of the so-called blaxploitation films to feature a female heroine. Previous movies of this genre such as *Shaft* (1971) and *Superfly* (1972) had strong, black male antiheroes; Coffy was a nurse who hunts down and kills the drug pushers who turned her little sister into an addict. Grier's statuesque beauty and tough style helped *Coffy* live up to its publicity that called her "the baddest one-chick hit squad that ever hit town." Her next film, *Foxy Brown* (1974), was even more violent and sexually explicit. Both movies were huge hits and Grier continued to play black superwomen in *Sheila Baby* and *Friday Foster*, both released in 1975.

By now, many women, both black and white, saw Grier as a symbol of women's liberation, despite the exploitative nature of her movies. By the late 1970s the cycle of blaxploitation films had played itself out, and Grier found some decent parts in mainstream films such as *Greased Lightning* (1977), where she played the wife of RICHARD PRYOR. Few good roles came her way in the 1980s, although she was frightfully convincing as a homicidal prostitute in the cop movie *Fort Apache, the Bronx* (1981).

Disillusioned with the roles she was offered, Grier turned to the theater and won a National Association for the Advancement of Colored People (NAACP) Image Award in 1986 for her performance in Sam Shepard's play *Fool for Love*. Two years later she was diagnosed with cancer and doctors gave her 18 months to live. But like one of her tough heroines, Grier fought the disease and made a full recovery.

Her big comeback took place when filmmaker Quentin Tarantino cast her as the title character in *Jackie Brown* (1997), his eagerly anticipated follow-up to *Pulp Fiction*. He wrote the part specifically for Grier, even naming the character in homage to Foxy Brown. Grier impressed critics and audiences with her acting, as she got the best of the head villain, a gunrunner played by SAMUEL L. JACKSON.

Since then she has appeared in a variety of movies including *In Too Deep* (1999) with rapper LL COOL J, *Holy Smoke* (2000), and *John Carpenter's Ghosts of Mars* (2001). In recent years, Grier has guest acted on a number of television shows. She earned two Emmy Award nominations for appearances on *The L Word* (2004–09) and *Law and Order—Special Victims Unit* (1999–).

"Before me, women weren't presented as action figures but, instead, as victims," Grier said in an interview. "That's not realistic. If a man is trying to take a woman's rent money, what is she going to do? She's going to kick his butt. That's what she's going to do. Those films were honest and simple."

Her cousin is former football player and actor Rosie Grier.

Further Reading

James, Darius. *That's Blaxploitation: Roots of the Baadasssss 'Tude (Rated X by an All 'Whyte Jury)*. New York: St. Martin's Press, 1995.

Schubart, Rikke. *Super Bitches and Action Babes: The Female Hero in Popular Cinema 1970–2006*. Jefferson, N.C.: McFarland, 2007.

Vincent, Mal. "Pam Grier Still a Woman of Action." *The Connecticut Post*, September 4, 2001, p. A9.

Further Viewing

Fox in a Box—Featuring Pam Grier (Sheba, Baby/Foxy Brown/Coffy). MGM Home Entertainment, DVD box set, 2005.

Jackie Brown (1997). Miramax Home Entertainment, Collector's Edition, 2 DVDs, 2002.

Guillaume, Robert
(Robert Peter Williams)
(1928–) *actor, singer*

A Broadway musical comedy star with a rich tenor voice, Robert Guillaume has found his greatest success playing a manipulative butler for nine seasons on television.

He was born Robert Peter Williams on November 30, 1928, in St. Louis, Missouri, and was raised by his maternal grandmother after his father abandoned the family. After serving briefly in the army, Guillaume studied business administration at St. Louis University. Opera singing interested him more than business, however, and he switched to music at Washington University and received a scholarship to study at the Aspen Music Festival in Colorado. He made his singing debut at Cleveland's Karama Theatre but then moved to New York City. About this time he changed his last name to "Guillaume," which means "William" in French because, he said, it sounded "prettier." Guillaume sang in New York productions of *Porgy* and *Bess* and *Jacque Brel Is Alive and Well* before reaching stardom as the captivating preacher in the musical *Purlie* (1970). He won a Tony Award for best actor in a musical for the role. Guillaume later earned another Tony nomination as best supporting actor in a musical when he played con man Nathan Detroit in the all-black Broadway production of *Guys and Dolls* (1977).

In 1977, Guillaume was cast as Benson, the outspoken butler in a family of crazies in prime-time television's soap opera spoof, *Soap.* His comic performance earned him an Emmy Award in 1979 as best supporting actor in a comedy series, and shortly after, he got his own spin-off series, *Benson.*

In the new series, Benson went to work in the household of scatter-brained Governor Gene Gatling, played by James Noble. Benson proved so indispensable to the governor that he was soon promoted to adviser, then state budget director, and during the 1984–85 season, lieutenant governor. That same year Guillaume won a second Emmy, this time as best actor in a comedy series. In *Benson*'s final season, Gatling's former butler ran against him for the governorship. The results of the election were cleverly kept a secret in the show's last episode.

Guillaume returned to prime time in *The Robert Guillaume Show* (1989), on which he also served as executive producer. He played a marriage counselor married to a white secretary. The show was not successful, but he had better luck on Broadway the following year, playing the Phantom in a national tour of the musical *Phantom of the Opera.* He was the first, and to date only, African American to play this famous role. *Sports Night* (1998), a comedy drama about a sports cable pro-gram on the Fox Network was Guillaume's next foray into series television. While on the set in January 1999 Guillaume suffered a mild stroke, but he recovered and returned to the show a few weeks later.

"I guess I'm a testament to the power of prayer and hard work," he said in an interview. "I want to be able to reassure people who have suffered strokes. There is life after a stroke."

There is apparently plenty of life left in Robert Guillaume. His interest in education led him to form a publishing company, the Confetti Company, with his wife, Donna Brown Guillaume, in 1992. They publish read-aloud books and audiocassettes of classic fairy tales told in a multiethnic style. They have also produced animated versions of their tales on the Public Broadcasting Service (PBS) and Home Box Office (HBO).

Guillaume lost a son to AIDS in 1990. Another son, Kevin, is also an actor.

Further Reading

Bogle, Donald. *Prime Time Blues: African Americans on Network Television.* New York: Farrar, Straus & Giroux, 2002, pp. 230–231.

"Robert Guillaume." The Internet Movie Database. Available online. URL: http://www.imdb.com/name/nm0347039/. Downloaded on February 5, 2009.

Further Listening

Purlie (1970). RCA Victor Broadway, CD, 1990.

Further Viewing

Benson: The Complete First Season (1979). Sony, DVD box set, 2007.

H

Handy, W. C.
(William Christopher Handy, "Father of the Blues")
(1873–1958) *blues musician, composer, bandleader*

W. C. Handy may not have invented the musical genre known as the blues, but in his artful compositions he brought this black folk music to the world's attention.

He was born William Christopher Handy on November 16, 1873, in Florence, Alabama. His father, Charles Bernard Handy, was a minister, and the only music he allowed in their home was church music. Young Handy, however, was attracted to the work songs and blues sung by the black laborers along the nearby Tennessee River. He began music lessons on the cornet, a small horn, in a local barbershop. He was at the same time arranging church choral music for choirs. In his late teens he tried his hand at teaching but gave it up for better wages at a factory in Bessemer, Alabama.

Handy continued to play his cornet in minstrel shows and in 1893 organized a quartet to perform at the World's Columbian Exposition in Chicago. He was inspired by the experience and decided to tour the country as a musician. For years he led a hand-to-mouth existence, often sleeping outdoors. In 1900, he accepted a teaching position at the Agricultural and Mechanical College in Hunts-

ville, Alabama. He left in 1902 to return to performing and formed a marching and dance band in Clarksville, Mississippi. About this time he heard the blues performed by black itinerant musicians. These earthy folk songs had more life and vitality than the kind of popular music he was playing. He eventually broke up his band and in 1905 formed the Python Band that played exclusively black folk music. He composed two blues numbers himself but couldn't interest a publisher in them.

Living then in Memphis, Tennessee, Handy wrote a campaign song for a local politician, Edward H. Crump. The catchy number, "Mr. Crump," helped Crump win the election. Handy felt the song had a wider appeal, changed the title to "The Memphis Blues," and published it himself in 1912. It may have been the first published blues song in American musical history. Unfortunately, a white song promoter brought all rights from Handy for $100, and Handy never got another penny once the song became popular. In the future, he was more careful in keeping the rights to his music.

Handy wrote more blues songs, the most popular of all being "St. Louis Blues" (1912). Although he faced bankruptcy when he wrote it, "St. Louis Blues" became Handy's most successful song. It has been recorded more times than almost any other song in musical history. A worldwide hit, it was even used as a battle hymn by the Ethiopian army of Africa in the 1930s in their war with the

Italians. By the 1940s, "St. Louis Blues" was earning Handy $25,000 a year in royalties.

Handy was a serious composer and his blue songs made up only a small part of his total output. His many other works include sacred songs that expressed his deep religious beliefs and ambitious symphonic pieces with such titles as *Afromerican Hymn.* In 1928 at Carnegie Hall in New York City, he conducted a large chorus and 30-piece orchestra in a musical history of the African American.

Handy never stopped being a teacher, writing books about the blues and other music and penning his autobiography in 1941. W. C. Handy died in New York City on March 28, 1958. The same year NAT KING COLE portrayed him in a highly fictitious biographical film, *St. Louis Blues.*

A statue of Handy stands in W. C. Handy Park in Memphis's Beale Street area, a street he immortalized in his "Beale St. Blues." He became the first African-American composer to be honored with a U.S. commemorative stamp in 1969.

Further Reading

Handy, W. C., and Miguel Covarrubias, eds. *Blues: An Anthology: Complete Words and Music of 53 Great Songs.* Carlisle, Mass.: Appleword Books, 2001.
———. *Father of the Blues: An Autobiography.* Reprint, New York: Da Capo Press, 1991.
Roberston, David. *W. C. Handy: The Life and Times of the Man Who Made the Blues.* New York: Knopf, 2009.

Further Listening

Louis Armstrong Plays W. C. Handy (1954). SBUE Special Mkts,. CD, 2008.
W. C. Handy's Beale Street—Where the Blues Began. Inside Sounds, CD, 2003.

Havens, Richie
(Richard Pierce Havens)
(1941–   ) *folk singer, guitarist, actor*

With his rough-as-sandpaper baritone and percussive guitar, Richie Havens was one of the most distinctive folk singers of the 1960s and one of the few to appeal to a rock and pop audience.

He was born Richard Pierce Havens in the Bedford-Stuyvesant section of Brooklyn, New York, on January 21, 1941, the eldest of nine children. His father played piano in New York bands but never learned to read music. Young Havens sang in local doo-wop groups through his teens and also performed with the McCrea Gospel Singers for a time. In 1961, he moved to Greenwich Village in Lower Manhattan, an area that was the center of a folk music boom. He made a living as a sidewalk portrait artist for two years while absorbing the folk music he heard nightly in small Village clubs. Havens soon learned to play guitar and began singing himself. He developed a musical style that was dynamic, expressive, and exciting. He would strum the guitar wildly and then sing rhythmically with his deep, ragged voice.

His big break came in 1967 when he signed with the jazz-folk label Verve and released *Mixed Bag,* considered by many to be his best album. It contained such classics as the stirring antiwar song "Handsome Johnny," which he cowrote with actor LOUIS GOSSETT, JR., and his heartfelt rendition of Bob Dylan's "Just Like a Woman."

Havens's next album, *Something Else Again* (1968), was his first to make the *Billboard* charts. He became a familiar figure on college campuses in the late 1960s and played the Newport Folk Festival in 1966 and the Monterey Jazz Festival in 1967. The festival that made him an international star, however, was the Woodstock Festival in upstate New York in the summer of 1969. Havens was the opening act at this historic three-day concert, and his galvanizing performance held the audience of 100,000 for nearly three hours. His improvised song "Freedom," which he based on the spiritual "Motherless Child," was one of the concert's most memorable moments.

Havens was then as popular with rock fans as with folkies. His rendition of the Beatles' "Here Comes the Sun" became a top-20 hit in 1971, and the following year he appeared in the first stage version of the rock opera *Tommy*. He played Othello in *Catch My Soul* (1974), the filmed rock version of the Shakespeare tragedy, and costarred with RICHARD PRYOR in the movie *Greased Lightning* (1977). He was the only act to appear on back-to-back programs of *The Tonight Show* with host Johnny Carson.

In the 1970s, Havens stopped recording and concentrated his energies on live performances and social causes, particularly the environment. He cofounded the Northwinds Undersea Institute in the Bronx, an oceanographic children's museum. In the 1980s, he became a familiar voice on commercial jingles for McDonald's, Amtrak, and Kodak, the last of which won him the Oscar of TV commercials, a Clio.

Havens returned to recording in 1988 with three albums. He came back to Woodstock in 1994, performing for old and new fans at Bethyl '94. His songs have been heard on the soundtracks of several recent movies, including *Collateral* (2004), *The Pursuit of Happyness* (2006), and *I'm Not There* (2007), a film about Bob Dylan in which Havens appeared as Old Man Arvin. Havens's most recent album, *Nobody Left to Crown*, was released in 2008. A unique troubadour for whom music is far more than entertainment, Havens has said, "I'm not in show business and never was. I'm in the communication business. That's what it's about for me."

Further Reading

Havens, Richie, and Steve Davidowitz. *They Can't Hide Us Anymore.* New York: Harper Entertainment, 2000.

The Richie Havens Official Web site. Available online. URL: http://www.richiehavens.com/. Downloaded on February 6, 2009.

Further Listening

Mixed Bag (1967). Polydor/Umgd, CD, 1990.
Nobody Left to Crown. Verve Forecast, CD, 2008.
Resume: The Best of Richie Havens. Rhino, CD, 1993.

Further Viewing

Woodstock: The Director's Cut (1970). Warner Home Video, VHS/DVD, 1992/1997.

Hayes, Isaac

(1942–2008) *R & B singer, musician, composer, record producer, actor*

The first African American to win an Academy Award for best musical score, Isaac Hayes was one of the principal architects, as both artist and composer, of 1970s soul music.

He was born in a tin shack in Covington, Tennessee, on August 29, 1942. His mother, Eula, died when he was about a year and a half old, and he was raised in Memphis by his grandparents, Mr. and Mrs. Willie Wade. Hayes played in the high school band and after graduation got a job as a musician playing recording sessions for Stax Records in Memphis. In a short time, Hayes became Stax's most prolific songwriter, turning out such classic soul anthems with his partner David Porter as "Hold On, I'm Coming," "You Don't Know Like I Know," and "Soul Man"—all recorded by the duo of Sam and Dave.

In 1967, Hayes released his first solo album, but *Presenting Isaac Hayes* sold few copies. Two years later, however, *Hot Buttered Soul* (1969) took the recording industry by storm. This single album changed the nature of soul music, replacing the catchy, three-minute song with long, extended, heavily orchestrated riffs infused by Hayes's soulful, reflective vocalizing, which ran nine minutes or longer. The album went gold and was followed quickly by *The Isaac Hayes Movement* and *To Be Continued* (both 1970).

But it was with his dazzling soundtrack for the pioneering blaxploitation film *Shaft* (1971) that Hayes reached his creative and commercial peak. Relentlessly rhythmic and moody, the "Theme from *Shaft*" became one of the most memorable movie themes of the decade and shot to number one on the charts, earning Hayes two Grammy

Awards and a National Association for the Advancement of Colored People (NAACP) Image Award. The entire score won him an Academy Award for best musical score in 1972.

While he continued to turn out best-selling albums filled with elaborate productions anchored by his ragged baritone, Hayes began acting in some of the blaxploitation movies he was scoring, including *Truck Turner* and *Three Tough Guys* (both 1974). Usually cast as an action hero or monstrous bad guy, he gave one of his best performances as the Duke of New York, the crime czar who held the president of the United States for ransom in the futuristic *Escape from New York* (1981). Hayes showed a talent for comedy in the blaxploitation spoof *I'm Gonna Get You Sucka* (1988) and Mel Brooks's *Robin Hood: Men in Tights* (1993), for which he also composed the score. More recently, he was the voice of the black cafeteria worker Jerome "Chef" McElroy in Comedy Central's animated television series *South Park*. He quit the show in 2006 after being offended by an episode that satirized Scientology, a new age religion he adhered to.

In contrast to his macho image in records and film, Hayes was in real life a sensitive and deeply concerned humanitarian who worked tirelessly for social relief in Africa and the United States. In 1992, he became the international spokesperson for the World Literacy Crusade. In the 1990s, Hayes tried his hand at a new career—radio disc jockey. For a time, as a DJ for KISS FM, he had the most popular morning radio show in New York City. After a long hiatus in 1995, he returned to recording with two albums—*Branded*, with vocals, and the all-instrumental *Raw and Refined*. Hayes was inducted into the Rock and Roll Hall of Fame in 2002. Isaac Hayes died of a stroke on August 10, 2008, at his home in East Memphis, Tennessee. He was 65 years old.

Further Reading

Bowman, Rob. *Soulsville, USA: The Story of Stax Records.* New York: Schirmer Trade Books, 2008.

Corio, David (photographer), Vivian Goldman (text), and Isaac Hayes (introduction). *Black Chord.* North Hollywood, Calif.: Universe Publishing, 1999.

Hayes, Isaac, and Susan Disesa. *Cooking with Heart and Soul.* New York: Putnam Publishing Group, 2000.

Further Listening

Shaft: Music from the Soundtrack (1971). Stax, CD, 1991.

The Very Best of Isaac Hayes. Stax, CD, 2007.

Further Viewing

Escape from New York (1981). MGM Home Entertainment, Special Edition DVD, 2003.

Isaac Hayes: Live at Montreaux 2005. Eagle Rock Entertainment, DVD, 2007.

Hayes, Roland

(1887–1976) *concert singer*

Called by some the greatest tenor born in America, Roland Hayes overcame prejudice and other obstacles to become the first successful black male concert singer in the United States and Europe.

He was born in 1887 in Curryville, Georgia, the son of former slaves. His family moved to Tennessee when he was 13, and he first studied music in Chattanooga and later at Fisk University in Nashville. Hayes began singing while at the university and in 1911 joined the Fisk Jubilee Singers, one of the first singing groups to bring Negro spirituals to a wide audience. He later left the group to further his musical studies in Boston, Massachusetts.

By 1916, Hayes felt confident enough to make a concert tour, but no managers would book him because he was black. So he became his own manager and arranged several national tours over a three-year period. Despite excellent reviews, audiences were small and the tours were a financial disaster.

Like other black performers before and after him, Hayes decided his talents might be better appreciated in Europe where there was less prejudice against blacks. Arriving in England, he performed his first concert while suffering from pneumonia and was hailed for his performance. On his return to the United States, Hayes finally received recognition for his gifted voice. He gave concerts across the nation, including a series of 30 concerts at Boston's Symphony Hall with the Boston Symphony.

Once he was famous, Hayes gave back to the African-American community. He kept a number of tickets for his concerts priced low enough for the poor to afford. He served as a mentor to young singers, providing them with encouragement and money to get them started in their careers. One obstacle he was unable to surmount was the color barrier in the world of opera. This great tenor never performed in a professional opera production. In later years, Hayes taught voice at Ohio State University.

Among the many honors Roland Hayes received in his long life was the National Association for the Advancement of Colored People's (NAACP) Spingarn Medal in 1924. He was also the recipient of the first Amistad Award for contributing creativity to the improvement of human relations. Roland Hayes died on December 31, 1976, at the age of 90. In 1996, the city of Boston held a weeklong celebration of Hayes's life. His daughter Afrika Hayes-Lambe is a singer, actress, and teacher in the Boston area.

Further Reading

Hayden, Robert C. *Singing for All People: Roland Hayes, a Biography.* Boston: Select Publications, 1995.

"Roland Hayes." The New Georgia Encyclopedia. Available online. URL: http://www.georgiaency-clopedia.org/nge/Article.jsp?id=h-1671. Downloaded on February 5, 2009.

Smith, Eunice Young. *A Trumpet Sounds: A Novel Based on the Life of Roland Hayes.* Westport, Conn.: Lawrence Hill, 1985.

Further Listening

Favorite Spirituals. Vanguard Classics, CD, 1998.

Haysbert, Dennis
(1954–　) *actor*

A commanding presence on screen, Dennis Haysbert has played a full range of interesting characters. In recent years he has cornered the market on authoritative figures, whether it be the first black president or the leader of an elite covert counterterrorism team on a hit television series.

He was born Dennis Dexter Haysbert on June 2, 1954, in San Mateo, California, the eighth of nine children. His father, Charles, was a deputy sheriff and his mother, Gladys, a homemaker. A defensive end on his high school football team, Haysbert was offered an athletic scholarship to college after graduation but turned it down to pursue acting. He studied at the American Academy of Dramatic Arts in New York City. Beginning in 1979, he started to get small roles in such television series as *Lou Grant, Laverne and Shirley,* and *Magnum P.I.* His first major film role was as a Cuban refugee baseball player who practices voodoo in the comedy *Major League* (1989). He would repeat the role twice in sequels and play another baseball player in *Mr. Baseball* (1992), starring Tom Selleck.

Haysbert's big break was playing a sensitive lover to Michelle Pfeiffer in the interracial romance/drama *Love Field* (1992), set during the assassination and funeral of President John F. Kennedy. Ten years later, he was involved in another interracial romance with Julianne Moore in *Far from Heaven* (2002), set in 1950s suburbia. The role earned him several acting awards. The previous year, Haysbert was cast as U.S. senator David Palmer in the hit action television series *24*. On the show, he would be elected the first black president.

After leaving *24*, Haysbert was cast as Jonas Blane, the commando head of a counterterrorism team on CBS's action series *The Unit* (2004–   ). The role has given the actor the exposure and fame he never enjoyed before. "I like Jonas a lot," Haysbert said in an interview with the *New York Times*, "It makes me feel good knowing that there are Jonases out there, fighting the good fight. He's a superpatriot, and race is not an issue."

Not content to be a popular actor, Haysbert is developing a production company that will produce the kind of intelligent films "we really want to see."

Married and divorced twice, Haysbert has two children by his second wife, actress Lynn Griffith.

Further Reading

"Dennis Haysbert." The Internet Movie Database. Available online. URL: http://www.imdb.com/name/nm0371660/. Downloaded on December 9, 2008.

Lee, Felicia R. "Latching on to the Role of a Lifetime Every Week." *New York Times*, September 27, 2008, pp. B7, 13.

Further Viewing

Far from Heaven (2002). Universal, DVD, 2003.

Love Field (1992). MGM Home Entertainment, DVD, 2001.

The Unit—The Complete First Season (2004). Fox Home Video, DVD box set, 2006.

Hemsley, Sherman
(1938–   ) *actor*

The star of one of the most popular black situation comedies ever aired on television, Sherman Hemsley has been a comic fixture on television for three decades.

He was born on February 1, 1938, in Philadelphia, Pennsylvania, and was a shy child. He served four years in the air force after high school and then got a job in the post office while attending Philadelphia's Academy of Dramatic Arts. Black actor Robert Hooks was impressed by Hemsley's acting in a

Sherman Hemsley's George Jefferson was one of the great comic characters of 1970s television. *(Photofest)*

local production and advised him to go to New York City and pursue the theater professionally. Hemsley followed his advice and soon found work in Off-Broadway productions, including an all-black production of *Alice in Wonderland*. He debuted on Broadway in the musical *Purlie* (1970) and also appeared in the Off-Broadway musical *Don't Bother Me I Can't Cope* (1973). It was this show that brought him to the attention of Norman Lear, producer of the groundbreaking TV sitcom *All in the Family*. Lear cast Hemsley as George Jefferson, neighbor of white bigot Archie Bunker.

Jefferson was as prejudiced in his way toward whites as Bunker was toward blacks. However, as played by Hemsley, the character was funny, entertaining and, because he was a little guy with a big mouth, not terribly offensive. George Jefferson was so popular that in 1975 Lear developed a spin-off series for him, *The Jeffersons*. In the new show, the Jeffersons moved from their middle-class Queens neighborhood to New York City's posh Upper East Side. If not the most relevant black series of the decade, *The Jeffersons* was probably the funniest, with Hemsley well supported by Isabel Sanford as his wife and Marla Gibbs as his nemesis, their maid Florence. *The Jeffersons* also featured the first married interracial couple on a TV series.

When *The Jeffersons* ended its long run in 1985, Hemsley returned the following year in a new show, *Amen*. This sitcom was about the members of a black church congregation. Hemsley's Deacon Ernest Frye, a lawyer by profession, was a close cousin to George Jefferson and just about as funny. After *Amen* folded in 1991, Hemsley lent his voice to construction company boss R. P. Richfield, who happened to be a dinosaur in the audio-animatronic sitcom *Dinosaurs* produced by Jim Henson.

In 1996, Hemsley starred in still another sitcom, *Goode Behavior*, in which he played Willie Goode, a con man released on parole and living with his son, a college professor. The show ran only two seasons.

For all his success, Hemsley has had serious financial problems. In the 1980s, he invested most of his money in the movie *Ghost Fever* (1987) in which he starred. The movie bombed. In June 1999, he sought bankruptcy when he could not pay a $1 million loan from a Las Vegas investment corporation.

Hemsley appeared briefly in the comedy *Mafia!* (1998) as George Jefferson. He continues to act in television specials and guest star on game shows such as *Who Wants to Be a Millionaire*. He played himself on a 2005 episode of the animated series *Family Guy*.

Further Reading

Bogle, Donald. *Prime Time Blues: African Americans on Network Television*. New York: Farrar, Straus & Giroux, 2002, pp. 210–217, 312–314.

Deane, Pamela S. "Hemsley, Sherman." The Encyclopedia of Television Online. The Museum of Broadcast Communications Web site. Available online. URL: http://www.museum.tv/archives/etv/H/hemsleysher/hemsleysher.htm. Downloaded on February 6, 2009.

Further Viewing

The Jeffersons. The Complete First Season (1975). Sony, 2 DVDs, 2002.

Hendrix, Jimi

(Johnny Allen Hendrix, Jimmy James)
(1942–1970) *rock singer, guitarist, songwriter*

One of the true pioneers of guitar-based rock, Jimi Hendrix fused rhythm and blues (R & B) with hard rock to create some of the most original and arresting music of the 1960s.

He was born Johnny Allen Hendrix into a middle-class family in Seattle, Washington, on November 27, 1942. His father, Al, was African American and a gardener. His mother, Lucille, was a full-blooded Cherokee Indian. After graduating from high school in 1959, Hendrix went into the army. In the early 1960s, Hendrix worked as a studio and backup guitarist for everyone from LITTLE RICHARD to Joey Dee and the Starliters. He had little confidence in his singing voice and hesitated to pursue a solo career. Then he heard Bob Dylan's flat, nasal monotone and decided he, too, had a chance at stardom.

He formed a band called Jimmy James and the Blue Flames in 1965 and played small clubs in New York's Greenwich Village. His experiments with feedback and fuzztone on the electric guitar began to attract attention in the pop world. Chas Chandler, former bassist with the British group the Animals, offered to be his manager and convinced Hendrix to move to England, where his talents would be more appreciated. In London, Chandler linked him with bassist Noel Redding and drummer Mitch Mitchell to form the Jimi Hendrix Experience. The trio took England and later the rest of Europe by storm.

In June 1967 the Jimi Hendrix Experience made one of the most celebrated debuts in American rock at the Monterey Pop Festival in California. Hendrix's skillful musicianship was matched by his over-the-top stage show. He played his guitar behind his back and then plucked the strings with his teeth. The act reached its climax with Hendrix setting his guitar on fire in front of thousands of screaming fans.

But Hendrix's act was more than pyrotechnics. His debut album, the classic *Are You Experienced?* (1967) was one of the most astonishing albums in rock, containing music that was both sonically exciting and deeply expressive. Such songs as "Purple Haze" (his first hit single), "Fire," and the haunting "The Wind Cries Mary," showed him to be an imaginative songwriter. Subsequent albums *Axis: Bold as Love* (1968) and *Electric Ladyland* (1969) showed Hendrix's music continuing to mature.

Having reached the height of his fame, Hendrix was suddenly torn between commercial success and artistic freedom. He disbanded the Experience and in 1969 hid out in upstate New York with a new group of musicians, only to emerge later that year at the historic Woodstock Music Festival with his fiery, unforgettable version of "The Star Spangled Banner."

His new group, Band of Gypsies, played harder, more recognizable black music and released a live album in May 1970, which was not as well received as his earlier studio albums. Again, Hendrix seemed uncertain what direction to take. He reformed the Jimi Hendrix Experience and soon disbanded it again. In August 1970, he returned to the origins of his success, England, played the Isle of Wight Festival, and then toured Europe.

In five short years, Jimi Hendrix changed the face of rock music before his untimely death from drugs in 1970. *(AP Photo)*

On September 18, 1970, Hendrix was staying at a girlfriend's apartment in London, when she found him unconscious and called the police. Jimi Hendrix, age 27, was pronounced dead of a drug overdose. Whether his death was suicide or an accident has never been fully determined.

The Jimi Hendrix Experience was inducted into the Rock and Roll Hall of Fame in 1992. The same year Hendrix posthumously received Grammy's Lifetime Achievement Award. While many have attempted to imitate the psychedelic sounds of Hendrix's guitar, no one has been able to use those sounds to create music of such power and imagination. "As the years go by," writes rock critic

John Morthland, "it becomes increasingly apparent that Hendrix created a branch on the pop tree that nobody else has ventured too far out on."

Further Reading

Cross, Charles R. *Room Full of Mirrors: A Biography of Jimi Hendrix*. New York: Hyperion, 2006.

Henderson, David. *'Scuse Me While I Kiss the Sky: Jimi Hendrix: Voodoo Child*. New York: Atria, 2008.

Lawrence, Sharon. *Jimi Hendrix: The Intimate Story of a Betrayed Musical Legend*. New York: Harper Paperbacks, 2006.

Further Listening

Are You Experienced? (1967). Experience Hendrix, CD, 1997.

Experience Hendrix: The Best of Jimi Hendrix. Experience Hendrix, CD, 1998.

Further Viewing

Jimi Hendrix: Live at Woodstock (1969). Experience Hendrix, DVD, 2003.

Jimi Hendrix: Live in Monterey, 1967 (1967). Experience Hendrix, DVD, 2007.

Hines, Gregory

(1946–2003) *dancer, actor*

The first entertainer to receive three consecutive Tony nominations for best actor in a musical, Gregory Hines almost single-handedly kept the art of tap dancing alive on Broadway and in Hollywood.

He was born on Valentine's Day, 1946, in New York City to Maurice Robert Hines, Sr., and Alma Iola Hines. Almost from the time he could walk, he was on stage as one-third of "Hines, Hines, and Dad" with his father, and his brother Maurice. Although Hines came to show business early, it was years before he achieved stardom. After a series of parts in Off-Broadway and Broadway shows, he scored big as a member of the cast of *Eubie!* (1978), a Broadway musical based on the music and career of composer EUBIE BLAKE. He received his first Tony nomination and repeated the achievement in 1979 in another black musical revue, *Comin' Uptown*. He topped these performances as a singer and dancer in *Sophisticated Ladies* (1981), a celebration of the music of DUKE ELLINGTON. That same year, Hines appeared in his first film, playing a Roman slave in Mel Brooks's comedy *The History of the World, Part 1*. The role was originally intended for RICHARD PRYOR, who dropped out due to illness. Hines immediately followed this with the role of a medical examiner in the horror film *Wolfen* (1981), playing opposite Albert Finney.

Hines was offered the leading role in the action-comedy *48 Hours* (1982), but he turned it down to make *The Cotton Club* (1984), a musical drama directed by Francis Ford Coppola. This film offered him the opportunity to dance with his brother Maurice as they portrayed two tap-dancing brothers modeled after the real-life NICHOLAS BROTHERS. Unfortunately, *The Cotton Club* was a flop, while *48 Hours* made a star of EDDIE MURPHY in the role Hines turned down.

But Hines continued to find good film roles. He got to dance opposite the Russian ballet dancer Mikhail Baryshnikov in *White Nights* (1985) and teamed up as Billy Crystal's cop partner in *Running Scared* (1986).

In *Tap* (1989), a project particularly dear to his heart, Hines played an ex-con finding a new life in tap dancing. In that film he danced with a number of living tap legends as well as a future one, his protégé SAVION GLOVER.

Hines returned to Broadway in 1992 to play the jazz pioneer JELLY ROLL MORTON in the musical *Jelly's Last Jam*. A showcase for his dancing, singing, and dramatic acting talents, the show finally earned him the long-sought Tony Award for best actor in a musical.

After that, Hines played one of the few sympathetic males in the women's picture *Waiting to Exhale* (1995). In 1997, he starred in his own short-lived television sitcom, *The Gregory Hines*

Show, and portrayed legendary tap dancer BILL ROBINSON in the television movie *Bojangles* (2001) on Showtime. Gregory Hines died of liver cancer on August 9, 2003.

Further Reading

Abrams, Dennis. *Gregory Hines: Entertainer.* Black Americans of Achievement. New York: Chelsea House, 2008 (YA).

Frank, Rusty E., foreword by Gregory Hines. *Tap: The Great Tap Dance Stars and Their Stories, 1900–1955.* New York: Da Capo Press, 1995.

Sommer, Sally R. "Gregory Hines: From Time Step to Timeless." *New York Times,* August 14, 2003, p. 3E.

Further Viewing

Tap (1989). Sony, DVD, 2006.

Holder, Geoffrey

(1930–) *actor, dancer, choreographer, costume designer*

Strikingly statuesque, bald-headed Geoffrey Holder has made his mark on stage and screen in a variety of capacities.

He was born on August 1, 1930, in Port of Spain, Trinidad, and studied there at Queens Royal College. He first danced professionally as a member of his brother Boscoe Holder's dance troupe, touring the West Indies and Puerto Rico. Holder began to choreograph revues such as *Ballet Congo* and *Bal Negre* for the group. In 1954, he made his New York stage debut in the Broadway musical *House of Flowers,* where he met his future wife, dancer Carmen de Lavallade. The Caribbean-set musical also featured future dance luminaries ARTHUR MITCHELL and ALVIN AILEY.

Holder formed his own dance troupe in 1956 and toured extensively. He appeared on Broadway and in Paris with legendary American expatriate dancer JOSEPHINE BAKER. He soon began choreographing dances for the Alvin Ailey American Dance Theater and other companies.

In 1957, Holder played his first major dramatic role as the hapless servant Lucky in an all-black production of Samuel Beckett's absurdist masterpiece, *Waiting for Godot.* The same year he choreographed the musical *Rosalie.* His greatest theatrical success was directing the Broadway hit musical *The Wiz* in 1974. The production won him two Tony Awards, one for direction and another for costume design. In 1978, he directed the all-black musical *Timbuktu* (1978), based on the musical *Kismet.* Among his other choreographic works are *Papa Clown* (1959), *Sports Illustrated* (1963), and *Suite and Light* (1967).

Holder's infrequent film roles have tended to be offbeat ones, befitting his striking appearance. He was memorably menacing as the voodoo man Baron Samedi in the James Bond movie *Live and Let Die* (1973) and played Daddy Warbucks's giant servant Punjab in the film adaptation of the Broadway musical *Annie* (1982). On television, Holder played the Cheshire Cat in *Alice in Wonderland* (1983) and is Ray the Sun in the children's television series *Bear in the Big Blue House* (1997–) on the Disney Channel.

He is probably best known to American audiences as "the Un-Cola Man," the laughing spokesperson for the soft drink 7-Up, in a series of 1970s television commercials. Holder also has made commercials for British West Indies Airlines. He narrated the film *Charlie and the Chocolate Factory* (2005).

A man of many talents, Geoffrey Holder is a respected painter whose work has earned him a Guggenheim fellowship and has appeared in many exhibitions. He is the author of several books, including a Caribbean cookbook. His elder brother, dancer and actor Boscoe, died in 2007.

Further Reading

Dunning, Jennifer. *Geoffrey Holder: A Life in Theater, Dance, and Art.* New York: Harry N. Abrams, 2001.

Holder, Geoffrey. *Moko Jumbies: The Dancing Spirits of Trinidad.* New York: Pointed Leaf Press, 2004.

Holiday, Billie
(Eleanora Fagan Gough, "Lady Day")
(1915–1959) *jazz singer, songwriter*

A singer of astonishing sensitivity and nuance, Billie Holiday is generally considered to be one of the great pop and jazz vocalists of the 20th century.

She was born Eleanora Fagan Gough on April 7, 1915, in Baltimore, Maryland, and had a harrowing childhood. Her father, Clarence Holiday, a jazz guitarist, called her "Billie" because of her tomboy ways. He abandoned her and her mother when she was very young. Eleanora lived with a series of relatives and was possibly raped at age 10 and sent to a Catholic reformatory. After the death of the cousin she was living with, Eleanora moved to New York to be with her mother in 1927. She helped support them by working part time as a prostitute.

At age 15, adopting her father's name, Holiday began singing in small clubs and was discovered by John Hammond of Columbia Records, who set up a recording date for her with Benny Goodman's Orchestra. Her first record was "Riffin' the Scotch," backed by "Your Mother's Son-In-Law." It sold poorly, but in 1935, she appeared at the legendary Apollo Theater in Harlem. Holiday was so nervous that when the time came to perform she had to be pushed onto the stage by the comic Pigmeat Markham. However, once she sang "Them There Eyes," with an arrangement she had written herself, the audience was entranced.

Through the 1930s, Holiday sang with a number of top big bands, including COUNT BASIE's orchestra. Lester Young, who played trumpet in the Basie band, gave her the nickname "Lady Day" because of her elegant manner and unique singing style. She in turn admired Young's playing and patterned her singing in part on his unique phrasing. She modulated and improvised as if her voice were a musical instrument.

Much of the pop material she was given to record was inferior, but she experimented with rhythm and singing ahead or behind the notes. This way Holiday often turned a forgettable pop song into a work of art. "More than technical ability, more than purity of voice," wrote music critic John Bush, "what made Billie Holiday one of the best vocalists of the century . . . was her relentlessly individualist temperament, a quality that colored every one of her endlessly nuanced performances."

Not everyone appreciated her talent or temperament. Rival singer ETHEL WATERS said of her, "She sounds like her feet hurt." Holiday became the first black woman to tour the South with a white band (led by Artie Shaw) but she was fired in 1938 for her jazzy interpretations of familiar songs. Song publishers banned her from radio broadcasts because they complained she strayed from their songs' melodies and lyrics. But black audiences loved her for her independence, her unique style of singing, and the elegant way she dressed.

Holiday hit her artistic peak in the early 1940s with her classic recordings of "Strange Fruit," about a lynching in the South, and "God Bless the Child," which she wrote herself. "Strange Fruit" was her most controversial song, and John Hammond would not let her record it for Columbia. When she finally recorded it on another label, many radio stations refused to play it. The song's stark honesty about racism in America nevertheless made it a standard.

The loneliness and alienation that comes through so clearly in Holiday's singing was very real. She attempted through the years to escape her demons through alcohol, marijuana, opium, and eventually heroin. In 1947, she was arrested for possession of heroin and sentenced to eight months in prison. This conviction prevented her from getting a cabaret card, without which she could not perform in nightclubs.

Holiday concentrated on recording and made a rare film appearance in the Hollywood movie *New Orleans* (1947) in which she played a maid and sang "Do You Know What It Means to Miss

New Orleans" backed by Louis Armstrong and his band. She continued to make memorable records into the mid-1950s backed by small, intimate groups consisting of such fine musicians as pianist Oscar Peterson. Although her voice was hoarse and ragged, the artistry remained.

Holiday gave perhaps her last great performance on the television special *The Sounds of Jazz* in 1958. After a tour of Europe in early 1959, she collapsed. Years of drinking and drug abuse left her with serious liver and heart disease. Even on her deathbed she was taking heroin to ease the pain and suffered the final indignity of being arrested for possession. Billie Holiday died on July 17, 1959, at age 44. Since her death, her fame has spread far beyond what it ever was in her lifetime.

A statue of Holiday stands in her hometown of Baltimore, and each year the city holds a contest in her name for new rising blues singers. Singer Diana Ross played Holiday in the biopic *Lady Sings the Blues* (1972). A U.S. postage stamp was issued in her honor in 1977. On it, she wears her trademark, a blue gardenia, in her hair.

Further Reading

Clarke, Donald. *Billie Holiday: Wishing on the Moon.* New York: Da Capo Press, 2002.

Holiday, Billie, with William Dufty. *Lady Sings the Blues: The 50th Anniversary Edition,* Reprint, New York: Harlem Moon, 2004.

O'Meally, Robert G. *Lady Day: The Many Faces of Billie Holiday.* New York: Da Capo Press, 2000.

Weatherford, Carole. *Becoming Billie Holiday.* Honesdale, Pa.: Wordsong, 2008 (YA).

Further Listening

The Ultimate Collection. Hip-O Records, 2 CDs, 1 DVD, 2005.

Further Viewing

Lady Day: The Many Faces of Billie Holiday. White Star, DVD, 2000.

Lady Sings the Blues (1972). Paramount Home Video, DVD, 2005.

New Orleans (1947). Kino Video, VHS/DVD, 2000.

Holmes, Odetta   See Odetta.

Hooker, John Lee
(John Lee Booker, Delta John, Texas Slim, the Boogie Man)
(1917–2001) *blues singer, guitarist, songwriter*

One of the last practitioners of raw, authentic Mississippi Delta blues, John Lee Hooker and his primitive but powerful music had a profound effect on rhythm and blues (R & B) and rock 'n' roll.

He was born on August 17, 1917, on a cotton plantation near Clarksdale, Mississippi, the fourth of eleven children of William and Minnie Hooker. As a child Hooker learned about the blues from his stepfather, musician William Moore, who married his mother after his parents divorced. Moore's friends included legendary bluesmen Charley Patton and Blind Lemon Jefferson. Until he had the money to buy a guitar, Hooker learned to play their "country boogie" on strings made from strips of inner tube nailed to a barn wall.

At age 14, he moved to Memphis, Tennessee, where he worked as an usher in the W. C. Handy Movie Theater on Beale Street. Hooker moved to Detroit, Michigan, in 1943, working days in an automobile factory and nights playing blues in local clubs. In 1948 he made his first recording for Sensation Records, "Boogie Chillun." It became a smash R & B hit, and Hooker quit his day job.

Record companies in the South were notorious for cheating blues musicians out of royalties. To fight back, Hooker recorded his songs for numerous labels under a number of pseudonyms including John Lee Booker, Delta John, Texas Slim, and the Boogie Man. Among his hit recordings through the early 1960s were "Crawling

Kingsnake Blues," "I'm in the Mood," and "Boom Boom." Hooker's stark, percussive blues songs were covered by many British and American rock groups in the 1960s, including the Rolling Stones, the Animals, the Yardbirds, Canned Heat, and Van Morrison. The latter two recorded with Hooker in the 1970s.

By 1980, Hooker was nearly forgotten until he appeared as a street musician in the comedy film *The Blues Brothers*. Filmmaker Steven Spielberg used his songs to underscore the earthy southern drama of his movie *The Color Purple* (1985). Then in 1990, at age 70, Hooker made a spectacular comeback with his album *The Healer*, which sold 1.5 million copies. It featured duets with rockers Robert Cray, Santana, and Bonnie Raitt. Hooker's duet with Raitt of his 1951 hit "I'm in the Mood" earned him his first Grammy Award. He won two more Grammys in 1997 for the album *Don't Look Back* and a duet with Van Morrison from the album.

Hooker's last years were spent in semi-retirement in Los Altos, California, near San Francisco, where he sang occasionally and appeared in advertisements for blue jeans and liquor. He died on June 21, 2001, at age 83, the last link with the legendary Mississippi Delta blues of the 1920s and 1930s.

When asked once what the blues were, Hooker replied, "No matter what anybody says, it all comes down to the same thing. A man and a woman, a broken heart and a broken home."

John Lee Hooker was inducted into the Rock and Roll Hall of Fame in 1991. He received the Grammy Lifetime Achievement Award in 2000.

Further Reading

Murray, Charles Shaar. *Boogie Man: The Adventures of John Lee Hooker in the American Twentieth Century*. New York: St. Martin's Griffin, 2002.

Trynka, Paul, and Val Wilmer. *Portrait of the Blues: America's Blues Musicians in Their Own Words*. London: Hamlyn, 1998.

Further Listening

John Lee Hooker: The Definitive Collection. Hip-O Records, CD, 2006.

Further Viewing

John Lee Hooker: Come and See About Me: The Definitive DVD: Eagle Rock Entertainment, DVD, 2004.

Horne, Lena
(Lena Mary Calhoun Horne, Helena Horne)
(1917–   ) *singer, actress*

The first African-American actress to appear in movies as a glamorous, mature woman, Lena Horne was, and remains today, an electrifying performer on stage, screen, and television.

She was born Lena Mary Calhoun Horne on June 30, 1917, in Brooklyn, New York. Her parents divorced when she was three, and she spent much of her childhood living with different relatives. Her mother was an aspiring actress, and her grandmother, Cora Calhoun Horne, was an early member of the National Association for the Advancement of Colored People (NAACP) and an activist for women's rights. Horne dropped out of school at age 16 to work as a chorus girl at Harlem's legendary Cotton Club. Two years later she made her Broadway debut as the "Quadroon Girl" of mixed racial background in the play *Dance with Your Gods*. Her sultry voice, copper skin, and dazzling looks made her a singing sensation in New York nightclubs. She was sometimes billed as "Helena Horne."

Horne starred on Broadway in the short-lived musical revue *Blackbirds of 1939* and after a brief marriage to Louis J. Jones that produced a daughter, moved to California in the early 1940s. She was singing in a club when she caught the attention of a talent scout for the MGM movie studios. The studio signed her to a long-term contract, the first ever offered to a black performer.

Her debut in the movie musical *Panama Hattie* (1942) was anticipated as a breakthrough for black performers who had previously been relegated to playing maids, servants, and fools. But this first film set a depressing pattern in which Horne made brief but memorable appearances in a musical number or two and then vanished from the film. MGM partly did this so that southern movie house operators, knowing a black actress in a movie would be intolerable for their white audiences, could cut her scenes out of their movies without ruining the continuity. Horne has referred to herself in these 1940s musicals as "a butterfly pinned to a column singing away in Movieland."

Two exceptions to this practice were the 1943 all-black musicals *Cabin in the Sky,* in which she played a sultry temptress sent by the devil, and *Stormy Weather,* where she played a nightclub singer not unlike herself. In the latter film Horne sang the title song with such expressive artistry that it became a hit and her signature number.

No other roles came close to fully showcasing her talents and by the late 1940s Horne was disillusioned with Hollywood. MGM Studios was equally unhappy with her relationship with white musician Lennie Hayton, whom she married secretly in 1947.

Horne desperately wanted the role of Julie, the tragic mulatto singer in the MGM remake of the classic musical *Show Boat* (1951). Unbelievably, the role went to white actress Ava Gardner. Horne's outspokenness on politics and her friendship with politically left-wing actor PAUL ROBESON got her blacklisted during the Communist-hunting years of the 1950s. She was banned from appearing in movies and television. Never one to give in to adversity, she took the lead role in the Broadway musical *Jamaica* (1957) and was a smash success. For the next decade, Horne toured as a singer on stage and in concert to enthusiastic reviews.

She finally returned to the movies in the western *Death of a Gunfighter* (1969), opposite actor Richard Widmark in her first dramatic role. Nearly 10 years later she played Glenda, the

Singer and actress Lena Horne is seen at the height of her fame as a sultry singer and sex symbol in 1940s Hollywood. *(Photo courtesy of Showtime Archives, Toronto)*

Good Witch, in the movie version of the hit black musical *The Wiz* (1978), based on *The Wizard of Oz.*

The indomitable Horne returned to Broadway in 1981 in her hit one-woman show *Lena Horne: The Lady and Her Music.* The show was taped on both public and cable television. In 1997, public television did a documentary on her life and career entitled *Lena Horne: In Her Own Voice.* Horne received a Grammy Lifetime Achievement Award in 1989 and 10 years later received an NAACP Image Award for outstanding jazz artist. Her album *Seasons of a Life,* recorded in 1999, was released in 2005.

Still glamorous in her 90s, Lena Horne remains a survivor of a studio system that never could figure out what to do with this uniquely gifted entertainer. Her daughter Gail Buckley is a journalist and the author of a history of African Americans in the U.S. military.

Further Reading

Buckley, Gail Lumet, and Lena Horne. *The Hornes: An American Family.* New York: Applause Books, 2002.

Gavin, James. *Stormy Weather: The Life of Lena Horne.* New York: Atria, 2008.

Horne, Lena, and Richard Schickel. *Lena.* New York: Limelight Editions, 1986.

Further Listening

Lena Horne: The Lady and Her Music (1981). Qwest/Wea, 2 CDs, 1995.

Further Viewing

Cabin in the Sky (1943). Warner Home Video, DVD, 2006.

The Incomparable Lena Horne. Mvd Visual, DVD, 2009.

Stormy Weather (1943). Fox Video, DVD, 2006.

Houston, Whitney

(1963–   ) *R & B singer, actress*

No pop singer of the 1980s made as spectacular a debut nor enjoyed such universal appeal as Whitney Houston.

She was born on August 9, 1963, in Newark, New Jersey. It could be said that singing was in her genes. Her mother, Cissy Houston, is a respected rhythm-and-blues (R & B) and gospel backup vocalist. Her father, John, was once her mother's manager and her cousin is celebrated pop singer DIONNE WARWICK.

Houston's own singing career began in the New Hope Baptist Junior Choir when she was 11. "It was something that was so natural to me that when I started singing, it was almost like speaking," she has said. She signed with manager Gene Harvey just before turning 18. He wisely decided not to rush her career and built her up slowly and steadily for stardom. She started her professional career singing backup vocals for her mother and singers LOU RAWLS and Chaka Khan. She also took advantage of her good looks and tried modeling, appearing on the cover of *Seventeen* and other fashion magazines.

In April 1983, Houston signed with Arista Records. Arista president Clive Davis took a personal interest in her and set about making her debut album as good as possible. Nearly two years and $250,000 later, *Whitney Houston* was released. It was a smash hit, staying on the *Billboard* charts for 78 weeks and selling 12 million copies. The album produced four hit singles, three of them going to number one on the charts. One song, "Saving All My Love for You," won her a Grammy Award for best pop vocal performance by a female. Houston's eagerly anticipated second album, named simply *Whitney,* entered the charts at number one, an unprecedented event for a female recording artist.

Houston's soaring love ballads appealed to both white and black listeners as well as young and older ones. This kind of crossover was most unusual in the divided listening markets of the 1980s. When she sang "The Star Spangled Banner" at Super Bowl XXV in January 1991, the live recording became a top-20 hit record in a matter of weeks.

The following year, Houston married singer Bobby Brown and later gave birth to a daughter, Bobbi Kristina. The marriage had its ups and downs, made worse by Brown's drug problems and charges of physical abuse. But Houston's career continued to soar. In 1992, she appeared in her first film, playing a pop diva opposite Kevin Costner in *The Bodyguard.* The soundtrack album produced three more hit singles, including "I Will Always Love You," which, according to record researcher Joel Whitburn, is one of the biggest hits of the rock era, which began in 1955. Since then, Houston has starred in two more movies, *Waiting to Exhale* (1995) with costar ANGELA BASSETT, and *The Preacher's Wife* (1996) opposite DENZEL WASH-

INGTON. In 1997, she played the Fairy Godmother with singer BRANDY as Cinderella in Disney's television version of *Rodgers and Hammerstein's Cinderella*. This multicultural production gave the ABC network its highest ratings on a Sunday night in more than a decade. The video version has outsold any other made-for-TV movie.

In 1998, Houston produced her first new album in eight years, *My Love Is Your Love,* which included the hit record "When You Believe," which she sang with Mariah Carey in the Disney animated film *The Prince of Egypt.* A singer who enjoys collaboration, Houston has recorded memorable duets with Teddy Pendergrass, ARETHA FRANKLIN, Cece Winons, and Bobby Brown.

Houston signed a record-breaking $100 million deal with Arista in August 2001 for seven albums. Up to then she had sold 140 million albums for the label. But her first effort, *Just Whitney* (2002), got mixed reviews and was her poorest selling album to date. In 2004, Houston went on a Soul Divas Tour with her cousin Dionne Warwick and Natalie Cole. That same year, Houston, who was having trouble with drugs, went into rehab and emerged clean in 2006. She divorced Brown in 2007 and retained custody of their daughter, Bobbi Kristina. Houston's long-awaited new album, *I Look to You,* was released on August 30, 2009.

The Whitney Houston Foundation for Children, a nonprofit organization she started, raises money for children with social and medical problems such as AIDS.

Further Reading

Cox, Ted. *Whitney Houston.* Black Americans of Achievement. New York: Chelsea House, 1998 (YA).

Parish, James Robert. *Whitney Houston: The Biography.* Worthington, U.K.: Aurum Press, 2003.

Further Listening

Whitney Houston: The Ultimate Collection. Arista Europe, CD, 2007.

Further Viewing

Rodgers and Hammerstein's Cinderella (1997). Walt Disney Video, VHS/DVD, 1998/2003.

Waiting to Exhale (1995). Fox Video, VHS/DVD, 1999/2001.

Whitney Houston Live. Hudson Street, DVD, 2008.

Hudson, Jennifer
(1981–   ) *singer, actress*

Called by one writer "a symbol of second chances," Jennifer Hudson surmounted obstacles to become a movie and recording star only to have her happiness marred by family tragedy.

She was born Jennifer Kate Hudson on September 12, 1981, in Chicago, Illinois, the youngest of three children. Her father, now deceased, was a bus driver. She began singing in gospel choirs from age seven. A talented child, she acted in community theater productions and attended Dunbar Vocational Career Academy, graduating in 1999. She continued to perform, touring as a singer in the Disney stage production of *Hercules: The Musical.* But with her less than sleek figure, Hudson did not seem destined to be a professional singer/actress. Between theater jobs she worked at a Burger King restaurant.

In 2004, at age 23, she auditioned for TV's *American Idol: The Search for a Superstar.* While she did well in the grueling competition, Hudson finished sixth among the 12 finalists. The winner, Fantasia Barrino, seemed destined for stardom, but Hudson did not do so badly herself. She performed on the *American Idol* summer tour and continued to perform on concert tours for the next two years. Then came the audition for the film version of the 1981 Broadway musical *Dreamgirls.*

Hudson, one of 782 singers who auditioned for the pivotal role of Effie Melody White, won the part. Among the losers, ironically, was Barrino. The film featured an all-star cast that included EDDIE MURPHY, BEYONCÉ KNOWLES, DANNY GLOVER, and

JAMIE FOXX, but it was Hudson who stole the film with her powerhouse performance of Effie's signature song, "And I Am Telling You I'm Not Going." Her portrayal won Hudson an Academy Award for best supporting actress, in addition to Golden Globe and Screen Actors Guild (SAG) Awards. She is one of only a select group of actors to receive an Oscar for their debut film performance.

After crushing disappointments, Hudson's life seemed to be a dream fulfilled. She signed a recording contract with Arista Records; had roles in several movies, including the film version of the hit television series *Sex and the City* (2007); and sang the national anthem at the start of the Democratic National Convention in August 2008 at the request of presidential candidate Barack Obama. A month later, her first album, *Jennifer Hudson*, was released, and she announced her engagement to David Otunga on her 27th birthday.

"It's like I came in through the back door," Hudson has said about her phenomenal success story. "Even I don't understand it. . . . I'm an actress, almost before being a singer, when that's almost all I've ever known?"

But amid all this happiness tragedy struck. On October 25, 2008, Hudson's mother, Darnell, and her brother, Jason, were found shot dead in their Chicago apartment. Her seven-year-old nephew, Julian, was missing, presumably kidnapped by the killer. Three days later, Julian's lifeless body was discovered in an abandoned SUV in Chicago. Soon after, Julian's stepfather, the estranged husband of Hudson's sister, was arrested and charged with the three murders. After months of seclusion, Hudson appeared in public in February 2009 to collect her first Grammy Award for best R & B album for *Jennifer Hudson*.

Further Reading

Sisario, Ben. "And She Is Telling You She Is Just Getting Started." *New York Times,* September 28, 2008, Arts & Leisure, pp. 1, 32.

West, Betsy. *Jennifer Hudson: American Dream Girl, An Unauthorized Biography.* New York: Price Stern Sloan, 2007.

Further Listening

Jennifer Hudson. Arista, CD, 2008.

Further Viewing

Dreamgirls (2006). DreamWorks Home Entertainment, DVD, 2007.

I

Ice Cube
(O'Shea Jackson)
(1969–) *rap singer, songwriter, actor, director, film producer, screenwriter*

Perhaps the most gifted and multitalented rap artist of his generation, Ice Cube has captured the fears and hopes of inner city youth in a string of deeply expressive, if often controversial, best-selling albums.

He was born O'Shea Jackson on June 15, 1969, to Hosea and Doris Jackson, a middle-class couple in South Central Los Angeles, California. He wrote his first rap song on a challenge from a fellow student in a high school typing class. Jackson adopted the name Ice Cube and began frequenting the South Central club scene. He formed his own rap group, CIA, in 1986. Together with DR. DRE and other rap artists he founded the group Niggaz with Attitude (NWA). Ice Cube wrote "Dopeman" and "8-ball" for NWA and recorded them. Then, unsure where his career was headed, he took some time off to study architecture at the Phoenix Institute of Technology in Arizona. When he graduated a year later, NWA, with Cube's raps, was a hit. The group's violent and sexist lyrics made them both commercially successful and extremely controversial.

Despite the group's success, Ice Cube felt he was not being treated fairly by the management and quit NWA in 1989. He moved to New York and formed the group, Da Lench Mob, that backed him on his first solo effort, *AmeriKKKa's Most Wanted* (1990). The album was both a critical and commercial success, quickly going gold. It is, wrote music critic John Floyd, "a stark and gripping portrait of life in America's inner cities. . . . one of rap's most unflinching bursts of rhythm and political fury."

The next year, Ice Cube made an impressive acting debut as Doughboy, the violent and resentful brother of a high school football star in John Singleton's *Boyz N the Hood,* which took its title from one of his songs. He appeared in other films including *The Glass Shield, Trespass,* which costarred ICE-T, and Singleton's next film *Higher Learning* (1993). In *Anaconda* (1997), he wrestled with a 40-foot snake in the Amazon jungle, and in *Three Kings* (1999) he was a Gulf War soldier in search of Kuwaiti gold.

Ice Cube proved an adept screenwriter, coscripting with DJ Pook *Friday* (1995), about a day in the life of two brothers in South Central Los Angeles. He also wrote and starred in two sequels, *Next Friday* (2000) and *Friday after Next* (2002). Perhaps his most impressive achievement in film was the hit *The Player's Club* (1998), which he wrote, coproduced, and directed. He has also directed more than 20 videos.

In albums such as *Kill at Will* (1990), *Death Certificate* (1991), and *Lethal Injection* (1993), Ice

In recent years, Ice Cube has become as well known as a film actor as he is as a rap singer. *(Photofest)*

Cube has unflinchingly explored gangland murder and the American justice system. After several years' hiatus from the recording studio, during which he joined the Nation of Islam and married Kimberly Woodruff, Ice Cube returned in 1999 and 2000 with the ambitious double album *War & Peace—Vol. 1 (The War Disc)* and *War & Peace—Vol. 2 (The Peace Disc)*. The second of these featured such guest artists as Dr. Dre, MC Ren, and comic CHRIS ROCK.

Ice Cube continues to act, appearing in such films as *xXx State of the Union* (2005), with SAMUEL JACKSON, and the comedy *First Sunday* (2008), opposite TRACY MORGAN. His most recent studio album, *Raw Footage* (2008), debuted at number one on *Billboard's* Top R & B/Hip-Hop Albums chart.

Further Reading

McIver, Joel. *Ice Cube: Attitude.* London: Sanctuary Publishing, 2002.

The Official Ice Cube Web site. Available online. URL: http://www.icecubemusic.com. Downloaded on February 13, 2009.

Orr, Tamra. *Ice Cube.* Blue Banner Biographies. Hockessin, Del.: Mitchell Lane Publishers, 2006 (children).

Further Listening

AmeriKKKa's Most Wanted. Priority, CD, 1990.
Ice Cube—Greatest Hits. Priority Records, CD, 2001.

Further Viewing

Boyz N the Hood (1991). Sony, Anniversary Edition 2 DVDs, 2003.

Ice-T
(Tracy Morrow)
(1958–   ) *rap singer, songwriter, actor*

Among the most expressive and outspoken of rap artists, Ice-T has won mainstream America's respect if not always its admiration, as a serious spokesman against censorship.

He was born Tracy Morrow on February 16, 1958, in Newark, New Jersey. After his parents died in a car accident, he moved to South Central Los Angeles in California with relatives. While in high school, Ice-T became infatuated with rap. He took his stage name from his favorite writer, pimp and poet, Iceberg Slim, and would recite Slim's poetry to friends.

After graduation, Ice-T cut a few forgettable rap records and was featured in the low-budget hip-hop movies *Rappin'*, *Breakin'*, and *Breakin' II: Electric Boogaloo*. He was still unknown when he signed with Sire Records in 1987 and released his debut album *Rhyme Pays*. The disk went gold, selling 500,000 copies. With his newfound fame Ice-T negotiated his own label, Rhyme Syndicate, in 1988, distributed by Sire. His next album, *Power,* was more confident and assured, and it also went gold. But with fame came strong criticism of the profanity and violence in his lyrics. Ice-T answered his critics with a book condemning censorship—*The Iceberg/Freedom of Speech. . . . Just Watch What You Say* (1989).

He appeared as a tough ex-cop in his first major Hollywood film, *New Jack City,* in 1991. The movie aroused more controversy for its violent portrayal of inner city life. The same year saw the release of Ice-T's most successful album to date, *O.G. Original Gangster.* The songs on this album etched a bitter picture of gangster and ghetto life with biting social commentary.

Ice-T next joined forces with the heavy-metal group Body Count and produced their self-titled album. It contained his most controversial song yet—"Cop Killer"—that described the shooting of Los Angeles policemen by an African American in revenge for the real-life beating by police of black man Rodney King. Police groups and the National Rifle Association (NRA) urged Sire's parent label, Time-Warner, to remove the song from the album. Instead, the company refused to issue Ice-T's next album, *Home Invasion.* Angered by this action, the rapper began speaking out in public on the issue of censorship, appearing on television and radio and talking on college campuses.

Home Invasion was finally released in 1993 on Priority Records to surprisingly poor sales. The next Body Count release, *Born Dead* (1994) raised little controversy. Ice-T seemed to be losing his black audience and becoming a pop phenomenon. Other critics claimed that without a strong collaborator, his records were losing their cutting edge. His most recent album, *Black Ice—Urban Legend,* was released in 2008.

Ice-T's acting career has flourished, and he has appeared in such action movies as *Trespass* (1992) with fellow rapper ICE CUBE, *Johnny Mnemonic* (1995), *Body Count* (1997), and *3000 Miles to Graceland* (2001). On television he hosted a documentary series *Beyond Tough* (2002) and has had

his own reality show, *Ice-T's Rap School* (2006), on VH1.

Further Reading

Jenkins, Sacha. *Ego Trip's Book of Rap Lists.* New York: St. Martin's Press, 1999.

Sigmund, Head, and Ice-T. *The Ice Opinion.* London: Pan Books, 1995.

Further Listening

Ice-T—Greatest Hits: The Evidence. Atomic Pop, CD, 2000.

Further Viewing

New Jack City (1991). Warner Home Video, Special Edition DVD, 2005.

Ingram, Rex
(1895–1969) *actor*

Rex Ingram, not to be confused with the silent film director of the same name, was one of the first black actors in Hollywood to break out of the stereotypes most African-American performers were trapped in. Yet for all his impressive talent, Ingram never achieved the star stature he might have had in a later era.

He claimed he was born aboard the riverboat *Robert E. Lee* not far from Cairo, Illinois, on October 20, 1895. His father was a ship's stoker who earned the money to send him to a military school in Chicago. Ingram went on to attend the medical school at Northeastern University in Boston, Massachusetts, and was the first black student in America to earn a Phi Beta Kappa key for academic excellence. Despite holding a medical degree, he decided he would rather be an actor and moved to Hollywood. There he played African natives in such silent films as *Tarzan of the Apes* (1918), the first Tarzan movie, and such early sound films as *Trader Horn* (1931) and *King Kong* (1933). His big breakthrough was his towering portrayal of De Lawd in the film version of the all-black biblical epic *The Green Pastures* (1936).

Ingram played a string of memorable roles in the next decade including the runaway slave Jim in *The Adventures of Huck Finn* (1939) and the giant genie who comes out of a lamp in *The Thief of Baghdad* (1940). He reprised the role in a remake, *A Thousand and One Nights* (1945). In the all-black musical *Cabin in the Sky* (1943), Ingram played Lucifer with as much energy and conviction as he had De Lawd. He was equally impressive as a Sudanese soldier who sacrifices himself for the Allied cause during World War II in *Sahara* (1943). His last major role was as a wise, old black outcast who encourages a young murderer to give himself up in *Moonrise* (1948).

The sad decline of Ingram's career followed his arrest and trial for transporting a 15-year-old white girl across state lines for immoral purposes. He pleaded guilty to the charges. Although he later returned to films, the charisma that made Ingram so dynamic on screen had faded. His roles in the 1950s and 1960s grew smaller and smaller. He had better luck in the theater, where in 1957 he joined Earle Hyman, Mantan Moreland, and GEOFFREY HOLDER in an all-black Broadway production of Samuel Beckett's *Waiting for Godot*. In 1962, he became the first African-American actor to be contracted to appear on a television soap opera, *The Brighter Day*. Ingram died of a heart attack on October 20, 1969.

Rex Ingram was a gifted actor who, along with PAUL ROBESON, helped pave the way for such strong and independent black leading men as SIDNEY POITIER and DENZEL WASHINGTON.

Further Reading

Bogle, Donald. *Toms, Coons, Mulattoes, Mammies & Bucks: An Interpretive History of Blacks in American Cinema.* New York: Continuum, 1997, pp. 69–71.

"Rex Ingram (I)." The Internet Movie Database. Available online. URL: http://www.imdb.com/name/nm000227/. Downloaded on February 6, 2009.

Further Viewing

The Green Pastures (1936). Warner Home Video, DVD, 2006.

The Thief of Baghdad (1940). Criterion Collection. 2 DVDs, 2008.

J

Jackson, Janet
(1966–) R & B singer, actress

The youngest of the nine talented Jackson children, Janet Jackson has surpassed them all in popularity, including, for a time, her famous brother MICHAEL JACKSON.

She was born on May 26, 1966, in Gary, Indiana to a working class couple, Joseph and Katherine Jackson. When she was three, her five brothers signed with Motown Records as the Jackson 5 and went on to have four back-to-back number-one hits. At age seven, Jackson made her professional debut at the MGM Grand Hotel in Las Vegas, opening for her brothers. Although she performed occasionally after that, her first big national exposure was as an actress, not a singer. She became a regular on the black sitcom *Good Times* in 1977, playing a battered child who is adopted by Ja'net DuBois. After *Good Times* folded, Jackson was seen in the short-lived sitcom *A New Kind of Family* (1979) and appeared for one season on the successful sitcom *Diff'rent Strokes* (1981) as a classmate of Gary Coleman's Arnold.

Her father wanted to turn her into another family singing superstar and pushed her into signing a recording contract with A & M Records in 1981. Her debut album, *Janet Jackson* (1982), sold more than a quarter million copies. It was her family name, more than Jackson's singing, however, that sold the records.

Like her siblings, Jackson rebelled against her father's iron control over her career, and in 1984, she married James DeBarge of another famous musical family group, DeBarge. A second LP, *Dreamstreet* (1984), sold poorly, and she came to the realization she needed her father's guidance. She had her marriage to DeBarge annulled and returned home. Her father put her future in the hands of record executive John McClain, who wanted to give her a new, more exciting image. He had Jackson lose weight and learn to dance. More important, he set her up with producers Jimmy Jam and Terry Lewis, formerly of the group The Time. They collaborated with her on the dazzling, upbeat, dance songs that made up her next album, *Control* (1986). It sold 10 million copies worldwide and produced five top-10 hits, including the title song, "Let's Wait Awhile," and the number-one hit "When I Think of You." With the help of Jam and Lewis, Jackson's voice, formerly not that impressive, now filled "each track with a breathless, believable presence," wrote music critic Mark Coleman.

Three years later, she released *Rhythm Nation 1814* (1989), which did even better than *Control* and brought a social consciousness to her dance beat that wasn't entirely convincing. However, the album produced seven top-10 hits, four of them,

115

including "Miss You Much" and "Love Will Never Do Without You," going to number one. The album's release was quickly followed by a world tour that helped make Janet Jackson as much an international star as her brother Michael.

In 1991, the self-assured singer left A & M and signed an unprecedented $32 million contract with Virgin Records for two albums. The first album, *janet* (1993), cast her in a more sexually mature light and sold more than 15 million copies. The same year, she made her big-screen debut in John Singleton's film *Poetic Justice* (1993). Jackson played a beauty parlor worker and poet who traveled from Los Angeles to Oakland, California, with a postal worker played by the late rapper TUPAC SHAKUR. The poems Jackson's character wrote were actually penned by African-American

Singer Janet Jackson shared with her brother Michael a love of dramatic stage costumes. *(Photo courtesy of Showtime Archives, Toronto, and Eddie Wolfl)*

writer Maya Angelou. The film was not successful, but Jackson's performance won her generally respectful reviews. *Poetic Justice* also produced her seventh number-one pop hit, "Again." Jackson's next film appearance was as EDDIE MURPHY's girlfriend in *The Nutty Professor II: The Klumps* (2001).

When Jackson signed another contract with Virgin Records in 1996, it was for $80 million, the highest amount paid to a recording artist up to that time. Her next effort, *The Velvet Rope* (1997), was considered by many critics to be her best and most personal album. Its songs dealt with such surprisingly dark subjects as psychological abuse and power in sexual relationships.

In 2001, having sold more than 50 million records, Janet Jackson was chosen by Music Television (MTV) as its first icon honoree, in recognition of her contributions to music, dance, video, and pop culture. "I thought, 'This isn't supposed to be happening now,'" Jackson said after hearing about the honor. "Not necessarily that it should be happening at all, but it's not supposed to happen until I have grandkids and I'm kicking back in my rocking chair."

Her next album, *All for You* (2001), again revealed an intensely personal side of the singer, but it showed Jackson in a more assertive mood. It celebrated her new single status after the breakup of her nine-year marriage to Rene Elizando, Jr., director of her music video "That's the Way Love Goes."

Performing during the halftime show at Super Bowl XXXVIII on February 1, 2004, Jackson's breast was briefly exposed in what she later claimed was a "wardrobe malfunction." The controversy hurt her career and may have ended plans for her to play singer LENA HORNE in a made-for-TV movie.

The albums *Damita Jo* (2004) and *20 Y.O.* (2006) were modest successes compared to her earlier work, but *Discipline* (2007) was an outright commercial failure. However, it did not stop Jackson from going on her first tour in seven years.

"She strutted through a full-tilt arena spectacle like those she had mounted since her multimillion-selling days in the 1980s and '90s," wrote Jon Pareles in the *New York Times* about her performance at New York's Madison Square Garden. In February 2009, Jackson won an Image Award for outstanding supporting actress in a motion picture for her role in the comedy *Why Did I Get Married?* (2007).

Further Reading

Andrews, Bart. *Out of the Madness: The Strictly Unauthorized Biography of Janet Jackson.* London: Headline Book Publishing, 1995.

Dyson, Cindy. *Janet Jackson.* Black Americans of Achievement. New York: Chelsea House, 2000 (YA).

Nathan, David. *The Soulful Divas: Personal Portraits of a Dozen Divine Divas from Nina Simone, Aretha Franklin & Diana Ross, to Patti LaBelle, Whitney Houston & Janet Jackson.* New York: Billboard Books, 2002.

Further Listening

Design of a Decade 1986/1996. A & M, CD, 1995.
The Velvet Rope. Virgin Records, CD, 1997.

Further Viewing

Janet Jackson: From Janet to Damita Jo. The Videos. Virgin Records, DVD, 2004.
Poetic Justice (1993). Sony, VHS/DVD, 1998/1999.

Jackson, Mahalia

(1911–1972) *gospel singer*

Possessed of a voice filled with the joy and pain of the African-American church, Mahalia Jackson, more than any other performer, has made black gospel music popular the world over.

She was born on October 26, 1911, in New Orleans, Louisiana, where her father was a Baptist minister who made his living as a stevedore and barber. Her mother died when Mahalia was five, and she was raised by an aunt who, like her father, was strict and deeply religious. Jackson sang in her father's church choir from an early age, but she was also intrigued by the music of the neighboring Sanctified Church that she found more expressive and joyous.

She quit school after the eighth grade and worked as a laundress 10 hours a day, saving nearly every penny she earned to move to Chicago when she was 16. There she pursued her gospel singing, joining the Great Salem Baptist Church choir and singing with the gospel group the Prince Johnson Singers. Her energetic and joyous contralto voice gained Jackson wide attention and by the 1930s she was touring solo across the country, singing at black churches and social organizations. Her debut record was of the gospel song "God Gonna Separate the Wheat from the Tares" (1934). Recordings and live performances on the gospel circuit, however, earned her little money, and she had to support herself by doing laundry for white families on Chicago's north side.

In 1938, Jackson married. Her husband, Isaac Hockenhull, urged her to record secular music, which would bring in more money and gain her the recognition she deserved. But she refused to sing any music that was not the Lord's. To finance her gospel tours, Jackson opened a beauty salon and flower shop.

Her big break finally came in 1946 when she was 35 years old. Her recording of "I Will Move on up a Little Higher" on Apollo Records became an unexpected hit, selling close to 2 million copies. The attention from the record got her an invitation to sing at a music symposium in western Massachusetts. Jackson's electrifying performance there gained her national attention. Before long she was singing at the National Baptist Convention and then made her national television debut on *The Ed Sullivan Show*.

Her biggest triumph was a concert at New York's Carnegie Hall in 1950. Her first European tour followed two years later. Jackson signed a recording contract with Columbia Records in

1954, and her records gained her a wide audience of both black and white listeners. Her 1959 recording of "He's Got the Whole World in His Hands" became a pop hit on the *Billboard* charts. But she continued to refuse to sing rhythm and blues (R & B) or rock 'n' roll. "Rock and roll was stolen out of the sanctified church," she declared.

She did, however, agree to sing DUKE ELLINGTON's serious jazz concert piece *Black, Brown and Beige* at the Newport Jazz Festival in 1958. Jackson also raised her voice for the cause of civil rights. She sang at civil rights rallies and gatherings in the 1950s and early 1960s. In August 1963, she joined in Martin Luther King, Jr.'s historic March on Washington and at King's request, sang on the steps of the Lincoln Memorial right before he delivered his famous "I Have a Dream" speech. Jackson also sang at the presidential inaugurations of Dwight D. Eisenhower and John F. Kennedy.

Mahalia Jackson continued to sing until her death from heart failure on January 27, 1972. That same year she received Grammy's Lifetime Achievement Award. In 1997, she was inducted into the Rock and Roll Hall of Fame as an early influence on rock, something that surely would have amused her. The following year she was one of four African-American gospel singers honored with a U.S. postage stamp.

Further Reading

Goreau, Laurraine. *Just Mahalia, Baby: The Mahalia Jackson Story.* Gretna, La.: Pelican Publishing, 1985.

Gourse, Leslie. *Mahalia Jackson: The Queen of Gospel Song.* Danbury, Conn.: Franklin Watts, 1996 (YA).

Kramer, Barbara. *Mahalia Jackson: The Voice of Gospel and Civil Rights.* Berkeley Heights, N.J.: Enslow Publishers, 2003.

Schwerin, Jules Victor. *Got to Tell It: Mahalia Jackson, Queen of Gospel.* New York: Oxford University Press, 1994.

Further Listening

The Essential Mahalia Jackson. Sony, 2 CDs, 2004.

Further Viewing

Mahalia Jackson 1947–1962. Video Artists International, DVD, 2007.

Jackson, Michael
("The King of Pop")
(1958–2009) *R & B singer, songwriter*

One of the few recording artists to make the difficult transition from child to adult performer successfully, Michael Jackson was one of the best-selling recording artist of all time, although controversy cost him much of his popularity in the 1990s.

He was born on August 29, 1958, in Gary, Indiana, the seventh of nine children of Joseph and Katherine Jackson. His family was working class but aspired to success. The three eldest brothers—Jermaine, Jackie, and Tito—formed a singing trio in the early 1960s, organized by their father. When Marlon and Michael joined the group a short time later, they became the Jackson 5. Michael, only five when he started performing, became the group's star with his high energy vocals and dance moves patterned after JAMES BROWN.

The Jackson 5 signed a recording contract in 1965 with Steeltown Records, a local label, and began touring as the opening act for big-name rhythm and blues (R & B) acts. In 1969, they signed with legendary Motown Records of Detroit, Michigan, which had relocated to Los Angeles, California. Motown's president, Berry Gordy, created a new image for the Jackson 5, from their clothes to their dance movements. They rocketed to the top of the charts with their first single "I Want You Back" (1969). It was followed by three more number-one hits—"ABC," "The Love You Save," and "I'll Be There" (all 1970). Jermaine, Jackie, and Michael each made solo records in 1971, with Michael scoring the greatest success with two plaintive ballads—"Got to Be There"

(1971) and "Ben" (1972)—and a remake of the old rocker "Rockin' Robin" (1972).

The Jackson 5 became displeased with Gordy's tight control on their careers and left Motown in 1976. They signed with Epic Records and had two gold albums in succession—*Enjoy Yourself* (1976) and *Destiny* (1979). Michael, now 20, saw it as his destiny to go out on his own. The previous year he had made his film debut as the Scarecrow in the movie version of the Broadway musical *The Wiz* (1978). QUINCY JONES had produced the film's soundtrack and Jackson asked him to produce his first solo album. The resulting *Off the Wall* (1979) was a smash, selling more than 7 million copies and producing four top-10 hit singles, including "Rock with You," "Don't Stop 'Til You Get Enough," and the title song.

The album heralded Jackson's arrival as a mature, adult pop artist, no longer the kinetic kid from the Jackson 5. Jones and Jackson went all out on their next collaboration, *Thriller* (1982). Out of the album's nine tracks, six became huge hits, including Jackson's duet with former Beatle Paul McCartney, "The Girl Is Mine." "Beat It" was a great dance number, as was "Billie Jean," which became a music video, the first one by a black artist to be featured regularly on cable's Music Television (MTV). Its success opened the way for a host of other black singers to appear on MTV.

Thriller eventually sold 40 million copies worldwide, making it the best-selling album in record history to date. The album and the songs on it won Jackson a record eight Grammy Awards. Michael Jackson was now more than a hit-maker, he was a cultural icon. He next starred in *Captain EO*, a 15-minute 3-D film directed by filmmaker George Lucas. The sci-fi film has been seen by millions of visitors to Disneyland and Disney World. In 1985, Jackson wrote and recorded the song "We Are the World" with LIONEL RICHIE, the profits of which went to help famine relief in Africa. His next album, *Victory* (1984), reunited him with his brothers and was followed by a national tour.

Having reached the peak of success, Jackson's career had nowhere to go but down. His next solo album, *Bad* (1987), sold 8 million copies, a modest success compared with *Thriller*. *Dangerous* (1991) fell even further behind *Thriller*'s sales. Jackson's private life began upstaging his public one. He underwent plastic surgery, supposedly to help correct a skin condition. He was accused of pedophilia with some of the children he surrounded himself with in his palatial home. Charges were dropped after monetary payments were made to families, but many people doubted Jackson's claims of innocence. Then, in 1994, he made headlines again, marrying Lisa Marie Presley, Elvis Presley's only child. The marriage lasted less than two years. Jackson then married Deborah Rowe, an assistant to his dermatologist, in late 1996, and they had a son the following year. In the spring of 1998, the couple had a daughter. Jackson and Rowe later divorced. In 2002, a second son was born to the singer. His mother remains unnamed.

In 1995, Jackson released *HIStory*, an anthology of past hits with new songs added. It was far from the smash hit Jackson and his label, Sony, were hoping for. At the same time, his sister, JANET JACKSON, was beginning to surpass her older brother in popularity and record sales. After several relatively quiet years, Jackson staged a comeback in 2001, with two all-star concerts in New York's Madison Square Garden to celebrate his 30th anniversary in show business. It reunited him with his brothers, except for Jermaine who stayed away, and featured a gallery of stars including WHITNEY HOUSTON, RAY CHARLES, and GLADYS KNIGHT. Within a month, Jackson released a new album, *Invincible* (2001), and a single, "You Rock My World."

Michael Jackson was inducted into the Rock and Roll Hall of Fame in 2001. He was honored with a birthday cake on his 44th birthday at the MTV Video Music Awards on September 1, 2002. During the event, pop singer Britney Spears called him the "artist of the millennium."

The following year, Michael Jackson was arrested and charged with seven counts of child molestation based on the accusations of a boy who slept over at his Neverland Ranch. The boy was under 14 at the time of the alleged incidents. In June 2005, Jackson was acquitted of all charges, but the controversy drove him into seclusion. In 2008, his record label marked the 25th anniversary of *Thriller* with *Thriller 25*, a special double disc edition. It sold 3 million copies in 12 weeks.

Jackson was rehearsing for a comeback tour when he suffered cardiac arrest at his Los Angeles home on June 25, 2009. He was rushed to the University of California–Los Angeles (UCLA) Medical Center, when he was pronounced dead at age 50. An investigation revealed that powerful prescription drugs he had been taking to sleep may have played a part in his untimely death. In October 2009, a film of Jackon in rehearsal for his never-to-be concert tour, *This Is It*, was released.

Further Reading

Jackson, Michael. *Moonwalk*. New York: Doubleday, 1988.

Jefferson, Margo. *On Michael Jackson*. New York: Vintage, 2007.

Nicholson, Lois P. *Michael Jackson*. Black Americans of Achievement. New York: Chelsea House, 1994 (YA).

Porter, Darwin. *Jacko, His Rise and Fall*. Staten Island, N.Y.: Blood Moon Productions, 2007.

Taraborrelli, Randy J. *Michael Jackson: The Magic and the Madness*. London: Pan Books, 2004.

Further Listening

Jackson 5: The Ultimate Collection. Motown, CD, 1996.

Number Ones. Sony, CD, 2003.

25th Anniversary of Thriller (1982). Sony, 2 CDs, 2008.

Further Viewing

Michael Jackson: Video Greatest Hits—HIStory. Sony, DVD, 2001.

Jackson, O'Shea   See ICE CUBE.

Jackson, Samuel L.
(Samuel Leroy Jackson)
(1948–) *actor*

One of the hardest-working actors in Hollywood, Samuel L. Jackson has brought an intensity and passion to a colorful gallery of film roles from a born-again hit man to a space-age Jedi knight.

He was born Samuel Leroy Jackson on December 21, 1948, in Washington, D.C., and raised in Chattanooga, Tennessee, by his mother and grandparents. He played the French horn and trumpet in school orchestras from the third grade through high school and was a high school cheerleader. Jackson attended Morehouse College in Atlanta, Georgia, where a speech therapist urged him to audition for a campus musical to help overcome a stuttering problem. He got the part and became enthralled with the theater. Jackson also became a dedicated student activist. He once held hostage several school trustees, among them Martin Luther King, Sr., during a student sit-in protesting the school's low number of black trustees.

After graduating in 1972, Jackson acted in theaters in the Atlanta area and appeared in his first film, *Together for Days*. He moved to New York City in 1976 and joined the Negro Ensemble Company (NEC). One of his fellow actors there was MORGAN FREEMAN. His first major Hollywood film was *Ragtime* (1981), in which he played the bit part of "Gang Member No. 2." The same year he appeared in the NEC's stage production of *A Soldier's Story* and caught the eye of fledgling filmmaker Spike Lee. He continued to appear in small roles in films through the 1980s. On Broadway, Jackson appeared in African-American playwright August Wilson's *The Piano Lesson* (1990). He originated a leading role in the Off-Broadway production of Wilson's *Two Trains Running*, but when the show's producers learned of his additions to alcohol and crack cocaine,

Hardworking Samuel L. Jackson may have appeared in more films in the 1990s than any other leading film actor. *(Photofest)*

they dropped him from the Broadway production. Jackson saw that drugs could destroy his career and entered drug rehabilitation.

About the same time, Spike Lee cast him as the crack addict Gator in his film *Jungle Fever* (1991). Jackson had previously appeared in three Lee films—*School Daze* (1988), *Do the Right Thing* (1989), and *Mo' Better Blues* (1990). But it was Gator that proved to be his breakthrough role. Drawing on his years as an addict, Jackson gave an electrifying performance. The judges of the Cannes Film Festival were so impressed by his work that they created a special category for best supporting actor to honor him.

Jackson quickly moved up to starring roles in two feeble comedies *Amos and Andrew* and *Loaded*

Weapon I (both 1993) and played one of the technicians in *Jurassic Park* (1993). Then came Jules, a Bible-quoting hit man who undergoes a spiritual conversion, in Quentin Tarantino's strikingly original crime saga *Pulp Fiction* (1994). Jackson stood out in a fine cast that included John Travolta, Bruce Willis, and VING RHAMES. His performance earned him an Academy Award nomination for best supporting actor.

Now a full-fledged star, Jackson appeared in perhaps more movies during the 1990s than any other Hollywood actor. From 1990 to 1998, he averaged four films a year. He was a black attorney opposite his wife, actress La Tanya Richardson, in *Losing Isaiah* (1995), a buddy to Bruce Willis in his first "good guy" leading role in *Die Hard with a Vengeance* (1995), and a vicious gunrunner in another Tarantino film, *Jackie Brown* (1997), for which he won a Silver Berlin Bear Award. More recent roles have included the Jedi knight Mace Windu in three *Star Wars* films, the title character in filmmaker John Singleton's remake of the blaxploitation classic *Shaft* (2000), an old blues man in *Black Snake Moan* (2006), and a psychopathic cop in *Lakeview Terrace* (2008).

Winner of a National Association for the Advancement of Colored People (NAACP) Image Award in 2001, Samuel Jackson and his wife are known for their work for numerous social causes.

Further Reading

Dils, Tracey E. *Samuel L. Jackson.* Black Americans of Achievement. New York: Chelsea House, 2000 (YA).

Hudson, Jeff. *Samuel L. Jackson: The Unauthorized Biography.* London: Virgin Books, 2004.

Further Viewing

Black Snake Moan. Paramount, DVD, 2007.

Jungle Fever (1991). Universal Studio Home Video, DVD, 1995.

Pulp Fiction (1994). Miramax Home Video, Collector's Edition, 2 DVDs, 2002.

Jamison, Judith
(1944–   ) *modern dancer, choreographer, dance company director*

One of the most strikingly elegant and statuesque of modern dancers, Judith Jamison returned to direct the dance company she helped make famous nine years after leaving it.

She was born in Philadelphia, Pennsylvania, on May 10, 1944, to John and Tessie Jamison. Her father was a sheet-metal mechanic and her mother a part-time teacher. Jamison began her dance studies at age six and was discovered in her teens by the great choreographer Agnes De Mille. She debuted in 1964 with the American Ballet Theatre and the following year joined ALVIN AILEY's American Dance Theater (AAADT). Jamison was a principal dancer with this African-American dance company for 15 years. A tall, elegant dancer with a feline grace, Jamison was featured prominently in such classic Ailey works as *The Lark Ascending* (1972), *The Mooch* (1975), and *Cry* (1971), in which she memorably danced the solo part.

After leaving Ailey in 1980, Jamison was a guest artist with such leading ballet and music companies as the Munich State Opera and the Vienna State Opera. She became a Broadway star in the musical revue *Sophisticated Ladies* (1981), based on the music of DUKE ELLINGTON. In 1988 she founded her own company, the Jamison Project, and was the subject of a Public Broadcasting Service (PBS) special *Judith Jamison: The Dancemaker.*

The following year Alvin Ailey died and Jamison returned to become artistic director of AAADT. She expanded the company's activities, helping to develop the Women's Choreography Initiative. Jamison brought the Ailey company to national attention by putting its dancers into American Express TV commercials and print advertisements. At the same time, she pursued her own career as a choreographer. AAADT performed her *Hymn* (1993), a moving tribute to

Ailey with a libretto by playwright-actress Anna Deavere Smith. Her other major works include *Rift* (1991), *Riverside* (1995), and *Sweet Release* (1996), which premiered at the Lincoln Center Festival in New York City with original music by WYNTON MARSALIS. Jamison was the recipient of the Kennedy Center Honors in 1999 and was awarded a National Medal of Arts in 2001.

"Dance is about never-ending aspiration," Jamison has said.

Further Reading
"Center Stage Interview." *Ebony,* June 1, 2005, p. 26.

Jamison, Judith, with Howard Kaplan. *Dancing Spirit: An Autobiography.* New York: Anchor Books, 1994.

Maynard, Olga. *Judith Jamison, Aspects of a Dancer.* Garden City, N.Y.: Doubleday, 1982.

Further Viewing
Richard Strauss—Josephs Legend. Deutsche Grammophon, DVD, 2007.

Jean, Wyclef
("Clef")
(1972–   ) *R & B singer, songwriter, record producer, social activist*

One of the most eclectic and creative talents in contemporary hip-hop, Wyclef Jean has carved out a unique niche, both as a member of the group the Fugees and as a solo artist.

He was born in Croix-des-Bouquets, Haiti, on October 17, 1972, and came with relatives to south Florida when he was nine. The family later moved to Brooklyn, New York, where Jean's father, Gesner, was a minister of the Nazarene Church, and then to South Orange, New Jersey. Jean's father bought him and his three siblings their first musical instruments with the idea they would play them in church. When he saw them playing secular music, however, he banned them from Sunday services. Jean continued to pursue pop music and formed a rap trio with his cousin Prakazrel "Pras" Michel and singer Lauryn Hill. They called themselves the Translater Crew but later changed their name to the Fugees. The name was short for refugee, which is both symbolic and political. Jean and Michel considered themselves refugees from their native Haiti. Their first album, *Blunted on Reality* (1993), gained some attention but sold poorly. Their second album, *The Score* (1996), scored a huge hit and made the Fugees famous for their intriguing mix of rap, reggae, and folk.

The following year Jean went solo and produced *Presents the Carnival Featuring the Refugee All Stars* (1997). This far-ranging album showcased Jean's playfulness and his sharp intellect. *The Carnival* contained everything from retro disco to an updated version of the folk song "Guantanamera." It boasted the former Fugees as well as the New York Philharmonic Orchestra conducted by Jean on the beautiful ballad "Gone Till November." The album's single hit was "We Trying to Stay Alive," which smartly sampled the old Bee Gees' hit "Stayin' Alive."

Jean's second solo album, *The Ecleftic: 2 Sides II a Book* (2000), was as deliciously eclectic as its predecessor. It "contains enough anger and righteous indignation to be real hip-hop, and enough humor and musical magic to be fun," wrote rock critic Lizz Mendez Berry. One highlight was the reggae-like "Diallo," a tribute to Amadou Diallo, a West African immigrant killed by New York police in 1999.

Jean's album *The Preacher's Son* (2003) was a follow-up to *The Carnival*. His most recent album, *Carnival II: Memoirs of an Immigrant*, appeared in 2007. He has written songs for the soundtracks of the documentary *The Agronomist* (2003), about Haitian activist Jean Dominique, and *Hotel Rwanda* (2004).

His Wyclef Jean Foundation is dedicated to helping the poor children of Haiti and the United States. In 2005, he established the Yéle Haiti Foundation after hurricane Jean struck his homeland.

Wyclef Jean is married to Haitian-American fashion designer Marie Claudinette Pierre-Jean. Their adopted daughter, Angelina Claudinelle, was born in 2005.

Further Reading
"Wyclef Jean" Wyclef Jean Official Web site. Available online. URL: http://www.wyclef.com/. Downloaded on February 6, 2009.
Yélehaiti Web site. Available online. URL: http//www.yele.org/. Downloaded on February 6, 2009.

Further Listening
Carnival II: Memoirs of an Immigrants. Sony, CD, 2007.
The Ecleftic: 2 Sides II a Book. Sony, CD, 2000.
Presents the Carnival Featuring the Refugee All Stars. Sony, CD, 1997.

Further Viewing
Wyclef Jean's All Star Jam at Carnegie Hall. Eagle Rock Entertainment, DVD, 2004.

Johnson, Caryn   See GOLDBERG, WHOOPI.

Johnson, Robert
(Robert Leroy Johnson)
(1911–1938) *blues singer, songwriter, guitarist*

Probably the most influential blues musician who ever lived, Robert Johnson led a life as shadowy and mysterious as his music is dark and foreboding.

Robert Leroy Johnson was born out of wedlock in Hazlehurst, Mississippi, on May 8, 1911, to Julia Dodds and Noah Johnson. At the time, Dodds was married to furniture maker and landowner Charles Dodds. When she ran off, Robert lived with her husband in Memphis, Tennessee. He later reunited with his mother and a new stepfather in Robinsonville, Mississippi. When he learned the identity of his real father he took the name Johnson. As a boy, Johnson played the mouth instrument called the Jew's harp and the harmonica, but he didn't take up the guitar until he was in his late teens. He learned the blues from its best practitioners in the Mississippi Delta region—Charley Patton and Son House. House would become a major influence on his music. Johnson married at age 17, but his wife died in childbirth two years later in 1930.

Johnson moved back to Hazelhurst where he practiced his guitar religiously and married an older woman with three children. He spent three years in Hazelhurst, the longest he would stay in one place for the remainder of his short life. By the time he returned to the Mississippi Delta, Johnson was a mature artist whose intricate and expressive guitar work and haunting, high-pitched vocals amazed the veteran bluesmen who heard him. Having abandoned his second wife, he became an itinerant musician, traveling from town to town and playing music at small clubs called "jook" joints, country fairs, and other social gatherings. He'd perform and then mysteriously disappear, only to reappear in the next town. Stories spread that Johnson's gift was a supernatural one. People said he had met the devil at midnight at a lonely crossroads and sold his soul in return for his extraordinary musical talent. Johnson perpetuated these stories in such classic songs as "Cross Roads Blues," "Me and the Devil Blues," and "Hell Hound on My Trail," one of the last songs he wrote.

In November 1936, Johnson recorded his music for the first time for the American Record Company in San Antonio, Texas. Within a year, he had recorded his entire catalogue of original songs, only one of which, "Terraplane Blues," about a big, fast car, became a hit.

After completing the recording sessions, Johnson took his most ambitious road tour with two fellow musicians. He went to St. Louis, Chicago, Detroit, New York, and even Windsor, Canada. Then he returned to Mississippi where his womanizing finally proved his undoing.

On August 13, 1938, Johnson appeared at Three Forks, a jook joint near Greenwood, Mississippi. He was having an affair with the wife of the club's owner who found out about it. During the evening, the jealous husband slipped Johnson a bottle of poisoned whiskey. The bluesman recklessly drank from the opened bottle and became violently sick. He was carried to a room and died in agony three days later at age 27. Not long after, a letter arrived for Johnson from record producer John Hammond, inviting him to perform at a gala concert at Carnegie Hall in New York City. If he had lived, that appearance might have made Robert Johnson a star.

But Johnson's music continued to exert a powerful influence on other bluesmen. Among them was MUDDY WATERS, who used it as the foundation of his new, electrified urban blues. In the 1960s, Johnson's songs were performed by such rock groups as Cream, the Rolling Stones, and Canned Heat. When his complete recordings were re-released in 1990, they became a commercial and critical hit and have sold nearly 2 million copies by 2004. Robert Johnson, who died more than 15 years before the birth of rock 'n' roll, was inducted into the Rock and Roll Hall of Fame in 1986 as an early influence. According to guitarist and singer Eric Clapton, a Johnson disciple, "His music remains the most powerful cry that I think you can find in the human voice."

Further Reading

Calt, Stephen. *Hellhound on My Trail: The Life and Legend of Robert Johnson.* New York: Grove Press, 2001.

Graves, Tom. *Crossroads: The Life and Afterlife of Blues Legend Robert Johnson.* Spokane, Wash.: Demers Books, 2008.

Guralnick, Peter. *Searching for Robert Johnson.* New York: Penguin USA, 1998.

Wald, Elijah. *Escaping the Delta: Robert Johnson and the Invention of the Blues.* New York: Amistad, 2004.

Further Listening

The Complete Recordings. Sony, 2 CDs, 1996.

Jones, Bill T.
(1951–   ) *modern dancer, choreographer, dance company director*

The surviving half of one of the best-known partnerships in contemporary dance, Bill T. Jones has broken new ground in modern dance by his daring exploring of such themes as racial prejudice, homosexuality, and AIDS.

He was born on February 15, 1951, either in Bunnell, Florida, or Steuben County, New York (sources differ) to migrant farmers. He went to the State University of New York at Binghamton on a sports scholarship as a runner. When he discovered dance, however, Jones changed his focus and studied classical ballet and modern dance. Jones met and fell in love with white photographer Arnie Zane, whom he persuaded to take up dance. The two men founded the American Dance Asylum in 1973 at Binghamton. In 1976, they dissolved the company and toured internationally as a duo, performing their unique athletic dance duets, which dance writer Allen Robertson has called "among the most evocative and autobiographical dance works of the era."

In 1982, they founded Bill T. Jones/Arnie Zane and Dancers, a 10-member multicultural dance company. Their original works became a fascinating combination of dance and theater. A good example is *Secret Pastures* (1984) in which Zane played a mad scientist who created a kind of Frankenstein creature (Jones) who then became a celebrity. Such works appealed to a wide, commercial audience, and soon the two men were developing new dance pieces for other companies including the ALVIN AILEY American Dance Theater, the Boston Ballet, and the Berlin Opera Ballet.

When Zane died of AIDS in 1988, Jones's work took on a new fierceness and immediacy. Jones held workshops around the country for people with life-threatening diseases and had them express their feelings about life and death in movement. He then incorporated these movements into his dance work *Still/Here* (1994), which deals with AIDS and survival. (Jones is HIV-positive.) The same year he received a MacArthur Fellowship. One of his recent works, *Ghostcatching* (1999), is a collaboration with abstract filmmakers Paul Kaiser and Shelley Eshkor in which Jones's movements are motion-captured using sensors attached to his body that translate into skeleton figures on a cube.

The Bill T. Jones/Arnie Zane Dance Company has performed in more than 100 American cities and 30 countries. Having completed a four-year residency at Aaron Davis Hall at New York's City College in 2001, Jones is raising money for a permanent home for his company in Harlem.

In 2007, Jones won a Tony Award for his choreography for the Broadway musical *Spring Awakening.* The following year, he directed and choreographed the Off-Broadway musical *Fela!* about the Nigerian bandleader and folk hero Fela Anikulapo Kuti who died of AIDS in 1997. *Fela!* opened on Broadway in 2009.

Writer Wendy Perron has called Bill T. Jones "[t]he Muhammad Ali of the dance world, he possess an audacity, eloquence and insolence that have elicited both awe and irritation."

Further Reading

Cunningham, Merce, ed. *Art Performs Life: Merce Cunningham/Meredith Monk/Bill T. Jones.* Minneapolis, Minn.: Walker Art Center, 1998.

Jones, Bill T., with Peggy Gillespie. *Last Night on Earth.* New York: Pantheon Books, 1997.

Kuklin, Susan. *Dance! With Bill T. Jones.* New York: Hyperion, 1998 (children).

Zimmer, Elizabeth. *Body against Body: The Dance and Other Collaborations of Bill T. Jones & Arnie Zane.* Barrytown, N.Y.: Station Hill Press, 1990.

Further Viewing

Bill T. Jones: Solos. Bel Air Classiques, DVD, 2008.

Jones, James Earl
(1931–) *actor*

One of the most distinguished living African-American actors, James Earl Jones is as well known for his rich, rumbling baritone as his imposing physical presence.

He was born on January 17, 1931, in Arkabutla, Mississippi. His father, Robert Earl Jones, was a prizefighter who turned to acting. His mother, Ruth, was a maid and former schoolteacher. Robert Jones left his family not long after Jones's birth, and the child was adopted and raised on a Michigan farm by his maternal grandparents.

Jones developed a strong stutter as a youth and, out of embarrassment, rarely talked until he was 15. A high school English teacher took an interest in him when he learned that Jones wrote poetry. He helped him overcome his stutter and win a scholarship to the University of Michigan, where he went in 1949. Jones started as a pre-med student and then switched to drama. He graduated magna cum laude in 1953 and served a stint in the army.

After his service time, Jones moved to New York City to pursue an acting career and for a time was reunited with his father, another struggling actor. Together they waxed floors for money to live on while auditioning for plays. Jones began getting small parts in Off-Broadway shows but did not land his first role on Broadway until 1957. His career got a big boost when he was invited to join the New York Shakespeare Festival, which performed Shakespeare's plays each summer in Central Park. Jones was impressive in such leading Shakespearean roles as Othello, King Lear, and Oberon, the king of the fairies in *A Midsummer Night's Dream*. During this time he made his film debut as a member of the flying squad that dropped a nuclear bomb on Russia in Stanley Kubrick's black comedy *Dr. Strangelove* (1964). Two years later he made his television debut on the daytime soap opera *As The World Turns*.

That same year Jones became a Broadway star when he was cast as a troubled black heavyweight boxer based on fighter Jack Johnson in the drama *The Great White Hope* (1966). His powerful performance earned him a Tony Award for best actor in a play. He later earned an Academy Award nomination for best actor when he reprised the role in the 1970 film version.

Jones gave strong performances in a handful of films in the 1970s. He played an eccentric psychiatrist in *The End of the Road* (1972), the first black president in *The Man* (1972) written by Rod Serling, and a black baseball player in *The Bingo Long Travelling All-Stars and Motor Kings* (1976). Jones gave a riveting performance as the great actor and human rights activist PAUL ROBESON in a controversial, one-man show on Broadway. He portrayed writer Alex Haley in television's *Roots: The Next Generation* (1979), the sequel to the blockbuster miniseries *Roots*, based on Haley's best-selling book.

Jones's most popular and probably best-known film role is one in which he was never seen. He was the threatening, mysterious voice of arch villain Darth Vader in *Star Wars* (1977) and its two sequels. The actor made a triumphant return to Broadway in 1985 as a defiant former baseball player in August Wilson's play *Fences*, which earned him his second Tony as best actor. He played another former baseball player and reclusive writer in the fantasy film *Field of Dreams* (1989), generally considered one of his finest screen roles.

In the 1990s, Jones, who had played an African chieftain on the 1960s TV series *Tarzan*, returned to series television as the ex-con and former cop Gabriel Bird in the dramatic series *Gabriel's Fire*. Despite generally good reviews, the series, retitled *Pros and Cons* in its second season, did not last. He has won three Emmys for his television work and has been nominated six other times most recently in 2004.

Jones has found few good screen roles in recent years but has played many solid supporting roles.

He was Admiral James Greer, Harrison Ford's mentor in *The Hunt for Red October* (1990), who reappears in *Patriot Games* (1992) and *Clear and Present Danger* (1994), all based on the techno-thrillers of novelist Tom Clancy. Younger viewers may know Jones best for his popular television commercials for American Telephone and Telegraph (AT&T) and other companies, where his rich voice has been a strong selling tool.

James Earl Jones received a Life Achievement Award from the Screen Actors Guild in January 2009. Regarding acting he has said, "It's important to say something that's from your heart."

Further Reading

Hasday, Judy L. *James Earl Jones*. Overcoming Adversity. New York: Chelsea House, 1999 (YA).

Jones, James Earl, with Penelope Niven. *Voices and Silences*. New York: Limelight Editions, 2004.

Further Viewing

Field of Dreams (1989). Universal Studios Home Video, Anniversary Edition, 2 DVDs, 2004.

The Great White Hope (1970). Fox Video, DVD, 2005.

James Earl Jones as Paul Robeson (1977). Kultur Video, DVD, 2005.

Jones, Quincy

(Quincy Delight Jones, Jr.)

(1933–   ) *composer; record, film, and television producer; arranger; musician; R & B singer*

Quincy Jones's dazzling accomplishments in the world of music, film, and television have made him one of the most versatile talents in show business for five decades.

He was born Quincy Delight Jones, Jr., on Chicago's impoverished South Side on March 14, 1933. His parents divorced when he was quite young and his mother, Sarah, was hospitalized for a time with schizophrenia. When Quincy was 10, Quincy Jones, Sr., a carpenter, moved the family

Quincy Jones at work in his favorite place—the recording studio *(Showtime Music Archives, Toronto)*

to Seattle, Washington. Jones was shocked to suddenly find himself the only black student in his grade school. He sang in a gospel quartet and played trumpet in the high school band. At 14, he met singer RAY CHARLES, who was two years older and had just moved to Seattle. Together they played rhythm and blues (R & B) music in black clubs. Jones wrote his first musical suite, *From the Four Winds*, when he was 16. He moved to Boston and attended the Berklee School of Music for a time. In 1950, he joined Lionel Hampton's jazz band and began to write arrangements for their music. Jones's skill as an arranger soon found him freelancing for such recording artists as COUNT BASIE, DUKE ELLINGTON, and SARAH VAUGHAN.

He moved to Paris in 1956 to study classical composition with the great American teacher

Nadia Boulanger. When he returned to the United States in 1961, he was hired as music director for Mercury Records and guided the careers of several vocalists, including singer Leslie Gore. He soon became Mercury's first African-American vice president. Jones then went to Los Angeles, California, where he began a new phase of his musical career. He became a film composer and scored some of the most memorable films of the 1960s, including *The Pawnbroker* (1965) and *In the Heat of the Night* (1967). One of his most celebrated scores was for the television miniseries *Roots* (1977), which earned him an Emmy Award.

The following year Jones scored the film *The Wiz*, a job he accepted reluctantly. On the set of the movie he met singer MICHAEL JACKSON, who played the Scarecrow. Jackson asked him if he would produce his next album. Jones was impressed with Jackson's professionalism and later agreed. The results were three albums, the second of which, *Thriller* (1982), became the biggest-selling album of all time and won both men Grammy Awards for album of the year and record of the year.

But Jones's restless energy was leading him into new creative territory. He started his own record label, Qwest, in 1981 and produced his first movie, *The Color Purple* (1985), for which he also composed the score. The same year, he produced the album and music video for Jackson's "We Are the World," a sing-a-long for a gallery of musical stars. The profits from the record and video sales went to aid relief for Africa.

Between 1970 and 1996, Jones had 13 *Billboard* pop chart top-100 hits on which he played or sang. His recording collaborators have included his old friend Ray Charles, Chaka Khan, BARRY WHITE, BABYFACE, and Tamia.

Jones merged his company with that of producer David Salzman to form Quincy Jones David Salzman Entertainment (QDE) in 1993. Their company produced the television situation comedy *Fresh Prince of Bel Air*, which starred WILL SMITH, and the comedy show *MAD TV*. In 1994, Jones formed Qwest Broadcasting with several partners, including broadcaster Geraldo Rivera. It is one of the largest minority-owned broadcasting companies in the nation.

"I've been driven all my life by a spirit of adventure and a criminal level of optimism," Jones wrote in his autobiography published in 2001. With all he has accomplished, Jones has reason to be optimistic. He has accrued 77 Grammy nominations, more than any other person has. He is tied with sound designer Willie D. Burton for the most Academy Award nominations—seven. He received Grammy's Trustees Award in 1989 and its Living Legends Award in 1990. The same year he was awarded the French Legion of Honor. He was the recipient of the Kennedy Center Honors in 2001 and received the Black Entertainment Television (BET) Humanitarian Award in 2008. Quincy Jones was married to actress Peggy Lipton, star of TV's *Mod Squad*, from 1974 to 1990. Their daughter Rashida Jones is an actress. He has five other children, including a daughter with actress Nastassja Kinski, who he lived with from 1991 to 1997.

Further Reading

Bayer, Linda N. *Quincy Jones*. Overcoming Adversity. New York: Chelsea House, 2000 (YA).

Jones, Quincy. *Q: The Autobiography of Quincy Jones*. New York: Harlem Moon, 2002.

———. *The Complete Quincy Jones: My Journeys & Passions*. San Rafael, Calif.: Insight Editions 2003.

Nelson, Ross and Courtney. *Listen Up: The Lives of Quincy Jones*. New York: Warner Books, 1990.

Further Listening

20th Century Masters—The Millennium Collection: The Best of Quincy Jones. Interscope Records, CD, 2001.

Ultimate Collection. Hip-O Records, CD, 2002.

Further Viewing

Listen Up! The Lives of Quincy Jones (1990). Warner Home Video, DVD, 2009.

Quincy Jones: 50 Years in Music—Live at Montreux 1996. Eagle Rock Entertainment, DVD, 2008.

Joplin, Scott
("King of Ragtime")
(1868–1917) *composer, pianist*

The man who popularized ragtime music and raised it to the heights of great art, Scott Joplin is today considered one of America's most important composers.

He was born in Bowie County, Texas, on November 24, 1868. His birthplace later became a part of the town of Texarkana. Joplin's father, Giles, was a former slave who played the fiddle at his master's parties. His mother, Florence, worked as a cleaning woman and took her son with her to play on the pianos at the white homes were she worked.

A musical prodigy, young Joplin left home at age 14 and traveled across the South, playing piano in bars and bordellos. Along the way, he learned about a new kind of music called ragtime, an intriguing mixture of popular black folk music and European classical forms. Principally played on the piano, ragtime had a strong rhythm line played by the left hand and an infectious melody line, usually three or four of them in a rag, played by the right hand. Joplin began to play ragtime, most prominently at the Chicago World's Fair of 1893, where he met many other talented musicians.

Two years later, Joplin's first compositions were published, two sentimental songs that showed little of the genius to come. In 1896 he wrote three compositions for piano, the most interesting of which was "The Great Crash Collision March." A stirring reenactment of a train wreck, it was Joplin's most original piece of music to date.

The fledging composer settled in Sedalia, Missouri, in 1897 and studied musical composition at George R. Smith College. He played piano nightly at the Maple Leaf Club, a local saloon. Among the most popular pieces he played was his own composition "Maple Leaf Rag," which he named in honor of the saloon. The piece was published in 1899 by local music publisher John Stark, who paid Joplin a royalty on each piece of sheet music sold, an unusual arrangement at the time. Most composers were paid outright for their work. The two men formed a partnership that lasted nine years.

Slowly, like a snowball rolling downhill, the "Maple Leaf Rag" became a success and within three years became the first piece of instrumental sheet music to sell more than 1 million copies. Its popularity set off a ragtime craze across America. Soon Joplin was able to quit performing and devote himself full time to composing. Over the next decade he wrote dozens of rags, marches, and songs. Among his most famous rags were "The Entertainer" (1902), "Weeping Willow" (1903), "The Cascades" (1904), and "Wall Street Rag" (1909). As ingenious and memorable as these rags were, Joplin aspired to greater things. In 1902 he wrote, and Stark published, *The Ragtime Dance*, a 20-minute folk ballet. The following year he staged a one-act "ragtime opera," *A Guest of Honor*, the score to which was later lost.

After a disastrous first marriage to Belle Hayden, Joplin left his home in St. Louis in 1905 and spent two years on the road. He played in vaudeville shows where he was billed as the "king of ragtime" and continued to compose. In 1909, he married Lottie Stokes and the two settled in New York City. Here Joplin began work on a full-length opera, *Treemonisha*.

Treemonisha was the story of a girl who was found under a tree by a childless couple, hence her unusual name. When Treemonisha reached her teens, she saved her all-black community from a band of evil conjurers and led them out of superstition and ignorance into a new day of peace, education, and harmony. This ambitious folk opera contained rags as well as many other styles of music, including Negro spirituals, church hymns, popular ballads, and European operatic arias, or songs. Stark refused to publish *Treemonisha*, feeling white audiences would never accept an opera composed by a black man, and the two men parted ways. Joplin published the opera himself at great expense in 1911 and four years later staged it at a Harlem theater for one night. The audience of mostly middle-class blacks dismissed Joplin's work, and he was heartbroken. With little money and in failing health, he suffered a major breakdown in early 1917. His wife put him in the Manhattan State Hospital on Ward's Island. He died there on April 1, 1917, probably from the effects of syphilis, which he contracted years earlier. With him died ragtime, which was soon replaced in popularity by a new kind of American music—jazz.

After decades of neglect, ragtime and its greatest composer experienced a revival in the 1970s. Pianist Joshua Rifkin released an album of Joplin rags, which became a best-seller, and in 1973 the popular movie *The Sting* used "The Entertainer" and other music by Joplin in its soundtrack. *Treemonisha* was performed professionally by the Houston Opera Company in 1975 and later went to Broadway exactly 60 years after it was first performed. The production was an artistic and commercial success and was instrumental in Joplin's posthumously receiving a special Pulitzer Prize in music in 1976. Today, Scott Joplin has finally found his place in the pantheon of great American composers.

Further Reading

Berlin, Edward A. *King of Ragtime: Scott Joplin and His Era.* New York: Oxford University Press, 1996.

Curtis, Susan. *Dancing the Black Man's Tune: A Life of Scott Joplin.* Columbia: University of Missouri Press, 2004.

Due, Tananarive. *Joplin's Ghost.* New York: Washington Square Press, 2006.

Hubbard, Brown Janet. *Scott Joplin.* Black Americans of Achievement. New York: Chelsea House, 2006 (YA).

Otfinoski, Steven. *Scott Joplin: A Life in Ragtime.* Danbury, Conn.: Franklin Watts, 1995 (YA).

Further Listening

The Complete Works of Scott Joplin (played by Richard Zimmerman). Bescal, CD box set, 1994.

Scott Joplin's Treemonisha. Deutsche Grammophon, 2 CDs, 1992.

Jordan, Louis
("King of the Juke Boxes")
(1908–1975) *R & B singer, saxophonist, bandleader, songwriter*

One of the most popular African-American singers of the 1940s, Louis Jordan was a true pioneer of both rhythm and blues (R & B) and rock 'n' roll.

He was born on July 8, 1908, in Brinkley, Arkansas. His father was the leader of Arkansas's famous Rabbit Foot Minstrels. Jordan studied music at Arkansas Baptist College and played alto sax with the Jungle Band in the late 1920s. In the early 1930s, he moved to Philadelphia and then New York City where he played in several jazz bands, including drummer CHICK WEBB's band. Jordan formed his own band, the Elks Rendezvous Band, in 1938, named after the Harlem nightclub where they played. They recorded their first record for Decca entitled "Honey in the Bee Ball." In 1939, Jordan changed the group's name to the Tympany Five, although the number of musicians in the band changed from year to year. At different times the group included such noteworthy musicians as keyboardists Wild Bill Davis and Bill Doggett and drummer Chris Columbus.

The Tympany Five played a wild mixture of jazz and blues that had a strong dance beat and outlandish, humorous lyrics sung with great verve by Jordan. Their music came to be called "jump jive," and it was the direct ancestor of the R & B that emerged in the early 1950s. The group had its first hit in 1942 with "I'm Gonna Leave You on the Outskirts of Town." It was the start of an impressive run of 57 hits on the "race charts," as black music was then referred to, including 18 number-one hits. Such songs as "Choo Choo Ch'

Boogie" and "Ain't Nobody Here But Us Chickens" (both 1946) earned Jordan the title "king of the juke boxes." A number of his hits also crossed over to the pop charts, making him one of the first African-American recording artists to reach a wide white audience.

Jordan's popularity hit its peak during World War II and immediately after, when he and his group made a number of short musical films. They also appeared in several feature-length Hollywood movie musicals including *Follow the Boys* (1944) and *Swing Parade of 1946*.

Jordan had his last hit in 1951 and formed a big band, a bad decision at a time when the big band era was ending. Three years later he left Decca Records for the Aladdin label in Los Angeles, California, but his jive novelty songs were now considered passé. Ironically, Jordan's career faded just as the music he championed—R & B—was becoming popular. Bill Haley and the Comets, one of the first rock 'n' roll bands, owed much to Jordan's delivery and shuffle beat, as Haley himself readily admitted. CHUCK BERRY was another early rocker who claims Jordan was his model and inspiration.

Jordan continued to make records, hoping for the big comeback that never came. He died, all but forgotten, on February 4, 1975, of a heart attack in Los Angeles. Since then, his music and his reputation have been on the rise. He was inducted posthumously into the Rock and Roll Hall of Fame in 1987 as an early influence. A Broadway revue, *Five Guys Named Moe* (1992), the title of one of his songs, was a hit. It was a musical tribute to Jordan, even though his name was not mentioned once in the show.

Further Reading

Chilton, John. *Let the Good Times Roll: The Story of Louis Jordan and His Music.* Ann Arbor: University of Michigan Press, 1997.

Rock and Roll Hall of Fame Inductees. "Louis Jordan." Rock and Roll Hall of Fame and Museum Web site. Available online. URL: http://www.rockhall.com/inductee/louis-jordan. Downloaded on February 7, 2009.

Further Listening

Essential Collection. West End, 2 CDs, 2007.

Further Viewing

Hey Everybody—It's Louis Jordan and His Tympany Five. Storyville Films, DVD, 2007.

K

King, B. B.
(Riley B. King)
(1925–   ) *blues singer, guitarist, songwriter*

One of the greatest practitioners of urban blues, whose expressive guitar work is as distinctive as his achingly pleading vocals, B. B. King did not reach full stardom until well into his 40s.

He was born Riley B. King in Itta Bena, Mississippi, on a cotton plantation on September 16, 1925. His parents, who were tenant farmers, separated when he was four. He lived with his churchgoing mother, who would not allow blues music in her home and made him sing in the church choir. She died when King was nine, and he went to work full time in the cotton fields. He moved in with his father, Albert, when he was 14 and a year later bought his first guitar for eight dollars. During World War II, King served in a black army unit, where he learned about the blues listening to other black soldiers play and sing.

After his discharge, he performed the blues on street corners for money but kept his doings a secret from his disapproving family. In 1947, he hitchhiked to Memphis, Tennessee, where he got a job singing commercials on WDIA, the first American radio station to play all-black music. King soon got his own radio show and became a disc jockey, often singing along with the blues records he played. He began to perform in local clubs, billing himself as "Riley King, the Blues Boy from Beale Street." Later he shortened this to Blues Boy and finally, "B. B." One night King got into a fight over a woman named Lucille. A fire broke out during the fight and his guitar was nearly destroyed. After that, he called all his guitars Lucille and does so to this day.

Sam Phillips, a radio engineer, heard him play and was inspired to open a studio to record black blues artists. King was one of the first musicians Phillips recorded, although his records were released on the Modern label out of Los Angeles, California. Phillips's studio was later renamed Sun Studios, and he would be the first to record Elvis Presley and other white rock singers. His recording of "Three O'Clock Blues" (1951) became King's first rhythm and blues (R & B) hit. King had many more hits on Modern through the 1950s. Yet his electric guitar blues was too sophisticated to appeal to the folk fans who made stars out of more traditional bluesmen such as JOHN LEE HOOKER. King remained little known outside of the black community until the early 1960s.

In 1963, he began recording for his first major record label, ABC-Paramount, and put out a number of highly successful albums. When the Beatles and other British rock groups came to America in 1964, they praised King as a major influence on their music. The 39-year-old blues singer suddenly became the idol of legions of young rock listeners.

In 1970, King had his biggest pop hit, "The Thrill Is Gone," which earned him his first Grammy Award for best R & B vocal performance, male. He won two more Grammys in 1981 for best ethnic or traditional recording and in 1983 for best traditional blues recording. His best-selling album *Live at Cook County Jail* (1971) has been called by *Rolling Stone* magazine one of the best live concert recordings ever made.

King toured extensively with his own band and in 1979 became the first blues musician to go on a major tour of the Soviet Union. He was inducted into the Rock and Roll Hall of Fame in 1987 and received Grammy's Lifetime Achievement Award in 1988. King has won a total of 15 Grammys as of 2009. He was the closing act at the 2008 Grammy Nominating Concert, performing with singer John Mayer.

The B. B. King Museum and Delta Interpretive Center, a $15 million museum, opened in September 2008 in his hometown of Indianola, Mississippi, in a building where King worked as a boy hauling cotton. His most recent album, *One Kind Favor*, released a month earlier, was called "one of the strongest studio sets of his career" by *Rolling Stone* magazine. When asked once about the future of his music, King replied, "As long as people have problems, the blues can never die."

Further Reading

King, B. B., with David Ritz. *Blues All around Me: The Autobiography of B. B. King.* New York: Harper Paperbacks, 1999.

McGee, David, and B. B. King. *B. B. King: There Is Always One More Time.* San Francisco: Backbeat Books, 2005.

Shirley, David. *Everyday I Sing the Blues: The Story of B. B. King.* Danbury, Conn.: Franklin Watts 1995, (YA).

Spillane, Stan. "At 83, B. B. King Still King of the road." *Connecticut Post,* September 25, 2008.

Further Listening

Live in Cook County Jail (1971). MCA, CD, 1998.

The Ultimate Collection. Geffen Records, CD, 2005.

Further Viewing

B. B. King: Live. Geffen Records, DVD, 2008.

Kitt, Eartha
(Eartha Mae Keith)
(1928–2008) *pop singer, actress*

With her exotic presence and seductive warbling, Eartha Kitt was one of the most distinctive performers of the 1950s, who gave new meaning to the term "sex kitten."

She was born Eartha Mae Keith on January 26, 1928, in North, South Carolina. She claimed that her father was the son of the owner of the farm where she was born and that he raped her mother. The woman she thought was her mother left Eartha and her half sister Pearl with a neighboring family who treated them poorly. In 1936, at age eight, Eartha moved to New York City, where she lived with an aunt, Mamie Kitt, who she later learned was her biological mother. Friction between the two eventually drove her to move out, quit school, and work for a time as a seamstress.

One day she auditioned for the KATHERINE DUNHAM Dance School and was accepted on a scholarship. By age 18, Kitt was touring professionally with Dunham's dance troupe throughout the United States, Latin America, and Europe. She left the troupe in Paris, France, in 1950 and began to sing in nightclubs. Her exotic looks and singing style made her popular in Europe. Actor-director-producer Orson Welles called her "the most exciting woman in the world" and cast her as Helen of Troy in his European production of *Doctor Faustus* (1951).

Kitt soon returned to the United States and became an overnight sensation singing the world-weary novelty song "Monotonous" in the Broadway

The ultimate "sex kitten" of the 1950s, Eartha Kitt was a unique talent and an outspoken personality. *(Photo courtesy of Showtime Archives, Toronto)*

musical revue *New Faces of 1952*. She became a star of cabarets and clubs across the country and began a successful recording career. In the hit Christmas novelty "Santa Baby" (1954), she turned Santa Claus into her own personal sugar daddy.

Kitt appeared in several movies, including *The Accused* (1957) and *St. Louis Blues* (1958) opposite NAT KING COLE. But her brittle, intense acting made her less than appealing on the big screen and she never became a movie star. Her 1960 marriage to William McDonald ended in divorce, but produced a daughter, Kitt McDonald, who later became her mother's manager. In the mid-1960s Eartha Kitt had some success on television playing the campy villain Catwoman on the series *Batman* (1966–68).

Always outspoken and politically liberal, Kitt publicly criticized the Vietnam War in the pres-

ence of First Lady Lady Bird Johnson at a White House luncheon in 1968. After that, her club dates in the United States dried up and she came under investigation by the Federal Bureau of Investigation (FBI) and the Central Intelligence Agency (CIA). For nearly a decade, she lived and worked mostly in Europe.

A well-known activist and charity worker, Eartha Kitt was a spokesperson for the United Nations Children's Fund (UNICEF) and established the Eartha Kitt Performing Arts Scholarship for needy dance students at Benedict College in South Carolina.

Kitt finally returned to Broadway triumphantly in the all-black musical *Timbuktu* (1978). She was nominated for a Tony Award as best actress in a musical and was invited back to the White House during the show's run in Washington, D.C. President Jimmy Carter greeted her with the words, "Welcome home, Eartha."

She recorded several new albums in the 1980s and was nominated for a Grammy Award in 1995 for the album *Back in Business*. She was the voice of Yzma in the Disney animated film *The Emperor's New Groove* (2000) and won an Emmy for a spin-off TV series *The Emperor's New School*. In 2003, she starred as Madame Zeroni in the film adaptation of the novel *Holes*.

She returned to Broadway several times, replacing Chita Rivera in the musical *Nine* in 2003. Kitt performed regularly on the New York cabaret circuit until the last year of her life. She died on December 25, 2008, of colon cancer at age 81.

Further Reading

Hoerburger, Rob. "Eartha Kitt, A Performer Who Seduced Audiences, Dies at 81." *New York Times*, December 26, 2008, Obituaries, p. A37.

Kitt, Eartha. *I'm Still Here: Confessions of a Sex Kitten.* Fort Lee, N.J.: Barricade Books, 1993.

Further Listening

The Collection. EMI Gold, CD, 2006.

Further Viewing

Most Exciting Woman in the World. Kultur Video, VHS, 1994.

New Faces (1954). Reel Enterprises, DVD, 2006.

Knight, Gladys
(1944–   ) *R & B singer*

One of the most successful female soul singers of the 1960s and 1970s, Gladys Knight, unlike most other black divas, achieved fame as the lead singer of a vocal group made up of family members.

She was born in Atlanta, Georgia, on May 28, 1944. Her parents, Merald and Elizabeth Knight, were both gospel singers in the Wings Over Jordan Choir. She made her public debut as a gospel singer at age four and made her first tour through Florida and Alabama as a gospel singer when she was five. Two years later, Knight won the grand prize of $2,000 on television's *Ted Mack's Original Amateur Hour.*

But the real turning point for her was at a birthday party given for her brother Merald in the late 1950s. She sang with Merald, a sister, and two cousins at the party. They were so good that another cousin, James Wood, offered to become their manager if they went professional. With Knight singing lead, the group called themselves the Pips, after Wood's nickname, Pip. After singing together for a couple of years, they landed a recording contract with Vee-Jay Records in 1961. Their first hit single was a doo-wop ballad, "Every Beat of My Heart" (1961), followed by the more upbeat "Letter Full of Tears" (1962).

The group didn't find stardom, however, until they signed with Motown Records of Detroit, Michigan, in 1966. Knight's gritty gospel voice backed by the smooth professionalism of the Pips brought them many hits at Motown. One of their first and biggest records was the pounding dance floor favorite, "I Heard It through the Grapevine" (1968), which would become an even bigger hit a year later for another Motown artist, MARVIN GAYE. In the early 1970s, the Pips developed a more sophisticated sound in two of their biggest Motown hits, "If I Were Your Woman" (1971) and "Neither One of Us (Wants to Be the First to Say Good-bye)" (1972).

In 1973, they left Motown and signed to the Buddah label. Here they recorded the song most closely identified with them to this day, "Midnight Train to Georgia" (1973), their first and only number-one pop hit. It won them their first of two Grammy Awards for best rhythm & blues (R & B) vocal performance by a duo, group or chorus.

Gladys Knight and the Pips had reached the pinnacle of pop success, but by the end of the 1970s their careers took a nosedive. Inferior albums failed to sell. The group got into an ugly fight with Buddah over unpaid royalties. A movie, *Pipe Dreams,* meant to be a star vehicle for Knight and in which she invested her own money, proved a disaster. Because the group had been around for so long, people were starting to derisively call them "Gladys Knight and the Fossils."

But these veterans proved they could change with the times. They updated their sound in their third album for Columbia Records, *Visions* (1982). It became a best-seller, producing the hit single "Save the Overtime for Me." While remaining part of the group, Knight ventured out on her own, singing with DIONNE WARWICK, STEVIE WONDER, and Elton John on the gold record, "That's What Friends Are For" (1986). Proceeds from the singles benefited the American Foundation for Acquired Immune Deficiency Syndrome (AIDS). In 1988, Gladys Knight and the Pips had their first top-20 single in a decade, "Love Overboard."

More recently the Pips have retired from performing, and Knight has continued as a solo act. While her voice is as good as ever, in recent years she has sung mostly middle-of-the-road adult contemporary music. Never the most dynamic or charismatic of her contemporaries, she has rarely let her audience down. As rock critic Paul Evans writes, she is "the most dependable of soul divas—

she's neither a visionary, nor a truly distinctive stylist, but consistently, she delivers."

Gladys Knight and the Pips were inducted into the Rock and Roll Hall of Fame in 1996. She joined the Mormon Church in 1997 and directs the choir Saints Unified Voices, which won a Grammy in 2006 for their first album, *One Voice*.

Further Reading

Knight, Gladys. *Between Each Line of Pain and Glory: My Life Story*. New York: Hyperion, 1998.

Rock and Roll Hall of Fame Inductees. "Gladys Knight and the Pips." The Rock and Roll Hall of Fame and Museum Web site. Available online. URL: http://www.rockhall.com/inductee/gladys-knight-and-the-pips. Downloaded on February 7, 2009.

Further Listening

Gold. Hip-O Records, 2 CDs, 2006.

Knowles, Beyoncé

(Beyoncé)

(1981–) *R & B singer, songwriter, actress, record producer*

One of the most visible and popular R & B singers working today, Beyoncé Knowles is equally well known for her glamorous looks, her sponsorships, and her film roles.

She was born Beyoncé Giselle Knowles on September 4, 1981, in Houston, Texas. Her father, Matthew, was a medical equipment salesman before becoming a successful music group manager. Her mother, Tina, a Creole of African-American, French, and Native American heritage, is a hairdresser and costume designer. Beyoncé's gift of song was first recognized when her dance instructor began humming a tune and she finished it, hitting high-pitched notes. A shy girl, she entered her first talent show at age seven, singing John Lennon's "Imagine" and winning with a standing ovation. She attended the High School for the Performing and Visual Arts in Houston for

a time and was soloist in her church choir for two years.

At age eight, she auditioned and became a part of a new singing group, Girls' Tyme, that would eventually become Destiny's Child. The trio competed on the television show *Star Search* but lost owing to poor material. It would be the first of many disappointments for the group. Destiny's Child, which acquired its new name in 1993, rehearsed in Beyoncé's mother's salon and group members' backyards. A contract with Elektra Records went nowhere, and until 1997, the group sang on the road as an opening act for bigger R & B artists. The group finally made its recording debut with the song "Killing Time" on the soundtrack of the film *Men in Black* (1997). Their debut album, *Destiny's Child*, followed the next year. The track "No, No, No" went on to become their first hit single. Real fame came with the release of their second album, *The Writing's on the Wall* (1999), which has sold more than 7 million copies and produced the Grammy-winning single "Say My Name." Lead singer for the group, Knowles went out on her own while still a group member. In 2003, she produced her first solo album, *Dangerously in Love*, which became one of the biggest selling albums of the year. The album earned her five Grammys in 2004. Destiny's Child, which had been experiencing problems for some time, disbanded in 2005.

By now, Beyoncé was a superstar with her own family fashion line, House of Dereon, and endorsement deals with such sponsors as Pepsi and the cosmetics company L'Oreal. In 2006, she moved from small film roles to starring roles in *The Pink Panther* and *Dreamgirls*, for which she received three Golden Globe nominations and played opposite EDDIE MURPHY, JENNIFER HUDSON, and JAMIE FOXX. Her second solo album, *B'Day* (2006), produced two number-one singles in the United Kingdom, one of which, "Beautiful Liar," was a duet with Colombian-born pop singer Shakira. In 2008, Beyoncé won her third Golden Globe nomination for her portrayal of pioneering R & B singer

Etta James in the film *Cadillac Records,* directed by Darnell Martin. Her third solo album, *I Am . . . Sasha Fierce,* released in November 2008, has produced another number-one hit, "Single Ladies (Put a Ring on It)."

After years of being in a relationship with rapper Jay-Z, Beyoncé married him in April 2008. Extremely private about her personal life, she rarely talks about her marriage. "I know it's not a secret," she said in a 2008 interview, "but I like keeping that part of my life for me." Her younger sister Solange, also a singer, has recently released her debut album. On January 20, 2009, Knowles performed "At Last" in honor of President Barack and First Lady Michelle Obama at the Neighborhood Inaugural Ball. In 2010, Beyoncé won a record six Grammys, including Song of the Year and Best Female Pop and Best Female R&B Vocal Performance.

Further Reading

Hodgson, Nicola. *Beyoncé Knowles.* Chicago: Raintree, 2005 (YA).

Knowles, Beyoncé, Kelly Ronald, and Michelle Williams. *Soul Survivors: The Official Autobiography of Destiny's Child.* New York: HarperEntertainment, 2002.

Ogunnaike, Lola. "Mrs. Irreplaceable." *USA Weekend,* December 5–7, 2008, pp. 6–7.

Waters, Rosa. *Beyoncé.* Hip Hop. Broomall, Pa.: Mason Crest Publishers, 2007 (YA).

Further Listening

I Am . . . Sasha Fierce. Sony, 2 CDs, 2008.

Dangerously in Love. Sony, CD, 2003.

Further Viewing

The Beyoncé Experience—Live! (2007). Sony, DVD, 2007.

Dreamgirls (2006). DreamWorks Home Entertainment, DVD, 2007.

L

LaBelle, Patti
(Patricia Louise Holt, Patricia Louise Holte)
(1944–) *R & B singer, songwriter*

One of the true survivors of soul music, Patti LaBelle has been belting out rhythm and blues for four decades in a career with more highs and lows than a weather map.

She was born Patricia Louise Holt, or Holte, on May 24, 1944, in Philadelphia, Pennsylvania, and was an extremely shy child. She would stay in the house and sing in front of the mirror rather than go outside and play with the other children. She soon found, however, that singing in public built up her confidence and helped her to overcome her inferiority complex. In high school she adopted the name LaBelle and formed a singing group, the Ordettes, which later became the Bluebelles. The other members were Nona Hendryx, Sarah Dash, and Cindy Birdsong, who would later leave to become a member of the Motown girl group the Supremes.

The Bluebelles signed with Newtown Records and in 1962 had their first hit, the irrepressible "I Sold My Heart to the Junkman." Rumors persist to this day that the record was actually made by another group, the Starlets. With LaBelle's powerhouse lead, the Bluebelles became one of the grittiest of the girl groups of the early 1960s and scored several more hits with their impassioned versions of "Down the Aisle" (1963) and "You'll Never Walk Alone" (1964). After 1966, they would not have another hit for nine years.

The group turned to singing backup to such major artists as Jerry Butler and later Laura Nyro. In 1967, LaBelle updated the look and sound of the group and renamed it LaBelle. By the 1970s, LaBelle were appearing in space-age costumes and singing their own brand of funk rock but to little avail. Then, in 1974, their album *Nightbirds* became a best seller and produced the hit single "Lady Marmalade," a down-and-dirty dance floor favorite that they introduced in a concert at the Metropolitan Opera House in New York City. They were the first African-American act to perform at this legendary venue. "Lady Marmalade" went straight to number one on the pop charts. The song, about a New Orleans prostitute, contained the memorable line, "Voulez-vous coucher avec moi ce soir?" which in English means: "Will you sleep with me tonight?" LaBelle claims she didn't know the English meaning when they recorded the song. "I just knew it sounded cute," she says. "Soon after that we found out, but we said, well, let's keep it anyway."

Despite their smash success, LaBelle had only one more hit single before Hendryx walked out and the group disbanded in 1977. Patti LaBelle wasn't sure what to do next. "I didn't think I could go out there by myself," she said in an interview,

After two decades of singing lead for a group, Patti LaBelle found stardom as a solo act. *(AP Photo/Kim D. Johnson)*

"because I wouldn't have anybody to blame if things went wrong."

She recorded several solo albums without attracting much attention and in 1982 costarred with singer AL GREEN in a Broadway revival of the black musical *Your Arms Too Short to Box with God.* LaBelle signed with the Philly International record label in 1983. The smooth sophisticated sound of Philly International was a perfect match for LaBelle's over-the-top vocals. Her albums started selling, and in 1985, "New Attitude" from the soundtrack of the EDDIE MURPHY movie *Beverly Hills Cop* became her first top-20 hit in a decade. It was followed a year later by a chart-topping romantic duet, "On My Own" with Michael McDonald, formerly of the rock group the Doobie Brothers. Since then, Patti LaBelle has emerged, along with TINA TURNER, as one of soul music's mature and seemingly ageless divas. Her 1996 memoir, *Don't Block the Blessings,* became a best seller.

LaBelle's signature song "Lady Marmalade" again reached number one in the summer of 2001 when sung by Christina Aguilera, Mya, Pink, and Lil' Kim. Patti LaBelle couldn't have been happier. "Whenever I hear it," she says, "I get a glow."

LaBelle's album *Timeless Journey* (2004) was her biggest-selling recording in 18 years, and *The Gospel According to Patti LaBelle* (2006) shot to number one on the gospel charts. She reunited with Labelle on the album *Back to Now* (2008), and the group went on a reunion tour.

MARY J. BLIGE has called LaBelle "the diva of all divas and the voice touched and blessed by God."

Further Reading

Ankeny, Jason. "Patti LaBelle." The Allmusic Web site. Available online. URL: http://allmusic.com/cg/amg.dll?p=amg&sql=11:3ifwxqe5ldde. Downloaded on February 13, 2009.

LaBelle, Patti, with Laura B. Randolph. *Don't Block the Blessings: Revelations of a Lifetime.* New York: Berkeley, 1998.

Further Listening

The Essential Patti LaBelle. Sony Legacy, 2 CDs, 2008.

Patti LaBelle and the Bluebelles: Golden Classics. Collectable Records, CD, 1993.

Further Viewing

The Best of Patti LaBelle DVD Collection. Universal Music Group, DVD, 2004.

Leadbelly

(Huddie Ledbetter)
(ca. 1885–1949) *folk and blues singer, songwriter, guitarist*

A powerful blues singer who wrote some of the most enduring songs of the modern folk movement, Leadbelly and his music might never have become known to the world if not for a chance meeting with a musicologist in a Louisiana prison.

He was born Huddie Ledbetter sometime around 1885 in Mooringsport, Louisiana. The exact date of his birth is unknown. His heritage was part black and part Cherokee Indian. He learned to sing from his mother, Sally, who led a church choir. Ledbetter left school at 15 to work with his father, Wes, on the family farm and soon was excelling as a singer and guitarist. While still in his teens, he worked summers on farms and winters playing guitar and singing in the bars and brothels of Dallas, Texas. His vast repertoire of songs included blues, cowboy songs, folk songs, and spirituals.

A big, strong man, Leadbelly, nicknamed for his powerful voice, also had a powerful temper. That and his reputation as a womanizer soon got him into trouble. He was arrested in 1917 for assault after attacking a woman who rejected him and served a year on a chain gang before escaping. He was caught and charged again with assault. After serving five years of his sentence, he was pardoned by the governor of Louisiana after singing him a song he wrote pleading for mercy.

Leadbelly got a steady job at an oil refinery and continued to perform his music. But again his violent temper got the better of him. In 1930, he was arrested for assaulting five men with intent to kill and sentenced to 10 years in Louisiana's Angola Penitentiary. In 1933, musicologist John Lomax and his son Alan were visiting southern prisons to record and collect authentic folk and prison songs for the Library of Congress. The Lomaxs heard Leadbelly singing his own songs and were overwhelmed by his talent. Their support helped earn him a pardon and they brought him to New York City, where he worked as John Lomax's chauffeur and performed his music in clubs, especially in the Greenwich Village area.

Despite one more brief term in jail for assault, Leadbelly spent most of the remaining 15 years of his life bringing his music to a wider audience of whites. He gained the friendship of such folk singers as Woody Guthrie and Pete Seeger and joined Guthrie, SONNY TERRY, and Brownie McGhee in the Headline Singers. Leadbelly recorded many of his own songs, including the classics "Rock Island Line," "Cotton Fields," and "The Midnight Special." Unfortunately, music publishers refused to publish his songs because they did not think they were commercial enough.

Leadbelly died of Lou Gehrig's disease on December 6, 1949, in New York City. Months later, the Weavers, a folk group that included Pete Seeger, had a number-one pop hit with his song "Goodnight, Irene." "It's a pure tragedy he didn't live another six months, because all his dreams as a performer would have come true," Seeger said many years later.

Black filmmaker Gordon Parks made biopic *Leadbelly* in 1976. Leadbelly was inducted into the Rock and Roll Hall of Fame as an early influence in 1988.

Further Reading

Jess, Tyehimba. *Lead Belly: A Life in Pictures.* London: Steidl, 2007.

Wolfe, Charles, and Kip Lornell. *The Life and Legend of Leadbelly.* New York: Da Capo Press, 1999.

Further Listening

Important Recordings 1934–1949. JSP Records, CD box set, 2006.

Further Viewing

A Vision Shared—A Tribute to Woody Guthrie and Leadbelly (1991). Sony Music Entertainment, VHS/DVD, 1998/2000.

Lee, Canada
(Leonard Lionel Cornelius Canegata)
(1907–1952) *actor*

A gifted actor of stage and screen, Canada Lee's career was tragically cut short during the Communist witch-hunt of the post–World War II years.

He was born Leonard Lionel Cornelius Canegata on March 3, 1907, in the Harlem section of New York City, to James and Lydia Canegata. Politician Adam Clayton Powell, Jr., was one of his childhood friends. Canegata ran away from home at age 14 to Saratoga, New York, with dreams of becoming a race jockey. Instead he became a boxer and went on to win the national amateur lightweight title. He turned professional in 1926 and changed his name to Canada Lee. He had married Juanita Waller the previous year.

For a time he was a leading contender for the welterweight championship, but a detached retina left one eye blind and forced him to retire from the ring in 1933. Lee began acting in plays at the Harlem Young Men's Christian Association (YMCA) in the mid-1930s. He received critical praise for his portrayal of Banquo in the Federal Theater's all-Negro production of Shakespeare's *Macbeth* in 1936.

Soon he was starring on Broadway in a string of successes. He played the title role in Shakespeare's *Othello*; Ben Chaplin, a black boxer, in *Body and Soul*; and Bigger Thomas, the protagonist of *Native Son*, the stage adaptation of Richard Wright's best-selling novel.

Lee moved to Hollywood to act in films in the late 1930s. He was memorable as one of the survivors of a Nazi attack adrift at sea during World War II in Alfred Hitchcock's *Lifeboat* (1944) and reprised the role of boxer Ben Chaplin in the film version of *Body and Soul* (1947). His last screen appearance was in the film adaptation of another classic novel, South African Alan Paton's *Cry, the Beloved Country* (1951), which dealt with life under apartheid. His costar was a young SIDNEY POITIER.

Lee was outspoken about the rights of African Americans and this got him into trouble with the House Committee on Un-American Activities (HUAC) in the early 1950s. He was accused of being a Communist for his liberal views and was ordered to testify before HUAC. When he refused to do so, he was blacklisted and could not find work in film or television. Lee publicly denied ever being a member of the Communist Party but continued to refuse to testify, knowing he would be expected to "name names" of other performers who might be Communists or Communist sympathizers.

"I can't take it anymore," he wrote to Walter White of the National Association for the Advancement of Colored People (NAACP) in April 1952. "I am going to get a shoeshine box and sit outside the Astor Theatre. My picture [*Cry, the Beloved Country*] is playing to capacity audiences and, my God, I can't get one day's work."

About a month later, on May 9, 1952, Canada Lee, age 45, died of a heart attack. Those who knew him best believed the stress he was under was responsible for his death. A fine actor, who exuded a quiet strength in all his roles, Lee's greatest role may have been the one he courageously played in real life. His son, Carl Lee (1926–86), was also a film actor.

Further Reading
"Canada Lee." The Internet Movie Database. Available online. URL: http://imdb.com/name/nm0496938/. Downloaded on February 7, 2009.
Smith, Mona Z. *Becoming Something: The Story of Canada Lee.* London: Faber & Faber, 2005.

Further Viewing
Body and Soul (1947). Republic Pictures, DVD, 2001.
Lifeboat (1944). Fox, DVD, 2005.

Lewis, Henry
(1932–1996) *orchestra conductor, classical musician*

The first African American to become the regular conductor of a major American symphony orchestra, Henry Lewis enjoyed a career as a musician and conductor that spanned nearly half a century.

He was born on October 16, 1932, in Los Angeles, California. His father, Henry, Sr., was an auto and real-estate dealer, and his mother, Josephine, was an administrative nurse. He began piano lessons at age five and later learned to play the clarinet, double bass, and other stringed instruments. At 16, Lewis was hired as a double-bassist with the Los Angeles Philharmonic (LAP) where he stayed for six years. He joined the army in 1955, where he played with, and then conducted, the Seventh Army Symphony. After his service stint, Lewis returned to the LAP and was appointed an assistant conductor in 1961 under head conductor Zubin Mehta. During this time, he also founded and directed the String Society of Los Angeles, also known as the Los Angeles Chamber Orchestra. He left the LAP in 1965 and served as guest conductor with a number of major orchestras including the Chicago Symphony and the London Symphony. In addition, he briefly served as a musical director of the Los Angeles Opera Company in 1965.

Lewis was invited in 1968 to become director of the New Jersey Symphony in the primarily black city of Newark. At the time, the group was a modest, community ensemble compromised of part-time musicians. Through hard work and discipline,

Lewis transformed it into a major, nationally recognized orchestra that performed more than 100 concerts each year.

Lewis took the New Jersey Symphony into ghetto areas to perform in neighborhoods largely destroyed by the riots of 1968. He attracted black families to concerts with low-priced tickets and special youth programs. "I tell the people that if they want to break in with applause after an exciting movement, that's fine," he said in an interview in the *New York Times.*

In 1972, Lewis made his first appearance as a guest conductor with the Metropolitan Opera in New York City conducting the opera *La Bohème.* After eight years as conductor and musical director, Lewis left the New Jersey Symphony in 1976 to take on two new jobs—musical director of the Opera-Music Theatre Institute of New Jersey and conductor of the Netherlands Radio Orchestra.

He continued to travel the world as a guest conductor until his death from a heart attack at age 63 on January 26, 1996. Lewis was married to opera singer Marilyn Horne from 1960 to 1979. She called him her "teacher and right hand." Together they recorded a number of operas.

Further Reading

"Henry Lewis." *Current Biography Yearbook 1973.* New York: H. W. Wilson, 1974.

Horne, Marilyn. *Marilyn Horne, My Life.* New York: Atheneum Books, 1984.

McFadden, Robert D. "Henry Lewis, Conductor Who Broke Racial Barriers at U.S. Orchestra Is Dead at 63." *New York Times,* January 29, 1996 Obituaries.

Conductor Henry Lewis transformed the New Jersey Symphony from an amateur community ensemble into a nationally recognized orchestra. *(Photofest)*

Lewis, John

(1920–2001) *jazz pianist, bandleader, composer*

The driving force behind the longest-running small ensemble in jazz history, John Lewis succeeded in making jazz respectable by bringing it out of smoky clubs and into concert halls.

He was born on May 3, 1920, in La Grange, Illinois, and grew up in Albuquerque, New Mexico. He started playing the piano at seven and studied both music and anthropology at the University of New Mexico. Lewis served in the army during World War II and was stationed in Europe. There he met Kenny Clarke, a drummer of the new bebop school of jazz. Clarke encouraged him to move to New York, where Clarke introduced him to trumpeter and bandleader DIZZY GILLESPIE. Gillespie used Lewis's arrangements in his new big band and hired him as his pianist. Over the next few years Lewis played with such great jazz performers as saxophonists CHARLIE PARKER and Lester Young and vocalist ELLA FITZGERALD.

In 1952, Lewis formed a quartet with Clarke, bassist Percy Heath, and vibraphonist Milt Jackson. At first, they called themselves the Milt Jackson Quartet but soon changed their name to the Modern Jazz Quartet. They were "modern" in that they played the complex, improvisational bebop jazz that Gillespie and Parker championed a few years earlier. Their style, however, was less raucous than most bebop music. It was often quiet and understated, with a classical elegance that reflected Lewis's training and interests.

Lewis felt jazz was as artistically valid as classical music. He booked the M.J.Q., as they came to be called, into as many concert halls as possible and insisted members wear tuxedos when they performed. The group drew in many listeners who had not previously listened to jazz. Lewis wrote most of their music, and among his best-known compositions are "Two Degrees East, Three Degrees West" and "Django," a moving tribute to the gypsy guitarist Django Reinhardt. Lewis always left room in his music for improvisation. "For me," he said in a 1999 interview, "improvisation is one of the most exciting parts of making music. You're not confined. If you have enough imagination, you don't have to repeat." Lewis's piano-playing was noted for its light touch, classical balance, and dramatic use of silences.

Except for a seven-year hiatus, the Modern Jazz Quartet performed and recorded from 1953 to the late 1990s. When Connie Kay, who replaced Clarke in 1955, died in 1994, bassist Heath's brother Albert replaced him. Milt Jackson's death in 1999 effectively ended the longest-running act in jazz.

All the group's members pursued separate careers during their years together, and Lewis was perhaps the busiest. He directed the Monterey Jazz Festival from 1958 to 1982. In the early 1960s, he led Orchestra U.S.A., an ensemble that pioneered "third stream music," a mixture of jazz and classical music. One of his most lasting contributions to jazz was helping to found the Lenox School of Jazz in Massachusetts in the late 1950s, perhaps the first institute in the world completely devoted to jazz.

One of modern jazz's greatest practitioners and supporters, John Lewis died on March 29, 2001.

Further Reading

Balliett, Whitney. *American Musicians II: Seventy-One Portraits in Jazz.* Jackson: University of Mississippi Press, 2006.

Doerschuk, Robert L. *88: The Giants of Jazz Piano.* San Francisco, Calif.: Backbeat Books, 2001.

Keepnews, Peter. "John Lewis, 80, Pianist, Composer and Creator of the Modern Jazz Quartet, Dies." *New York Times* March 31, 2001, Obituaries, p. B9.

Further Listening

The Complete Modern Jazz Quartet Prestige & Pablo Recording. Prestige, CD box set, 2003.

The Wonderful World of Jazz/Evolution (solo piano album). Collectables Records, 2 CDs, 2007.

Further Viewing

Jazz, Part 8: Risk. Paramount Home Video, VHS/DVD, 2004.

The Modern Jazz Quartet: 35th Anniversary Tour (1984). TDK DVD Video, DVD, 2005.

Little Richard

(Richard Wayne Penniman, "Georgia Peach,"
"The Bronze Liberace")
(1932–   ) *rock and R & B singer, pianist,
songwriter, actor*

One of the founding fathers of rock 'n' roll, Little Richard's flamboyant stage presence and driving music make him one of rock's first and greatest icons.

He was born Richard Wayne Penniman on December 5, 1932, in Macon, Georgia, one of 12 children. His father, Bud, was a devout Seventh-Day Adventist and a bartender who sold bootleg whiskey on the side. He married Richard's mother, Leva Mae, when she was 14. Richard's grandfather and two uncles were preachers. His nickname had little to do with his height, which was above aver-

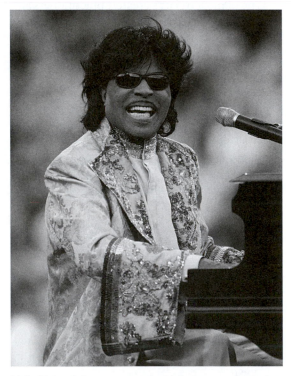

Little Richard demonstrates the high-octane energy that made him one of rock's most exciting performers. *(AP Photo/Mark Humphrey)*

age. "Since I was the middle child in my family it was always 'lil Richard,'" he explained once. "After a while I was hearing it so much that it became a part of me."

Another part of Little Richard was his homosexuality, which exhibited itself at an early age. His family frowned on his sexual orientation as well as the rhythm and blues (R & B) music he liked and threw him out of the house at age 13. He eventually was taken in by a white couple, Ann and Johnny Johnson, who ran a local nightspot, the Tick Tock Club. The Johnsons took care of Richard and let him perform his R & B music in the club. He was forever grateful to the family and wrote the song "Miss Ann" (1957) in Ann Johnson's honor.

At 19, Little Richard entered a talent contest sponsored by RCA Records and won a recording contract. He recorded a number of songs, but they were considered too derivative of other artists and went nowhere. He next recorded for Peacock, a small label in Houston, Texas, in 1954 and again met with no success. The following year he tried his luck with Los Angeles-based Specialty Records. Specialty producer Robert "Bumps" Blackwell thought Richard had talent but needed the right atmosphere to bring it out. Blackwell took him to New Orleans to record with a group of veteran R & B musicians. The session, to Blackwell's disappointment, produced nothing special, until Richard decided to try a nonsense song he had cowritten with the outrageous opening line "A Wop Wop Alu Bop a Wop Bam Boom!" When Blackwell heard the energy and pure joy of "Tutti Frutti," he knew they had a hit. Once recorded, "Tutti Frutti" shot into the top 20 and sold more than a million copies. It was quickly recognized as one of the first classic anthems of rock 'n' roll.

With the same crack musicians and his own pounding piano and inimitable frenetic vocals, Little Richard proceeded to turn out a string of rock classics over the next year and a half that included his biggest hit, "Long Tall Sally," as well as "Rip It Up," "Lucille," "Jenny, Jenny," and

"Good Golly, Miss Molly." He performed in three rock 'n' roll movies, including what is considered one of the best of the genre, *The Girl Can't Help It* (1956), in which he sang the title song and two others.

Then, in 1957, Richard's career came to a grinding halt. Torn between his music and homosexuality and the strict Christian religion he grew up with, he had a dramatic conversion. He enrolled in Oakwood Theological College in Huntsville, Alabama, and for the next six years recorded only gospel music. In 1961, he became an ordained minister of the Seventh-Day Adventist Church.

But rock 'n' roll was as much in his blood as religion, and Richard launched a comeback rock 'n' roll tour in Britain in late 1962. Among his biggest British fans was a new group called The Beatles, who would later adopt his signature high whoop on several of their hit records. Richard had a minor hit with "Bama Lama Bama Loo" (1964), but the wild style of rock he helped invent had gone out of style.

Richard continued to tour and tapped into the rock revival of the 1970s. He also recorded with such young white groups as Canned Heat and Bachman-Turner Overdrive. Then, in 1977, struggling with drug and alcohol abuse, he returned to evangelism and became a traveling Bible salesman. He recorded gospel music exclusively but, predictably, bounced back to rock in the 1980s. In 1986, he had a small role in the comedy *Down and Out in Beverly Hills* and recorded his last hit single to date, the movie's title song, "Great Gosh A'Mighty! (It's a Matter of Time)."

Little Richard continues to be a spokesperson for his music and era, appearing in concerts and frequently on television. He was among the first artists to be inducted into the Rock and Roll Hall of Fame in 1986 and received Grammy's Lifetime Achievement Award in 1993. In 2002, Little Richard received the National Association for the Advancement of Color People's (NAACP) Image Hall of Fame Award. He portrayed himself in the 1997 biographical film *Why Do Fools Fall in Love* about his friend and contemporary doo-wop singer FRANKIE LYMON. In 2000, Robert Townsend directed a made-for-TV biopic of his life through 1962, with Leon Robinson giving an Emmy-nominated performance as Richard. *Rolling Stone* magazine ranked Little Richard as number eight on its 2004 list of the 100 Greatest Artists of All Time.

Further Reading
The Rock and Roll Hall of Fame Inductees. "Little Richard." The Rock and Roll Hall of Fame and Museum Web site. Available online. URL: http://www.rockhall.com/inductee/little-richard. Downloaded on February 7, 2009.

White, Charles. *The Life and Times of Little Richard: The Authorized Biography*. New York: Da Capo Press, 2003.

Further Listening
Very Best of Little Richard. Specialty, CD, 2008.

Further Viewing
Little Richard (2000). Live/Artisan, DVD, 2002.
Little Richard: Keep On Rockin' (1969). Pioneer Video, VHS/DVD, 1992/2002.

LL Cool J
(James Todd Smith, Ladies Love Cool James)
(1968–   ) *rap singer, actor*

One of the world's best-selling rap artists, LL Cool J is known for his blending of rap and pop that has gained him legions of pop fans while costing him much of his following in the rap world.

He was born James Todd Smith on August 16, 1968, in Queens, New York. He was drawn to rap at age nine, but got serious about it only when his grandfather bought him his own mixing table when he was 16. Cool, whose stage name stands for "Ladies Love Cool James," recorded tapes of his rapping and sent them to various record labels. Def Jam showed interest in his music and signed him to a contract in 1984. His first album, *Radio* (1985), established his rap sound and went platinum, selling 1 million copies. His next album, *Big and Deffer* (1987) produced the hit single and ballad "I Need You," that went to number one on the rhythm and blues (R & B) charts. His next hit, "Going Back to Cali" (1988) was from the soundtrack of the movie *Less Than Zero*. His increasing use of pop elements in his music earned Cool J harsh criticism from rap fans.

Cool J's next album, *Walking with a Panther* (1989) demonstrated a new maturity and a widening range of musical interests. He reached his greatest success with *Mama Said Knock You Out* (1990), which mixed warm love songs with some of his best upbeat hip-hop material. The album produced four hits including the title track and the top-10 tune "Around the Way Girl."

Cool J has followed the lead of other rap artists by also working as an actor. He played himself in the hop-hop film *Krush Groove* (1985) and starred in the NBC television situation comedy *In the House* (1995–98), playing opposite DEBBIE ALLEN. He was a cook who fights off a pack of super sharks in *Deep Blue Sea* (1999), a cop in *S.W.A.T.* (2003), and an actor playing a 19th-century British prime ministry in the satire *The Deal* (2008). In 2009, Cool J starred on *NCIS: Los Angeles* as Special Agent Sam Hanna.

His next two albums, *14 Shots to the Dome* (1993) and *Mr. Smith* (1995), were seen as less successful than *Mama Said Knock You Out,* but nevertheless sold well. Cool J has released five more studio albums to date, including his first number one on the *Billboard* charts, G.O.A.T. (2000), and *Exit 13* (2008), his last album for Def Jam. He lives with his wife and four children in Manhasset, New York.

Further Reading

LL Cool J, with Karen Hunter. *I Make My Own Rules.* New York: St. Martin's Press, 1998.
Murphy, John. *LL Cool J.* Hip Hop. Broomall, Pa.: Mason Crest Publishers, 2007 (YA).
Shekell, Dustin. *LL Cool J.* Hip Hop Stars. New York: Chelsea House, 2007 (YA).

Further Listening

All-World: Greatest Hits. Def Jam, CD, 1996.
Mama Said Knock You Out (1990). Def Jam, CD, 1994.

Further Viewing

Deep Blue Sea (1999). Warner Home Video, VHS/DVD, 1999.

Lymon, Frankie
(Franklin Lymon)
(1942–1968) *R & B singer, songwriter*

One of the most dynamic performers of the early rock era, Frankie Lymon was the first and, some would argue, the greatest of rock 'n' roll's "child stars."

He was born Franklin Lymon on September 30, 1942, in New York City. At age 13, while working in a grocery store, Lymon joined four older boys in the neighborhood in a doo-wop harmony vocal group called the Premieres. The group rehearsed on a tenement rooftop and sang on street corners to passersby for loose change. They soon changed their name to the Teenagers. Frankie, the lead singer and the youngest, had a vibrant high tenor full of irrepressible energy. Richard Barrett, leader of the doo-wop group the Valentines, heard them and brought them to the office of his recording label, Gee. They sang their song, "Why Do Fools Fall in Love," written by Lymon, for Gee president George Goldner, and he had them record it the next day. None of the group, including Lymon, could write music, so it was recorded without a written arrangement.

"Why Do Fools Fall in Love" was released in January 1956, and it shot to number one on the rhythm and blues (R & B) charts and number six on the pop charts. It sold more than 2 million copies worldwide. The Teenagers had four more hits that year, including "I Want You to Be My Girl," "I Promise to Remember," and "The ABC's of Love." They sang their song "I'm Not a Juvenile Delinquent" in the rock movie *Rock, Rock, Rock* (1956).

Lymon, despite the song title, *was* a bit of a delinquent, loved to party, and had plenty of adoring older girlfriends. In 1957, he left the Teenagers for a solo career. The move proved professionally fatal for both him and the group. The Teenagers continued to record but never had another hit record. Lymon scored with the oldie "Goody Goody" (1958), but then his career stalled. To make matters worse, his voice began to change and within two years he could no longer sing the high notes that made his plaintive tenor so distinctive. Discouraged, Lymon turned to drugs and became a heroin addict. To get money for drugs, in 1965 he sold all rights to "Why Do Fools Fall in Love" to a record executive for $1,500.

Lymon joined the army in 1966 and this straightened him out for a time. When he was discharged in 1968, Roulette Records set up a recording session for him. But by then he was back on heroin. On February 28, 1968, the day before his recording session, Lymon was found dead on the floor of his grandmother's apartment from a heroin overdose. He was 25 years old.

Although he died penniless, royalties for his music began to accrue, and in the early 1990s they became the center of a courtroom battle among three women who all claimed to have been married to Lymon at different times. The case became the subject of a 1998 film, *Why Do Fools Fall in Love,* which starred HALLE BERRY and Larenz Tate as Frankie Lymon.

Frankie Lymon and the Teenagers were inducted into the Rock and Roll Hall of Fame in 1993.

Further Reading

Groia, Philip. *They All Sang on the Corner: A Second Look at New York City's Rhythm and Blues Vocal Groups.* Port Jefferson, N.Y.: Phillie Dee Enterprises, 1983.

Rock and Roll Hall of Fame Inductees. "Frankie Lymon and the Teenagers." Rock and Roll Hall of Fame and Museum Web site. Available online. URL: http//www.rockhall.com/inductee/frankie-lymon-and-the-teenagers. Downloaded on February 7, 2009.

Further Listening

The Very Best of Frankie Lymon and the Teenagers. Rhino, CD, 1998.

Further Viewing

Rock, Rock, Rock (1956). A2ZCDS.com, DVD, 2009.

Why Do Fools Fall in Love (1998). Warner Home Video, VHS/DVD, 1999.

M

Mabley, Moms
(Loretta Mary Aiken, Jackie Mabley, Jackie Mayble)
(1897–1975) *comedian, actress*

The first successful African-American female stand-up comedian with a solo act, Moms Mabley had a 60-year career in show business that spanned everything from minstrel shows to television.

She was born Loretta Mary Aiken on March 19, 1897, in Brevard, North Carolina. The "funniest woman in the world," as she was known, had a childhood that was anything but funny. Her father, a volunteer firefighter, was killed when his fire truck overturned and exploded. A short time later she was raped by two men, one of them the town's white sheriff. She ran away at 16 to Cleveland, Ohio, where she lived for a time with a minister and his family. She changed her named to Jackie Mabley, after her boyfriend Jack Mabley, and decided to become a singer and dancer. She went on tour on the black vaudeville, or variety show, circuit and eventually worked her way to New York City. The other performers dubbed her "Moms" because she looked after them like a mother on the road.

Mabley developed a folksy act, sprinkled with ribald humor, all in the guise of a wise, old grandmother figure, which she based on her own grandmother. Her trademark costume included outlandish polka-dot dresses, floppy shoes, droopy socks, and an oversized hat. She carefully made herself up to appear as nonthreatening and endearing as possible, to get by in the male-dominated world of black vaudeville comics. The approach worked, and soon she was a popular favorite at Harlem's Cotton Club and later the Apollo Theater, where she was a mainstay for a quarter century.

In 1933, she appeared in her first film, *The Emperor Jones,* which starred PAUL ROBESON. She was billed as "Jackie Mayble." She appeared in a few more Hollywood films in the 1940s but didn't become a nationally recognized figure until the 1960s. Then her feisty personality and raucous humor made her a cult figure for a new generation. She was one of the stars of the television special *A Time for Laughter,* a celebration of black humor, and made appearances on *The Flip Wilson Show* (see FLIP WILSON) and other variety programs.

Mabley recorded many comedy albums, more than a dozen of which made the pop charts. She even had a top-40 single, a moving rendition of "Abraham, Martin and John" (1969), which had been a huge hit the previous year for the rock singer Dion.

In 1974, she had her first starring role in the film comedy *Amazing Grace,* playing a woman named Grace who takes on corrupt politicians in Baltimore, Maryland. Always keeping up with the times, she included political humor in her stand-up act and even made jokes about President Richard Nixon and Watergate. Another popular subject was young men, who she boasted she couldn't get enough of. In real life, Mabley was a lesbian.

Moms Mabley died on May 23, 1975, at age 78, one of the most beloved black entertainers of her time.

Further Reading

Dance, Daryl Cumber, ed. *Honey, Hush!: An Anthology of African American Women's Humor*. New York: W. W. Norton, 1998.

Williams, Elsie A. *The Humor of Jackie Moms Mabley: An African American Comedic Talent*. Studies in African American History and Culture. New York: Routledge, 1995.

Further Listening

Comedy Ain't Pretty. Varese Sarabande, CD, 2004.

Further Viewing

Amazing Grace (1974). MGM Home Video, DVD, 2001.

Killer Diller (1948). Alpha Home Entertainment, DVD, 2006.

Marsalis, Wynton

(1961–   ) *jazz trumpeter, composer, musical director, educator*

The first jazz composer to win a Pulitzer Prize for music, Wynton Marsalis has done more to keep jazz alive for future generations than any other living American.

He was born in New Orleans, Louisiana, on October 18, 1961, the second of six sons. Music, particularly jazz, was in his blood. His father, Ellis Marsalis, is a jazz musician and teacher, and his mother, Dolores, was a jazz singer. His brothers Branford and Delfrayo also became jazz musicians.

Marsalis got his first trumpet from New Orleans trumpet legend Al Hirt when he was six. His father played in Hirt's band at the time. Until he was 12, however, he was more interested in baseball than music. He studied music theory and harmony at the New Orleans Center for the Creative Arts and at age 14 won a state classical music competition. His prize was appearing with the New Orleans Philharmonic Orchestra and playing the Trumpet Concerto by composer Franz Haydn. Marsalis's love of music took him in several directions. While in high school, he played classical music with the New Orleans Civic Orchestra, jazz with several local groups, and rock music in a band with his brother Branton and some friends. At age 18, he won a scholarship to study at the prestigious Juilliard School of Music in New York City.

Marsalis quickly became disillusioned with the school. "When you played jazz at Juilliard," he said later, "people laugh." During his stay there he spent a summer touring with Art Blakey's Jazz Messengers and played in the pit orchestra of the Broadway musical *Sweeney Todd*. He left Juilliard after two years without earning a degree.

Wynton Marsalis is the first musician to win Grammy Awards in both the jazz and classical music categories. *(AP Photo/Frank Franklin II)*

Marsalis immersed himself in jazz, and he toured Japan with Herbie Hancock's quartet. When he was 20, Columbia Records offered him an unprecedented recording contract that allowed him to record both jazz and classical music. His debut album, *Wynton Marsalis* (1982), sold 125,000, an impressive number for a jazz album. A year later his first classical album, *Trumpet Concertos*, was released along with another jazz work, *Think of One,* featuring his own quintet with his brother Branford on saxophone. He won Grammy Awards for both albums, becoming the first person to ever win or even be nominated in both the jazz and classical categories.

Although he continued to play and record classical music, jazz became Marsalis's central focus. He has called jazz "the ultimate 20th century music" and spreading the word about it has become his life's passion. In 1987, Marsalis helped found Jazz at Lincoln Center in New York, a regular series of concerts that included many of the biggest names in jazz. In 1995, he also organized a regular series of Saturday morning concerts at Lincoln Center to educate young audiences about jazz. The concerts were broadcast on the Public Broadcasting Service (PBS). Another series hosted by Marsalis, called *Making the Music,* was aired on National Public Radio (NPR) in 1996.

As a composer, Marsalis has used his classical training and love of New Orleans's roots music (blues and rhythm and blues) to create exciting jazz compositions. His impressive body of work includes ballet scores ("Jazz: Six Syncopated Movements"), jazz compositions ("In This House"), film scores, and even a string quartet ("Octoroon's Ball"). In 1997, he became the first jazz composer to win the Pulitzer Prize, the honor given for his moving oratorio dedicated to the Civil War and slavery, *Blood on the Fields.* As of 2009, Marsalis has won nine Grammy Awards for jazz and classical recording.

Marsalis's appearances in the epic, 12-hour documentary *Jazz* (2000) by filmmaker Ken Burns have reinforced his position as the leading spokesperson for jazz, as well as one of its most prolific practitioners.

A strong supporter of New Orleans's recovery after the devastation of Hurricane Katrina in 2005, Marsalis organized a stellar benefit at Lincoln Center for New Orleans residents. The same year, he was awarded a National Medal of Arts. Wynton Marsalis has never married but has two sons, the second with actress Victoria Rowell.

"Jazz," said Marsalis in an interview in *American Heritage* magazine, "is a music of conversation, and that's what you need in a democracy. You have to be willing to hear another person's point of view and respond to it."

Further Reading

Gourse, Leslie. *Wynton Marsalis: Skain's Domain: A Biography.* New York: Music Sales Corporation, 2003.

Marsalis, Wynton. *Marsalis on Music.* New York: W. W. Norton, 1995.

Malone, Margaret Gay. *Jazz Is the Word: Wynton Marsalis.* Tarrytown, N.Y.: Benchmark Books, 1998 (YA).

Marsalis, Wynton, and Geoffrey Ward. *Moving to Higher Ground: How Jazz Can Change Your Life.* New York: Random House, 2008.

Further Listening

Blood on the Fields. Sony, CD box set, 1997.

The London Concert: Haydn/Hummel/Mozart/Fasch. Sony, CD, 2009.

Standards & Ballads. Sony Legacy, CD, 2008.

Further Viewing

In This House, On This Morning (1992). Pioneer, DVD, 2006.

Mathis, Johnny
(John Royce Mathis)
(1935–   ) *pop singer*

One of the most successful non-rock singers of the last 45 years, Johnny Mathis's smooth, ethereal tenor has made him one of the great romantic vocalists of pop music.

He was born John Royce Mathis in Gilmer, Texas, on September 30, 1935, and grew up in a poor neighborhood in San Francisco, California. His father Clem Mathis was a former vaudeville singer and dancer who encouraged his son's gift for singing, which initially turned to classical music and opera. His first voice teacher was so impressed by his voice that she gave him free lessons for six years.

Mathis was also attracted to athletics and played basketball and track in high school, excelling in the hurdles and the high jump. He won a track scholarship to San Francisco State College and planned to be an English teacher or athletic coach. At the same time, he continued to sing with a jazz sextet at local clubs.

Mathis was invited to try out for the 1956 U.S. Olympic track and field team, but in the summer of 1955 his life took a new turn. Columbia Record executive George Avakian was on vacation in San Francisco when he heard Mathis sing in a club and immediately signed him to his record label. Mathis left college and moved to New York City to record for Columbia. His first releases were in a jazzy vein and sold poorly. Then Mitch Miller, Columbia's artists and repertory (A & R) man, convinced the young singer to try soft ballads. His next single, "Wonderful! Wonderful!" (1957) became a top-20 hit. His next, "It's Not for Me to Say" went to number five on the pop charts and "Chances Are" soared to number one. In six short months in 1957, Johnny Mathis had become one of America's top pop vocalists.

He found himself busy touring late that year and unable to return to the studio to record a new album. Miller put together his first few hits along with some other material and released it as *Johnny Mathis's Greatest Hits*. The album became a best-seller and remained on *Billboard*'s album charts for an unprecedented nine years. Over the next six years, Mathis had many more hit records,

all of them romantic ballads. Among his biggest hits were "The Twelfth of Never" (1957), "A Certain Smile" (1958), "Misty" (1959), "Gina" (1962), and "What Will Mary Say" (1963). A poll taken by *Ebony* magazine in 1962 listed Mathis as the only one of 35 "Negro millionaires" in show business.

The arrival of The Beatles and other British rock groups on the American charts in 1964 hurt Mathis as a singles artist, although his albums continued to sell well for years. He returned to the pop charts in 1978 with his first number-one hit in 21 years—"Too Much, Too Little, Too Late," a duet with singer Deniece Williams. He teamed up with DIONNE WARWICK for another hit, "Friends in Love," in 1982.

The recipient of three Grammys, Mathis has sold more than 350 million records. He was awarded the Lifetime Achievement Award of the Academy of Recording Arts and Sciences in 2003. He still performs limited concert engagements, and his most recent recording, *A Night to Remember* (2008), marked his 52nd anniversary as a recording artist.

After all these years of performing, Johnny Mathis still has what people call the "Mathis Magic." He himself has described it as a sound "that seems to float a few inches off the ground, never landing with a thud."

Further Reading

Jasper, Tony. *Johnny: The Authorised Biography of Johnny Mathis*. London: Comet, 1984.
The Official Johnny Mathis Web site. Available online. URL: http://www.johnnymathis.com. Downloaded on February 13, 2009.

Further Listening

The Essential Johnny Mathis. Sony, 2 CDs, 2004.

Further Viewing

Johnny Mathis: Live—Wonderful, Wonderful—A Gold 50th Anniversary Celebration (2006). Sony, DVD, 2007.

Mayfield, Curtis
(1942–1999) *R & B singer, songwriter, group leader, record producer*

One of the primary architects of 1960s and 1970s soul music as both performer and writer, Curtis Mayfield created gospel-tinged music that reflected a deep and abiding faith in God and humankind.

He was born on June 3, 1942, on the mostly black North Side of Chicago, Illinois. His attraction to gospel music and his religious faith came from his loving grandmother, whom he was close to until her death. He began writing and singing gospel when he was 10. About that time he met Jerry Butler, three years his senior, in a church choir, and their careers would be inextricably entwined. At age 14, Mayfield was singing and playing guitar with the Alphatones, a gospel group. In 1957, Butler invited him to join him and singers Fred Cash and Sam Gooden in a rhythm and blues (R & B) group called the Roosters. When two more members joined, they changed their name to the Impressions. Their first recording for Abner Records was a Mayfield composition, "For Your Precious Love" (1958), with Butler singing lead. The ballad became a hit and is regarded by many as the first soul record, artfully combining gospel music with rock doo-wop harmony.

When the record company released the record as by "Jerry Butler and the Impressions," it stirred up bad feelings and the group disbanded. Butler went on to a successful solo career and took Mayfield along as his guitar player and songwriter. Mayfield's song "He Will Break Your Heart" (1960) became a top-10 hit for Butler. With the money from his royalties, Mayfield reformed the Impressions with Fred Cash as lead singer. Their initial release for ABC-Paramount, the exotic and lyrical "Gypsy Woman" (1961), was the first of an impressive string of hit records that would continue into the mid-1970s. The songs, nearly all written by Mayfield, reflected his belief in the power of faith and the individual to overcome the obstacles of poverty, race, and failed love. Such classic hits as "It's All Right" (1963), "I'm So Proud" (1964), "Keep On Pushing" (1964), "People Get Ready" (1965), and "We're a Winner" (1967), put the Impressions in the front ranks of soul singing groups. Their smooth, tight harmonizing became the hallmark of "the Chicago Sound."

"We're complimented that people look on us as spokesmen," Mayfield said, "but we think we're just saying what all the brothers feel."

In 1969, Mayfield felt the need to strike out on his own. While he continued to write and produce for the Impressions, he began recording his own solo efforts. He produced both the Impressions' and his own records on his new label, Curtom.

His first solo hit was the uncharacteristically angry "(Don't Worry) If There's a Hell We're All Going to Go" (1970). Then, in 1972, Mayfield reached the peak of his commercial success with the soundtrack for the blaxploitation film *Superfly*. The soundtrack album went gold, selling 500,000 copies. Two tracks, "Freddie's Dead" and the title theme, became top-10 hits. Mayfield's score may well have earned him an Academy Award, but because the songs were not sung in the movie but only played instrumentally, it was ruled ineligible to compete.

Mayfield continued to write film scores for black-oriented movies such as *Claudine* (1974), *A Piece of the Action* (1976), *Sparkle* (1976), and *Short Eyes* (1977), which he also acted in. He charted 31 R & B hits in the 1970s, after which he concentrated more on film scores and producing other artists, including ARETHA FRANKLIN. He reunited for a tour with the original Impressions, including Jerry Butler, in 1983.

A solo tour ended in disaster when a stage light tower fell on Mayfield shortly before a concert on August 13, 1990. It left him paralyzed from the chest down. He took his personal tragedy with the same good spirits he had lived all his life, continuing to record and produce. His medical expenses were high, however, and a group of artists made a tribute album to him in 1993, with the proceeds going to Mayfield. He received Grammy's Lifetime Achievement Award in 1995. One of the few artists to be inducted twice into the Rock and Roll Hall of Fame, he entered as a member of the Impressions in 1991 and as a solo artist in 1999. He died that same year on December 26, in Roswell, Georgia.

Further Reading

Burns, Peter. *Curtis Mayfield.* London: Sanctuary Publishing, 2003.

Mayfield, Curtis. *Poetic License: In Poem and Song.* Beverly Hills, Calif.: Dove Books, 2006.

Werner, Craig. *Higher Ground: Stevie Wonder, Aretha Franklin, Curtis Mayfield and the Rise and Fall of American Soul.* New York: Three Rivers Press, 2005.

Further Listening

Curtis Mayfield and the Impressions: The Anthology 1961–1977. MCA, 2 CDs, 1992.

The Definitive Soul Collection—Curtis Mayfield. Rhino, 2 CDs, 2006.

Further Viewing

The Music and Message of Curtis Mayfield and the Impressions. Hip-O Records, DVD, 2008.

McDaniel, Hattie
(1895–1952) *actress, singer*

The first African American to win an Academy Award, Hattie McDaniel rose above the stereotypical roles of mammy and servant in Hollywood films to create memorable characters brimming with life and humanity.

She was born in Wichita, Kansas, on June 10, 1895, the 13th child of Henry McDaniel, a Baptist minister. Her singing talent came from her mother, Susan, who sang in church. The family soon moved to Denver, Colorado, where McDaniel

started performing in black minstrel shows while still in high school. She won a gold medal for reciting the poem "Convict Jones" before the Women's Christian Temperance Union.

Encouraged by this success, she quit school and became a full-time entertainer in touring minstrel shows on the West Coast. When the booking agency for these shows went bankrupt, she found herself stranded in Milwaukee, Wisconsin. To support herself, McDaniel worked as an attendant in a ladies' washroom. When patrons heard her singing, she was hired as an entertainer. As her singing career blossomed, she was often billed as "the colored Sophie Tucker," after the most popular white female singer in vaudeville. McDaniel recorded songs she wrote for herself and may have been the first black woman to sing live on American radio.

Although relegated to roles as maids and mammies, Hattie McDaniel usually endowed her film performances with her own indomitable spirit. *(Photofest)*

She arrived in Hollywood in 1931 to break into movies. Her first professional acting job was playing an outspoken maid, Hi-Hat Hattie, on a weekly radio show. McDaniel landed her first film role in 1932, and two years later was noticed by critics and audiences in the role of a washerwoman in the Will Rogers comedy *Judge Priest* (1934), which also starred black comic actor STEPIN FETCHIT.

She was hilarious as a drunken maid wreaking havoc during a family dinner in *Alice Adams* (1935) and was PAUL ROBESON's domineering but loving spouse in the musical *Show Boat* (1936). *Show Boat* was one of the rare times she got to display her singing talent in a film. Although invariably cast as a servant or maid, McDaniel's powerful personality—whether kindly or ornery—always made her stand out.

Her finest moment came in 1939 when she played heroine Scarlett O'Hara's Mammy in the Civil War saga *Gone With the Wind* (1939). McDaniel's elemental strength and simple dignity made Mammy one of the film's most admirable and memorable characters. The role earned her the Academy Award for best supporting actress, the first time a black actor had won an Oscar.

"Hattie sobbed her gratitude, clutched the statuette to her breast, and sobbed her way back to her seat, through a standing ovation—one of the Academy's great moments," recalled film director Frank Capra, who was present at the ceremony.

Although she played in scores of films through the 1940s, McDaniel never again had a role as good as Mammy. Failing health forced her to leave films, and in 1947, she took the less-demanding role of the warm-hearted maid Beulah in the radio series of the same name. In late 1950's, she took over as Beulah on the television series from ETHEL WATERS, but she completed only six episodes before illness caused her to leave the show. She died of breast cancer in October 26, 1952, at age 57.

Although she was criticized sharply by organizations such as the National Association for the Advancement of Colored People (NAACP) for the roles she took, McDaniel's talent broke through the stereotypes and gave black audiences a positive and enduring image in Hollywood films of the 1930s and 1940s. As McDaniel herself once explained, "I could play a maid for $700 a week, or end up working as a maid for $7 a week." She chose the former, and American movies were all the richer for it.

Further Reading

"Hattie McDaniel." ClassicMovieMusicals.com. Available online. URL: http://www.classicmoviemusicals.com/mcdaniel.htm. Downloaded on February 7, 2009.

Jackson, Carlton. *Hattie: The Life of Hattie McDaniel.* Lanham, Md.: Madison Books, 1993.

Watts, Jill. *Hattie McDaniel: Black Ambition, White Hollywood.* New York: Amistad, 2007.

Further Viewing

Alice Adams (1935). Turner Home Entertainment, DVD, 2003.

Gone With the Wind (1939). Warner Home Video, 2 DVDs, 2006.

Show Boat (1936). Warner Home Video, VHS, 1990.

McDonald, Audra
(1970–) *singer, actress*

The youngest actress ever to win three Tony Awards for her work on Broadway, Audra McDonald is both a gifted classically trained singer and a first-class dramatic actress.

She was born Audra Ann McDonald on July 3, 1970, in Berlin, Germany, the elder of two daughters. A hyperactive child, she was encouraged to study acting to counteract her problems. Her gift for singing came naturally. In the 1970s, five of her aunts toured as the gospel group "The McDonald Sisters." She attended Roosevelt High School's School of the Arts in Fresno, California, where she spent most of her childhood, and went to the famed Juilliard School in New York City after graduation. As impressive as her soprano voice was, McDonald almost did not graduate from Juilliard, due to a disinterest in classical music.

What did interest McDonald was musical theater. While auditioning for a Broadway revival of the Rodgers-Hammerstein musical *Carousel* in 1994, she fainted onstage but got the second female lead, Carrie Pepperidge, nonetheless. Her sublime performance earned McDonald her first Tony Award for best featured actress in a musical. But musicals were not McDonald's only love. Two years later she appeared in the play *Master Class* and won her second Tony for best featured actress in a play. In 1998, at age 28, she won a third Tony for best featured actress in a musical for her role in *Ragtime,* a first in Broadway history.

Among McDonald's many admirers is composer/playwright Michael John LaChiusa, who wrote his musical *Marie Christine* (2000) with her in mind for the leading role. Her performance earned McDonald her first Tony nomination for best actress in a musical. She received a fourth Tony, however, four years later for her role as Ruth Younger, a struggling black mother, in the Broadway revival of Lorraine Hansberry's drama *A Raisin in the Sun.* When the play was brought to television in 2008, McDonald was reunited with her Broadway costar SEAN COMBS and won an Emmy for her performance.

While continuing to perform on Broadway in such musicals as *110 in the Shade* (2007 revival), McDonald has sung opera at the Houston Grand Opera and the Los Angeles Opera. She has recorded four solo albums to date, the most recent being *Build a Bridge* (2006), featuring pop songs by Neil Young, John Mayer, and Laura Nyro. She has acted in movies and television and portrays Dr. Naomi Bennett on the ABC series *Private Practice* (2007–), a spin-off from the medical series *Grey's Anatomy.*

McDonald has been married since 2000 to bass player Peter Donovan, a fellow former student

In both musicals and straight plays, Audra McDonald has been one of Broadway's most gifted performers for a decade and a half. *(AP Photo/Peter Kramer)*

at Juilliard. Their daughter, Zoe Madeline, was born in 2001.

Further Reading

"Audra McDonald." IMG Artists Web site. Available online. URL: http://www.imgartists.com/?page= artist&id=89. Downloaded on February 12, 2009.

"Audra McDonald." The Internet Movie Database. Available online. URL: http://www.imdb.com/ name/nm0567653/. Downloaded on December 10, 2008.

Further Listening

110 in the Shade (2007, Broadway revival). P.S. Classics, CD, 2007.

Way Back to Paradise. Nonesuch, CD, 1998.

Further Viewing

A Raisin in the Sun (2008). Sony Pictures, DVD, 2008.

Wonderful Town (2002, concert performance). Euroarts, DVD, 2005.

McFerrin, Bobby

(1950–) *jazz singer, musician, composer, conductor*

Called by music critic Paul Evans "an a cappella one-man band," Bobby McFerrin has created his own unique musical genre by combining elements of jazz, rock, pop, and classical music in his engaging vocal performances.

He was born on March 11, 1950, in New York City. His father, Robert, was a baritone singer with the Metropolitan Opera Company, and his mother, Sara, was a classical soprano. He began playing the piano at age six and later studied at the Juilliard School of Music and then Sacramento State College in California.

In his 20s, McFerrin worked as a pianist and accompanist for dance companies and the Ice Follies. In 1977, he moved to New Orleans where he began singing with the band Astral Projects. McFerrin developed a unique singing style by overdubbing his own voice and using backing vocal sound effects and hand and body slaps.

He got his big break when he met actor and comedian BILL COSBY in California in 1980. Cosby was impressed with McFerrin's talent and helped arrange his debut at the Playboy Jazz Festival. Later McFerrin recorded the theme song for television's *The Cosby Show*. He soon signed a recording contract with Elektra Records, and his first album, *Bobby McFerrin*, was released in 1982. In 1985, he and Jon Hendricks won a Grammy Award for best jazz vocal performance, male, for the album *Another Night in Tunisia*. McFerrin won another Grammy the following year for the soundtrack of the jazz film *Round Midnight* (1986).

He reached the peak of his commercial success in 1988, when his calypso-style song "Don't Worry, Be Happy" from the Tom Cruise film *Cocktail*, soared to number one on the pop charts. It earned him four more Grammys, including ones for record of the year and song of the year. His next effort, *Medicine Music* (1990), teamed him as orchestrator for Voicestra, a 10-person vocal ensemble. *Hush* (1992) featured duets with Asian-American cellist Yo-Yo Ma.

McFerrin made his conducting debut in 1990 with the San Francisco Symphony Orchestra. He has since conducted major orchestras in Chicago, Philadelphia, and London. In 1994, he was appointed the creative chair of the St. Paul Chamber Orchestra in St. Paul, Minnesota. He also plays and tours with his jazz trio Bang! Zoom and vocal ensemble Hard Choral.

McFerrin's most recent albums are *Mouth Music* (2001) and *Beyond Words* (2003), a collaboration with pianist Chick Corea and other jazz artists. In July 2009, McFerrin performed his wordless opera *Bobble* about the biblical Tower of Babel at the Stimmen Festival in Basel, Switzerland. He and his wife, Debbie Green, have three children. McFerrin's son Taylor is a singer and rapper who has collaborated with him on music projects.

Further Reading

Bobby McFerrin's Official Web site. Available online. URL: http://www.bobbymcferrin.com/. Downloaded on February 8, 2009.

McFerrin, Bobby, and Alexander Calder, illustrator. *Don't Worry, Be Happy*. New York: Welcome Books, 2001.

Further Listening

The Best of Bobby McFerrin. Blue Note Records, CD, 1996.

Further Viewing

Bobby McFerrin: Spontaneous Inventions (1987). Blue Note Records, DVD, 2005.

M. C. Hammer
(Stanley Kirk Burrell, Hammer)
(1963–   ) *rap singer, record producer, actor*

An uncanny hit-maker who brought dance and sampling to their peaks of popularity, M. C. Hammer has been both praised and criticized for his ability to combine elements of rap and pop into catchy, commercial music.

He was born Stanley Kirk Burrell in Oakland, California, on March 29, 1963. His father, Lewis, managed a neighborhood social club. As a youth, Stanley was a batboy for the Oakland Athletics baseball team. Team members dubbed him "Little Hammer" because of his resemblance to baseball great "Hammerin'" Hank Aaron.

He tried out for the San Francisco Giants baseball team but failed to make the team. Burrell dropped out of high school and enlisted in the navy for a three-year hitch. After leaving the service Hammer adopted his baseball name and formed the Posse, an energetic, eight-member group that included singers, dancers, and deejays. *Let's Get It Started* (1988), his debut album on Capitol Records, captured the public's interest with its infectious dance beat. His next album, *Please Hammer Don't Hurt 'Em* (1990), sold more than 10 million copies. It stayed at number one on the album charts for 21 weeks and produced three top-10 singles—"U Can't Touch This," "Have You Seen Her," and "Pray." Rap fans, however, were vehement in their condemnation of Hammer as a sellout to pop stardom. To further demonstrate that stardom, he became the first rap artist to get his own animated television series, *Hammerman* (1991), for which he provided his cartoon character's voice. Hammer also played himself in the television movie *Hammer from the Heart* (1992).

However, M. C. Hammer took the criticism from rap fans seriously and tried to change his image. He dropped the "M. C." from his stage name and released *Too Legit to Quit* (1991), which contained fewer samplings of other people's songs than on his previous album and had a harder and leaner rhythm and blues (R & B) sound. The album sold 3 million copies but was seen by many as inferior to his previous albums. *The Funky Headhunter* (1994) continued the move to a tougher rap sound and sold only 500,000 copies.

In 1995, Hammer added the "M. C." back to his name. He played himself in *Private Parts* (1997), a film about the life of radio personality Howard Stern and more recently starred with rapper ICE-T in *Rhapsody* (2001), a thriller about the rap music industry.

His popularity in sharp decline, Hammer filed for bankruptcy in 1996. His next three albums sold poorly, but he rebounded briefly with *Look Look Look* (2006), his best seller in a decade. In 2008, he cofounded a dance Web site, DanceJam.com. He performs only occasionally and lives in Tracy, California, with his wife and six children. In June 2009, his reality series, *Hammertime*, debuted on the television cable station A & E.

Further Reading
Hildebrand, Lee. *Hammertime.* New York: Avon Books, 1992.
Huey, Steve. "MC Hammer Biography." The Allmusic Web site. Available online. URL: http://allmusic.com/cg/amg.dll?p=ang&sql=ll:kitrxq95ld6e. Downloaded on February 8, 2009.

Further Listening
Greatest Hits. Capitol, CD, 1996.
Please Hammer Don't Hurt 'Em. Capitol, CD, 1990.

McQueen, Butterfly
(Thelma McQueen)
(1911–1995) *actress*

A marvelously unique character actress with a squeaky voice and a waif-like presence. Butterfly McQueen refused to be locked into Hollywood racial stereotype roles and walked away from a promising career with her dignity intact.

She was born Thelma McQueen on January 8, 1911, in Tampa, Florida. Her father was a stevedore and her mother a housemaid. The family moved to Augusta, Georgia, and then to New York City, where she attended high school. At age 13, McQueen joined a theater company in Harlem, then a predominantly black section of New York City. In a production of William Shakespeare's *A Midsummer Night's Dream,* she danced in the Butterfly Ballet and ever after was known as "Butterfly" McQueen. She made her Broadway debut at age 26 in the musical revue *Brown Sugar.* A year later, in Hollywood, she auditioned for the role of Prissy, a young black servant in the Civil War saga *Gone With the Wind* (1939). The producers rejected her at first, finding her "too old, too plump, and too dignified" for the part. She auditioned again and won the role and a place in Hollywood history. Although HATTIE MCDANIEL won an Academy Award for best supporting actress as Mammy in the picture, nearly as memorable was McQueen's Prissy—the flustered, weepy servant girl who declared to Miss Scarlet in a moment of crisis, "I don't know nothin' 'bout birthin' babies!"

"It was not a pleasant part to play," she later recalled. "I didn't want to be that little slave. But I did my best, my very best."

Unlike McDaniel and other black actresses, McQueen resisted playing servants, although she played her share of them through the 1940s. When she found a line she had in one movie to be ridiculously demeaning, she refused to say it and walked off the set. After appearing in the western *Duel in the Sun* (1946) for *Gone With the Wind* producer David Selznick, she quit Hollywood and moved back to Augusta. For the next two decades, she divided her time between Georgia and New York, where she continued to audition for parts in stage plays. In Augusta, McQueen took a course in nursing at the Georgia Medical College. She returned to California in the early 1950s to play the daffy Oriole, Beulah's friend in the TV series *Beulah* (1950–53). She returned to

movies in the comedy *Amazing Grace* (1974) and the following year, at age 64, went to college. McQueen earned her bachelor of arts (B.A.) degree in political science at the City College of New York.

She devoted most of her remaining years to the welfare of children. She patrolled the playground of a local school in Augusta, picking up litter and watching out for the students. On December 22, 1995, the kerosene heater in her one-bedroom cottage caught fire, and Butterfly McQueen, age 84, died in the blaze.

Further Reading

Bogle, Donald. *Toms, Coons, Mulattoes, Mammies & Bucks: An Interpretive History of Blacks in American Films.* New York: Continuum, 1997, pp. 89–94.

Bourne, Stephen. *Butterfly McQueen Remembered.* Lanham, Md.: The Scarecrow Press, 2007.

Further Viewing

Amazing Grace (1974). MGM, DVD, 2001.
Duel in the Sun (1946). MGM, DVD, 2004.
Gone With the Wind (1939). Warner Home Video, 2 DVDs, 2006.

Mingus, Charles
(1922–1979) *jazz bassist, composer, bandleader, record producer*

Considered the greatest jazz composer after DUKE ELLINGTON, Charles Mingus was an uncompromising visionary whose music reflects his far-ranging intellect and interests.

He was born in Nogales, Arizona, on April 22, 1922, and grew up in the Watts section of Los Angeles, California. He came from a diverse ethnic background of black, white, Native American, and Asian ancestry. In a similar way, Mingus's music was incredibly eclectic, drawing on traditional jazz, gospel, blues, classical, and Mexican music. All these influences came through in a freewheeling blend that was uniquely his own.

While growing up, Mingus suffered rejection from both blacks and whites because of his light skin. He came to see himself as an outcast, apart from society. He carried this feeling with him throughout his life. He took up the bass and played it in his high school band and later in several jazz bands in the 1940s. In 1950, Mingus joined the Red Norvo Trio. Traditionally the bass provided the rhythm and backup for other, more prominent instruments in jazz. Mingus was the first jazz musician to give the bass a "voice" of its own, and he made it as important as any other instrument in the ensemble.

In 1951, he moved to New York City, where he played with Duke Ellington and CHARLIE PARKER, among other jazz artists. Together with drummer Max Roach, Mingus formed the record company Debut in 1952. He wrote and recorded prolifically for Debut as well as for Columbia, Atlantic, and other record labels. Mingus also gave young, talented jazz musicians such as Thad Jones the opportunity to record on Debut.

Mingus's music was precise but often left room for the improvisation of the other players. He was appalled by the commercialism of much of the jazz performed and recorded in the 1950s and 1960s. "I've come to the point, musically and personally," he declared, "where I have to play the way I want to. I just can't compromise anymore." In 1958, he developed the Jazz Workshop, which evolved out of the Jazz Composers' Workshop, to play his pure, personal jazz.

His greatest compositions were ambitious but eminently listenable. "Like Ellington," wrote music critic Paul Evans, "so much of his music, for all of its innovative force, offers such sheer accessible joy." Mingus could be playful and rambunctious in such pieces as "Hog Callin' Blues" and "Eat That Chicken" (both 1961) and then turn introspective and moody in the masterful "Pithecanthropus Erectus" (1956), which in 10 and a half minutes sums up the rise and fall of humankind.

Mingus's uncompromising stance cost him dearly, both financially and emotionally. By the late 1960s he was wandering the streets, nearly destitute. He thought he was going mad. He fortunately recovered from this depression and resumed his brilliant career, winning a Guggenheim fellowship in composition. Mingus was diagnosed with Lou Gehrig's disease in 1977, but he continued to write music, even when he could no longer play the piano, dictating new melodies into a tape recorder. He died on January 5, 1979, in Cuernavaca, Mexico.

Charles Mingus was the first jazz artist whose papers were admitted into the Library of Congress's archives. His musical legacy lived on in the Mingus Dynasty, a group that continued to play and record his more than 300 compositions.

"Mingus has given us a remarkable musical autobiography," wrote jazz critic Nat Hentoff, "the record of a man who has persisted in finding his own way by continually penetrating as deeply as he can into the possibilities, the dangers, the confusions, the affirmations of an uncompromising existence among many who regarded such fierce honesty as an aberration."

Further Reading

Jenkins, Todd S. *I Know What I Know: The Music of Charles Mingus.* Santa Barbara, Calif.: Praeger Publishers, 2006.

Mingus, Charles. *Beneath the Underdog: His Worlds as Explained by Mingus.* New York: Vintage Books, 1991.

Priestly, Brian. *Mingus: A Critical Biography.* New York: Da Capo Press, 1984.

Santoro, Gene. *Myself When I Am Real: The Life and Music of Charles Mingus.* New York: Oxford University Press, 2001.

Further Listening

The Great Concert of Charles Mingus. Verve, 2 CDs, 2004.

The Very Best of Charles Mingus. Rhino, CD, 2001.

Further Viewing

Charles Mingus: Triumph of the Underdog (1997). Shanachie Video, VHS/DVD, 1998/1999.

Jazz Icons: Charles Mingus Live in '64. Jazz Icons, DVD, 2007.

Mitchell, Arthur

(1934–) *ballet dancer, choreographer, teacher, dance company director*

The first African American to be a principal dancer with a major American classical ballet company, Arthur Mitchell has brought the world of ballet to thousands of underprivileged black youth through his world-famous Dance Theater of Harlem (DTH).

He was born in New York City's Harlem section on March 27, 1934. His father, Arthur, was a contracting engineer, and his mother, Willie Mae, a homemaker. Mitchell discovered a love of dance early, and when a guidance counselor watched him dance a jitterbug, he recommended that Mitchell attend the High School of the Performing Arts. He later became the school's first male student to win its annual dance award. Mitchell won a scholarship to the School of American Ballet, a training ground for the New York City Ballet. He debuted with the City Ballet in 1955 in the *Western Symphony.* Over the next 15 years, he danced many memorable roles with the company. His most acclaimed role was as Puck, the mischievous fairy, in *A Midsummer Night's Dream* (1964). The part was especially created for him by the legendary choreographer George Balanchine.

Mitchell was deeply moved when civil rights leader Martin Luther King, Jr., was assassinated in April 1968, and he decided he had to give something back to the Harlem community. He began giving dance lessons for underprivileged neighborhood children in a Harlem church basement that summer. Within a year he converted a garage into a more permanent space using his personal savings. After a few months the original 30 students had grown to 400. With the help of the Ford Foundation, Mitchell incorporated the Dance Theater of Harlem (DTH) in 1969. It was the first black classical ballet company in the United States.

As the company grew, it became both a teaching and a performing institute. Mitchell directed the company, taught classes, and choreographed new works for his dancers. Many of his works, although ballet, have dealt with black subjects, such as *Ode to Otis* (1969), his tribute to the late soul singer OTIS REDDING. Other works include *Rhythmetron* (1972) and *Manifestation* (1976).

The DTH toured not only the United States but foreign countries as well. In 1988, it became the first American ballet company to perform in the Soviet Union at the invitation of the United States Information Agency.

In 1993, Arthur Mitchell became one of the youngest recipients of the Kennedy Center Honors. He received a National Medal of Arts from President Bill Clinton in 1995. Mitchell is a member of the Council for the National Endowment for the Arts and holds honorary doctorate degrees from a number of institutions, including Harvard University, Princeton, and the City College of the City University of New York. In 2006, he and the DTH were honored a dinner at the White House.

Looking back on his distinguished career in dance, Mitchell has said, "The myth was that because you were black that you could not do classical dance. I proved that to be wrong."

Further Reading

"Arthur Mitchell." The Kennedy Center Honors Web site. Available online. URL: http//www.kennedy-center.org/calendar/index.cfm?fuseaction-showIndividual&entitY_id=3515&source_type-A. Downloaded on February 8, 2009.

Harrison, Paul Carter. *Black Light: The African American Hero.* New York: Thunder's Mouth Press, 1993.

Tobias, Tobi. *Arthur Mitchell.* New York: Thomas Y. Crowell Company, 1975 (children).

Further Viewing

Dance Theatre of Harlem: Creole Giselle (1987). Kultur Video, DVD, 2005.

Monk, Thelonious

(Thelonius Sphere Monk)
(1917–1982) *jazz pianist, composer, bandleader*

A uniquely gifted jazz musician, Thelonious Monk was one of the genre's finest composers and one of its most intriguing and colorful characters.

He was born Thelonius Sphere Monk on October 10, 1917, in Rocky Mountain, North Carolina, but moved with his family to New York City while still a child. His father, Thelonious, became seriously ill and returned to North Carolina. His mother, Barbara, supported her three children on her meager salary as a civil service worker. He took piano lessons from an early age and by 13 had won the amateur contests held weekly at the Apollo Theatre in Harlem so many times that he was barred from it. He soon met jazz pianist MARY LOU WILLIAMS, who became his mentor and a lifelong friend. When he was 19, Monk became part of the stellar house band at Harlem's Minton's Playhouse. Other members included CHARLIE PARKER and DIZZY GILLESPIE. Together they created a revolutionary new kind of jazz called bebop, noted for its frenetic pace and wildly inventive improvising.

By about 1945, Monk was leading his own combos while playing in other groups as well. He soon moved beyond bebop to his own highly personal and eccentric style of jazz. Monk's music was full of odd-sounding angular themes, classical intricacy, joyful humor, and sharp wit. His personal behavior was often as enigmatic as his music. Filmmaker Ken Burns has called him the "most mysterious man ever to play jazz." Monk's eccentricities were legendary. He would wear funny hats when he performed and when moved by his own music would get up and spontaneously

dance by himself. He could be ebullient and talkative one day and then not speak a word for a week.

In the 1950s, Monk made a series of classic recordings for Riverside Records. Among the most famous of his more than 70 compositions are the jazz perennials "Round Midnight" and "Straight, No Chaser." The Thelonious Monk Quartet, which included saxophonist JOHN COLTRANE, toured the United States and Europe. In 1964, Monk became one of the very few jazz musicians to be featured on the cover of *Time* magazine.

After two decades of feverish creativity and growing fame, Monk suddenly withdrew from view and retired from playing and recording in the early 1970s. An intensely private person, he gave no explanation for his withdrawal, but it is now known he suffered from a mysterious debilitating disease. In the last decade of his life he

Eccentric jazz pianist and composer Thelonious Monk shows off one of his unusual hats. *(Photo courtesy of Showtime Archives, Toronto)*

made only rare appearances at concerts at New York's Carnegie Hall and at the Newport Jazz Festival in Rhode Island. Thelonious Monk died on February 5, 1982 in Englewood, New Jersey.

While much of his music has unfortunately gone out of print since his death, Monk's legacy looms large in the world of jazz, and his musical archives reside with the Smithsonian Institution in Washington, D.C. His greatest legacy is the Thelonious Monk Institute of Jazz, a nonprofit educational organization founded by his family in 1986. With headquarters in Washington, D.C., and Los Angeles, California, the institute's mission is "to offer the world's most promising young musicians college level training by America's jazz masters and to present public schools-band jazz educational programs for young people and the world."

Further Reading

Fitterling, Thomas. *Thelonious Monk: His Life and Music.* Berkeley, Calif.: Berkeley Hills Books, 1997.

Gourse, Leslie. *Straight, No Chaser: The Life and Genius of Thelonious Monk.* New York: Schirmer Books, 1998.

Van der Bliek, Rob. *The Thelonious Monk Reader.* New York: Oxford University Press, 2001.

Further Listening

The Essential Thelonius Monk. Sony, CD, 2003.

Monk's Dream (1963). Sony, CD, 2002.

Further Viewing

Thelonious Monk—Straight No Chaser (1988). Warner Home Video, VHS/DVD, 1999/2001.

Morgan, Tracy

("The Hammer")

(1968–) *comedian, actor*

Arguably the most gifted African-American comic actor to come out of *Saturday Night Live* since EDDIE MURPHY, Tracy Morgan does a perfect caricature of himself and the show that made him famous on the NBC sitcom *30 Rock.*

He was born on November 10, 1968, in the Bronx, New York, and grew up in the mean streets of Brooklyn's Bedford-Stuyvesant district. His father, Jimmy, was a musician and Vietnam vet who became a drug addict and died of AIDS in 1987. His older brother, Jimmy Jr., was born with cerebral palsy. Tracy married early and in his early 20s was living on welfare with his wife and three sons. But a talent for humor saved him from his father's fate. He began performing stand-up on local radio shows and then moved his act to the Uptown Comedy club in Harlem where he learned how to transform the people he knew growing up on the streets into funny, memorable characters. Like RICHARD PRYOR, Morgan had a genius for making racial caricatures funny and satirical. But like Pryor, he also has a self-destructive streak that has accompanied his rise to success.

By the time he was cast as a regular member of NBC's *Saturday Night Live (SNL)*, after a featured role on Martin Lawrence's sitcom *Martin*, he was developing a serious drinking problem. In the seven seasons Morgan starred on *SNL*, he created a memorable gallery of likeable but outlandish, goofy characters, like Brian Fellow, the animal enthusiast, and Astronaut Jones, his personal favorite.

In 2003, he starred in his own series, *The Tracy Morgan Show*, produced by *SNL* producer Lorne Michaels. The show, however, was an unremarkable working-class sitcom, and it was canceled four months later. The move to Los Angeles to do the show was a bad one for Morgan and his family. His drinking got worse, and the future of his career was in doubt. Then fellow *SNL* alumnus Tina Fey cast him in her sitcom *30 Rock* (2005–), about the backstage machinations of a fictional NBC comedy show. Morgan plays Tracy Jordan, the show's star, whose outrageous behavior is remarkably similar to the actor playing him. The show was a critical success from the start but built an audience slowly. The security of a successful show, however, did not calm Morgan's demons. He was arrested for drunk drinking in 2005 and 2006 and the following year was fitted with an ankle bracelet to monitor the alcohol in his blood. In January 2008, Sabina, his wife of 22 years, filed for divorce. In a November 2008 interview with the *New York Times*, Morgan claimed to be sober for nearly a year and in a better place. "You get somebody to crack a smile, that's a beautiful thing," he said. "So I think all comedians are earning their wings into heaven."

Further Reading

Itzkoff, Dave. "Each Room Is a Stage, Every Day Is a Show." *New York Times*, November 2, 2008, Arts & Leisure, pp. 1, 12.

Morgan, Tracy, and Anthony Bozza. *I Am the New Black*. New York: Spiegel & Grau, 2009.

Tracy Morgan's Official Web site. Available online. URL: http://www.tracymorgan.net/. Downloaded on February 12, 2009.

Further Viewing

Saturday Night Live—The Best of Tracy Morgan. Lions Gate, DVD, 2004.

30 Rock—Season 1 (2006). Universal, DVD box set, 2007.

Morrow, Tracy   See ICE-T.

Morton, Jelly Roll
(Ferdinand Lamothe, Ferdinand Mouton)
(1899–1941) *jazz pianist, composer, bandleader*

A pianist and composer whose inventive music bridged the gap between ragtime and jazz, Jelly Roll Morton may not have, as he often claimed, "invented" jazz, but he undoubtedly was one of its most creative pioneers.

He was born Ferdinand Lamothe in New Orleans, Louisiana, on October 20, 1890, of French, Native American, and African-American descent. He changed his name early on from Lamothe to Mouton, the surname of his stepfather, and anglicized it to "Morton."

His father was a carpenter and part-time trombonist who left home when Morton was young. His mother died when he was 14, and he was mostly on his own after that, playing piano in local bars and brothels from age 15. He composed his first jazz number, "New Orleans Blues," in 1906. Other early classics—"Jelly Roll Blues" and "King Porter Stomp"—quickly followed. In 1907, Morton left New Orleans and for the next 15 years traveled the country playing piano in bars and clubs and soaking up all the kinds of contemporary popular music.

He finally settled in Chicago, Illinois, in 1923 and became part of the lively jazz scene there. Morton published many of his compositions and began recording with trumpeter and bandleader Joe "King" Oliver and other musicians. He formed a jazz band, the Red Hot Peppers, and from 1926 to 1928 made a series of disks that today are considered among the greatest of early jazz recordings. With his fine, expensive clothes and a diamond-inlaid tooth that flashed when he smiled, Jelly Roll Morton was one of the most famous and colorful characters of jazz in the Roaring Twenties. But by 1930, his career was in swift decline. Many viewed his music as old-fashioned, as new "swing" jazz bands emerged. In the meantime, Walter Melrose, Morton's music publisher, was stealing money from his works and claiming to be his coauthor.

Unhappy and broke, Morton left Chicago and moved to New York City where he played piano in seedy bars on Seventh Avenue. In 1934, he bought his own saloon in Washington, D.C., where he kept bar and played piano, entertaining his patrons with stories of how he had invented jazz nearly 30 years earlier. In 1938, musicologist Alan Lomax interviewed Morton and recorded eight hours of him playing and talking for the archives of the Library of Congress. The experience inspired Morton to record again on the Bluebird jazz label, but his comeback was brief. His lawsuits against Melrose and others were largely unsuccessful.

Morton went to Los Angeles, California, in 1939 to collect some diamonds that his godmother supposedly left to him. He never got the diamonds but decided to stay on in Los Angeles, where, plagued by ill-health, he died on July 10, 1941. This "old man" of jazz's earliest days was only 56 years old.

In 1992, *Jelly's Last Jam,* a Broadway musical based on his life and work, opened to rave reviews. Morton was played by actor and dancer GREGORY HINES.

Further Reading

Lomax, Alan. *Mister Jelly Roll: The Fortunes of Jelly Roll Morton, New Orleans Creole and 'Inventor of Jazz.'* Berkeley: University of California Press, 2001.

Reich, Howard, and William Gaines. *Jelly's Blues: The Life, Music, and Redemption of Jelly Roll Morton.* New York: Da Capo Press, 2008.

Wolfe, George C., and Susan Birkenhead. *Jelly's Last Jam.* New York: Theatre Communications Group, 1993.

Further Listening

The Complete Library of Congress Recordings. Rounder/Umgd, CD box set, 2005.

Jelly's Last Jam (1992). Decca Broadway, CD, 1994.

Mr. T

(Laurence Tureaud, Lawrence Tero)
(1952–   ) *actor*

A former bodyguard and professional bouncer, Mr. T used his ferocious image to become a film and television star, then more important, became a prominent role model for young people.

He was born Laurence Tureaud on May 21, 1952, in Chicago, Illinois. He grew up in a three-room apartment in a housing project with 11 siblings and a single mother who raised them on a $38-a-week welfare check. Tureaud was encouraged by his older brothers to build up his body so he could defend himself in their rough neighborhood.

By high school he had a formidable physique and played football and wrestled. After graduation, he was accepted at Prairie View A & M University in Texas on a football scholarship. He left school after a year and soon found work as a bouncer in nightclubs and then as a bodyguard. Among his celebrity clients were heavyweight champion Muhammad Ali and singers MICHAEL JACKSON and DIANA ROSS.

Interested in becoming a celebrity himself, Tureaud changed his name to Mr. T, shaved his hair in a Mohawk cut, and started wearing lots of heavy jewelry. He appeared on the television game show *Games People Play* competing for the title the "World's Toughest Bouncer." After playing himself in the film *Penitentiary II,* actor Sylvester Stallone cast Mr. T in the third of his *Rocky* movies. He played Clubber Lang, a nasty boxer and Rocky's nemesis, in *Rocky III* (1982). In the film, he originated the famous catchphrase, "I pity the fool." The role made Mr. T a star and led directly to a role in the new NBC television action-adventure series *The A-Team,* which premiered in January 1983.

Mr. T played Sergeant Bosco "B.A." (Bad Attitude) Baracus, one of a rogue band of Vietnam veterans who roam the world taking on good causes. The show, which also starred George Peppard and Dirk Benedict, was largely tongue-in-cheek and Baracus was a good "bad guy" with a heart of gold.

The show was a hit, and Mr. T quickly became a national phenomenon. His popularity with young children led NBC to quickly put in production a Saturday morning animated series, *Mr. T.* The cartoon Mr. T was involved in adventures with a group of teenage friends. Each program taught a moral lesson more fully explicated by the real Mr. T, who appeared at the start and end of each show.

Over the next several years Mr. T's popularity peaked. He starred in several television movies, including *The Toughest Man in the World;* made guest appearances as himself in several situation comedies; and wrote a book. He even dressed up as Santa Claus at a White House Christmas party where First Lady Nancy Reagan sat on his lap. There was a Mr. T cereal and a Mr. T doll.

By the time *The A-Team* went off the air in 1987, Mr. T's popularity had waned. He appeared occasionally as a guest on television programs in the 1990s and was in a few movies, including *Inspector Gadget* (1999). In 1995, at age 43, he was diagnosed with T-cell lymphoma. He fought it tenaciously and was declared cancer free in 2001. In 2006, he starred in a short-lived reality TV series called *I Pity the Fool*. A graphic novel based on his adventures was published in 2008. Mr. T is single and divides his time between his home in Sherman Oaks, California, and a ranch in New Mexico where he breeds horses.

Further Reading

Bunting, Christopher. *Mr. T: Advanced Edition Graphic Novel*. Mohawk Media, 2008.

"Mr. T." The Internet Movie Database. Available online. URL: http://www.imdb.com/name/nm0001558/. Downloaded on February 8, 2009.

Mr. T. *Mr. T: The Man with the Gold: An Autobiography*. New York: St. Martin's Press, 1985.

Further Viewing

The A-Team: Season One. Universal, DVD box set, 2008.

Rocky III (1982). MGM Home Video, DVD, 2005.

Murphy, Eddie
(Edward Regan Murphy)
(1961–) *actor, comedian, film producer*

One of the biggest box office names in movies today, Eddie Murphy moved from stand-up comedy to Hollywood stardom with a keen intelligence and a wise guy personality.

He was born Edward Regan Murphy in the Bushwick section of Brooklyn, New York, on April 3, 1961. His father, Charles, was a police officer

Despite the unevenness of his films, Eddie Murphy continues to be one of the biggest stars in Hollywood today. *(AP Photo/Laurent Rebours, File)*

and an amateur comedian. The family moved to Long Island when Murphy was still a child. His parents divorced when he was three, and his mother, Lillian, remarried. Murphy would amuse family members by impersonating different television celebrities and set up insult contests with his friends.

As a teenager he formed a band with some buddies and would do stand-up comedy between songs. He began performing in local clubs and after high school got a chance to perform at the Comic Strip, a well-known Manhattan comedy club. The club's owners were so impressed by Murphy that they agreed to manage his career. They got him dates at leading comedy clubs all along the East Coast and an audition in 1980 for the NBC television comedy show, *Saturday Night Live (SNL)*. Murphy was hired as a featured player on the long-running show but quickly was promoted to a full cast member of the Not-Ready-for-Prime-Time Players. He created such memorable characters on *SNL* as Buckwheat, Velvet Jones, an unhappy Gumby, and Mr. Robinson, a ghetto version of Fred Rogers of *Mister Rogers' Neighborhood,* a highly successful children's television program.

Murphy stayed with the show for four seasons, during which time he appeared in his first movie, *48 Hours* (1982). The action-comedy featured Murphy as a small-time hood who is released from jail for two days in order to help a white cop track down a killer. His big-mouthed, con man character was a hit with audiences and established a persona that Murphy would refine in film after film. In *Trading Places* (1983), he played a hustler who switches places with a preppy stockbroker played by Dan Aykroyd, another *SNL* alumnus.

Then came the movie that propelled Eddie Murphy into the top ranks of movie stardom—*Beverly Hills Cop* (1984). He played Alex Foley, a Detroit street cop, whose hunt for the men who killed his best friend takes him to luxurious, upper-class Beverly Hills, California. Murphy was hilarious as the "fish out of water" and the film became one of the top grossers of the decade. Murphy was offered an attractive five-picture deal from Paramount Pictures for $15 million. His next three films, including *The Golden Child* (1986) and *Beverly Hills Cop II* (1987), were mediocre efforts but made millions because of Murphy's star power. A concert film, *Eddie Murphy Raw* (1987), raised disturbing questions of taste with its derisive jokes made at the expense of homosexuals and women. He partly recovered with *Coming to America* (1988), in which he played an African prince looking for an American bride. Despite this charming film, Murphy continued to receive criticism from some in the African-American community for not making more black-centered films that showcased black actors. He responded

by writing, directing, producing, and starring in *Harlem Nights* (1989), a period gangster film with a cast that included RICHARD PRYOR, REDD FOXX, and DELLA REESE. Although well intended, the film was a critical and commercial flop. Murphy's film career declined further with several more dismal efforts, including two pointless sequels, *Another 48 Hours* (1990), and *Beverly Hills Cop III* (1994).

Murphy finally regained his comic footing in the hit *The Nutty Professor* (1996), a clever remake of a classic Jerry Lewis comedy. Murphy played the overweight Professor Sherman Klump who discovers a drug that turns him into a sexy, ruthless playboy. The film gave Murphy the opportunity to play a handful of zany minor characters, including most of Klump's outrageous relatives. He again struck gold with the reworking of another old film, *Doctor Doolittle* (1998), in which he plays a veterinarian who suddenly discovers that he can communicate with animals. Murphy's frantic efforts to hide his gift from the rest of the world and the film's special effects made *Doctor Doolittle* a family hit. Murphy kidded his own movie-star persona in *Bowfinger* (1999), in which he played Kitt Riley, a self-obsessed movie star, who is made the accidental star of a grade-Z science-fiction film. He also played Riley's look-alike brother, his stand-in in the hilarious movie-within-a-movie.

This superstar tends to play it safe, as illustrated by two more sequels—*Nutty Professor II: The Klumps* (2000) and *Doctor Doolittle 2* (2001). The worst in a string of bad movies was *The Adventures of Pluto Nash* (2002), rated one of the biggest bombs in recent movie history. Murphy fared far better as the voice of the wise-cracking donkey in the animated film *Shrek* (2001) and its three sequels. He was also impressive as the rhythm-and-blues singer James "Thunder" Early in the film version of the Broadway musical *Dreamgirls* (2006). Murphy's performance earned him an Academy Award nomination for best supporting actor.

Murphy divorced wife Nicole Mitchell in 2006. They have five children.

Further Reading

"Eddie Murphy." The Internet Movie Database. Available online. URL: http://www.imdb.com/name/nm0000552/. Downloaded on February 8, 2009.

Sanello, Frank. *Eddie Murphy: The Life and Times of a Comic on the Edge.* Secaucus, N.J.: Birch Lane Press, 1997.

Wilborn, Deborah A. *Eddie Murphy.* Black Americans of Achievement. New York: Chelsea House, 1993 (YA).

Further Viewing

Beverly Hills Cop Collection (1987). Paramount Home Video, DVD box set, 2007.

Bowfinger (1999). Universal, VHS/DVD, 2000.

Saturday Night Live—The Best of Eddie Murphy (1989). Lions Gate, DVD, 2004.

N

Nelson, Prince Rogers   See PRINCE.

Neville, Aaron
(1941–   ) *R & B singer*

Possessed of a feathery tenor that music critic Colin Escott has called "one of the truly great, eccentric voices in black music," Aaron Neville experienced pop celebrity early, only to fight his way back from obscurity to reach even greater fame.

He was born in New Orleans, Louisiana, on January 24, 1941. His father, Art, Sr., was a day laborer, while his mother, Amelia, was once half of a song-and-dance team with her brother George "Big Chief Jolly" Landry. All four Neville brothers turned to music for a living. Art Neville was the first, founding a band called the Hawkettes in the early 1950s. Renamed the Meters, the group became a legendary New Orleans rhythm and blues (R & B) band in the 1960s.

Aaron's road to music fame was more circuitous. He dropped out of high school to help support his pregnant girlfriend Joel, who he later married, and went to jail at age 17 for stealing a car. By the early 1960s, he began singing in local clubs and recording for several small independent labels. He struck gold in 1966 when he recorded the soulful ballad "Tell It Like It Is." The record went to number one on the R & B charts and

number two on the pop charts. Neville claims, however, he never saw any money from his hit because the record company and distributor declared bankruptcy. Even while his record was peaking, he was forced to make a living as a dock worker and ditchdigger.

Neville joined forces with his brothers, Art, Charles, and Cyril, in 1976 to form the Wild Tchoupitoulas. The unusual name came from the "tribe" their Uncle George belonged to in the yearly New Orleans Mardi Gras festivities. The following year they wisely renamed themselves the Neville Brothers and released a string of albums of eclectic music that gained critical praise but little commercial success.

After years of hard work, the Neville Brothers finally found fame with their album *Yellow Moon* (1989), which produced the Grammy Award–winning instrumental "Healing Chant." The brothers' success brought Aaron the fame he long deserved. His duet with Linda Ronstadt, "Don't Know Much" (1991), won a Grammy for best duo or pop group vocal. He teamed up with country singer Trisha Yearwood on the best-selling album *Rhythm, Country and Blues* (1994) and found further success on the solo album *To Make Me Who I Am* (1997). Among his most recent albums is *Bring It On Home: The Soul Classics* (2000), composed of songs by Sam Cooke, Otis Redding, and others.

A large, menacing-looking man with tattoos and a birthmark on his face, Aaron Neville has a sensitive, spiritual nature. He believes his angelic voice is "God in me touching God in others." A supporter of many causes, Neville founded the Uptown Youth Center, a New Orleans recreation center, and the New Orleans Artists Against Hunger and Homelessness in the 1980s. Neville himself was left homeless when Hurricane Katrina destroyed his New Orleans residence in August 2005. He relocated to Nashville, Tennessee, and moved back to New Orleans in 2008 and sang with his brothers in the city's Jazzfest that year. His son Ivan is also a recording artist.

Further Reading

Broven, John. *Rhythm and Blues in New Orleans.* New York: Pelican Publishing Company, 1983.

Ritz, David, and The Neville Brothers. *The Brothers: An Autobiography.* New York: Da Capo Press, 2001.

Further Listening

The Best of the Neville Brothers—20th Century Masters. A & M, CD, 2004.

Gold. Hip-O Records, 2 CDs, 2008.

Further Viewing

The Neville Brothers & Friends—Tell It Like It Is. Image Entertainment, DVD, 2004.

Nicholas, Fayard (1914–2006), and Harold Nicholas (1921–2000)
(The Nicholas Brothers)
tap specialty dancers, singers, actors

Undoubtedly the most daring and acrobatic dance team ever to stride across a stage or enliven a movie, the Nicholas Brothers became dance legends with their gravity-defying routines.

Fayard, the older of the two, was born on October 20, 1914, in Mobile, Alabama. Harold was born on March 27, 1921, in Winston-Salem, North Carolina. Their parents for years ran an orchestra in a Philadelphia theater. The brothers developed their unique dance act from watching dancers and circus acrobats. They began dancing and singing in Philadelphia clubs and by 1932, when Harold was only 11, were starring at New York's Cotton Club, performing with the jazz bands of DUKE ELLINGTON and CAB CALLOWAY, among others.

They called what they did "classical tap" and one of their specialties was leaping into splits, legs spread wide apart, over one another's heads. They repeated this astonishing feat up and down a gigantic staircase in their favorite movie, *Stormy Weather* (1943). The Nicholas Brothers appeared in their first film, *Pie, Pie Blackbird*, in 1932. It costarred pianist and composer EUBIE BLAKE and was shot in New York. Hollywood producer Sam Goldwyn caught their act at the Cotton Club and invited them to come to Hollywood to appear in the movie musical *Kid Millions* (1934). Soon after, they were featured in their first Broadway show, *Ziegfeld Follies* (1935), with exotic dancer JOSEPHINE BAKER. After that, they traveled to London, England, where they starred on stage in the musical *Blackbirds of 1936*.

In the early 1940s, the Nicholas Brothers appeared in a string of movies for the studio Twentieth Century–Fox. They received no credit in their first Fox musical, *Down Argentina Way* (1940) and were never given speaking roles in any of their Fox musicals. "They never did write us into the story," recalled Harold Nicholas in an interview. "I guess it was because we weren't the type they wanted." Like LENA HORNE and other black film performers of the 1940s, the Nicholas Brothers were brought in to do their act and then disappeared from the film. Despite this, the brothers' dazzling footwork was usually the most anticipated part of these movies for both black and white viewers.

Their Hollywood years reached a climax in MGM's *The Pirate* (1948), where they danced with

The Nicholas Brothers demonstrate one of their gravity-defying dance moves in the 1940s musical film *Sun Valley Serenade. (Photo courtesy of Showtime Archives, Toronto)*

Gene Kelly in the famous "Be a Clown" number. It would be their last appearance together in a Hollywood film.

Through the next two decades, the brothers concentrated on concert, stage, and television work. They toured the nation and took their act to Europe, Latin America, and Africa. Fayard mostly retired from performing in the late 1960s, but Harold continued to dance and sing on Broadway in the musicals *Sophisticated Ladies* (1981), which he also choreographed, and *The Tap Dance Kid* (1984). He danced and acted in the films *Tap* (1989) and *The Five Heartbeats* (1991), directed by black filmmaker Robert Townsend.

Fayard acted in a few films and won a Tony Award for his choreography in the Broadway musical revue *Black and Blue* (1989). He and Har-old also danced together in two JANET JACKSON music videos in the 1990s.

The Nicholas Brothers were inducted into the Black Film Makers Hall of Fame in 1978 and were recipients of the Kennedy Center Honors in 1991. They received a star on Hollywood's Walk of Fame in 1994. "Nowadays when black movie stars meet us, they say, 'You were the pioneers,'" Harold Nicholas said. "We're proud of that."

Harold Nicholas died of heart failure on July 3, 2000, in New York City at age 79. Fayard died of pneumonia on January 24, 2006, in Toluca Lake, California, at age 91.

Further Reading

Hill, Constance Valis. *Brotherhood in Rhythm: The Jazz Dancing of the Nicholas Brothers.* Lanham, Md.: Cooper Square Press, 2002.

Kennedy Center Honors. "The Nicholas Brothers." The Kennedy Center Web site. Available online. URL: http://www.kennedy-center.org/calendar/index.cfm?fuseaction=showIndividual&entity-id=370. Downloaded on February 8, 2009.

Further Viewing

The Pirate (1948). Warner Home Video, DVD, 2007.

Stormy Weather (1943). Twentieth Century Fox Video, DVD, 2006.

Norman, Jessye

(1945–) *opera and concert singer*

A soprano known for her dynamic range and extraordinary stage presence, Jessye Norman is one of America's most renowned contemporary opera singers.

She was born on September 15, 1945, in Augusta, Georgia, one of five children. Her father, Silas, was an insurance broker and her mother, Janie, a secretary and amateur pianist. Norman began singing at age four and sang publicly in church, at Parent-Teacher Association meetings, and at Girl Scouts meetings.

Despite her love of singing, Norman's career goal through high school was to become a nurse. In her senior year, however, her choral director urged her to compete for a music scholarship given by the MARIAN ANDERSON Foundation of Philadelphia, Pennsylvania. They traveled together to the competition where Norman failed to make an impression. On the trip back to Augusta, her teacher stopped in Washington, D.C., where she had Norman sing for a music professor at Howard University, a well-known black institute of higher learning. The professor was so impressed by Norman's voice that she offered her a full scholarship to attend Howard, which she did two years later.

After graduating from Howard with honors in 1967, Norman received a scholarship to travel to Germany, where she won first prize in a competition sponsored by Munich Radio. She was employed to sing at several leading German opera houses. After returning briefly to the United States, she settled in West Berlin and sang in several major European opera houses. She made her professional American debut in 1972, singing a concert version of the opera *Aida* at the Hollywood Bowl in California. Her first American recital took place the following year at Lincoln Center for the Performing Arts in New York City. "Miss Norman's recital stamped her a singer of extraordinary intelligence, taste and emotional depth," wrote Donal Henhan in *The New York Times.*

At age 38, Norman made a long-anticipated debut at New York's Metropolitan Opera in its centennial year of 1983, singing two roles in Hector Berlioz's opera *Les Troyens* (The Trojans). She continued to perform in opera through the 1990s, but gradually moved from soprano to mezzo-soprano parts. On March 11, 2002, she sang "America the Beautiful" at a memorial service for the victims of the World Trade Center (WTC) terrorist attack of September 11, 2001. Now in her sixties, Norman no longer sings on the opera stage but performs a regular schedule of concerts and recitals, combining opera arias with art songs and spirituals. In March 2009, she curated Honor!, a New York City festival honoring African-American cultural heroes with a series of concerts, lectures, discussions, and exhibits.

Norman was named an honorary ambassador to the United Nations (UN) in 1990 and was the recipient of the Kennedy Center Honors in the Performing Arts in 1997. She is probably one of the few opera singers to have an orchid named after her.

Speaking of her life, Norman has said that she "would like it to be that it made a difference to some people that I came and went, that I was here."

Further Reading

Kennedy Center Honors. "Jessye Norman." The Kennedy Center Web site. Available online. URL:

http://kennedy-center.org/calendar/index.cfm?fus
eaction=showIndividual&entity-id =378. Down-
loaded on February 8, 2009.
Story, Rosalyn M. *And So I Sing: African-American
Divas of Opera and Concert.* New York: Amistad
Press, 2000.

Further Listening
Very Best of Jessye Norman. EMI Classics, 2 CDs,
2003.

Further Viewing
Jessye Norman: A Portrait (2005). Decca, DVD, 2008.

Norwood, Brandy   See BRANDY.

Odetta
(Odetta Holmes, Odetta Felious)
(1930–2008) *folk singer, guitarist, actress*

Possessed of a powerful contralto voice and an imposing stage presence, Odetta was a mainstay of the American folk music scene for more than half a century.

She was born Odetta Holmes on December 30, 1930, in Birmingham, Alabama. Her father, Reuben, was a steel mill worker who died before she was born. Her mother, Flora, remarried, and Odetta took the surname of her stepfather, Zadock Felious, who worked as a janitor. The family moved to Los Angeles, California, when Odetta was six. She took piano lessons and sang in the school glee club. After graduating from high school, she attended Los Angeles City College where she studied classical music at night while earning a living as a housekeeper by day.

While she was performing in the chorus of a production of the musical *Finian's Rainbow* in San Francisco in 1949, some friends introduced her to folk music. Remembering the experience, she has said, "I knew I was home." She learned to play the guitar and started singing traditional folk songs. She was partial to work and prison songs but mastered a wide repertoire, including ballads, spirituals, and blues.

A classically trained singer, Odetta did not turn to folk music until she was nearly 30 and became one of the leading lights of the folk movement. *(AP Photo/Stuart Ramson)*

Odetta debuted as a folk singer at the Tin Angel, a club in San Francisco, and ended up performing there for a year. She came to New York for a month's engagement at the Blue Angel, where she met folksinger HARRY BELAFONTE, who became one of her strongest supporters. She appeared with him on his 1959 television special.

Her first of more than two dozen albums, *Odetta Sings Ballads and Blues*, was released in 1956. Reviewing a later album, *The New York Times* critic Robert Shelton called her "the most glorious new voice in American folk music." Odetta sang in the film *Cinerama Holiday* (1955) and made her dramatic acting debut as the crazed servant Nancy in the film adaptation of the William Faulkner novel *Sanctuary* (1960).

Like many folksingers of her generation, Odetta was strongly committed to social change. She participated in the Civil Rights movement; marched in Selma, Alabama; and performed on stage with civil rights leader Martin Luther King, Jr. She received the Martin Luther King Medal from George Washington University in 1992. The same year, she performed and campaigned for Democratic presidential candidate Bill Clinton.

Odetta toured throughout the United States and Canada and performed in the Soviet Union for the first time in 1974. She received the World Folk Music Association's first Lifetime Achievement Award in 1994 for "incorporating a social message in song."

Odetta continued to perform into her seventies despite health problems. At a Carnegie Hall tribute to rock musician Bruce Springsteen in April 2007, she sang Springsteen's song "57 Channels." The composer called it "the greatest version" of the song he'd heard. Odetta died of heart disease on December 2, 2008, at age 77.

Further Reading

Hood, Phil, ed. *Artists of American Folk Music: The Legends of Traditional Folk, the Stars of the Sixties, the Virtuosi of New Acoustic Music.* New York: William Morrow, 1988.

"Odetta." *Current Biography Yearbook 1998.* New York: H. W. Wilson, 1998.

Weiner, Tim. "Odetta 77, a Voice of the Civil Rights Movements, Dies." *New York Times,* December 3, 2003, Obituaries, p. A24.

Further Listening

Absolutely the Best. Varese Sarabande, CD, 2000.

Further Viewing

Festival—The Newport Folk Festival. Eagle Vision Media, DVD, 2005.

Owens, Dana   See QUEEN LATIFAH.

P

Parker, Charlie
(Charles Christopher Parker, Jr., "Bird")
(1920–1955) *jazz saxophonist, composer*

One of jazz's greatest innovators and the cofounder of the bebop movement, Charlie Parker is as much a legend for his tragic and dissolute life as he is for the incredible music he created.

He was born Charles Christopher Parker, Jr., on August 24, 1920, in Kansas City, Kansas. His father, Charles, Sr., left home when his son was very young, and the boy was raised by his loving mother, Addie. She wanted him to be a doctor, but Parker fell in love with jazz and the alto saxophone in high school and never looked back. He formed his first band, the Deans of Swing, while still in high school. He quit school at age 15 when told he would have to stay back a year. Soon after, he married his girlfriend, 19-year-old Rebecca Ruffing. Parker's first attempt to play a solo at a local club's jam session was so bad that he was hooted off the stage. This rejection made him all the more determined to succeed, and he practiced for months before going off alone on the road.

He arrived in New York City in 1939 and was hired to play in Jay McShann's jazz band. He made his first recordings with McShann and went on to work with several other big bands in the early 1940s. Fellow musicians called him "Yardbird" because of his fondness for chicken. This was later shortened to "Bird."

Parker began to experiment with his music. He speeded up the playing tempo, created irregular rhythms, played with a fierce aggressiveness, and improvised far more than most traditional jazz musicians did. This revolutionary style of jazz playing would soon come to be called bebop.

The bebop movement solidified when Parker teamed up with trumpeter DIZZY GILLESPIE, bassist Ray Brown, pianist Bud Powell, and drummer Max Roach in a new quintet in 1944. Their first recordings are classics of bebop jazz and include "Salt Peanuts," "Hot House," and "Groovin' High," all recorded in 1945. When Gillespie left the group that same year, Parker formed his own small combo. Among the talented musicians who played with him was the young MILES DAVIS. The group's distinctive music began to develop a small following of devoted listeners, but most listeners found bebop too disjointed, fast, and unmelodic to listen to. Parker traveled to Los Angeles, California, with his combo and introduced bebop to the West Coast, where a number of jazz musicians adapted the style.

Despite his success, Parker's personal life was a shambles. He divorced his first wife and a second marriage to Geraldine Scott also failed. (He would marry two more times.) He had been addicted to heroin since age 17 and had an appetite for life that was truly self-destructive. He once downed 16 double whiskies in two hours and ate 20 hamburgers at one time. He would fail to appear for shows, record when he was on drugs with disastrous results, and not always pay his musicians. In late 1946, Parker suffered a complete nervous breakdown and was confined for seven months to a state hospital in California.

He made a full recovery and returned to New York, where he experienced several productive years. He recorded a number of classic albums for Verve Records including *Bird with Strings* and *Bird and Dizzy,* which reunited him with Gillespie after a break in their relationship. Charlie Parker was so famous in the jazz world that two jazz clubs were named after him, Birdland in New York and Birdhouse in Chicago, Illinois.

By the early 1950s, Parker was taking heroin again and drinking heavily. After he was arrested for drugs, he could not get a permit to play in nightclubs. He continued to record and play wherever he could, but his health declined and he could not afford his own apartment. He began living with friends, moving from one apartment to another. He was staying at a friend's in New York City on March 12, 1955, when he suffered a fatal heart attack while watching television. He was only 34 years old.

Parker's legacy has grown steadily in the nearly five decades since his death. Today, he is seen as one of jazz's true greats whose inventive mind and musical ability is still looked on with awe and respect. "He brought a new level of psychological complexity, and he had an incredible sense of thematic organization," jazz musician WYNTON MARSALIS has said. "You combine that kind of intellectual capability with that type of deep soul and you've got something to contend with."

In 1988, actor and jazz enthusiast Clint Eastwood directed *Bird,* a biographical film about Charlie Parker, starring FOREST WHITAKER in the lead role.

Further Reading

Giddins, Gary. *Celebrating Bird: The Triumph of Charlie Parker.* New York: Da Capo Press, 1999.

Priestley, Brian. *Chasin' The Bird: The Life and Legacy of Charlie Parker.* New York: Oxford University Press, 2007.

Russell, Ross. *Bird Lives!: The High Life and Hard Times of Charlie (Yardbird) Parker.* New York: Da Capo Press, 1996.

Woideck, Carl, ed. *The Charlie Parker Companion: Six Decades of Commentary.* New York: Schirmer Books, 2000.

Further Listening

The Best of Charlie Parker: 20th Century Masters. Verve, CD, 2004.

Ken Burns JAZZ Collection: Charlie Parker. Polygram Records, CD, 2000.

Further Viewing

Bird (1988). Warner Home Video, Special Edition, 2 DVDs, 2008.

Charlie Parker: Celebrating Bird (1987). Pioneer, VHS/DVD, 1991/1999.

P Diddy   See COMBS, SEAN "PUFFY."

Peterson, Oscar
(Oscar Emmanuel Peterson)
(1925–2007) *jazz pianist, group leader, composer*

One of the finest of modern jazz pianists, Oscar Peterson and his trio were also one of the longest-running acts in jazz, having played and recorded for half a century.

He was born Oscar Emmanuel Peterson in Montreal, in the Canadian province of Quebec, on August 15, 1925. His father, Daniel, taught him the piano and the trumpet when he was five. By seven he had dropped the trumpet to concentrate on the piano. When Peterson was 15, he won first prize on a local radio show and was soon playing with the Johnny Holmes Orchestra. He formed his first trio in 1947 and had a weekly radio show broadcast live from Montreal's Albert Lounge. Two years later, record producer and manager Norman Granz, who would revive the career of jazz singer ELLA FITZGERALD, heard Peterson at the lounge and signed him on as a client. Granz brought Peterson to the United States to play at Carnegie Hall in New York City. Then the pianist toured with Granz's celebrated "Jazz at the Philharmonic" group.

In 1953, Peterson formed a new trio with two Americans—Ray Brown on bass and Herb Ellis on guitar. In later years, Brown would be replaced by Danish bassist Neils-Henning Orsted Pederson, and Ellis by American guitarist Joe Pass. The Oscar Peterson Trio recorded extensively for Granz's Verve label and later for the MPS German label. Peterson was nominated for 11 Grammy Awards and won eight, including two in 1990 for jazz instrumental performance, soloist and group (with the trio). He was also known as a top accompanist and worked with singer Ella Fitzgerald, among many other performers.

Peterson was less well known as a composer, although he wrote many pieces, suites, and film scores. His more ambitious works include the *Canadian Suite* (1963) and *Easter Suite* (1984), considered by many to be his finest work. His *Hymn to Freedom* became a crusade hymn of the Civil Rights movement in the 1960s. He won a Canadian Film Award for his edgy score for the thriller *The Silent Partner* (1978). Peterson also wrote the music for the award-winning animated films *Celebration* and *Begone Dull Care* by famed Canadian animator Norman McLaren.

Oscar Peterson was voted best jazz pianist by the readers of *Down Beat* magazine for 12 years and received Grammy's Lifetime Achievement Award in 1997. He died of kidney failure on December 23, 2007, at his home outside of Toronto, Canada, at age 82.

Further Reading

Lees, Gene. *Oscar Peterson: The Will to Swing.* Lanham, Md.: Cooper Square Press, 2000.

Marin, Reva. *Oscar: The Life and Music of Oscar Peterson.* Toronto, Canada: Groundwood Books, 2008 (YA).

The Oscar Peterson Official Web site. Available online. URL: http://www.oscarpeterson.com. Downloaded on February 8, 2009.

Peterson, Oscar. *A Jazz Odyssey: The Life of Oscar Peterson.* Edited by Richard Palmer. New York: Continuum, 2003.

Further Listening

Live at the Blue Note. Telarc, CD box set, 2009.

Further Viewing

Jazz Icons: Oscar Peterson—Live in '63, '64 & '65. Naxos of America, DVD, 2008.

Phifer, Mekhi
(1974–   )   *actor*

One of the most visible and talented of the new generation of black actors, Mekhi Phifer is best known as the easygoing but confident Dr. Gregory Pratt on TV's long-running medical series *ER.*

He was born Mekhi Thira Phifer on December 29, 1974, in Harlem, New York. He and his twin brother were raised by their single mother, Rhoda, who later became a high school teacher. He never met his father, who left before he was born, and Phifer felt his seven uncles provided the male role models he needed growing up. He attended Lincoln Square Auxiliary Service High School and after graduation intended on going to college to study electrical engineering. A chance decision to attend an open casting call for director Spike Lee's film *Clockers* changed the course of his life. Despite the fact that he had no formal training as an actor, Phifer beat out a thousand other young black men for the leading role of Strike, a drug dealer. Phifer found his calling and never looked back.

Other teen roles quickly followed, including the comic spoof *High School High* (1996), where he met his first wife, actress Malinda Williams; the thriller *I Still Know What You Did Last Summer* (1998); and *A Lesson before Dying* (1999), a made-for-television movie in which he played a man on death row opposite DON CHEADLE and CICELY TYSON. Phifer played Odin, the captain of a high school basketball team, in a contemporary version of Shakespeare's Othello called *O* (2001). The following year he had his most prominent screen role to date opposite the rapper Eminem in *8 Mile*.

As interesting as some of these roles were, Phifer was tired of playing teen heroes and villains, and when the opportunity to become a regular cast member of *ER* presented itself, he jumped at the chance. "I definitely thought [*ER*] could take me to another level of manhood as far as how people see me," he has said. Phifer quickly became one of the show's mainstays. In the opening episode of the 2008–09 season, *ER*'s last, Pratt dies from the effects of an ambulance explosion engineered by the Mob to kill a man in a witness-protection program whom Pratt had befriended. In his six seasons on the show, Phifer was twice nominated for an National Association for Advancement of Colored People (NAACP) Image Award.

Phifer's marriage to Williams, which produced a daughter, ended in divorce. He married Oni Souratha from the African nation of Malagasy in 2007. The couple has a son also born in 2007. Phifer is a champion poker player and has participated on the World Poker Tour in Hollywood Home games for charity. He is also chairman of the board of trustees of the Vine Group USA, a nonprofit organization that aids African universities.

Further Reading

"Mekhi Phifer." The Internet Movie Database. Available online. URL: http://www.imdb.com/name/nm0001616/. Downloaded on December 10, 2008.

Morrison, Mark. "A Prescription for Change." *USA Weekend,* November 22–24, 2002, p. 22.

Further Viewing

8 Mile (2002). Universal, DVD, 2003.
ER—The Complete Tenth Season (2003–2004). Warner Home Video, DVD box set, 2009.
O (2001). Lions Gate, DVD, 2001.

Pickett, Wilson
("The Wicked Pickett")
(1941–2006) *R & B singer, songwriter*

One of the grittiest soul singers to come to prominence in the 1960s, Wilson Pickett enjoyed more than a decade of recording success, far more than most of his contemporaries.

He was born on March 18, 1941, in Pratville, Alabama, not far from Montgomery, the youngest of 11 children. Physically abused by his mother, Pickett moved to Detroit, Michigan, where his father lived, when he was 14. He began his singing career there in a local gospel-harmony group called the Violinaires. In 1959, he joined the rhythm and blues (R & B) group the Falcons. He began contributing songs to the group's repertoire, including "I Found a Love," which became the Falcons' only pop hit in 1962. The following year he became a solo act for a small, independent record company. One of his first recordings was the self-penned "If You Need Me." It became a minor hit for Pickett but a much larger hit for R & B singer Solomon Burke. Atlantic Records, a major label, bought Pickett's contract in 1964, but his first few Atlantic releases failed to sell.

Atlantic producer Jerry Wexler traveled with the singer to Memphis, Tennessee, to record some songs at the Stax Record studios. Stax's trademark southern soul was just the recipe for success for Wilson Pickett. Stax guitarist and producer Steve Cropper wrote a song with the singer based on a peculiar phrase that Pickett heard while performing in a club. The singer's frayed vocals backed by punchy Memphis horns and a powerhouse bass line sent "In the Midnight Hour" (1965) to number one on the R & B charts, and it became a soul classic. He quickly consolidated his fame with a string of outstanding, hard-hitting records—"634-5789," "Land of 1000 Dances," and "Mustang Sally" (all 1966) among many others. When Stax closed its doors to Atlantic artists, Wexler sent Pickett to the legendary Muscle Shoals Studio in Florence, Alabama, where ARETHA FRANKLIN would soon make her mark.

Although he made upbeat dance songs his specialty, Pickett showed he could also be an effective ballad singer, with such hits as "I'm in Love" (1967) and a surprisingly moving cover of the Beatles' song "Hey Jude" (1968). He freely drew material from every genre of pop music, including bubble gum music ("Sugar, Sugar") and 1970s rock ("Mama Told Me Not to Come"), putting his inimitable stamp on everything he sang.

In 1973, Pickett left Atlantic for RCA, where he had two more minor hits. He continued to record into the 1980s on a number of labels, including Motown and his own Wicked Records, but without any appreciable success. He toured through the 1980s, remaining an exciting and spontaneous performer. "There isn't a rock group with soul leanings that hasn't performed [his] songs and borrowed more than a little from Pickett," wrote writer Lillian Roxon. The Alan Parker film *The Commitments* (1991), about an Irish band that plays American R & B, paid tribute to Pickett when the group excitedly anticipated his visit to Ireland to hear them. Wilson Pickett was inducted into the Rock and Roll Hall of Fame in 1991.

The man who dubbed himself "The Wicked Pickett" unfortunately lived up to that name in later years. In 1992 he was sentenced to a year in prison for hitting a pedestrian in New Jersey while driving drunk, and he had other run-ins with the police.

It's Harder Now (1999), Pickett's first album in a decade, received a Grammy nomination for best traditional R & B vocal performance and was honored with a Blues Foundation W. C. HANDY Award for Comeback Album of the Year in 2000. Wilson Pickett died of a heart attack on January 19, 2006, at age 64.

Further Reading

Guralnick, Peter. *Sweet Soul Music: Rhythm and Blues and the Southern Dream of Freedom.* San Francisco, Calif.: Back Bay Books, 1999.

Leeds, Jeff. "Wilson Pickett, 64, Soul Singer of Great Passion, Dies." *New York Times,* January 20, 2006, Obituaries, p. B8.

Rock and Roll Hall of Fame Inductees. "Wilson Pickett." Rock and Roll Hall of Fame and Museum Web site. Available online. URL: http://www.rockhall.com/inductee/wilson-pickett. Downloaded on February 8, 2009.

Further Listening

The Definitive Collection. Atlantic, 2 CDs, 2006.

Further Viewing

Only the Strong Survive: A Celebration of Soul (2002). Miramax Home Entertainment, DVD, 2009.

Poitier, Sidney
(1927–   ) *actor, director*

The first African-American actor to achieve international stardom, Sidney Poitier has created a gallery of memorable characters marked by their intelligence, compassion, and immense personal appeal. In the process, he broke the old Hollywood stereotypes of blacks and blazed a trail for many other black actors to follow.

He was born in Miami, Florida, on February 20, 1927, while his parents, Evelyn and Reginald Poitier, were visiting relatives from their native Bahamas. Poitier grew up on a poor tomato farm on Cat Island in the Bahamas with seven brothers and a sister. He attended school for less than two years and was permitted to return to Miami by his parents when he was 15. They were afraid that if

Sidney Poitier's fame as the first major black film star has often overshadowed his fine acting ability. *(Photofest)*

appeared in bit roles in several Off-Broadway productions and won critical notice in the Greek comedy *Lysistrata.*

When producer Darryl F. Zanuck auditioned him for his first film role in 1949, Poitier added five years to his age (he was 22) to land the part. The movie, *No Way Out* (1950), was one of the first Hollywood films to deal head-on with racism in America. Poitier played a young doctor who is marked for vengeance by a bigoted hood who thinks he deliberately killed his brother. Poitier's intelligence and passion in the role made him an actor worth watching. This was followed by a leading role in the South African drama, *Cry, the Beloved Country* (1952), costarring veteran black actor CANADA LEE, and three years later, *Blackboard Jungle* (1955), where Poitier played a troubled high school student who is befriended by a new teacher.

His next important role was as a black convict on the run who is chained to a white prisoner (Tony Curtis) during a prison break in *The Defiant Ones* (1958). Poitier's tough and embittered, but ultimately compassionate, convict earned him his first Academy Award nomination for best actor. By the early 1960s, Poitier had established himself as not only the leading black actor in Hollywood but also a top box-office draw. In two years during the 1960s, he was named the top male movie star in the United States. He moved effortlessly from musicals (*Porgy and Bess*) to action-adventure films (*Red Ball Express, The Long Ships*) to contemporary dramas (*A Raisin in the Sun, Paris Blues*). Poitier won the Academy Award for best actor for his easygoing but caring handyman who helps a group of German nuns build a chapel in *Lilies of the Field* (1963). He was the first African-American actor to be so honored.

Poitier's biggest year was 1967 when he starred in three box-office hits. He played Virgil Tibbs, a big-city detective who helps a small-town southern sheriff solve a murder in *In the Heat of the Night.* In *To Sir, With Love* he was an understanding teacher in a tough British school and in

he stayed in the Bahamas he would become a juvenile delinquent.

Poitier lived with his relatives for a time and then at age 18 moved to New York City with $1.50 in his pocket. He found menial jobs and slept for a time in a bus terminal bathroom. He served in the army briefly, working in a veteran's hospital, and then returned to New York. Poitier found more menial work in the Harlem section of the city while he pursued acting. He auditioned for the American Negro Theater (ANT) in 1946 but was rejected because of his thick Caribbean accent. The rejection only made Poitier more determined to succeed. For six months he listened to radio announcers and imitated their way of speaking. He went back to ANT, and this time he was accepted into the company. One of his fellow fledging actors was HARRY BELAFONTE. He

Guess Who's Coming to Dinner he was Katharine Hepburn and Spencer Tracy's prospective son-in-law.

Ironically, Poitier's very success made him a target for sharp criticism from many leading lights in the black community. They called him an Uncle Tom and cardboard "noble Negro" whose very goodness was unreal and robbed his characters of any real individuality and blackness. Much of this criticism had its point, but to blame it all on Poitier was unfair. He tried to extend the range of his film roles, sometimes successfully and other times not so. He turned to directing and made four entertaining comedy-adventure films in which he also starred—*Buck and the Preacher* (1972), *Uptown Saturday Night* (1974), *Let's Do It Again* (1976), and *A Piece of the Action* (1977). His costars in these films included his good friends Harry Belafonte and BILL COSBY. Poitier acted in no films from 1978 to 1987, but he directed the prison comedy *Stir Crazy* (1980) with RICHARD PRYOR and Gene Wilder.

He finally returned to film acting in the excellent crime thriller *Shoot to Kill* (1987). In the 1990s Poitier found better roles on television than in the movies. He played lawyer and first black Supreme Court Justice Thurgood Marshall in the Emmy Award–winning television drama *Separate but Equal* (1991). Two years later he received the Thurgood Marshall Lifetime Achievement Award given by the National Association for the Advancement of Colored People (NAACP). In 1997, he was named ambassador to Japan from his native Bahamas. His last big screen appearance to date was the same year in *The Jackal*. He has not appeared in a TV movie since 2001.

A person of great charisma both on and off the screen, Sidney Poitier is today recognized as one of Hollywood's finest actors and the man who paved the way for every black film actor who came after him. Poitier received a second, honorary Academy Award in 2002 for his impressive body of work in film. President Barack Obama pre-sented Poitier with the Presidential Medal of Freedom in August 2009. He has been married to actress-model Joanna Shimkus since 1976.

Further Reading

Bergman, Carol. *Sidney Poitier.* Black American Series. Los Angeles: Holloway House, 1990 (YA).

Goudsouzian, Aram. *Sidney Poitier: Man, Actor, Icon.* Chapel Hill: University of North Carolina Press, 2003.

Poitier, Sidney. *Life Beyond Measure: Letters to My Great-Granddaughter.* New York: HarperOne, 2008.

———. *The Measure of a Man: A Spiritual Autobiography.* San Francisco: HarperSanFrancisco, 2007.

Further Viewing

The Defiant Ones (1958). MGM Home Video, VHS/DVD, 1999/2001.

In the Heat of the Night (1967). MGM Home Video, VHS/DVD, 2001.

Lilies of the Field (1963). MGM Home Video, VHS/DVD, 1999/2001.

Price, Leontyne
(Mary Violent Leontine Price)
(1927–   ) *opera singer*

The first African-American star of the opera stage, Leontyne Price's warm and expressive soprano has been called "the voice of the century."

She was born Mary Violent Leontine Price in Laurel, Mississippi, on February 10, 1927. When she was nine her mother, Kate, a nurse and midwife, took her to see MARIAN ANDERSON in concert at Jackson, Mississippi. "I said to myself, 'I don't know what she's doing, but I sure want to do some of that one of these days,'" Price later recalled. In 1944, she attended the College of Educational and Industrial Arts in Wilberforce, Ohio. Her goal was to become a music teacher, but when the college's president heard her sing he encouraged her to change her major to voice. Another early supporter was actor-singer PAUL ROBESON, who started a scholarship fund for her after hearing her sing in college.

Price went on to the Juilliard School of Music in 1948 and made her operatic debut as Mistress Ford in a school production of Giuseppe Verdi's *Falstaff.* She sang opposite baritone William Warfield, whom she would later marry. American composer Virgil Thomson attended the production and immediately asked her to sing in the Broadway revival of his opera *Four Saints in Three Acts.* She no sooner completed that production than she was chosen by lyricist Ira Gershwin to star as Bess in the revival of his brother George's opera *Porgy and Bess.* She later toured with the Broadway production across the United States, Europe, and the Soviet Union.

In 1955, Price became the first African-American singer in a television opera production. She sang the title role in Verdi's *Tosca* on the NBC Network. The next year she appeared on NBC in Mozart's *The Magic Flute.* Price made a belated but stunning debut at the Metropolitan Opera Company in New York in 1961 in the opera *Il Trovatore.* A reviewer in the *New York Times* wrote, "Her voice, warm and luscious, had enough volume to fill the house with ease. . . ." At the performance's conclusion Price received a 42-minute ovation, one of the longest in opera history. She went on to sing many major roles at the Met over the next two decades, including the title role in *Aida* and Minnie in *The Girl of the Golden West.*

In 1965, the Metropolitan Opera moved to its new home in New York's Lincoln Center for the Performing Arts. American composer Samuel Barber wrote the opera *Cleopatra* especially for the occasion with Price in the leading role. The singer rehearsed the demanding role of Cleopatra for a year before the dazzling premiere.

Having sung in nearly every major opera house in America and Europe, Price retired from the opera stage in 1985, but continued to record and sing recitals for many years, giving her last recital in 1997 at age 71. She has won 15 Grammy Awards in the classical music division. In 1980, she was the recipient of the Kennedy Center Honors. Price was one of four recipients of the first Opera Honors given by the National Endowment for the Arts in October 2008. Her children's book version of the Verdi opera *Aida,* published in 1997, was the basis for the 2000 Broadway musical by Elton John and Tim Rice.

With her amazing voice and star presence, Leontyne Price has widened the appeal of opera in America and paved the way for such other African-American divas as JESSYE NORMAN.

Leontyne Price's expressive soprano has been called "the voice of the century." *(Photofest)*

Further Reading

Lyon, Hugh Lee. *Leontyne Price: Highlights of a Prima Donna* (1993). Toronto, Canada: Author's Choice, 2007.

Story, Rosalyn M. *And So I Sing: African-American Divas of Opera and Concert.* New York: Warner Books, 1990.

Woronoff, Kristen. *Leontyne Price*. Library of Famous Women Juniors. Farmington Hills, Mich.: Blackbirch Press, 2002 (children).

Further Listening

Leontyne Price: The Ultimate Collection. RCA, 2 CDs, 1999.

Further Viewing

The Art of Leontyne Price. Video Artists International, DVD, 2004.

Pride, Charley
(1939–   ) *country singer*

The most successful African-American country singer, Charley Pride blazed a trail that very few blacks have followed.

He was born on March 18, 1939, in Sledge, Mississippi, on a 40-acre cotton farm. Pride bought his first guitar from Sears and Roebuck with money he earned picking cotton. His father, Mack Pride, Sr., played a large role in his becoming a country musician. The elder Pride, a sharecropper, was strictly opposed on religious grounds to the blues, but he loved country music. Charley grew up listening with his dad to the Grand Ole Opry, country music's greatest institution, on the radio.

Pride's other great love was baseball. At age 16 he joined the Negro American League. Two years later he joined the army, got married, and returned to civilian life, determined to become a pro baseball player. He tried out for the California Angels team in the early 1960s, but an injured throwing arm dashed his hopes of playing pro ball.

Country singer Red Sovine heard Pride singing one night in a club and helped him obtain an audition at RCA Records in Nashville, Tennessee. RCA producer Chet Atkins wanted to sign Pride and did so before his bosses found out he was black and might have objected. His first single record, "The Snakes Crawl at Night," was

released in early 1966. "Just Between You and Me," his third single, shot to the top-10 on the country charts. "All I Have to Offer You (Is Me)" (1969) was his first record to cross over to the pop charts. Pride's mellow, unadorned tenor and his good choice of material quickly made him a favorite with country listeners. He was invited to perform at the Grand Ole Opry, every country performer's dream, in 1967. But another 26 years would pass before he was asked to become a regular cast member of the Opry. He became only the second black performer to receive that honor, nearly 52 years after harmonica player DeFore Bailey. Pride's biggest pop hit was "Kiss an Angel Good Mornin'" (1971), which was a number-one country hit. By 1989, Pride had 29 number-one country hits.

His recording career peaked in the 1970s, and in the 1980s he focused on his growing business interests. He is one of country music's most astute and successful businessmen. Pride controls a large share of First Texas Bank; owns Chardon, his own booking and management company; and is a part owner of Pi-Gem, a song publisher.

Charley Pride was named the Country Music Association's entertainer of the year in 1971 and was twice voted male vocalist of the year in 1971 and 1972. In 2000, he was inducted into the Country Music Hall of Fame. He still occasionally records. *Pride and Joy: A Gospel Music Collection* was released in 2006.

Further Reading
Barclay, P. *Charley Pride*. Mankato, Minn.: Creative Paperbacks Inc., 1981 (YA).
Pride, Charley, with Jim Henderson. *Pride: The Charley Pride Story*. North Yorkshire, U.K.: Quill, 1995.

Further Listening
The Essential Charley Pride. RCA, 2 CDs, 2006.

Further Viewing
Live in Concert: March 15th 1975. Forever DVD N1, DVD, 2008.

Primus, Pearl

(1919–1994) *modern dancer, choreographer, dance company director, anthropologist*

An athletic dancer of dramatic intensity, Pearl Primus transformed African and Caribbean dance forms into powerful political and social statements.

She was born on November 26, 1919, in Trinidad, an island in the West Indies. When she was two, her parents, Edward and Emily Primus, immigrated with her to the United States. Primus grew up in New York City and attended Hunter College, where she studied medicine. Racial prejudice, however, prevented her from getting a laboratory position after graduation. A good athlete, she decided to give dance a try and became an understudy in a dance troupe under the National Youth Administration. In 1941, at age 22, she won a scholarship to the New Dance Group. She began to study African dance styles and made her solo debut in her original dance work *African Ceremonial* (1943). The response to this performance was so positive that she formed her own dance company the following year. Racial and social issues figured prominently in such Primus works as *Strange Fruit* (1945), based on the song made popular by BILLIE HOLIDAY that deals with the lynching of blacks in the South.

Primus traveled to Africa to study traditional native dances on a Julius Rosenwald Fellowship in 1948. One result was the work *Fangs* (1949), based on a Liberian ritual dance. On another research trip to her homeland of Trinidad in 1953, Primus met and married dancer and choreographer Percival Borde. In 1959, the couple traveled to the African nation of Liberia, where Primus became the first director of the Liberian Performing Arts Center. Returning to the United States, she established the African-Caribbean-American Institute of Dance in New York City in 1963. She combined her dance work with teaching through the 1960s, stressing the importance of dance as a means of cultural expression and communication. She earned a doctorate in anthropology, the study of human societies, from Columbia University in 1978. The same year, she founded the Pearl Primus Dance Language Institute in New Rochelle, New York.

Her husband and close collaborator died in 1979, and Primus stopped dancing professionally in her 60s. She continued to teach at Hunter College until her death on October 29, 1994. She was awarded the National Medal of Art by President George H. W. Bush in 1991.

Further Reading

Emery, Lynne Fauley. *Black Dance: From 1619 to Today.* Princeton, N.J.: Princeton Book, 1989.

Glover, Jean Ruth. *Pearl Primus: Cross-cultural Pioneer of American Dance.* Ann Arbor, Mich.: UMI, 1989.

Thorpe, Edward. *Black Dance.* New York: Overlook Press, 1994.

Further Viewing

Dancing in the Light: Six Dance Compositions by African-American Choreographers / Asadata Dafora, Katherine Dunham, Pearl Primus, Talley Beatty, Donald McKayle, Bill T. Jones. Kultur Video, DVD, 2007.

Prince

(Prince Rogers Nelson, The Artist Formerly Known as Prince)
(1958–   ) *rock singer, songwriter, actor, musician, record and film producer, director*

Called by music critic Stephen Thomas Erlewine "one of the most singular talents of the rock & roll era," Prince has always taken his own road, from his first self-produced album to his mysterious retirement from recording 15 years later.

He was born Prince Rogers Nelson on June 7, 1958, in Minneapolis, Minnesota. The name Prince came from his father, John, a musician, whose stage name was Prince Rogers. His mother, Nattie, sang with his father's jazz trio. By age seven, Prince was playing television theme songs on the family piano and by 12 could play a number of different musical instruments. The same year he formed his first band, Champagne, which played the Minneapolis area for five years.

Prince, now using only his Christian name, began to write songs and record them, often playing all the instruments on different recording tracks himself. He submitted a demo tape with three songs to Warner Brothers Records. The company was so impressed by Prince's abilities that they gave him more than $100,000 to produce a debut album. At age 19, he became the youngest performer ever to produce an album for the label. That album, *Prince-For-You* (1978), and its follow-up, *Prince* (1979), were solid efforts and sold well but did not prepare anyone for what came next.

Dirty Mind (1980) and *Controversy* (1981) contained songs that dealt with human sexuality and social and political issues with a directness never before seen in pop music. While Prince's lyrics were often controversial, his music was a mesmerizing blend of pop, rock, funk, and folk. Prince reached a creative peak with *1999* (1982) and *Purple Rain* (1984), which was the soundtrack for the movie of the same name. The film, released later that year, was both a concert film and a semi-autobiographical look into the life of a rising rock star, with Prince in the central role. Many critics hailed it as one of the best rock films ever made and Prince won an Academy Award for the best original song score.

Prince put together a new band, the Revolution, and went on a national concert tour that was as successful as the album and the movie. He was now one of rock's true superstars, but like other artists in that position, he made a number of missteps. A second film, *Under the Cherry Moon* (1986), was a commercial and critical flop. A new studio album, *Lovesexy* (1988), was attacked for its

lyrics and a nude photo of Prince on the cover. His soundtrack for the movie *Batman* (1989) was a commercial smash, but it was less innovative than his earlier albums. *Graffiti Bridge* (1990), a sequel movie to *Purple Rain,* was another box-office failure.

Prince recovered from this slump and formed a new band, the New Power Generation. Their subsequent album, *Diamonds and Pearls* (1991), contained some of his best music in years. His next album perplexed many fans with its strange title—a graphic that combined male and female symbols. It became known as the *Love Symbol Album* (1992). In April 1993 Prince stunned the music world by announcing that he would no longer record. A short time later, on his 35th birthday, he officially changed his name to the love symbol. Since no one could say the symbol, journalists began to refer to him as the Artist Formerly Known as Prince.

Despite his retirement, more albums were released after 1993. *Black Album,* another exploration of sexual relationships, was actually recorded back in 1987 but withheld from release by Prince. *Come* (1994), one of his weakest efforts, was recorded to meet a contractual agreement with Warner Brothers.

Despite his promise, this "former artist" returned in 1995 with a new album, *The Gold Experience,* which proved he had not lost his golden touch with music. In May 2000, he officially declared himself Prince once more, following the expiration of a publishing contract.

His instrumental album *N.E.W.S.* (2003) was nominated for a Grammy. Prince's next album, *Musicology* (2004), was his most successful in years, and two songs from it earned him two Grammys for best male R & B vocal performance and best traditional R & B vocal performance. His *Indigo Nights* (2008) is a live album accompanied by a book of poems and lyrics. In March 2009, Prince released a three-disc set, *Lotus Flow3r/Mp/sound/Elixir.* Prince was inducted into the Rock and Roll Hall of Fame in 2004.

Further Reading

Hahn, Alex. *Possessed: The Rise and Fall of Prince.* New York: Billboard Books, 2003.

Jones, Liz. *Purple Reign: The Artist Formerly Known as Prince.* Secaucus: N.J.: Carol Publishing Group, 1999.

Nilsen, Per. *Dancemusicsexromance: Prince—The First Decade.* U.K.: Firefly Publishing, 2001.

Perone, James E. *The Words and Music of Prince.* Santa Barbara, Calif.: Praeger, 2008.

Further Listening

Music from the Motion Picture Purple Rain (1984). Warner Bros, CD, 1990.

Ultimate Prince. Rhino, 2 CDs, 2006.

Further Viewing

Purple Rain (1984). Warner Home Video, 2 DVDs, 2004.

Pryor, Richard

(1940–2005) *comedian, film actor, writer*

The most gifted and influential black comic of the past three decades, Richard Pryor turned his personal problems into insightful and trenchant humor. The first black comic to become a major Hollywood movie star, his unflinching honesty and manic energy struck a chord with black and white audiences alike.

Pryor's early life was harrowing and explained much of the self-destructive streak that haunted him most of his adult life. He was born in a poor section of Peoria, Illinois, on December 1, 1940. He grew up in a brothel run by his paternal grandmother in which his mother worked as a prostitute. His parents married after he was born and later divorced. Pryor was a problem child in school and was expelled from high school at 16 for striking a teacher. He worked for a time in his father's trucking company and then joined the army. On his return to civilian life in 1960 he settled in Peoria, married, and started doing stand-up comedy in midwestern clubs. Pryor moved to New York City in 1963, where he patterned his stand-up comedy act after BILL COSBY's nonracial, inoffensive brand of humor. He became popular enough to break into television, performing on *The Ed Sullivan Show* and other variety and talk shows.

Soon after, he moved to Los Angeles, California, and began to get small parts in movies. His first film role was as a comic detective in *The Busy Body* (1966). By 1970, his act underwent a remarkable transformation. He started delving into the dark side of ghetto life, creating an unforgettable gallery of junkies, pimps, winos, and prostitutes, the kind of people he knew growing up in Peoria. The new Richard Pryor was brilliantly showcased in his first concert film, *Richard Pryor—Live and Smokin'* (1971). This led to his first fully realized dramatic role as BILLIE HOLIDAY's accompanist, the Piano Man, in *Lady Sings the Blues* (1972). Pryor's affecting performance earned him his first and only Academy Award nomination for best supporting actor.

Through the mid-1970s, he was extremely busy as both a writer and supporting film actor. He won an Emmy Award in 1973 for writing the TV special *Lily* for comedian Lily Tomlin and gave the award to his former junior high school teacher who had encouraged him years earlier. He cowrote the script for the western spoof *Blazing Saddles* (1974) with its director Mel Brooks and was slated to star in the picture, but the film's backers refused to let Brooks cast Pryor because he was considered too controversial.

Pryor played a supporting role in the comedy-thriller *Silver Streak* (1976), which he also helped write. His unconventional petty thief virtually stole the picture from its nominal star, Gene Wilder. His manic energy helped made *Silver Streak* a runaway hit and Pryor an overnight movie star. He was quickly cast in a handful of films over the next several years, none of which capitalized fully on his comic genius. He portrayed real-life Wendell Scott, the first black racing car driver, in

The same manic energy that made Richard Pryor a comic superstar in the 1970s also led him to self-destruct in the 1980s. *(Photo courtesy of Showtime Archives, Toronto)*

Greased Lightning (1978) and was an auto factory worker whose allegiance shifts when he becomes a union representative in *Blue Collar* (1978), one of his best dramatic roles.

All of these film performances pale, however, when compared to his stand-up comedy act, which became more daring and dazzling with each year. Two comedy albums, *That Nigger's Crazy* (1974) and *Bicentennial Nigger* (1976), were million sellers and earned him Grammy Awards for best comedy album. His concert films, *Richard Pryor Live in Concert* (1979) and *Live on Sunset Strip* (1982), were without a doubt his best film work. In the latter he transformed tragedy into blistering comedy in routines about his 1978 heart attack (in which he played his own heart)

and an incident when he riddled his third wife's car with bullets. He even was able to find humor in the terrible accident that nearly ended his career—and his life. On June 9, 1980, Pryor was freebasing cocaine, lighting up volatile drug compounds, when a fiery explosion set him on fire. His upper body suffered third degree burns and he underwent months of agonizing hospitalization and therapy.

The much-publicized accident, which may have been a suicide attempt, and his fight back to health only served to increase Pryor's box office appeal. In 1983, he signed a historic three-movie deal with Columbia Pictures for $15 million. Unfortunately, nearly all the films he made after his accident were far below his abilities. Some of them, such as *The Toy* (1983) and *Critical Condition* (1987), were abysmal. The one film he really cared about and took seriously was the frankly autobiographical *Jo Jo Dancer, Your Life Is Calling* (1986), which bombed at the box office.

That same year Pryor was diagnosed with multiple sclerosis (MS). Although he made a few more films, including two that reunited him with Gene Wilder, his film career was drawing to a close. In 1992, Pryor made a return to stand-up comedy, although during his monologue at the Comedy Store in Los Angeles he sat in an easy chair. He began a stand-up tour but had to cancel it the following year due to the debilitating effects of MS. It was a sad ending to a truly brilliant talent.

Richard Pryor was the 1998 recipient of the Mark Twain Prize for humor at the Kennedy Center, in Washington, D.C. He died from a heart attack on December 10, 2005, in Los Angeles at age 65.

Richard Pryor's influence can be seen in many of the young, irreverent comedians and comic actors who have followed him, from EDDIE MURPHY to TRACY MORGAN. While most of them have been highly talented, none has displayed the brilliance and imagination of Richard Pryor.

Further Reading

McCluskey, Audrey Thomas. *Richard Pryor: The Life and Legacy of a "Crazy" Black Man.* Bloomington: Indiana University Press, 2008.

Pryor, Rain. *Jokes My Father Never Taught Me: Life, Love, and Loss with Richard Pryor.* New York: Harper Paperbacks, 2007.

Pryor, Richard, with Todd Gold. *Pryor Convictions and Other Life Sentences.* Beverly Hills, Calif.: Revolver Books, 2005.

Williams, John A., and Dennis A. Williams. *If I Stop I'll Die: The Comedy and Tragedy of Richard Pryor.* New York: Da Capo Press, 2006.

Further Listening

And It's Deep Too! The Complete Warner Bros. Recordings 1968–1992. Rhino, CD box set, 2000.

Further Viewing

Lady Sings the Blues (1972). Paramount Home Video, DVD, 2005.

Richard Pryor: Live in Concert (1979). HBO Home Video, VHS/DVD, 1996/2006.

Richard Pryor: Live on the Sunset Strip (1982). Sony, VHS/DVD, 1995/2000.

Puff Daddy   See COMBS, SEAN "PUFFY."

Q

Queen Latifah
(Dana Owens)
(1970–) *rap singer, actress, talk show host, record, film, and television producer*

The most successful female rapper, Queen Latifah has gone on to fame in nearly every area of show business, most recently as a television talk show host.

She was born Dana Owens on March 18, 1970, in Newark, New Jersey, but was raised in East Orange, New Jersey. Her father, Lance, was a police officer and her mother, Rita, a high school art teacher. A powerful athlete at six feet tall, she played forward on her high school basketball team. About this time she took the Arabic name Latifah, meaning delicate and sensible. She added the "Queen" later.

After graduating from high school, Latifah attended Manhattan Community College for a short time while working as a fast food cashier. She began writing songs and performing rap locally. She submitted a demo tape of her work to the cable station Music Television (MTV) and won a recording contract. Her debut album, *All Hail the Queen* (1989), was a smash hit and produced the hit single "Ladies First," an attack on the male chauvinism and anti-feminism of much rap music.

A charismatic and appealing presence, Latifah was signed to star in the Warner Bros (WB) Net-

work's television series *Living Single* in 1993. She played Khadijah James, a magazine editor and leader of a group of professional African-American

It was rap music that made Queen Latifah famous, but she soon proved herself to be a gifted actress and television personality as well. *(AP Photo/Matt Sayles)*

women. While Latifah's character was mature and realistic, her friends were interested in little else but men. This drew sharp criticism from many viewers. However, the show ran five seasons, and for a time it was the most-watched television program among black viewers.

Latifah continued to record and in 1994 won a Grammy Award for best rap solo performance for her song "U.N.I.T.Y.," which encouraged women to find self-empowerment by joining together as one. In 1999, Latifah brought her feminist stand to daytime television in her own daily syndicated talk show, *The Queen Latifah Show*. She was also the popular program's executive producer. The show went off the air in 2001. Latifah is a cofounder of Flavor Unit Entertainment, a record label and artists management company, and owns a television and film production company. In 1993, she formed the Lancelot H. Owens Foundation, named for her late brother, which helps needy students with outstanding ability.

As an actress, Latifah has appeared in many films since the early 1990s including *Jungle Fever* (1991), *Set It Off* (1996), *Hoodlum* (1997), *Living Out Loud* (1998), and *The Bone Collector* (1999) with DENZEL WASHINGTON. She was seen in Disney's *The Country Bears* and the film adaptation of the Broadway musical *Chicago* (both 2002) for which she was nominated for an Academy Award for best supporting actress. Other recent performances include *Bringing down the House* (2003) with Steve Martin, *Hairspray* (2007), and *The Secret Lives of Bees* (2008). Queen Latifah received an Emmy nomination for her portrayal of an HIV-positive woman in the TV film *Life Support* (2007), and it earned her her first Golden Globe Award.

Further Reading

Bloom, Sarah R. *Queen Latifah*. Black Americans of Achievement. New York: Chelsea House, 2001 (YA).

Galens, Judy. *Queen Latifah*. People in the News. Farmington Hills, Mich.: Lucent Books, 2007 (YA).

Queen Latifah. *Ladies First: Revelations of a Strong Woman*. North Yorkshire, U.K.: Quill, 2000.

Further Listening

All Hail the Queen (1989). Collection's Choice, CD, 2007.

The Best of Queen Latifah: 20th Century Masters. Motown, CD, 2005.

Further Viewing

Life Support (2007). HBO Home Video, DVD, 2007.

Set It Off (1996). New Line Home Video, VHS/DVD, 1998/1999.

R

Rashad, Phylicia
(Phylicia Ayers-Allen)
(1948–   ) *actress, singer, television producer*

One of the most popular television actresses of the 1980s, Phylicia Rashad returned to her roots in the theater after 2004 and became the first African-American actress to win a Tony Award for leading actress in a play.

She was born Phylicia Ayers-Allen on June 19, 1948, in Houston, Texas. Her father, Andrew, a full-blooded Cherokee, was a dentist, and her African-American mother, Vivian Ayers, a Pulitzer Prize–nominated poet and playwright. The family moved to Mexico when Phylicia was a child to escape the racism of the United States. She attended Howard University and, after graduating in the early 1970s, taught drama there. Then she moved to New York City to pursue a stage career.

Rashad made her Broadway debut in 1975 as a replacement in the musical *The Wiz*, in which she played, at different times, a Munchkin, an Emerald City citizen, and a field mouse. A struggling actress, she did not assume a Broadway role again until 1981, when she was an ensemble player and an understudy for a lead role in the musical *Dreamgirls*. By the early eighties, Rashad was finding work in television in episodes of such series as *The Love Boat*. Her big break came in 1984 when she was cast as BILL COSBY's lawyer wife, Clair Huxtable, in *The Cosby Show*, one of the most popular and respected sitcoms of the decade. Rashad stayed with the show until it went off the air in 1992 and continued to play Cosby's wife in a new series *Cosby* (1996–2000). The comedian later promoted her to executive producer of this series.

Although she had returned to Broadway twice during her years of television stardom, her first major dramatic role was playing Ruth Younger, matriarch of a struggling black family, in a revival of Lorraine Hansberry's classic drama *A Raisin in the Sun* in 2004. The all-star cast included AUDRA MCDONALD and SEAN COMBS. Her stirring performance earned Rashad her first Tony for best leading actress in a play. "Often I've wondered what it takes for this to happen," she said in her emotional acceptance speech. "Now I know it was effort and grace, tremendous self-effort, and amazing grace." She later reprised the role in a 2006 television adaptation of the play.

Rashad was again nominated for a Tony as best leading actress the following year for her role in August Wilson's *Gem of the Ocean*. In 2008, she starred with JAMES EARL JONES in an all-black Broadway revival of Tennessee Williams's *Cat on a Hot Tin Roof*, directed by her sister DEBBIE ALLEN. She appeared in the Pulitzer Prize–winning play *August: Osage County* in 2009.

Rashad has been married and divorced three times. Her second husband was Victor Willis, lead singer of the rock group Village People. Her third husband was sportscaster Ahmad Rashad, who proposed to her on national television during the halftime show of a Thanksgiving Day football game. She has one child from her first marriage.

Further Reading

Bogle, Donald. *Prime Time Blues: African Americans on Network Television*. New York: Farrar, Straus & Giroux, 2002, pp. 286, 290, 301, 355, 449.

"Phylicia Rashad." Answer.com. Available online. URL: http://www.answers.com/topic/phylicia-rashad. Downloaded on February 12, 2009.

"Phylicia Rashad." The Internet Movie Database. Available online. URL: http://www.imdb.com/name/nm0711118/. Downloaded on December 11, 2008.

Further Viewing

The Cosby Show—Season 1 (1984). Urban Works, DVD box set, 2005.

A Raisin in the Sun (2008). Sony, DVD, 2008.

Rawls, Lou
(Louis Allen Rawls)
(1936–2006) *R & B singer, record producer*

The epitome of smooth, sophisticated soul, Lou Rawls used his mellow baritone for more than four decades to sell everything from disco ballads to beer.

He was born Louis Allen Rawls on December 1, 1936, in Chicago, Illinois. His father, Virgil, a Baptist minister, abandoned the family shortly after he was born. Raised by his mother, Evelyn, and grandmother, Eliza, Rawls began singing in the church choir at age seven. By 15, he was touring the country with the professional gospel group the Pilgrim Travelers. Rawls was drafted into the army in 1956 and served as a paratrooper. Discharged in 1958, he returned to the Pilgrim Trav-elers, which now included future soul star SAM COOKE.

Cooke and Rawls became fast friends, and in November 1958, they were traveling to their next singing date when their car had a serious accident. Cooke was only slightly injured, but the 21-year-old Rawls suffered a brain concussion and was in a coma for five days. He made a full recovery and returned to the group. When the Travelers broke up in 1959, Rawls went solo as a rhythm and blues (R & B) singer, but it was years before his career caught fire. In 1962, he sang backup to Cooke on the hit ballad "Bring It on Home to Me." The same year his first solo album, *Stormy Monday*, was released on Capitol Records.

While his albums sold respectably, Rawls did not hit the big time until 1966 when his single "Love Is a Hurtin' Thing" reached the top 15 on the pop charts. He began prefacing his songs with unique monologues about growing up in poverty and crime. The technique worked most effectively on the hit song "Dead End Street" (1967). In 1971, Rawls left Capitol for MGM Records and had a big hit with "A Natural Man" (1971), which again had an arresting opening monologue. But he resisted MGM's pressure to sing more commercial material, and he left the label to sign with Philadelphia International, one of the premier soul labels of the 1970s. "You'll Never Find Another Love Like Mine" (1976), a smooth, romantic ballad set to a pulsating disco beat, became his biggest hit, going to number two on the pop charts. Rawls's next album, *Unmistakably Lou* (1977), won a Grammy for best R & B vocal performance, male. "Lady Love" (1978), another disco floor favorite, was his last top-40 hit. By then, Rawls's distinctive cool voice could be heard on television and radio commercials for Budweiser and Michelob beer and other products. His rendition of "This Bud's for You" is an advertising classic.

An astute businessman, Rawls began to invest his money in the late 1960s in a travel service, an office building in Hollywood, California, and his own music publishing company. His record company, Dead End Productions, gives underprivileged youth a chance to start a music career. In the late 1980s, his annual telethon, the Lou Rawls Parade of Stars, raised more than $100 million for the United Negro College Fund.

In 2003, Rawls moved to Scottsdale, Arizona, and released an album of gospel and spiritual music. In 2004, after marrying his third wife, a former flight attendant, he was diagnosed with lung cancer. Lou Rawls died on January 6, 2006, in Los Angeles at age 72. Singer Frank Sinatra once said Rawls had the "silkiest chops in the singing game."

Further Reading

Huey, Steve. "Lou Rawls." The Allmusic Web site. Available online. URL: http://allmusic.com/cg/amg.dll?p=amg&sql=11:hfexqr5ldje. Downloaded on February 9, 2009.

Lou Rawls Official Web site. Available online. URL: http://www.lourawls.com/. Downloaded on February 9, 2009.

Ratliff, Ben. "Lou Rawls, Singer of Pop and Gospel, Dies at 72." *New York Times*, January 7, 2006, Obituaries, C14.

Further Listening

The Essential Lou Rawls. Sony Legacy, 2 CDs, 2007.

Further Viewing

The Jazz Channel Presents Lou Rawls. (BET on Jazz). Image Entertainment, VHS/DVD, 2000.

Redding, Otis

(Otis Redding, Jr.)
(1941–1967) *R & B singer, songwriter, record producer*

One of the great soul singers of the rock era, Otis Redding was on the verge of super stardom when death cut his career tragically short.

He was born on September 9, 1941, in Dawson, Georgia, and was raised in nearby Macon, home of RAY CHARLES, LITTLE RICHARD, and JAMES BROWN. "He was a shy old country boy," said Stax Records president Jim Stewart, when he first met Redding at an audition in 1962. Shy or not, Redding was a seasoned rhythm and blues (R & B) singer when he arrived at Stax in Memphis, Tennessee. He had been lead singer for Johnny Jenkins and the Pinetoppers, a local Macon band, for several years. The group performed throughout the South, mainly at college parties and made their first recordings in 1960.

For some reason, when Jenkins got the call to audition for Stax, Redding was not part of the package. However, he agreed to drive the group to Memphis. Jim Stewart was not impressed by the Pinetoppers, but the group insisted that Otis get his chance to audition, too. After some coaxing, he sang an up-tempo number in the style of his idol, Little Richard. "I told them the world didn't need another Little Richard," recalled Stewart later.

Then Redding sang "These Arms of Mine," a slow ballad he'd written himself. "No one flipped over it," said Stewart, but he was impressed by Redding's intensely emotional delivery and agreed to record the song. "These Arms of Mine" became a local hit and then made the national charts. Stewart immediately signed Redding to a recording contract, and over the next two years he recorded a string of his own ballads in a voice that ached with longing. These songs sold modestly, but when he went more upbeat with "Mr. Pitiful" (1964), backed by the tightly orchestrated Stax horn section, he just missed the top 40.

The real turning point in Redding's career came the following year. Artists such as WILSON PICKETT and James Brown were modernizing soul music and appealing to a larger pop market. Redding finally broke into that market with perhaps his finest ballad, "I've Been Loving You Too Long," and the explosive "Respect," which two years later became a much bigger hit for ARETHA FRANKLIN. In 1966, Stax released *The Otis Redding Dictionary of Soul*, considered by many critics as the finest album of soul music ever recorded. Its highlights included his stirring renditions of the old pop song "Try a Little Tenderness" and the Beatles' "Day Tripper." Despite Redding's growing popularity with black listeners, he was not a top recording artist with white Americans. This was not the case in Europe, where he toured in 1966 and 1967 and was a major star. In 1967, Otis Redding was voted the top male singer in Great Britain.

In the summer of 1967, he appeared at the Monterey Pop Festival in California, where he was suddenly "discovered," along with another American musician more popular in England than at home, JIMI HENDRIX. Back in Memphis, a few months later, Redding wrote a mellow ballad with Stax producer and guitarist Steve Cropper called "(Sittin' on) The Dock of the Bay." "He knew this was the number that was going to open a door long nailed shut; he just never got to step inside," writes Redding's biographer Scott Freeman.

Three days after recording the new song, Redding left on a cross-country tour with his backup band, the Bar-Kays. Their Beechcraft twin-engine plane was lost in thick fog over Wisconsin on December 10, 1967, when it crashed into frozen Lake Monona. Redding and four members of his band drowned in the icy waters. He left behind his wife, Zelma, and two small sons. A few weeks later "The Dock of the Bay" was released and sold about 4 million copies. It was Otis Redding's first and only number-one hit. In death, Redding became a bigger recording star than he ever was in life. Over the next 18 months, he had 10 more hit singles of previously recorded material, including the infectious "The Happy Song (Dum Dum)" and a live version of the James Brown hit, "Papa's Got a Brand New Bag."

Otis Redding was inducted into the Rock and Roll Hall of Fame in 1989. His sons, Dexter and Otis III, formed a group in the early 1980s called the Reddings. Their recording of their father's "The Dock of the Bay" became a hit 14 years after the release of the original.

Further Reading
Bowman, Rob. *Soulsville, U.S.A.: The Story of Stax Records.* New York: Schirmer Books, 2003.

Brown, Geoff. *Otis Redding: Try a Little Tenderness.* Edinburgh, U.K.: Canongate Books, 2003.

Freeman, Scott. *Otis! The Otis Redding Story.* New York: St. Martin's Griffin, 2002.

Further Listening
The Definitive Soul Collection. Atlantic, 2 CDs, 2006.

Further Viewing
Dreams to Remember: The Legacy of Otis Redding. Stax, DVD, 2007.

Reese, Della
(Deloreese Patricia Early)
(1931–) *actress, singer*

A top pop singer of the 1950s, Della Reese found even greater fame in her 60s as the star of one of television's most popular dramatic series.

She was born Deloreese Patricia Early on July 6, 1931, in Detroit, Michigan, where her father, Richard, worked in a steel mill. Her mother, Nellie, was a full-blooded Cherokee Indian. She started singing at age six and by 13 was touring with a gospel music group led by MAHALIA JACKSON. She founded her own group, the Meditation Singers, when she was 18 and later sang with the Erskine Hawkins Orchestra. Reese first recorded in 1954 for the local Great Lakes label and had her first top-20 pop hit, "And That Reminds Me," three years later. She reached her commercial peak with the majestic ballad "Don't You Know" (1959), a number-two hit. She continued to record hit songs into the early 1960s, but after that her singing career declined sharply as she became a popular personality on television. Reese appeared many times on the variety program *The Ed Sullivan Show* and in 1969 became the first African-American woman to host her own syndicated talk show, *Della.* She later was the first woman to guest-host *The Tonight Show.*

An angel on the popular television program *Touched by an Angel,* Della Reese is an ordained minister in real life. *(Photofest)*

But life was not all roses for Della Reese. Her first husband, Vermont Adolphus Ben Taliaferro, abused her, and during a stage performance she suffered a massive aneurysm that nearly killed her. Reese's faith got her through these experiences and prepared her for the most successful role of her life—that of an angel on the television series *Touched by an Angel.*

By the time that series premiered on the CBS network in 1994, Reese was a television veteran, having appeared as a regular on a number of situation comedies, including *Chico and the Man, It Takes Two,* and *The Royal Family,* in which she costarred with REDD FOXX. *Touched by an Angel* was a different challenge, an hour-long dramatic series that featured a trio of "undercover" angels who enter the lives of desperate people in crisis. The show was initially criticized for being too sweet and sentimental, but it gradually found a large and loyal audience. As Tess, the experienced, supervising angel, Reese became the show's anchor

and a spiritual symbol of faith and comfort for millions of viewers. *Touched by an Angel* went off the air in 2003. Since then, Reese has made only occasional appearances in film and on television.

In real life, Reese is an ordained minister in the Church of "Understanding Principals for a Better Living" in Los Angeles, California. In this role, she performed the marriage of her television costar Roma Downey. A type-2 diabetic, Reese is a spokesperson for the American Diabetes Association. She has been married since 1983 to Franklin Thomas Lett, Jr., a concert and film producer. The couple has four children.

Further Reading

Dean, Tanya. *Della Reese.* Black Americans of Achievement. New York: Chelsea House, 2001 (YA).

Reese, Della, with Franklin Lett and Mim Eichler. *Angels along the Way: My Life with Help from Above.* New York: Boulevard, 2001.

Further Listening

Legendary. BMG, CD box set, 2001.

My Soul Feels Better Right Now. Homeland Records, CD, 1998.

Further Viewing

Biography: Della Reese—Outspoken. A & E Home Video, VHS, 2000.

Touched by an Angel—The Complete First Season (1994). Paramount Home Video, DVD box set, 2004.

Rhames, Ving
(Irving Rhames)
(1959–) *actor*

A classically trained actor known for playing tough good and bad guys in movies, Ving Rhames plays character parts with strength and conviction.

He was born Irving Rhames on May 12, 1959, in New York City, where his father was an auto mechanic. Growing up in the mean streets of Harlem, the city's black section, Rhames managed to avoid the pitfalls of drugs and crime. A poetry reading he attended with some friends in ninth grade inspired him to pursue the theater, and he applied to New York's High School of Performing Arts. He became the only person in the history of his junior high school to be accepted by this prestigious institute. When Rhames graduated in 1978, he won a scholarship to the Juilliard School of Drama. While there, he became friendly with fellow student Eriq La Salle.

Success on the stage came quickly for Rhames. Two days after graduating from Juilliard in 1983, he was hired to perform with the New York Shakespeare Festival in New York's Central Park. He made his Broadway debut in *The Winter Boys* (1985) costarring Matt Dillon. He began to appear in tough guy roles on such television series as *Miami Vice* and had a supporting part in the television adaptation of James Baldwin's novel *Go Tell It on the Mountain* (1984).

Rhames gained critical praise for his portrayal of the ruthless Cinque, the leader of the revolutionary Symbionese Liberation Army, in *Patty Hearst* (1988). He played an American soldier in Vietnam in *Casualties of War* (1989) and a Secret Service agent in the comedy *Dave* (1993). His breakthrough role was as the crime boss Marsellus Wallace in Quentin Tarantino's crime saga *Pulp Fiction* (1994), who experienced a surprising reversal in the film's second half. Rhames's friendship with Eriq La Salle, a star of the television medical series *ER*, led him to have a recurring role on the show as the brother-in-law of La Salle's character, Dr. Peter Benton.

When Rhames won the Golden Globe Award as best actor in a miniseries or special for his vivid portrayal of boxing promoter Don King in the Home Box Office (HBO) special *Don King: Only in America*, he handed it to veteran actor and fellow nominee Jack Lemmon. Rhames declared Lemmon was more deserving of the award.

Rhames has played strong supporting roles in *Out of Sight* (1998) opposite George Clooney,

Entrapment (1999) with Sean Connery, and the three *Mission: Impossible* films (1996, 2000, 2006) with Tom Cruise. In 2005, he played police detective Theo Kojak in a remake of the 1970s television series *Kojak* that lasted only 10 episodes. Rhames portrayed boxer Sonny Liston in the biopic *Phantom Punch* (2009), directed by Robert Townsend, and played a leading role in the film adaptation of South African playwright Athol Fugard's *Master Harold . . . and the Boys* (2010).

"I didn't choose acting. Acting chose me," he has said. "My purpose on this planet is to teach human beings about being human to one another."

Further Reading

"Ving Rhames." Answers.com. Available online. URL: http://www.answers.com/topic/ving-rhames. Downloaded on February 9, 2009.
"Ving Rhames." The Internet Movie Database. Available online. URL: http://us.imdb.com/name/nm0000609/. Downloaded on February 9, 2009.

Further Viewing

Don King: Only in America (1997). HBO Home Video, DVD, 2002.
Out of Sight (1998). Universal Studios Home Video, VHS/DVD, 2001/2006.
Pulp Fiction (1994). Miramax Home Entertainment, 2 DVDs, 2002.

Richie, Lionel

(Lionel Brockman Richie, Jr.)
(1949–) *R & B singer, songwriter, musician, record producer*

The premier male singer and songwriter of the early 1980s, Lionel Richie is one of the contemporary masters of the romantic pop ballad, both as songwriter and performer.

He was born Lionel Brockman Richie, Jr., on June 20, 1949, in Tuskegee, Alabama, across the street from the prestigious Tuskegee Institute, a traditionally black university established by African-American leader Booker T. Washington. Richie's grandfather worked in the college's business office and his grandmother, Adlaide Foster, was a classical pianist and piano teacher. His father, Lionel Richie, Sr., was an army captain and his mother worked as a school principal in Joliet, Illinois.

Richie's uncle Bertram played in a big band and gave him his first musical instrument, a saxophone. He attended Tuskegee on a tennis scholarship and majored in accounting and economics. At college, he formed his first band, the Mighty Mystics. When they merged with another band, the Jays, they chose the name the Commodores, picked randomly from a dictionary.

The Commodores played professionally in Europe and elsewhere during the summers and eventually found themselves opening for the Jackson Five on a 1971 tour. Richie left college to perform with the group but later returned to Tuskegee to earn a degree in 1974. The Commodores signed with Motown Records in 1972 but didn't have a hit record until "Machine Gun," an instrumental, two years later. Richie, the group's lead singer and sax player, began writing songs under the tutelage of Motown songwriters Norman Whitfield and Hal Davis. He specialized in soft ballads and provided the Commodores with their first top-10 hits, "Sweet Love" (1975), "Just to Be Close to You" (1976), and "Easy" (1977). He also wrote "Three Times a Lady" (1978), the group's first number-one hit. Richie was soon writing hit songs for other artists, including Kenny Rogers ("Lady") and DIANA ROSS, who had the biggest hit of her career with Richie's "Endless Love" (1981), which they recorded as a duet.

"Endless Love" marked the beginning of Richie's solo career, which included the number-one songs "Truly" (1982), "Hello" (1984), and "Say You, Say Me" (1985). "All Night Long (All Night)" (1983) was so popular that Richie was asked to sing it in the closing ceremonies of the 1984 Olympics in Los Angeles, California, surrounded in the L.A. Coliseum by 200 break dancers. His 1984 album *Can't Slow Down* won him two Grammy Awards for album of the year and producer of the year. The American Society of Composers, Authors and Producers (ASCAP) named him writer of the year for 1984 and 1985. One of Richie's proudest achievements was the cowriting with MICHAEL JACKSON of "We Are the World," which they recorded with more than 30 other top artists. The millions in profits from the record's sale went to relief aid for Africa.

After 1986, Richie recorded no new songs for seven years. His comeback album, *Back to Front* (1992), sold well but was considered not up to the level of his previous work. *Coming Home* (2006) produced his biggest hit single stateside in ten years—"I Call It Love." In May 2008, Richie was the recipient of the George and Ira Gershwin Lifetime Achievement Award at the University of California at Los Angeles (UCLA). Nate Chinen, writing in the *New York Times*, called Richie's most recent album *Just Go* (2009) "a textbook adult-contemporary album" in which "Richie doesn't sound out of his element singing on tracks provided by contemporary R&B hitmakers."

Further Reading

Huey, Steve. "Lionel Richie." The Allmusic Web site. Available online. URL: http://allmusic.com/cg/amg.dll?p=amg&sql=ll:oifyxqr5ldje~T1. Downloaded on February 9, 2009.

Nathan, David. *Lionel Richie: An Illustrated Biography.* New York: McGraw-Hill, 1985.

Plutzik, Roberta. *Lionel Richie.* New York: Dell, 1985.

Further Listening

Gold. Hip-O Records, 2 CDs, 2006.

Further Viewing

The Collection. Motown, DVD, 2003.

Robeson, Paul
(Paul Leroy Robeson)
(1898–1976) *actor, singer, social activist*

A giant in 20th-century culture, Paul Robeson led a life that was so full of promise and achievement but that ended in almost Shakespearean tragedy, like that of Othello whom he played so memorably on the stage.

He was born Paul Leroy Robeson in Princeton, New Jersey, on April 9, 1898, into a family that was among the elite of African-American society. His father, William Robeson, was a former slave who ran away when he was 15, went to college and became a Presbyterian minister. His mother, Anna Louisa, was a teacher and a member of the leading black family of Philadelphia, Pennsylvania. She died when he was six. After high school Robeson won a scholarship to Rutgers College in New Jersey and became the third black to attend the school. He excelled at everything he put his hand to. He was a four-letter athlete, the top student in his class, an actor in college plays, and a champion debater. Football was his first sport, and he is still considered one of the best offensive tackles ever to play the game in college.

After graduation, Robeson went to Columbia University Law School in New York City. There he met and married Eslanda Cardozo Goode, a chemistry student. Robeson received his law degree in 1923 but was already being drawn to an acting career. He appeared on Broadway in the play *Taboo* (1922) and two years later the Provincetown Players in Greenwich Village asked him to join their company. The group's resident playwright, Eugene O'Neill, personally cast Robeson in a revival of his expressionistic play *The Emperor Jones* and then in his new play about an interracial marriage, *All God's Chillun Got Wings*. Robeson, with his imposing physique and rich baritone voice, gained rave reviews in these and other New York productions. In 1925, he gave a music recital of spirituals, becoming the first African American to commit an entire evening to this black folk music. The same year he appeared in his first film, the silent movie *Body and Soul*, directed by black filmmaker Oscar Micheaux.

Hailed as one of the finest American actors of the day, Robeson's reputation soared still higher when he played Shakespeare's tragic Moor, *Othello*, in London, England, in 1930. It was a century since African-American actor IRA ALDRIDGE had played the part in England. One British critic praised Robeson's performance as having the effect "of a soul bombarded by thunder and torn by lightning."

He scored another stage triumph on Broadway in a revival of the musical *Show Boat* (1932), stopping the show with his stirring rendition of the song "Ol' Man River." Four years later, he reprised his role in the film version, playing opposite HATTIE MCDANIEL. Robeson made a handful of Hollywood films in the 1930s, including a memorable adaptation of *The Emperor Jones* (1933). He also made several films in England, one of which, *The Proud Valley* (1940), was the only one of his films he was truly pleased with. Most of his roles, such as the African warrior in *Sanders of the River* (1936), were black stereotypes, reflecting a racist white society. In search of a better life for black people, Robeson began to study socialism and visited the Soviet Union in 1934. He became increasingly more radical in his politics, supported unionism in America, and took a deep interest in African political affairs.

In 1943, he played Othello on the New York stage to critical and public praise. The production ran for 296 performances, the record for a Shakespearean play on Broadway. The National Association for the Advancement of Colored People (NAACP) awarded Robeson the Spingarn Medal for artistry in song and theater in 1945.

As the cold war between the United States and the Soviet Union developed after World War II, Robeson's admiration of communism and political activism drew sharp criticism. In 1950, the government revoked his passport, and he was blacklisted not only in Hollywood, where he made his last picture in 1942, but also on the Broadway stage and in the concert hall. The Supreme Court finally allowed him to travel outside the United States in 1958. He traveled to Europe and revisited the Soviet Union to receive the Stalin Peace Prize, which had been awarded to him six years earlier. He returned in triumph to England in 1959, where he appeared again as Othello at the Shakespeare Memorial Theater at Stratford-on-Avon for its 100th anniversary season.

Although he was hailed as a great man abroad, Robeson was still an outcast in his own country. The stress of this wore on him, and in March 1961, he suffered a nervous breakdown. He returned to the United States in poor health in 1963. A victim of manic depression, Robeson spent most of the remainder of his life in isolated retirement. His final public appearance was at a Student Non-Violent Coordinating Committee (SNCC) benefit dinner in honor of his 67th birthday in 1966.

But these late honors did little to alleviate the bitterness and isolation that darkened the last decade of his life. Paul Robeson died on January 23, 1976, in Philadelphia. A great and complex man, his struggle to overcome racism and social injustice put him at odds with the country he had so enriched with his genius. Actor JAMES EARL JONES portrayed Robeson in a one-person play in 1977–78. He was also honored on a 2004 U.S. postage stamp in the Black Heritage Series.

Further Reading

Boyle, Sheila Tully, and Andrew Buni. *Paul Robeson: The Years of Promise and Achievement*. Amherst: University of Massachusetts Press, 2005.

Dorinson, Joseph, and William A. Pencak, eds. *Paul Robeson: Essays on His Life and Legacy*. Jefferson, N.C.: McFarland & Co., 2004.

Duberman, Martin. *Paul Robeson: A Biography*. New York: New Press, 2005.

Robeson, Paul. *Here I Stand*. (1958). Boston: Beacon Press, 1988.

Robeson, Paul, Jr. *The Undiscovered Paul Robeson: An Artist's Journey 1898–1939*. New York: John Wiley & Sons, 2001.

Further Listening

Best of Paul Robeson. Import, CD, 2005.

Further Viewing

Paul Robeson: Portraits of the Artist. Criterion Collection, DVD box set of seven films, 2007.

Show Boat (1936). Warner Home Video, VHS, 1990.

Robinson, Bill
(Luther Robinson, "Bojangles")
(1878–1949) *tap dancer, singer, actor*

Hailed by no less a talent than Fred Astaire as "the greatest dancer of all time," Bill Robinson was arguably, along with LOUIS ARMSTRONG, the most popular and beloved black entertainer of the 20th century.

He was born Luther Robinson on May 25, 1878, in Richmond, Virginia. Orphaned as an infant, he was raised by his grandmother, an emancipated slave, in abject poverty. As a child Robinson danced on street corners and in bars for spare change, a practice his grandmother strongly disapproved of. He ran away to Washington, D.C., at age eight and got a job as a stable boy at a racetrack. He developed his uniquely rhythmic style of tap dancing by watching the dancers in the popular minstrel shows of the day. Tired of being teased by other boys about his name, he changed it from Luther to his brother's name, Bill, forcing poor Bill to comply. But by the time he was dancing professionally in clubs and later vaudeville, most people called him Bojangles because of the happy-go-lucky way he danced. Robinson slowly but surely worked his way up the vaudeville circuit, until he became the first black dancer to do a solo act on the American stage. By 1908, he was regularly earning more than $3,000 a week.

When the United States entered World War I, Robinson enlisted, even though he was in his late 30s. He was the drum major of the 369th Infantry Regiment, better known as the Harlem

Tap dancer Bill Robinson shows some of the exuberance that made him the most popular black entertainer of his time. *(Photofest)*

brated routines. The high point of their collaboration was *The Littlest Rebel* (1935), set during the Civil War. Robinson becomes Temple's protector and guardian when her Confederate father is thrown into a Yankee jail. Their other films together were *Rebecca of Sunnybrook Farm* and *Just Around the Corner,* both made in 1938.

By the mid-1930s, Robinson was the most famous black man in America, if not the world. He performed before presidents and kings. Jerome Kern, one of the greatest of American songwriters, wrote "Bojangles of Harlem" in tribute to him, and Fred Astaire sang and danced it in blackface in the movie musical *Swing Time* (1936).

On stage and in films Robinson was the epitome of "copasetic," a word he himself coined, meaning everything's fine and dandy. He was extremely generous and gave his money and time to many charities. But there was a darker side to this great entertainer. He could be cold, suspicious, and egotistical among his colleagues. He was a notorious gambler and womanizer, and often carried a gun. His difficult childhood and years of subjection to white racism on the stage and in Hollywood well may have shaped his personality.

To celebrate his 61st birthday in 1939, Robinson danced down Broadway from Columbus Circle at 59th Street to 44th Street. The same year he made a triumphant return to Broadway in *The Hot Mikado* (1939), an all-black version of the famous Gilbert and Sullivan operetta. In 1943, after years of playing servants and butlers, Robinson finally got to play the leading man in the black musical movie *Stormy Weather.* As good as he was in the dancing sequences—in one of which he tapped his way across a stageful of drums—at 65, he was past his peak. His costar, the young and beautiful LENA HORNE, outshined him.

Stormy Weather would be Bill Robinson's last film. He died six years later on November 25, 1949, bitter and nearly broke, having gambled away a fortune. His funeral was an occasion for national mourning. All public schools in Harlem closed and thousands of people lined the streets to

Hellfighters. By the time he returned to civilian life, he was a national star. He came to Broadway in the smash musical *Blackbirds of 1928* and went on to star in two more all-black musical revues, *Brown Buddies* (1930) and *Blackbirds of 1933.*

In 1930, Robinson went to Hollywood where he appeared in *Dixiana,* the first of 14 films he would make there. In 1935, he costarred with child star Shirley Temple in *The Little Colonel.* It would be the first of four pictures they would make together in what became one of the most memorable partnerships in American film musicals. The tall, grandfatherly Robinson and the tiny, curly-haired tot would dance their cares away, up and down a staircase, in one of Robinson's most cele-

watch his funeral procession pass slowly down Broadway and on to Brooklyn, where he was buried. His honorary pallbearers were baseball player Jackie Robinson, jazz great DUKE ELLINGTON, and famed songwriters Cole Porter and Irving Berlin.

In 1989, the U.S. Congress officially named Robinson's birthday National Tap Dancing Day. GREGORY HINES portrayed Robinson in the Showtime television movie *Bojangles* (2000). More than half a century after his death, Bill Robinson remains the consummate entertainer, whose expressive, joyful tapping feet made the whole world forget their troubles.

Further Reading

"Bill Robinson." The Internet Movie Database. Available online. URL: http://imdb.com/name/nm0732408/. Downloaded on February 9, 2009.

Frank, Rusty E. *Tap! The Greatest Tap Dance Stars and Their Stories 1900–1955*. New York: Da Capo Press, 1995.

Haskins, Jim, and N. R. Mitgang. *Mr. Bojangles: The Biography of Bill Robinson*. New York: Welcome Rain, 1999.

Further Viewing

Bojangles (2001). Showtime Entertainment, DVD, 2002.

The Littlest Rebel (1935). Twentieth Century Fox Video, VHS/DVD, 2001/2006.

Stormy Weather (1943). Twentieth Century Fox Video, VHS/DVD, 1991/2006.

Robinson, Smokey
(William Robinson)
(1940–   ) *R & B singer, songwriter, record producer*

Called "America's greatest living poet" by songwriter-singer Bob Dylan, Smokey Robinson is one of the principal architects, as singer, songwriter, and producer, of the "Motown sound," one of the glories of modern pop music.

He was born William Robinson in Detroit, Michigan, on February 19, 1940. His father, known as Daddy Five, stacked pins in a bowling alley. His mother, Flossie, died when he was 10. Robinson, nicknamed Smokey Joe by an uncle when he was two, started writing songs when he was six and composed the musical score for a class play in which he portrayed the storyteller Uncle Remus. In high school he formed a singing group, the Matadors, with four friends. They later changed their name to the Miracles in consideration of the group's sole girl member, Claudette Rogers, whom Robinson married in 1963. The Miracles auditioned for singer JACKIE WILSON's manager in 1957, but he turned them down. Robinson became friends with Wilson's songwriter, Berry Gordy, Jr. When Gordy started his own record company, named Motown, in 1958, Robinson went to work for him. "We were all young black people from the same neighborhood," Robinson recalled years later, "and we all had one goal in mind—to make good records."

The Miracles were one of the first groups that Gordy signed to record for Motown. They got off to a slow start but in late 1960 had one of Motown's first big hits, the number-two record "Shop Around," written by Robinson. With his lyrical tenor and soaring falsetto, Robinson and the Miracles became one of Motown's most consistent hit-makers through the 1960s. They scored with such classic songs as "You've Really Got a Hold on Me" (1962), "Mickey's Monkey" (1963), "OOO Baby Baby" (1965), "The Tracks of My Tears" (1965), "Going to a Go-Go" (1966), and "I Second That Emotion" (1967).

Robinson's songs were characterized by inventive rhymes, imaginative metaphors and similes, and lyrical phrasing. Besides writing virtually all the Miracles' material, he also wrote many hits for other leading Motown artists, including Mary Wells ("My Guy"), The Temptations ("The Way You Do the Things You Do," "My Girl"), MARVIN GAYE ("Ain't That Peculiar"), and the Marvelettes ("Don't Mess with Bill," "The Hunter Gets Captured by the Game").

In 1970, the Miracles had their first number-one hit with "The Tears of a Clown," a Robinson song they had actually recorded three years earlier. Pop critic Paul Evans has called it "one of pop's few perfect singles." In 1972, Robinson left the group and became a solo artist, although he continued to write songs for the Miracles.

Robinson, along with Gaye and STEVIE WONDER, was one of the few Motown artists to remain a creative force in music into the 1970s and 1980s. His material as a solo artist may have been less remarkable than his 1960s output, but it was marked by a new jazzlike freedom and lyricism that culminated in three outstanding albums—*Where There's Smoke* (1979), *Warm Thoughts* (1980), and *Being with You* (1981).

In 1985, Robinson was named a vice president of Motown Records. He divorced his wife in 1986, but remains close to her and their two children Berry and Tamla, who was named for the Motown label the Miracles recorded on. Plagued by a cocaine addiction in the 1980s, he overcame it through prayer and religion. Smokey Robinson was inducted into the Rock and Roll Hall of Fame in 1987 and received Grammy's Living Legends Award in 1989. In 2006, he was a recipient of the Kennedy Center Honors. Robinson continues to tour and record. Recent releases include *Food for the Spirit* (2004), a gospel collection, and *Timeless Love* (2006), an album of pop standards. In March 2009, Robinson appeared on television's *American Idol*, coaching the top ten contestants who sang classic Motown songs.

Proud of his accomplishments as a songwriter and producer, Robinson is more modest about his achievements as a vocalist. "I'm a song feeler who has sung some of his songs thousands and thousands of times," he explained in one interview. "But each time is a new time for me."

Further Reading

George, Nathan. *Where Did Our Love Go?: The Rise and Fall of the Motown Sound.* Champaign: University of Illinois Press, 2007.

Robinson, Smokey, and David Ritz. *Smokey: Inside My Life.* New York: Jive, 1990.

Unterberger, Richie. "Smokey Robinson." The Allmusic Web site. Available online. URL: http://www.all-music.com/cg/amg.dll?p=amg&sql=ll:wifixqr5/dje. Downloaded on February 9, 2009.

Further Listening

Smokey Robinson: The Solo Anthology. Motown, 2 CDs, 2001.

The Ultimate Collection: Smokey Robinson and the Miracles. Motown, CD, 1998.

Further Viewing

The Definitive Performances: 1963–1987. Motown, DVD, 2006.

Rock, Chris
(1966–) *comedian, actor, screenwriter*

One of the brightest and funniest of the crop of black comic-actors to come to prominence in the 1990s, Chris Rock combines the manic energy of EDDIE MURPHY with the satiric bite of RICHARD PRYOR.

He was born on February 7, 1966, in Andrews, South Carolina. His father, Julius, a truck driver, moved the family to Brooklyn, New York, when Rock was still young. His mother, Rose, was a teacher. He attended a nearly all-white school and used the racial discrimination he faced as material for humor. Once out of high school, Rock began performing at New York City comedy clubs and was discovered by Eddie Murphy doing stand-up at the Comic Strip. Murphy cast him in a small role in his film *Beverly Hills Cop II* (1987), and the following year filmmaker Keenan Ivory Wayons starred him in his spoof of blaxploitation, *I'm Gonna Get You Sucka*.

In 1990, Rock joined the cast of television's *Saturday Night Live* (SNL), but in his three seasons on the show he rarely was given good material to work with. He was shown to better effect in his first comedy album *Born Suspect* (1991), which revealed his gift for political and social satire. The same year he played his first dramatic role as a drug-addicted informant in the black crime drama *New Jack City* (1991), which starred WESLEY SNIPES.

Rock's career got a big boost with his first Home Box Office (HBO) television special, *Bring the Pain* (1996), which earned him two Emmy Awards. This success led to HBO's regularly scheduled *The Chris Rock Show* (1997). The comedy albums *Roll with the New* (1997) and *Bigger and Blacker* (1999) won Grammy Awards for best comedy album. Rock aimed his satire at blacks as well as whites: *Bigger and Blacker* featured a devastatingly funny take-off on the rap group Niggaz With Attitude (N.W.A.).

While he continued to play comic roles in films, Rock was also impressive as a hit man on the trail of a delusional housewife in the dark comedy *Nurse Betty* (2000). Critics generally panned *Down to Earth* (2001) and *Head of State* (2003), two films he wrote and starred in. Rock has had better success on television. The sitcom *Everybody Hates Chris*, which he created and narrates, debuted in 2005 and was inspired by his youth in Bedford-Stuyvesant. The show was nominated for two Emmys in its first season and is still on the air as of 2009. Rock hosted the Academy Awards ceremony in 2005. His fifth HBO special, *Kill the Messenger*, aired in 2008.

Further Reading

"Chris Rock." The Internet Movie Database. Available online. URL: http://www.imdb.com/name/nm000 1674/. Downloaded on February 9, 2009.
Rock, Chris. *Rock This!* New York: Hyperion, 2000.

Further Listening

Bigger and Blacker. DreamWorks Records, CD, 1999.
Cheese and Crackers: The Greatest Bits. Geffen Records, CD, 2007.

Further Viewing

Chris Rock: Kill the Messenger. HBO Home Video, DVD box set, 2009.

The Chris Rock Triple Feature (Down to Earth, Head of State, Pootie Tang). Paramount Home Video, DVD box set, 2007.

Rolle, Esther
(1920–1998)   *actress*

The strong-willed but loving matriarch of one of the best black comedy series of the 1970s, Esther Rolle brought honesty and depth to every role she played on stage and screen in a 50-year acting career.

She was born on November 8, 1920, in Pompano Beach, Florida, the ninth of 18 children. Her parents came to the United States from the Bahamas in the Caribbean and scraped a living from a small vegetable farm. As a child, Rolle saw her mother give birth to triplets, all of whom died within 24 hours. After high school, she moved to New York City, where one of her sisters was pursuing an acting career. Rolle decided to try acting, too, and took drama classes at the New School for Social Research. Later she joined the newly formed Negro Ensemble Company (NEC). She appeared on Broadway in two plays by black author James Baldwin—*The Amen Corner* and *Blues for Mister Charlie,* as well as OSSIE DAVIS's *Purlie Victorious.* Rolle made her film debut as a churchwoman in the groundbreaking black drama *Nothing But a Man* (1964).

In 1971, she won rave reviews for her performance in the Broadway musical *Don't Play Us Cheap.* Television producer Norman Lear saw the play and offered her the role of a maid on the TV situation comedy *Maude,* but Rolle turned the part down. She told Lear she would not play a stereotyped black maid on television. Her talent and her convictions impressed him, and he assured her that she would have a say in developing the character of Florida, Maude Findley's maid. Under those conditions, Rolle accepted the part.

As Florida, Rolle was funny, sassy, and opinionated but more real than the Hollywood maids previously played so well by HATTIE MCDANIEL. The character became so popular that Lear created a spin-off sitcom for her. Florida left the Findley home and joined her husband and three children on the south side of Chicago, Illinois, in the sitcom *Good Times* (1974–1979).

Good Times stood out from the other black sitcoms of the 1970s, largely due to good writing and the solid performances of Rolle and John Amos, who played her husband. The actress insisted that the family have a strong father figure, to counteract the belief that black fathers were largely invisible in the black community. As time went on, J. J., the couple's eldest son played by Jimmie Walker, became increasingly popular. J. J. was funny, lazy, and always scheming. Rolle was so disgusted with the character of J. J., whom she saw as a bad role model for black children, that she quit the show during its third season. The producers persuaded her to return the next season.

After *Good Times* went off the air in 1979, Rolle found few roles worthy of her talents. She often was cast as a maid and earned an Emmy for best supporting actress in a limited series or special as the maid in the TV movie *The Summer of My German Soldier* (1978). She played another strong matriarch in a television adaptation of Lorraine Hansberry's play *A Raisin in the Sun* (1989) with DANNY GLOVER as her headstrong son.

For her work in improving the image of African Americans, in 1990 Rolle became the first woman to receive the Chairman's Civil Rights Leadership Award from the National Association for the Advancement of Colored People (NAACP). Esther Rolle died on November 17, 1998, from complications of diabetes. "Wherever she was, you knew she was there," Norman Lear said at the time of her death. "The woman had strong conviction."

Further Reading

Bogle, Donald. *Prime Time Blues: African Americans on Network Television.* New York: Farrar, Straus & Giroux, 2002, pp. 197–198, 203–206.

"Esther Rolle." The Internet Movie Database. Available online. URL: http://www.imdb.com/name/0738354/. Downloaded on February 9, 2009.

Further Viewing

Good Times: The Complete First Season (1974). Sony, 2 DVDs, 2005.

A Raisin in the Sun (1989). Monterey Home Video, VHS, 2001.

Ross, Diana
(1944–   ) *R & B and pop singer, actress*

The lead singer of the most successful pop female singing group of all time, Diana Ross went on to become one of the great pop divas of the 1970s and 1980s.

She was born on March 26, 1944, in Detroit, Michigan, one of six children. Her father, Fred, was a factory worker, and her mother, Ernestine, a homemaker. During high school she formed a singing group with two friends from the housing project where she lived—Florence Ballard and Mary Wilson. In 1954, they became the Primettes with a fourth singer, Betty Travis, and played local dates. When the Primettes auditioned for Berry Gordy, Jr., head of Motown Records, he told them to come back when they had more experience. Undaunted, they finished high school and did some recording. Travis and her replacement, Barbara Martin, left the group before their second audition for Motown, but this time Gordy signed the trio to his label and gave them a new name—the Supremes.

The Supremes' road to success was a bumpy one. Of their first eight singles, only three made the lower end of the charts. Their greatest success at Motown was singing backup for such established stars as Mary Wells and MARVIN GAYE. But Gordy still believed in the Supremes and turned them over to his top songwriting team of Eddie Holland, Lamont Dozier, and Brian Holland. Their first record with the group, "When the

Lovelight Starts Shining Through His Eyes" (1963), was a modest hit. A year later the slow-tempo "Where Did Our Love Go?" with Ross's seductive, shrill lead vocal, went to number-one on the charts. It was the start of one of the most extraordinary runs in pop history. Of the next 14 singles the Supremes released through 1967, all but one made the top-10 and nine went to number one. Among their classic songs from this period were "Come See About Me" (1964), "Stop! In the Name of Love" (1965), "You Can't Hurry Love" (1966), and "Love Is Here and Now You're Gone" (1967). In 1968 they reached number one with a rare social message song, "Love Child" (1968).

The Supremes were the first black vocal group to play in such sophisticated venues as supper clubs. They were the ultimate crossover group, beloved by white and black audiences alike. In 1967, the group's name was changed to "Diana Ross and the Supremes," reflecting the growing popularity of Ross and Berry Gordy's infatuation with her. Divisions grew between Ross and the other two singers, and Florence Ballard left in 1967 to be replaced by Cindy Birdsong. Ballard, once a potential star herself, eventually lost all the money she had made at Motown, went on welfare, and died in 1976 at age 33.

Ross left the Supremes for a solo career in 1970. Her last hit record with the Supremes was the ironically titled "Someday We'll Be Together" (1969). The Supremes, with new lead singer Jean Terrell, continued to record and have hit records through 1976. Ross, however, did not immediately become the superstar that Gordy envisioned she would be. She reached number one with the upbeat ballad "Ain't No Mountain High Enough" (1970), but for a year after that she had no major hit records. Then she made her movie debut in the Motown-produced *Lady Sings the Blues* (1972), in which she portrayed blues singer BILLIE HOLIDAY. As biography, the film was pure hokum, but Ross's star quality shone through and she won a Golden Globe Award for best actress and an Academy Award

Motown Records's top diva, Diana Ross went from being lead singer of the Supremes to having a successful solo career. *(Photo courtesy of Showtime Archives, Toronto)*

nomination in the same category. Soon after, she had her second number-one hit with "Tell Me in the Morning" (1973), followed by a hit album that teamed her with Marvin Gaye and produced three hit singles.

Ross's second film, *Mahogany* (1975), cast her as a top fashion model who must choose between her career and her lover. The critics panned the film, but it managed to do well enough at the box office and produced another number-one hit for Ross, the film's theme song, "Do You Know Where You're Going To." In 1976, Ross starred on Broadway in *An Evening with Diana Ross*, and she hit number one again with the discolike "Love Hangover."

Her third movie, *The Wiz* (1978), was the film version of the hit Broadway musical based on *The Wizard of Oz*. Ross played the lead part of Dorothy, for which she was far too old. *The Wiz* was a dismal flop, and Ross has only starred in one other feature film to date. She continued to be a top recording artist, however, and hit her commercial peak at Motown with "Endless Love" (1981), a duet with LIONEL RICHIE, who also wrote the song. It stayed at number one on the charts for nine weeks, Ross's biggest hit record to date.

Wanting to get tighter control over her career, Ross left Motown in 1981 and signed with RCA Records. Her first album for the label, *Why Do Fools Fall in Love* (1981), was a million seller. Her next album, *Silk Electric* (1982), produced the hit single "Muscles," written and produced for her by her close friend, singer MICHAEL JACKSON. By the mid-1980s, however, the hit records dried up, and Ross returned to Motown in 1989. Her first new Motown album was a flop, and she has found far greater success in the subsequent years in live concerts than in the recording studio. Her recording career revived somewhat in 2005 when a duet with Rod Stewart of "I Got a Crush on You" became an adult contemporary hit. Her 2007 studio album *I Love You* became her best-selling album in more than two decades.

Ross, with the other members of the Supremes, was inducted into the Rock and Roll Hall of Fame in 1988. In 2007, she received the Lifetime Achievement Award from Black Entertainment Television (BET) and was a recipient of the Kennedy Center Honors. Ross's two marriages, to her business manager and to a Norwegian businessman, both ended in divorce. She has five children; four of whom are in show business.

A grand and glamorous diva known both for her ego and her talent, Diana Ross remains a living pop icon.

Further Reading

Adrahtas, Thomas. *A Lifetime to Get Here: Diana Ross: The American Dreamgirl.* Bloomington, Ind.: Author House, 2006.

Ross, Diana. *Secrets of a Sparrow: Memoirs.* New York: Random House, 1995.

Taraborrelli, J. Randy. *Diana Ross: An Unauthorized Biography.* New York: Citadel Press, 2007.

Wyeth, John. *Diana Ross: Entertainer.* Black Americans of Achievement. New York: Chelsea House, 1995 (YA).

Further Listening

Diana Ross and the Supremes: The Definitive Collection. Motown, CD, 2008.

Diana Ross: The Definitive Collection. Motown, CD, 2006.

Further Viewing

Diana Ross Live—The Lady Sings . . . Jazz & Blues (1992). Motown, DVD, 2002.

Lady Sings the Blues (1972). Paramount Home Video, DVD, 2005.

Roundtree, Richard
(1942–   )   *actor*

Forever identified with the tough black detective John Shaft that he played in three films, Richard Roundtree, unlike other black male action heroes of the 1970s, has managed to keep an acting career going for three decades after *Shaft*.

He was born on September 7, 1942, in New Rochelle, New York, where his father worked as a chauffeur and his mother was a housekeeper. He went to Southern Illinois University on a football scholarship but dropped out in his sophomore year. His good looks got him a job as a male model on the Ebony Fashion Fair tour. After the tour ended, he studied acting in New York City and in 1967 joined the Negro Ensemble Company. He appeared in a number of Off-Broadway productions before getting the leading role of a black boxer in the drama *The Great White Hope* (1970), where he replaced JAMES EARL JONES on Broadway.

He had a small role in his first film *What Do You Say to a Naked Lady?* (1970), directed by *Candid Camera*'s Allan Funt. Then, he was cast in his signature role of black private eye John Shaft in the film *Shaft*. Shaft was a new kind of black hero who was tough and attractive to women (both black and white) and took no lip from white people. The film, with Roundtree's hard-hitting performance and a pulsating score by ISAAC HAYES, became a smash hit in 1971 and set the pattern for a long line of what came to be called "blaxploitation" movies. Roundtree starred in two sequels, *Shaft's Big Score* (1972) and *Shaft in Africa* (1973). He even appeared in a 90-minute *Shaft* television series that ran briefly during the 1973–74 season.

Roundtree appeared in a number of action-adventure films through the 1970s and into the early 1980s, including *Earthquake* (1974), *Escape to Athena* (1979), and *Q* (1982). As the years went on, the parts he played got more stereotyped and the films lower-budget. In more recent years he has had good character parts in such films as the comedy *George of the Jungle* (1998) and the black drama *Soul Food* (2000), where he played a senior citizen. *Shaft* was remade in 2001 with SAMUEL L.

JACKSON in the title role and Roundtree portraying his uncle, the original John Shaft. Since then, he has appeared mostly on television, playing recurring roles on the series *Desperate Housewives* (2004–   ) and *Heroes* (2006–   ).

In 1993, Richard Roundtree was diagnosed with breast cancer and later made a full recovery. He remains a spokesperson and fundraiser for breast cancer research.

Further Reading

Bogle, Donald. *Toms, Coons, Mulattoes, Mammies & Bucks: An Interpretive History of Blacks in American Films.* New York: Continuum, 1997, pp. 237, 239.

James, Darius. *That's Blaxploitation: Roots of the Baadasss 'Tude (Rated X by an All 'Whyte Jury).* New York: St. Martin's Griffin, 1995.

Further Viewing

Shaft/Shaft in Africa (1971). Warner Home Video, 2 DVDs, 2003.

S

Scott, Hazel
(Hazel Dorothy Scott)
(1920–1981) *jazz pianist, singer, television and film performer*

The first African-American woman to host her own television show, Hazel Scott is as well remembered for her image as a courageous, intellectual black woman as she is as a leading jazz entertainer.

She was born Hazel Dorothy Scott on June 11, 1920, in Port of Spain, Trinidad, an island in the West Indies. Her father, R. Thomas Scott, was a college professor and scholar, and her mother, Alma, was a musician. Scott was a child prodigy who made her debut at the piano at age three and was improvising her own music by five. When she was a teenager, the family moved to New York City, where she furthered her musical studies, and in a few years she was performing professionally in nightclubs. Scott's act was something of a novelty in the jazz world—she would take serious classical pieces and "jazz them up" on the piano. She had her own radio program in 1936 and appeared on the Broadway stage two years later. In the 1940s Scott went to Hollywood where she appeared in five movies. Like LENA HORNE, she was never a part of the film's story but was simply brought on to perform a number

or two. A telling moment in the Red Skelton comedy, *I Dood It* (1941), occurs when Scott and her entourage arrived backstage at a theater. The gatekeeper asks her where she's going, and she announces who she is. Impressed, the gatekeeper lets her proceed. Such a moment must have been exhilarating for black viewers for whom racial segregation meant having to sit in the back of theaters if they were allowed in at all.

In 1945, Scott married minister and Harlem congressman Adam Clayton Powell, Jr. They became one of the most celebrated black couples of the decade. *The Hazel Scott Show* debuted on the DuMont Television network in July 1950. The 15-minute program was set upon a penthouse terrace, where Scott, elegantly dressed, played pop, jazz, and classical music on the piano and sometimes the organ.

About the same time Scott's name was listed in the anticommunist publication *Red Channels* that exposed television and film entertainers who were supposedly pro-Communist. She insisted on being allowed to testify at the hearings of the House Committee on Un-American Activities (HUAC) in September. In her testimony she denied being a Communist but also courageously spoke out against *Red Channels*, calling it "Un-American." Her testimony finished off her television show, already in trouble and unable to keep a steady sponsor because of the controversy.

In 1956, Scott divorced Powell and moved to Europe for several years during the 1960s. She returned to the States and enjoyed a full career as a performer in clubs, on records, and on television as a guest star on variety shows. She died in New York City on October 2, 1981.

Further Reading

Chilton, Karen. *Hazel Scott: The Pioneering Journey of a Jazz Pianist from Cafe Society to Hollywood to HUAC.* Ann Arbor: University of Michigan Press, 2008.

Placksin, Sally. *American Women in Jazz 1900 to the Present: Their Words, Lives, and Music.* New York: Putnam Adult, 1982.

Further Listening

Hazel Scott 1946–47. Classics France, CD, 2007.

Shakur, Tupac

(Tupac Amaru Shakur, 2Pac)
(1971–1996) *rap singer, songwriter, actor*

Considered one of the most influential and creative of rap artists to emerge in the 1990s, Tupac Shakur lived the gangsta life he celebrated in song and paid dearly for it.

He was born Tupac Amaru Shakur on June 16, 1971, in Brooklyn, New York. His mother, Afeni Shakur, was a member of the black radical group the Black Panthers and named him for the Inca leader Tupac who rebelled against the Spanish in 16th-century Peru. He and his sister led a vagabond existence, traveling from city to city with their politically radical mother. He never knew his father. Along the way, Shakur attended acting classes at a Harlem theater group in New York City and spent a year at the Baltimore School of the Arts in Maryland, where he wrote his first rap songs.

When the family settled in California, however, Shakur became involved in the life of the streets, selling drugs and getting into other trouble. In 1990, he met Shock-G (George Jacobs), who led the rap group Digital Underground (D.U.) in Oakland, California. He worked with D.U. as a dancer on tour and sang on two of their albums. In 1992, Shakur signed a recording contract with Interscope Records and released his first solo album, *2Pacalypse Now,* a pun on his rap name "2Pac."

The same year he returned to his first love, acting, and appeared in the movie *Juice.* This was immediately followed by director John Singleton's *Poetic Justice* (1993), in which Shakur played opposite singer JANET JACKSON. His second album, *Strictly 4 My N.I.G.G.A.Z.* (1993), was a smash and produced the hit singles "I Get Around" and "Keep Ya Head Up." Shakur was a star in the rap world, but his lifestyle emulated the gangsta life he sang about. He was arrested in 1992 in connection with a shootout in which a six-year-old child was killed, but he was released without charges being pressed. The next year, he was sentenced to 15 days in jail for assaulting the director of a film he was appearing in. The more serious charge of sexual assault was brought against him in 1994, and this time he was sentenced to four and a half years in prison. The day after the verdict was passed, Shakur was shot five times in an apparent mugging outside a recording studio in New York City. He later celebrated his close call with death in the lyrics of one his songs.

When he recovered from his wounds, Shakur began his jail sentence in February 1994. A month later, his new album, appropriately titled *Me Against the World,* soared to number one on the charts. The notorious record producer Suge Knight took notice and put up $1.4 million in bond money to get Shakur out of prison after serving eight months. Free again, Shakur made up for lost time. In a creative burst, he recorded a new album for Knight's Death Row Records, *All Eyez on Me* (1996), and made two more films, *Bullet* and *Gridlock'd,* all within a year.

On September 13, 1996, Knight and Shakur were in Las Vegas, Nevada, on their way to a charity event in Knight's car. Suddenly another car pulled up alongside and shots were fired. Shakur took four bullets and was rushed to a hospital. Six days later, he died, never having regained consciousness. He was only 25 years old.

His assailants and the motive for the shooting remain a mystery to this day. Tupac Shakur's violent death has only increased the mystique around his name. A steady stream of previously recorded material has been released, including the double album *Until the End of Time* (2001).

More than any other contemporary rap artist, Shakur has come to symbolize the hopes and despair of the gangsta world. According to his biographer Michael Eric Dyson, he "articulated a generation's defining moods—its confusion and pain, its nobility and courage . . . its hopelessness and self-destruction."

Further Reading

Dyson, Michael Eric. *Holler If You Hear Me: Searching for Tupac Shakur.* New York: Basic Civitas Books, 2006.

Golus, Carrie. *Tupac Shakur* (Just the Facts Biographies). Minneapolis, Minn.: Lerner Publications, 2006 (YA).

Joseph, Jamal. *Tupac Shakur Legacy.* New York: Atria, 2006.

Moniauze, Molly, ed. *Tupac Remembered.* San Francisco, Calif.: Chronicle Books, 2008.

Shakur, Tupac. *The Rose That Grew from Concrete.* New York: MTV, 2009 (YA).

White, Armond. *Rebel for the Hell of It: The Life of Tupac Shakur.* New York: Da Capo Press, 2002.

Further Listening

2Pac—Greatest Hits. Interscope, 2 CDs, 1998.

Further Viewing

Poetic Justice (1993). Sony, VHS/DVD, 1998/1999.

Tupac: The Complete Live Performances. Eagle Rock Entertainment, DVD, 2006.

Short, Bobby
(Robert Waltrip Short)
(1924–2005) *cabaret singer, pianist*

Called by connoisseurs "the best saloon singer in the world," Bobby Short celebrated the golden age of American popular song in concerts, on records, and in cabarets for more than half a century.

He was born Robert Waltrip Short in Danville, Illinois, on September 15, 1924. The ninth of 10 children, he grew up in an integrated neighborhood. Short's father, Rodman, was, in turn, a coal miner, a mailman, a notary public, and finally, a justice of the peace. By age 10, Short was playing piano and singing locally. Two talent agents who happened to be attending an American Legion convention heard Short sing and persuaded his mother to let them take her 12-year-old son on the road. She consented, and Short played clubs and theaters between Danville and Chicago for two years. He returned to Danville to complete high school and then became a full-time performer in 1942.

Short traveled to Europe and played and sang in the clubs of London and Paris. Returning to the United States, he appeared in his first and only Hollywood movie musical, *Call Me Mister* (1951). He recorded his first album, *Songs by Bobby Short*, in 1954. By that time, the singer specialized in the popular songs of the 1920s, 1930s, and 1940s. His flawless diction, charm, and magnetic personality made him a favorite on the cabaret circuit in New York and other American cities.

The year 1968 proved a turning point in Short's until-then modest career. He appeared in a memorable concert at New York's Town Hall with legendary cabaret singer Mabel Mercer, who was a central influence on his own style. The same year, Short was invited to replace the regular pianist at the elegant Café Carlyle in the Carlyle Hotel on New York's fashionable East Side. Short was an instant hit with the Carlyle's sophisticated clientele, and he became an institution there, playing every spring and fall for more than three decades.

The 1970s saw him produce some of his best and most successful recordings, several of them devoted to his favorite songwriters. These include *Bobby Short Loves Cole Porter* (1971), *Bobby Short Is K-RA-ZY for Gershwin* (1973), and *Bobby Short Celebrates Rodgers and Hart* (1982).

Bobby Short lived in New York City during the spring and fall while playing at the Carlyle and spent his summers at his home in France. He appeared as himself in the Woody Allen movie *Hannah and Her Sisters* (1986) and played a dramatic role opposite Michael Caine in the crime thriller *Blue Ice* (1992).

Bobby Short died of leukemia on March 21, 2005, in New York City at age 80.

Further Reading

Boedicker, Mike. "The Bobby Short Saloon." Danville Library Web site. Available online. URL: http://www.danville.lib.il.us/Pathfinder/short.htm. Downloaded on February 10, 2009.

Short, Bobby. *Black and White Baby.* New York: Dodd, Mead, 1971.

Short, Bobby, and Robert G. Mackintosh. *Bobby Short, The Life and Times of a Saloon Singer.* New York: Clarkson Potter, 1995.

Further Listening

50 by Bobby Short (1986). Atlantic, 2 CDs, 1990.

Live at the Café Carlyle (1974). Collectables, CD, 2006.

Further Viewing

At the Café Carlyle (2003). View Video, DVD, 2004.

Simone, Nina

(Eunice Kathleen Waymon, "The High Priestess of Soul")
(1933–2003) *singer, pianist, songwriter*

A singer who defied classification, Nina Simone often used her dramatic voice and vibrant music to speak out against racism and social injustice.

She was born Eunice Kathleen Waymon on February 21, 1933, in Tryon, South Carolina, the sixth of seven children. Her father, John, was a gardener and her mother, Mary Kate, an ordained Methodist minister. Eunice began playing the piano at age four and, although her family was poor, was able to study at the Juilliard School of Music in New York City, thanks to funds raised by her music teacher.

Her first professional job was as an accompanist and then singer in an Irish bar in Atlantic City, New Jersey. She took the name "Nina," which means "little one" in Spanish, and "Simone," for the French actress Simone Signoret. Her taste in music reflected a similar eclecticism. She sang jazz, spirituals, classical, folk, blues, pop, and gospel. But all her songs are filtered through her own sensitive sensibility, and her personal, sometimes eccentric, interpretations of songs have often led to her being labeled a jazz singer.

Simone began recording in the late 1950s. Her first and biggest pop hit was a heartfelt rendition of "I Loves You, Porgy" (1959) from the George Gershwin folk opera *Porgy and Bess.* She began writing original songs about the same time, often reflecting her preoccupation with racism and other social issues. "Mississippi Goddam" was written about the 1963 bombing of a black church in Birmingham, Alabama. "Backlash Blues" was inspired by a poem by black writer Langston Hughes, and "To Be Young, Gifted and Black" was inspired by the play of the same name by Lorraine Hansberry.

A challenging artist who sang whatever she pleased and often became angry with audiences that gave her less than their full attention, Nina Simone left the United States in 1974. She moved to the Caribbean island of Barbados and settled in the south of France, where she recorded in both French and English. She was very active in the 1990s, publishing her autobiography, *I Put a Spell on You* (1991), and a new studio album, *A Single Woman* (1993). Her songs have been featured on the soundtracks of several movies including *Point* of No Return (1993), Ghosts of Mississippi (1996), and One Night Stand (1997).

A citizen of the world, Nina Simone received the Diamond Award for Excellence in Music from the Association of African American Music in Philadelphia, Pennsylvania, in June 2000.

"In her singular phrasing, we hear wickedness, wit, defiance and yearning," wrote Somini Sengupta in the New York Times. For women who see themselves as outsiders, "Nine Simone offers us a canvas on which to project our own desires." She died on April 21, 2003, after a long illness at her home in Carry-le-Rouet, France. Her daughter Lisa Stroud, is a stage actress and starred in the Broadway Music Elton John's Aida.

Further Reading

Brun-Lambert, David. Nina Simone: The Biography. Worthington, U.K.: Aurum Press, 2009.
Hampton, Sylvia, and David Nathan. Nina Simone: Break Down and Let It All Out. London: Sanctuary Publishing, 2004.
Simone, Nina, with Stephen Cleary. I Put a Spell on You: The Autobiography of Nina Simone. New York: Da Capo Press, 2003.

Further Listening

To Be Free. Sony Legacy, CD box set, 2008.

Further Viewing

Jazz Icons: Nina Simone—Live in '65 & '68. Naxos of America, DVD, 2008.

Smith, Bessie
(Elizabeth Smith, "The Empress of the Blues")
(ca. 1894–1937) blues singer

Perhaps the greatest female blues singer ever, Bessie Smith sang of good times and broken hearts in a voice of overwhelming power and intensity.

She was born Elizabeth Smith sometime between 1894 and 1900 in Chattanooga, Tennessee, into a childhood of grinding poverty. She was reluctant to give the date of her birth throughout her career, and the exact year and day remain unknown. Her father was a part-time Baptist minister and both parents died when she was nine. She earned a precarious living singing for pennies on the streets of Chattanooga until she was rescued by blues singer Ma Rainey. Rainey heard Smith sing while passing through with her Rabbit Foot Minstrel Revue and hired her to sing in her show. For the next several years Smith struggled to make a living singing and dancing with minstrel and traveling tent shows throughout the South.

In the early 1920s, she settled in Philadelphia, Pennsylvania, where she established herself as a major blues singer and married Jack Gee, a former police officer. After being turned down by three record companies who found her singing not commercial enough, she signed with Columbia Records in 1923. Smith's first record, "Down Hearted Blues," sold more than 2 million copies within a year. Over the next decade, she made 160 recordings, some of them with such major jazz musicians as LOUIS ARMSTRONG, Benny Goodman, and Fletcher Henderson.

Smith toured the South and other regions with her own show. At her peak in the 1920s, she earned $2,000 a week, making her the highest-paid black entertainer in the country. Smith was then called "the empress of the blues," and she lived like one. Legendary stories of her high living, expensive cars, and days-long drinking parties are still retold. A large, big-boned woman, Smith was a powerhouse on stage, always dressed spectacularly in spangled dresses and fancy hats. She proclaimed her independence as a woman who lived her life exactly as she wanted to in such classic songs as "'Tain't Nobody's Bizness If I Do" and "Gimme a Pigfoot and a Bottle of Beer."

The good times, however, came to an end by 1930. Changing musical tastes and a lack of good new material ended Smith's time in the limelight. Her fortune was wiped out by the Great Depression, her husband left her for another singer, and her drinking grew out of control. In 1933, she made her last recordings for Columbia. Three days later, a young new blues singer, BILLIE

Bessie Smith was known as the "Empress of the Blues" and lived up to that title by living in high style. *(Photo courtesy of Showtime Archives, Toronto)*

HOLIDAY, made her debut as a Columbia recording artist. She would soon eclipse Smith as a blues singer.

Despite all these problems, Smith continued to sing in one seedy venue after another, desperately looking for a comeback. She was on a southern singing tour when Columbia record producer John Hammond headed for Mississippi, hoping to take her to New York for a new recording session. Before he could catch up with Smith, her touring car crashed into a truck on a lonely road near Clarksdale, Mississippi, on September 27, 1937. Smith's right arm was nearly severed in the crash, and it took hours for help to arrive on the scene.

By the time she was taken to a hospital, she had lost too much blood and died. Rumors spread by John Hammond and others claimed she had been denied admittance to one hospital because she was black and died by the time she reached one farther away. This is no evidence to substantiate this story, but it persists to this day, reinforced by the play *The Death of Bessie Smith* (1959) by Edward Albee.

In death, as in life, Bessie Smith seems a larger-than-life personality—the first black female performer to become a part of mainstream American culture.

Further Reading

Albertson, Chris. *Bessie.* New Haven, Conn.: Yale University Press, 2005.

Davis, Angela Y. *Blues Legacies and Black Feminism: Gertrude 'Ma' Rainey, Bessie Smith, and Billie Holiday.* New York: Vintage, 1999.

Manera, Alexandria. *Bessie Smith.* African-American Biographies. Chicago: Raintree, 2003 (YA).

Scott, Michelle R. *Blues Empress in Black Chattonooga: Bessie Smith and the Emerging Urban South.* Champaign: University of Illinois Press, 2008.

Further Listening

Best of the Empress of the Blues. Blues Forever, CD, 2004.

Further Viewing

St. Louis Blues (1929). Unforgettable, DVD, 2008.

Smith, James Todd   See LL COOL J.

Smith, Will
(Willard Christopher Smith, Jr., "Fresh Prince")
(1968–   ) *actor, comedian, rap singer, television producer, screenwriter*

An appealing leading man in films, Will Smith has gracefully moved from rap artist to movie star with a stopover as a TV sitcom actor.

Will Smith is one of the most bankable stars in Hollywood today. *(AP Photo/Richard Drew)*

He was born Willard Christopher Smith, Jr., on September 25, 1968, in Philadelphia, Pennsylvania. His family was solidly middle class, and his father, Willard Smith, Sr., owned a refrigeration company. His mother, Caroline, worked for the Philadelphia Board of Education. In elementary school, his classmates called him "Prince," because he could charm his way out of any trouble. At age 14, Smith met Jeff Townes at a party and the two formed a rap duo, DJ Jazzy Jeff and the Fresh Prince. They sang at local gatherings in high school. After graduation, Smith was offered a scholarship to the Massachusetts Institute of Technology (MIT) but turned it down to pursue a singing career. DJ Jazzy Jeff and the Fresh Prince recorded their first single in 1987 and a year later

had a hit record, "Parents Just Don't Understand" (1988). The song earned them a Grammy Award for the best rap performance, the first time this award was given. Their first album, *He's the DJ, I'm the Rapper* (1989), sold 2 million copies, almost unheard of at the time for a rap album. Townes and Smith were sharply criticized by other rap artists for watering down rap music for the commercial marketplace.

However, they were just the kind of noncontroversial rap artists that TV producers were looking for to cash in on the rap phenomenon. In 1990, Smith was cast as a character very much like himself in the sitcom *The Fresh Prince of Bel Air,* produced by QUINCY JONES. He played a teen who is sent by his mother to live with his relatives in the upper-class Los Angeles suburb of Bel Air. The humor came out of the clashes between the lower-class rapper and his well-to-do relatives. The show got off to a rocky start, and Smith himself has admitted, "My performances were horrible" during the show's first season. With time, however, Smith got better and so did the writing. *The Fresh Prince* soon became a hit show and ran for six seasons.

Smith's easy charm and quick sense of humor led Hollywood producers to take notice and in 1992 he appeared in his first movie, *Wherever the Day Takes You,* about a group of teen runaways. He showed his ability as a dramatic actor in the film adaptation of John Guare's award-winning play *Six Degrees of Separation* (1993). In it he played a young con man who insinuates himself into an upper-class Manhattan family by claiming to be the son of the actor SIDNEY POITIER. Smith next teamed up with comedian Martin Lawrence in the action adventure *Bad Boys* (1995).

He was catapulted to movie stardom as a Marine Corps captain who saves the world from an alien invasion in the sci-fi spectacle *Independence Day* (1996). Smith claimed he modeled his performance on action hero Harrison Ford. In *Men in Black* (1997) he again fought aliens, but this time it was more for laughs. Since then, he has portrayed 19th-century government agent Jim West in an overproduced film version of the 1960s television series *Wild, Wild West* (1999) and was a mysterious golf caddy in the charming *Legend of Bagger Vance* (2000), directed by actor Robert Redford.

Smith's biggest acting challenge to date was playing world heavyweight boxing champ Muhammad Ali in the biographical drama *Ali* (2001). To prepare for the role Smith brought his weight up to 215 pounds and worked out for months with a boxing trainer. Smith received an Academy Award nomination for best actor for the role, losing to DENZEL WASHINGTON.

He reprised his role as Agent J in *Men in Black II* (2002). In 2003, Smith and his wife, actress Jada Pinkett, created a television sitcom, *All of Us,* based on their lives. The couple also wrote for the series, which was directed mostly by DEBBIE ALLEN and ran for four seasons.

Smith was nominated for a second best actor Oscar for his portrayal of a struggling salesman with a son in *The Pursuit of Happyness* (2006). The same year, he played the last man in New York City, battling zombies in *I Am Legend.* More recently, he has been a rehabilitated superhero in the comedy *Hancock* (2008) and a guilt-ridden man responsible for a deadly accident in *Seven Pounds* (2008). As of 2009, Smith is the only leading screen actor to have eight consecutive films open domestically as number-one box office hits.

Further Reading

Doeden, Matt. *Will Smith* (Just the Facts Biographies). Minneapolis, Minn.: Lerner Publications, 2006 (YA).

Robb, Brian J. *Will Smith: King of Cool.* Medford, N.J.: Plexus Publishing, 2000.

Schuman, Michael A. *Will Smith: "I Like Blending a Message with Comedy."* African-American Biography Library. Berkeley Heights, N.J.: Enslow Publishers, 2006 (YA).

Further Listening

Will Smith—Greatest Hits. Sony, CD, 2002.

Further Viewing

Ali (2001). Sony, VHS/DVD, 2002.

The Fresh Prince of Bel-Air—The Complete First Season (1990). DVD box set, 2003.

Men in Black (1997). Sony, Deluxe Edition, 2 DVDs, 2002.

The Pursuit of Happyness (2006). Sony, DVD, 2007.

Snipes, Wesley
(1962–   ) *actor*

A charismatic actor who is convincing in both action roles and more serious dramatic parts, Wesley Snipes was among the most popular and busiest of African-American leading men in films until he ran afoul of the Internal Revenue Service (IRS).

He was born in Orlando, Florida, on July 31, 1962. His mother, Marian, a teacher's assistant, divorced his father, an aircraft engineer, when he was a toddler, and moved to the Bronx, New York. Snipes attended the High School of Performing Arts in New York City but moved back to Florida with his mother before graduating. There he pursued acting and worked in dinner theater. An agent saw him perform and helped him land his first film role as a football player in the Goldie Hawn comedy *Wildcats* (1986). His wiry build and natural athleticism got him other roles as an athlete. Snipes played a boxer in *Streets of Gold* (1986) and a baseball player in *Major League* (1989).

But it was his tough demeanor as a gang leader who goes after MICHAEL JACKSON in Jackson's music video *Bad* (1989) that brought Snipes to critical attention. After that, filmmaker Spike Lee cast him as a jazz musician opposite DENZEL WASHINGTON in *Mo' Better Blues* (1990). The following year Snipes scored big with audiences as a charismatic but ruthless drug kingpin in *New Jack City* (1991), a movie that set off a cycle of black gangster movies. Snipes showed his versatility by next playing a black professional entangled in an interracial extramarital affair in Spike Lee's *Jungle Fever* (1991). He followed this with one of his best performances as a paraplegic in *The Waterdance* (1992).

After that, Snipes became the first prominent black action hero since the 1970s in such films as *Passenger 57* (1992), *Rising Sun* (1993) opposite Sean Connery, *Boiling Point* (1993), and *Murder at 1600 Pennsylvania Avenue* (1997). The quality of these films was uneven, but Snipes always delivered a solid and energetic performance. He relished the opportunity to play an over-the-top futuristic villain in the Sylvester Stallone vehicle *Demolition Man* (1993), even going so far as to bleach his hair blond. He showed a surprising gift for comedy as a hoop hustler in *White Men Can't Jump* (1992) and as a drag queen in *To Wong Foo: Thanks for Everything, Julie Newmar* (1995).

Snipes continued to skillfully mix genres, playing the comic book hero of *Blade* (1998) and its sequel *Blade II* (2002) and a member of a large southern family in *Down in the Delta* (1998), directed by author Maya Angelou.

By 2002, Snipes was making $15 million a picture and was among the highest-paid stars in Hollywood. However, the government claimed he hadn't paid taxes on his hefty income since 1998. A long battle with the IRS ended in April 2008 when Snipes was sentenced to three years in prison on three counts of willful failure to file income tax. As late as November 2009, Snipes was still appealing the convictions while free on bail.

The tax controversy has seriously hurt Snipes's career. Since 2005, he has only made a handful of low-quality action films that have gone directly to DVD. *Gallowwalker* (2009), a horror western, is his first theatrical release since 2004.

Further Reading

Blue, Rose, and Corinne J. Naden. *Wesley Snipes*. Black Americans of Achievement. New York: Chelsea House, 2001 (YA).

"Wesley Snipes." The Internet Movie Database. Available online. URL: http://www.indb.com/name/nm0000648/. Downloaded on February 10, 2009.

Zannos, Susan. *Male Fitness Stars of TV and the Movies: Featuring Profiles of Sylvester Stallone, John Travolta, Bruce Willis, and Wesley Snipes*. Legends of Health. Hockessin, Del.: Mitchell Lane Publishers, 2000 (YA).

Further Viewing

Jungle Fever (1991). Universal Home Entertainment, DVD, 1998.

New Jack City (1991). Warner Home Video, Special Edition, 2 DVD, 2005.

The Waterdance (1992). Sony, VHS/DVD, 1999/2001.

Snoop Dogg

(Calvin Broadus, Snoopy, Snoop Doggy Dogg) (1972–   ) *rap singer, songwriter, actor*

One of the most celebrated rappers of the mid-1990s, Snoop Dogg found his career both boosted and diminished by the violent gangsta lifestyle he pursued.

He was born Calvin Broadus on October 20, 1972, in Long Beach, California. His father, Vernell Varnado, gave him the nickname "Snoopy" because he was cute like the dog in the comic strip *Peanuts*. But the life he lived as a youth on the streets was anything but cute. Broadus got in trouble with the law numerous times and after graduating from high school was arrested and charged with possession of cocaine. Snoop was in and out of prison for the next several years. His growing interest in rap music saved him from a life of crime.

He began to record his own tapes of original rap songs. His friend Warren G, another rapper, was the stepbrother of DR. DRE, producer of the hit rap group Niggaz With Attitude (N.W.A.). Warren G. shared one of Snoop's tapes with Dre and he was impressed by his talent. Dre soon began a fruitful collaboration with Snoop that resulted in the popular theme song for the film

Deep Cover and Dre's debut album *The Chronic* (1992) on which Snoop sang under the name Snoop Doggy Dogg.

Snoop became Dre's right-hand man, epitomizing gangsta rap with his drawled vocals and nimble rhymes. With Dre producing, Snoop began to work on his own debut album, one of the most eagerly anticipated albums of 1994. It was nearly completed when disaster struck. On August 25, 1995, while Snoop was driving, his bodyguard allegedly shot a man named Phillip Woldermarian, who was in another car. In September, Snoop turned himself in to police, claiming the shooting was in self-defense and that Woldermarian had been stalking him for some time.

Two months later, his album *Doggystyle* (1994) was finally released. With Snoop Dogg's popularity at its peak since the shooting, it became the first debut album to enter the charts at number one. *Doggystyle* eventually sold 4 million copies and produced five hit singles, including "What's My Name?" and "Gin and Juice."

In February 1996, the long, drawn-out case against Snoop ended, and he was cleared of all charges. The time he lost in court, however, stalled his career. By the time he produced his second album, *The Doggfather* (1996), gangsta rap was in decline. Only a few weeks before the album's release, rapper TUPAC SHAKUR, a friend of Snoop Dogg, had been killed in another drive-by shooting. The album managed to sell about 2 million copies, but its critical reception was decidedly mixed.

Reacting to this change of fortune, Dogg tried to move away from gangsta rap and establish himself as more of a rocker. He signed with the No Limit label and released the albums *Da Game Is to Be Sold, Not to Be Told* (1998), *No Limit Top Dogg* (1999), and *Tha Last Meal* (2000). While his music remained captivating, some critics attacked the gratuitous violence in his lyrics. In 2004, Snoop signed with Geffen Records and released the album *R & G (Rhythm, and Gangsta): The Masterpiece*, which produced his first number-one

single, "Drop It Like It's Hot." In July 2007, Snoop Dogg became the first recording artist to release a track as a ring tone.

He began acting in movies in 1998 and has appeared in such major films as director John Singleton's *Baby Boy* and *Training Day* (both 2001) with DENZEL WASHINGTON. He has also guest starred on various television shows, including *Monk* (2002–) and the soap opera *One Life to Live*. He continues to live up to his gangsta reputation and was sentenced in April 2007 to five years of probation for gun and drug possession. He is the star of the reality sitcom *Snoop Dogg's Father Hood* (2007–) on the cable station E!

Snoop's cousin Nate Dogg is also a rap singer. They teamed up for Nate's top-40 hit, "Never Leave Me Alone" (1996).

Further Reading

Carlson-Berne, Emma. *Snoop Dogg.* Hip-Hop. Broomall, Pa.: Mason Crest Publishers, 2007 (YA).

The Official Snoop Dogg Web site. Available online. URL: http://www.snoopdogg.com/. Downloaded on February 10, 2009.

Snoop Doggy Dogg, with Davin Seay. *The Doggfather: The Times, Trials, and Hardcore Truths of Snoop Dogg.* New York: Harper Paperbacks, 2000.

Further Listening

The Best of Snoop Dogg. Priority Records, CD, 2005.

Further Viewing

Bigg Snoop Dogg Presents: The Adventures of the Blue Carpet Treatment. Cache Black Entertainment, DVD, 2008.

Summer, Donna

(LaDonna Adrian Gaines, "The Queen of Disco")
(1948–) *disco and R & B singer*

Considered little more than a sexy novelty act when she first appeared on the American musical

Donna Summer was a national singing star in Germany before disco music brought her fame in her native country. *(Photo courtesy of Showtime Archives, Toronto, and Brian Arias)*

scene, Donna Summer proved she had the staying power of a true superstar, her career long outliving the disco music that first brought her to fame.

She was born LaDonna Adrian Gaines on New Year's Eve, 1948, in Boston, Massachusetts, one of eight children. Her father, Ernest, was a butcher, an electrician, and a janitor. Gaines's first love was gospel music and by age 10 she was singing with several gospel groups around Boston. At 18, she moved to New York City and auditioned for the Broadway rock musical *Hair* with two of her sisters. She hoped to be the replacement for the show's star Melba Moore, but instead she was offered a role in the German company. She accepted and 10 days later left for Europe. The young black singer from Boston became an unlikely star in Germany. "Being a star in Germany is more low-key than it is in America," she later explained. "It is more quaint." After playing *Hair* in Vienna, Austria, Summer starred in the musicals *Porgy and Bess* and *Show Boat* with the

Vienna Folk Opera. There she met and later married actor Helmut Sommer. After they divorced, she kept the English spelling of her married name.

Summer became a session vocalist and had a major hit record in Europe with the song "The Hostage." In 1975, she recorded a dance track built around the repeated phrase "Love to Love You Baby." Neil Bogart of Casablanca Records in the States heard the track and liked it but felt it needed to be much longer to appeal to the disco dance crowd. Summer added about 18 minutes of moans and groans, making "Love to Love You Baby" the most erotic dance tune of its day. Still living in Germany, Summer suddenly found herself with the number-two hit record in the United States.

"The Queen of Disco" was first dubbed "the First Lady of Lust" by the American press and viewed as more of a joke than a serious recording artist. There were even rumors that she was a female impersonator. Summer proved a consistent hit-maker and even had a movie built around her, *Thank God It's Friday* (1978), which produced the number-three hit "Last Dance."

As disco faded, most people expected Summer's career to fade with it, but she surprised everyone by exhibiting the talent and creativity to adapt to other musical styles. In 1979, she scored three number-one records. "Hot Stuff" and "Bad Girls" effectively blended rock 'n' roll with the disco beat. "No More Tears (Enough Is Enough)" was a ballad sung with Barbra Streisand. Summer exhibited a quirky sense of humor in the infectious "The Wanderer" (1980) and brought a social conscience to the hard-driving "She Works Hard for the Money" (1983). "This Time I Know It's for Real" (1989) was her last top-ten hit to date. Summer's career seemed all but over when in 1998 her recording of "Carry On" earned her a Grammy for Best Dance Recording, the first time that category was honored. In 2003, Summer published her revealing autobiography, and the following year she was one of the first artists to be inducted into the Dance Music Hall of Fame. *Crayons,* released in 2008, is her first studio album of new material in 17 years. In a review, the *New York Times* called one track, "I'm a Fire," "a seven-minute throwback to the Hi-NRG disco of the 70s" and "a beacon of promise."

Further Reading

Howard, Josiah. *Donna Summer: Her Life and Music.* Cranbery Township, Pa.: Tiny Ripple Books, 2003.

Summer, Donna, and Marc Eliot. *Ordinary Girl: The Journey.* New York, Villard, 2003.

Further Listening

Gold. Hip-O Records, 2 CDs, 2005.

Further Viewing

Disc Queen. Hudson Street, DVD, 2008.

T

Tero, Lawrence   See Mr. T.

Terry, Sonny
(Saunders Terrell)
(1911–1986) *blues and folk harmonica player, singer*

One of the most influential and best known of blues harmonica players, Sonny Terry, with his long-time partner, guitarist Brownie McGhee, took his blend of blues and folk music to coffee houses, concerts halls, and even the Broadway stage.

He was born Saunders Terrell on October 24, 1911, in Greensboro, Georgia. His father played harmonica at dances and other gatherings. When he was five, Terry lost his sight in one eye in an accident. At age 18, another accident robbed him of sight in his other eye.

Falling back on music for his living, Terry teamed up with guitarist Blind Boy Fuller and the two recorded together for the first time in 1937. The following year Terry's musical career received a big boost when he was invited to perform at New York's Carnegie Hall in the legendary *From Spirituals to Swing* concert. Terry's so-called Piedmont Blues style of playing and singing was lighter and more accessible than the deep Delta blues of the Mississippi bluesmen. But his music was nonetheless colorful and exciting, full of whoops, wails, and a high falsetto that he often sang in.

When Fuller died in 1940, Terry traveled to Washington, D.C., for a concert. He was accompanied by guitarist Brownie McGhee, whose job it was to see that the blind musician got safely around the unfamiliar city. They decided to play together in Washington and were an immediate hit. They soon decided to become a team and moved to New York City, where they were embraced by the growing folk scene, led by such talented musicians as Leadbelly and Woody Guthrie. The duo appeared on Broadway in the musical *Finian's Rainbow* (1946–48) and a decade later sang onstage in Tennessee William's Broadway play *Cat on a Hot Tin Roof*. By the early 1960s, McGhee and Terry were performing for a largely white audience in clubs and at numerous folk festivals in the United States and Europe. The duo also made many appearances on television and in film documentaries.

The two friends had a falling out in the 1970s and went their separate ways after three decades together. Sonny Terry continued to play, wail, and moan until his death on March 11, 1986, in Mineola, New York. The same year, he was inducted into the Blues Foundation's Hall of

Fame. Brownie McGhee died 10 years later in 1996.

Further Reading

Campbell, Al. "Sonny Terry." The Allmusic Guide Web site. Available online. URL: http://allmusic.com/cg/amg.dll?p=amg&sql=ll:oifrxq95/d9e. Downloaded on February 10, 2009.

Terry, Sonny. *The Sourcebook of Sonny Terry Licks for Harmonica*. Milwaukee, Wisc.: Centerstream Publications, 1996 (YA).

Further Listening

Absolutely the Best. Varese Sarabande, CD, 2000.

Sonny Terry: The Folkways Years 1944–1963. Smithsonian Folkways, CD, 1992.

Further Viewing

Sonny Terry—Whoopin' the Blues 1958–1974 (1997). Grossman's Guitar Workshop, DVD, 2004.

Tupac   See SHAKUR, TUPAC.

Turner, Tina
(Anna Mae Bullock)
(1939–   ) *R & B singer, actress*

One of rock's greatest soul singers, Tina Turner overcame years of an abusive marriage to reemerge as a major star and a symbol of independent womanhood in the 1980s.

She was born Anna Mae Bullock on November 26, 1939, in Brownsville, Tennessee, although some sources give her birth year as 1938 or 1940. As a child she sang in a church choir and then worked as a singer and dancer with trombonist Bootsie Whitelaw. Her parents divorced when she was 11, and she lived for a time with her maternal grandmother. Bullock moved to St. Louis, Missouri, in 1956 to live with her mother and met guitarist Ike Turner, who led the rhythm and blues

(R & B) band The Kings of Rhythm. Turner, who was a shrewd judge of talent, hired Anna Mae as a singer in 1957. They were living together by 1958, although they may not have been legally married until 1962.

In 1960, Ike gave his lead singer the name Tina and the Kings of Rhythm became the Ike and Tina Turner Revue, backed by a girl chorus called the Ikettes. The same year, they signed a recording contract with Sue Records and had a top-30 pop hit record with their first release, "A Fool in Love" (1960). Tina's wild cries and groans, backed by the muddy, primitive sound of the Kings of Rhythm, made it one of the raunchiest R & B records ever to hit the pop charts. Tina's free and gravelly vocalizing in the studio was matched by her wild, seemingly spontaneous moves on stage. She helped make the Ike and Tina Turner Revue one of the most popular and exciting acts in the world of black music. Fame, however, came at a high price for Tina Turner. Ike controlled her every move and heaped both mental and physical abuse on her.

The team continued to have hit records for several years, including Tina's sly duet with Ike, "It's Gonna Work Out Fine" (1961). In 1966, producer Phil Spector released what should have been their biggest success, a spectacular production number "River Deep—Mountain High." Although the song became a top-10 hit in England, it barely made the charts in the United States. Spector was so disillusioned by its failure that he went into seclusion for three years. Ike and Tina did not have another major hit for four years. Tina and her talent were continuing to overshadow Ike, and in 1969, she went on tour with the British rock band the Rolling Stones.

A new, more contemporary sound resulted in two hits in 1970. Then Ike and Tina had their biggest hit together in 1971, a pounding, high-energy version of the song "Proud Mary." It also earned them their first Grammy Award. Tina made her film debut as the Acid Queen in the film adaptation of the rock opera *Tommy* (1975), a role that was first intended for rock star David Bowie.

As Tina became more famous, Ike became more abusive of her. Finally, one night in 1976, she fled from their home and checked into a hotel. Although their divorce would not be finalized for another two years, the relationship was over. Encouraged and helped by such British musicians as Rod Stewart, David Bowie, and Mick Jagger of the Rolling Stones, Tina launched a solo career. Her career stalled until she signed a contract with Capitol Records in 1983. The next year her debut album *Private Dancer* exploded on the music scene. It revealed a new and different Tina Turner. Her voice, while still full of grit, was more seductive, and the music was cool high-tech rock rather than raunchy R & B. The album sold more than 25 million copies, earned her three Grammys, and produced five hit singles, including the number-one "What's Love Got to Do with It" and the title song, about an erotic dancer who is only in it for the money.

Music critics and the public embraced the new Tina Turner as a woman who had suffered much and emerged from being a victim to an independent woman in full control of her life. As such, she became a symbol for women everywhere. In 1985, she returned to film acting, appearing as Aunty Entity, the Queen of Bartertown and Mad Max's nemesis, in the futuristic thriller *Mad Max Beyond Thunderdome.* She obviously relished the role and so did her fans. Over the next decade, Turner had 15 more hit singles, received two more Grammies, and published her autobiography *I, Tina: My Life Story* (1986). The book was adapted into a biographical film, *What's Love Got to Do with It* (1993), starring ANGELA BASSETT as Tina and LAURENCE FISHBURNE as Ike. Ike and Tina Turner were inducted into the Rock and Roll Hall of Fame in 1991. Turner gave what she said would be her last stadium tour, the much celebrated "Twenty-Four Seven Millenium Tour," in 2000.

In 2004, Turner released a greatest hits album that reached number two on the Billboard album charts, her highest debut. The following year, she was a recipient of the Kennedy Center Honors. Still ready to rock at age 69, in October 2008 she set off on the *Tina: Live in Concert Tour,* a world tour that ran through April 2009, ending in Europe. "It's a hopeful voice," a *New York Times* critic said of her Madison Square Garden performance in New York City. "It connotes ambition and longing, never misery." Ike Turner died on December 12, 2007.

Further Reading

Bego, Mark. *Tina Turner: Break Every Rule.* Lanham, Md.: Taylor Trade Publishing, 2005.

Hasday, Judy L. *Tina Turner.* Black Americans of Achievement. New York: Chelsea House, 1999 (YA).

Turner, Ike. *Takin' Back My Name: The Confessions of Ike Turner.* London: Virgin Books, 1999.

Turner, Tina, with Kurt Loder. *I, Tina: My Life Story.* New York: Avon, 1987.

Further Listening

All the Best. Capitol, 2 CDs, 2004.

Proud Mary: The Best of Ike and Tina Turner. Capitol, CD, 1991.

Further Viewing

Mad Max Beyond Thunderdome (1985). Warner Home Video, VHS/DVD, 1993/1997.

Tina Turner—One Last Time: Live in Concert (2000). Eagle Vision, VHS/DVD, 2001.

What's Love Got to Do with It (1993). Walt Disney Video, VHS/DVD, 1997/1999.

Tyson, Cicely
(1933–) *actress*

Considered by many to be the finest dramatic actress of her generation, Cicely Tyson never became the major movie star she could have been but has had far greater success in television drama.

She was born in New York City on December 19, 1933. Her father, William, was a carpenter, and her mother, Theodosia, was a domestic. To help with the family income, Tyson sold shopping bags on the streets at age nine. She attended New York University, and her first job was as a typist for the Red Cross. One day she declared to the entire office, "God didn't intend me to sit at a typewriter all my life." With her striking, statuesque looks, she had no trouble getting work as a fashion model. Tyson took courses at the Actors' Studio in New York City and soon was performing in small roles in Off-Broadway plays. In 1959, she got her first screen role as hoodlum HARRY BELAFONTE's girlfriend in the crime thriller *Odds Against Tomorrow* (1959). She got rave reviews Off-Broadway in a production of Jean Genet's *The Blacks* (1961), which also launched the acting careers of JAMES EARL JONES, GODFREY CAMBRIDGE, and ROSCOE LEE BROWNE. The role earned her the Drama Desk Award as outstanding Off-Broadway performer of the year.

In 1963, Tyson starred as a social worker opposite George C. Scott in the dramatic TV series *East Side, West Side*. "I really didn't do much on the series," she later recalled. "But people always remember me on it." A black woman on any television series at the time was a rarity, and it led to the program's cancellation when 26 southern stations refused to carry it because of her.

Tyson found few movie roles in the 1960s. Then, at age 39, she shot to stardom in *Sounder* (1972) as a sharecropper's wife struggling to hold her family together when her husband, played by PAUL WINFIELD, is sent to prison. The small movie was a surprise hit and Tyson was nominated for an Academy Award as best actress, along with DIANA ROSS for *Lady Sings the Blues*. Neither actress won, but it was a shining moment for the black community in Hollywood.

Despite her stardom, most of the film roles offered to Tyson after *Sounder* were inferior parts

Cicely Tyson has portrayed black women of determination and dignity on television and in movies. *(Photofest)*

and she refused them. Instead, she turned to television where she quickly found a role as meaningful as her part in *Sounder*. In the TV movie *The Autobiography of Miss Jane Pittman* (1974), she played an ordinary black woman, beginning in her youth at the end of the Civil War and spanning her life to old age during the civil rights era of the 1960s. In the film's climactic scene, the 110-year-old Pittman makes her stand against the prejudice she has endured all her life and takes a drink from a water fountain reserved for whites only. Tyson's performance was a true tour de force. The film won nine Emmys, two of them going to Tyson for outstanding actress in a drama and outstanding actress of the year in a special. Over the next several years she was featured in a string of outstanding television dramas including *Roots* (1977); *King* (1978), playing Coretta Scott King, wife of civil rights leader Martin Luther King, Jr.; and *A Woman Called Moses* (1978), in which she was Underground Railroad guide Harriet Tubman.

Tyson was seen less frequently in films, few of which were as successful or as satisfying as her television roles. She was reunited with Paul Winfield in *A Hero Ain't Nothing but a Sandwich* (1977) and costarred with RICHARD PRYOR in *Bustin' Loose* (1981). Less active in the 1980s, she played a strong-willed grandmother during the 1965 race riots in the Watts section of Los Angeles in the TV movie *Heat Wave* (1990) and played Rosa Parks's mother in the TV movie *The Rosa Parks Story* (2002) opposite ANGELA BASSETT. More recently she had a leading role in *Because of Winn-Dixie* (2005), based on a children's book, and played the role of Myrtle in the black comedy *Diary of a Mad Black Woman* (2005) and its sequel *Madea's Family Reunion* (2006), both written by and starring Tyler Perry. A high school of performing and fine arts in East Orange, New Jersey, has been renamed in Tyson's honor.

An actress who brings integrity and strength to every role she plays, Cicely Tyson continues to be one of the most admired black actresses in America. "The choice of roles I made had to do with educating and entertaining," she has said. "And as a result I found myself working only every two or three years."

Further Reading

Bogle, Donald. *Prime Time Blues: African Americans on Network Television.* New York: Farrar, Straus and Giroux, 2002, pp. 111–113, 234–239, 404–405.

"Cicely Tyson." The Internet Movie Database. Available online. URL: http://us.imdb.com/name/nm0001807/. Downloaded on February 11, 2009.

Further Viewing

The Autobiography of Miss Jane Pittman (1974). Classic Media, 2 DVDs, 2005.

Sounder (1972). Koch Vision, DVD, 2008.

A Woman Called Moses (1978). Xenon Studios. VHS/DVD, 1999/2001.

U

Uggams, Leslie
(1943–) *singer, actress*

A cheerful pop vocalist on television from age seven, Leslie Uggams emerged as a serious dramatic actress in the late 1970s via two outstanding television miniseries.

She was born on May 25, 1943, in New York City of black, Scotch, Irish, Cherokee, and Seminole ancestry. Her father, Harold, was an elevator operator and her mother, Juanita, had been a chorus girl before her marriage. A precocious child entertainer, she made her network television debut at age six on *Beulah* (1950–53), the first situation comedy to star a black performer. She played star ETHEL WATERS's niece. After singing on a number of leading television variety shows, Uggams became a full-fledged star at 18 as a featured vocalist on the musical variety show *Sing Along with Mitch* (1961–64), hosted by musical producer and conductor Mitch Miller. In 1969, she was the star of the short-lived *Leslie Uggams Show,* becoming the first black woman since HAZEL SCOTT nearly 20 years earlier to host her own network variety series. The previous year she had won a Tony for best actress in a Broadway musical comedy for her role in *Hallelujah, Baby!* (1968).

Uggams's image through the mid-1970s was clean-cut, cheerful, and more than a little plastic. Then came the miniseries *Roots.* In this saga of a black family from slavery to freedom, Uggams played Kizzy, the daughter of Kunta Kinte, an African brought to America as a slave in the early 1800s. Uggams gave a powerful performance in the role, leading writer Donald Bogle to comment that she "attained a newfound maturity, washing away any signs of the eager-to-please child star. . . . Here was a real woman suddenly coming to life." She was nominated for an Emmy Award as best leading actress.

Two years later, Uggams starred in another excellent black miniseries, *Backstairs at the White House,* in which she played Lillian Rogers Parks, a domestic who grows up working at the White House from the Taft through the Eisenhower administrations.

Uggams has continued to work in television in a variety of capacities. In 1982, she was cohost of the daytime game show *Fantasy* and earned an Emmy Award for outstanding host/hostess in a variety series. She had a continuing role on the popular soap opera *All My Children* in 1996. She has been very active on the stage in recent years and toured with the show *Stringbean* in 1991, based on the early career of singer/actress Ethel Waters. In 2001, Leslie Uggams was nominated for a Tony Award as best leading actress in a play for her performance in black playwright August Wilson's drama *King Headley.* She returned to Broadway in a revival of the musical *Thoroughly*

Modern Millie in 2003 and a limited revival of the drama *On Golden Pond* in 2005, playing opposite JAMES EARL JONES. More recently, Uggams played the grandmother in a 2008 revival of *First Breeze of Summer*. The *New York Times* reviewer called her performance a "subtle, contradiction-embracing portrayal."

Leslie Uggams has been married to Graham Pratt since 1965. Their son and daughter are both actors.

Further Reading

Bogle, Donald. *Prime Time Blues: African Americans on Network Television.* New York: Farrar, Straus & Giroux, 2002, pp. 241, 243–245, 247, 248.

"Leslie Uggams—Online!" Available online. URL: http://www.leslieuggams.com/. Downloaded on February 11, 2009.

Further Listening

On My Way to You: Songs of Alan and Marilyn Bergman (2003). Lml Music, CD, 2007.

Further Viewing

Backstairs at the White House (1979). Acorn Media, DVD box set, 2005.

Roots (1977). Warner Home Video, 30th-Year Anniversary DVD box set, 2007.

Underwood, Blair

(1964–   ) *actor*

A star of one of the most highly praised dramatic television series of the 1980s and early 1990s, Blair Underwood played TV's most popular "buppie" (black urban professional) for seven seasons.

He was born on August 25, 1964, in Tacoma, Washington. His father was a colonel in the U.S. Army, and he spent his childhood in Germany, Colorado, Michigan, and finally Alexandria, Virginia, where the family settled down. His mother is an interior decorator.

Underwood's good looks earned him the award for prettiest smile in junior high school. He attended Carnegie Mellon University in Pittsburgh, Pennsylvania, and after graduation pursued a modeling career. A prominent modeling agency turned him down because of several childhood scars on his face. He decided to forsake modeling for acting and made his film debut in the musical *Krush Groove* (1985).

Underwood's big break came two years later when he joined the cast of the TV dramatic series *L.A. Law* (1986–94) in its second season. Underwood played Jonathan Rollins, an Ivy League–educated black lawyer who is hired by a prominent Los Angeles law firm. In the first few seasons, the Rollins character was rather shallow, the kind of lawyer who would do anything to win a case. Little note was taken of Rollins's identity as a black man. Later in the series Rollins became more humanized, and Underwood began to shine in the part. In one episode he was a victim of racial profiling and falsely arrested as a mugger. Another time, he was caught up in the racial riots that followed the real-life police beating of black man Rodney King. Toward the end of the series' run, Rollins decides to run for City Council in the ghetto neighborhood of South Central Los Angeles.

During his time on *L. A. Law,* Underwood was involved in another race riot in the excellent TV movie *Heat Wave* (1990). He played real-life Robert Richardson, who became the first black reporter for the *L.A. Times* during the 1965 race riots in the black Los Angeles neighborhood of Watts. Two years after *L. A. Law* left the air, Underwood played another real person, black baseball player Jackie Robinson in the Home Box Office (HBO) television movie *Soul of the Game* (1996). Also in 1996, he appeared in the movie *Set It Off,* with QUEEN LATIFAH, as an upwardly mobile banker. In recent years, Underwood has again concentrated on television, playing recurring roles in such series as *Sex in the City* (1998–2004), *The New Adventures of Old Christine*

(2006–   ), and *Dirty Sexy Money* (2007–   ). Underwood is also the author of several books, including a mystery series.

Further Reading

"Blair Underwood." The Internet Movie Database. Available online. URL: http://us.imdb.com/name/nm0005516/. Downloaded on February 11, 2009.

Bogle, Donald. *Prime Time Blues: African Americans on Network Television.* New York: Farrar, Straus & Giroux, 2002, pp. 334, 335, 455, 456, 459.

Underwood, Blair. *Before I Got Here: The Wondrous Things We Hear When We Listen to the Souls of Our Children.* New York: Atria, 2005.

Further Viewing

Heat Wave (1990). Turner Home Entertainment, DVD, 2006.

Soul of the Game (1996). HBO Home Video, VHS/DVD, 2001.

Usher
(Usher Raymond IV, Big Ush,
Mr. Entertainment)
(1978–   ) *R & B singer, actor, songwriter*

Usher reveals the charm and personality that has helped make him a top recording artist. *(AP Photo/Jeff Christensen)*

One of the most popular and celebrated R & B singers of his generation, Usher made a smooth transition from teen idol to mature singer and along the way has sold more than 35 million albums to date.

Born Usher Raymond IV on October 14, 1978, in Chattanooga, Tennessee, at age six, Usher began singing in a church choir directed by his single-parent mother, Jonetta Patton. His godfather is actor and singer BEN VEREEN. When he was 12, the family moved to Atlanta, Georgia, where Usher continued to sing. Still in high school, he entered a talent show and was heard by a record executive from the La Face label. At the age of 16, his first album for La Face, *Usher* (1994), was released, coproduced by SEAN COMBS. The album sold well, and a single from it, "Think of You,"

went gold. His second album, *My Way* (1997), showcased both his voice and his talent as a composer. Usher wrote six of the album's nine songs. Three singles from the album sold well, with "Nice and Slow" becoming Usher's first number-one pop hit.

With his fourth album, *8701* (2001), Usher made a smooth shift from a teen star to a mature, lovelorn, adult singer. The single "U Got It Bad" went to number one in 2002, and his subsequent album, *Confessions* (2004), has to date sold more than 9 million copies. In 2008, *Billboard* magazine ranked Usher 21 in its All Time Hot 100 Artists. He has won five Grammy Awards to date and has his own vanity label, US Records.

"Usher's smooth-featured voice and taut, efficient hooks come pretty close to a sure thing, at a time when pop-music blockbusters are few and far between," wrote Nate Chinen in a review of a June 2008 concert at New York's Apollo Theater.

Usher has proved to be a creditable actor in a number of films, beginning with the horror movie *The Faculty* (1998). He has also acted in episodes of such television series as *The Twilight Zone, Moesha,* and *American Dreams,* in which he portrayed Motown soul singer MARVIN GAYE. Usher was nominated for an NAACP Image Award in 1999 for his acting on the soap opera *The Bold and the Beautiful.*

Further Reading

Chinen, Nate. "In the Hands of a Pro, the Moves Meet the Grooves." *New York Times,* June 9, 2008, p. E5.

Malkin, Marc S. *Usher: The Ultimate Entertainer.* Kansas City, Mo.: Andrews McMeel Publishing, 1998.

Nickson, Chris. *Usher: The Godson of Soul.* New York: Simon Spotlight, 2005 (YA).

Raymond, Lord. *Usher* (Hip Hop). Broomall, Pa.: Mason Crest Publishers, 2007 (YA).

Usher's Official Web site. Available online. URL: http://www.usherworld.com. Forthcoming.

Further Listening

Confessions. La Face, CD, 2004.

8701. La Face, CD, 2001.

Further Viewing

Live: 8701 Evolution Tour (2002). Eagle Rock Entertainment, DVD, 2002.

V

Vaughan, Sarah
("The Divine One," "Sassy")
(1924–1990) *jazz and pop singer*

Considered one of the greatest female jazz singers along with ELLA FITZGERALD and BILLIE HOLIDAY, Sarah Vaughan was unsurpassed in her stylistic virtuosity and tight control over her rich, husky voice.

She was born on March 27, 1924, in Newark, New Jersey, where her father, Ashbury Vaughan, was a carpenter. Her mother, Ada, was a laundress and played piano in the Mt. Zion Baptist Church Choir where Vaughan sang as a child. She began piano lessons at age six. When she was 18, she won Amateur Night at the Apollo Theater in Harlem, in New York City. Singer and bandleader Billy Eckstine heard her there and was so impressed by Vaughan's performance that he got her a job in Earl Hines's band. When Eckstine left Hines's band, he took her with him.

She recorded with Eckstine in 1944 and first recorded solo the following year. While singing in a New York club, she met and married trumpeter George Treadwell, who later became her manager. Vaughan signed a recording contract with Columbia Records in 1949 and began a successful recording career, alternating between pop and jazz songs. She left Columbia for Mercury Records in 1954.

Through the 1950s, she had numerous pop hits, her biggest singles including "Nature Boy" (1948), "Make Yourself Comfortable" (1954), "Whatever Lola Wants" (1956), and "Broken-Hearted Melody" (1959). She divorced Treadwell in 1959 and married four more times, once to football player Clyde Atkins.

Possessed of an incredible three-octave range, Vaughan's voice was a finely tuned instrument that she could use to amazing effect. Her ability to improvise on a tune was the envy of many other singers, among them Frank Sinatra. "Sassy is so good that when I listen to her I want to cut my wrists with a dull razor," Sinatra once said.

In her long career, Vaughan recorded with many great jazz musicians including Benny Carter, COUNT BASIE, and pianist OSCAR PETERSON. She is considered one of the finest interpreters of the music of DUKE ELLINGTON and recorded three albums of his work. After years of losing out in the Grammy Award competition to Ella Fitzgerald, "The Divine One" won her first and only Grammy for best vocal jazz performance, female, for the album *Gershwin Live!* in 1982. In 1989, she was the recipient of Grammy's Lifetime Achievement Award. She died on April 3, 1990, of lung cancer.

"Her vocal signatures," wrote music critic David McGee, "were so distinctly her own that she became a genre unto herself."

Further Reading

Gourse, Leslie. *Sassy: The Life of Sarah Vaughan*. New York: Da Capo Press, 1994.

Ruuth, Marianne. *Sarah Vaughan*. Black American Series. Los Angeles: Holloway House, 1994.

Further Listening

After Hours (1961). Blue Note Records, CD, 1997.

The Divine One (1961). CFP Domestic, CD, 2007.

Further Viewing

Jazz Icons: Sarah Vaughan Live in '58 and '64. Jazz Icons, DVD, 2007.

Vereen, Ben

(Benjamin Augustus Middleton)
(1946–   ) *actor, dancer, singer*

An all-around entertainer in the SAMMY DAVIS, JR., tradition, Ben Vereen has excelled on the Broadway stage, on television, and in movies. Like Sammy Davis, he has overcome tremendous odds to succeed.

He was born Benjamin Augustus Middleton on October 10, 1946, in Miami, Florida, and grew up in Brooklyn, New York. His father, James Vereen, was a carpenter, and his mother, Pauline, a theater matron. After graduating from high school, he entered the Pentecostal Theological Seminary, planning to become a minister. He left within six months to pursue an acting career. Vereen made his New York stage debut in 1964 and was SAMMY DAVIS, JR.'s understudy in the Broadway musical *Golden Boy* (1964). He landed a part in the national tour of the Broadway musical *Sweet Charity* in 1967 and two years later replaced another actor in the rock musical *Hair*. Vereen got his biggest break playing Judas in the musical *Jesus Christ Superstar* (1971). He became a theatrical star when he played the key role of the Leading Player in the musical *Pippin* (1972) and won the Tony Award for best actor in a musical as well as a Drama Desk Award.

A star of the Broadway stage, Ben Vereen achieved his greatest success as Chicken George in the television saga *Roots*. *(Photofest)*

Vereen was soon guest-starring on television variety shows and in the summer of 1975 had his own four-week variety program, *Ben Vereen—Comin' at Ya*. The following year he was cast as a young LOUIS ARMSTRONG in the television movie *Louis Armstrong—Chicago Style*. His greatest dramatic role came in 1977 when he joined a gallery of fine black actors and actresses in the miniseries *Roots*, the saga of four generations in an African-American family. Vereen was utterly appealing as Chicken George Moore, grandson of slave Kunta Kinte. He played the part of the happy-go-lucky hustler and fight cock trainer with joyful abandon, but he was also able to reach dramatic depths when he finally learns that his white master is also his father. Nominated for an Emmy Award as best actor in a single performance in a dramatic or comedy series, Vereen lost to *Roots* costar Louis Gossett, Jr.

As renowned on television as on the Broadway stage, Vereen then starred in his own TV special, *Ben Vereen: His Roots* (1978), which won seven Emmys. He was also a success in movies, with fine performances as song-and-dance men in *Funny Lady* (1975), a film sequel to the musical *Funny Girl*, and Bob Fosse's *All That Jazz* (1979).

Returning to television in his first starring role in a series, he played reformed con man E. L. "Tenspeed" Turner in *Tenspeed and Brown Shoe* (1980), about a pair of Los Angeles private detectives. Although Vereen was memorable in the part, the series could not find an audience and disappeared after half a season. However, he went on to appear as a regular character in a handful of sitcoms, including *J. J. Starbuck*, *Booker*, and *Webster*, where he played Webster's Uncle Phillip.

Then, in 1992, Vereen's extraordinary career nearly came to an end. While walking along a roadway, the performer suffered a stroke and was struck by a truck. Through determination and a strong faith, Vereen survived and made a full recovery. Within a year he was back on Broadway as the Chimney Man in the musical *Jelly's Last Jam* (1993), based on the life and music of jazz musician Jelly Roll Morton. He followed this with a role in *Fosse* a musical tribute to his late mentor in 2001. Most recently, he was seen as the Wizard of Oz in the Broadway musical *Wicked* in 2005.

Vereen has traveled the world with his one-man show in which he sings, dances, and shares his life's experiences with the audience. A devoted humanitarian, Ben Vereen has worked to raise money for many good causes and in 1991 established his own Celebrities for a Drug Free America. He received the National Association for the Advancement of Colored People's (NAACP) Image Awards in 1978 and 1979. Vereen is the godfather and acting coach of the singer Usher.

Further Reading

The Ben Vereen Official Web site. Available online. URL: http://www.benvereen.tv/onlyofficialBen-Vereensite/home.html. Downloaded on February 11, 2009.

Summers, Kim. "Ben Vereen." The Allmusic Web site. Available online. URL: http://allmusic.com/cg/amg.dll?p=ang&sql=ll.3zfuxqegld9e. Downloaded on February 11, 2009.

Further Listening

Pippin (1972). Decca Broadway, CD, 2000.

Further Viewing

Pippin (1981). VCI Home Video, VHS/DVD, 2000.

Roots (1977). Warner Home Video, 30th-Anniversary Edition DVD box set, 2007.

W–Y

Waller, Fats
(Thomas Wright Waller)
(1904–1943) *jazz singer, pianist, songwriter*

One of the greatest of jazz pianists, as well as a fine songwriter, Fats Waller was better known in his lifetime as a superb singer of novelty songs.

He was born Thomas Wright Waller on May 21, 1904, in New York City. His father, Reverend Edward Waller, was a prominent Baptist minister, and as a youth, Waller played the organ and sang in the choir of Harlem's Abyssinian Baptist Church. But soon secular music, particularly jazz and ragtime, excited him more and at age 15, to his father's disappointment, Waller took a job as organist in the Lincoln Theater in Harlem. Within a year, he was studying piano with pianist James P. Johnson, a master of the rollicking style of playing known as "stride." Waller adapted this style, giving it his own unique twist. While he is best known for his piano playing, Waller's favorite instrument remained the pump organ, and he was one of the first jazz musicians to play this instrument.

Waller earned the nickname Fats for his size, reaching close to 300 pounds by adulthood. He supplemented his income by playing in local cabarets and clubs and accompanied blues singer BESSIE SMITH on the vaudeville theater circuit. The theater attracted Waller, and he wrote songs with his mentor James Johnson for a show *Keep Shufflin'* (1928). He later teamed up with lyricist Andy Razaf and together they wrote the successful black musical *Hot Chocolates* (1929) that produced their best-known song "Ain't Misbehavin'." Jazz musician LOUIS ARMSTRONG joined the cast six weeks into the run and played the show's music on his trumpet during intermission. Waller and Razaf wrote a wealth of fine songs including the ballad "Honeysuckle Rose," the upbeat "The Joint Is Jumpin'," and the hilarious "Your Feets Too Big."

Waller's comic delivery of a lyric and his effervescent personality soon proved to be something of a liability. Though he was a hit recording artist, his label RCA Victor forced him to record many throwaway novelty songs and old standards, many of them far below the quality of his own material. But like Louis Armstrong, Waller could make any song sound good, enlivening the stalest of lyrics with his own clever asides. However, his success in this area far overshadowed his greatness as a pianist. His playing strongly influenced such jazz musicians as COUNT BASIE, Erroll Garner, and others.

In 1932, Waller debuted on his own radio show on WLW in Cincinnati, Ohio. *The Fats Waller Rhythm Club* became a huge hit and, along with his recordings, helped make him a national star. Waller's charismatic personality was captured on celluloid in only three films—*King of Burlesque, Hooray for Love* (both 1935), and the all-black musical *Stormy Weather* (1943), which starred BILL

ROBINSON and LENA HORNE. After completing this film, Waller left Hollywood, where he had spent some time, and took a train back to New York. En route, he became ill with pneumonia and died in Kansas City, Missouri, on December 15, 1943. Waller, so full of fun and life, was only 39 years old. "Exuberance is the spontaneity of life," Waller once said. In that sense, he lived his short life to the fullest.

In 1978, Waller's music became the basis of a Broadway musical revue, *Ain't Misbehavin'*. It became a huge hit, won the Tony Award for best musical, introduced a handful of gifted black performers, and brought Fats Waller a new generation of enthusiastic fans.

Further Reading

"Fats" Waller Web page. Available online. URL: http://www.geocities.com/BourbonStreet/Delta/6704/. Downloaded on December 16, 2001.

Kirkeby, Ed, with Duncan P. Schiedt and Sinclair Traill. *Ain't Misbehavin': The Story of Fats Waller.* New York: Da Capo Press, 1988.

Shipton, Alyn. *Fats Waller: The Cheerful Little Earful.* New York: Continuum, 2005.

Waller, Maurice, and Anthony Calabrese. *Fats Waller.* New York: Macmillan, 1979.

Further Listening

If You Got to Ask, You Ain't Got It! RCA, DVD box set, 2006.

Further Viewing

Stormy Weather (1943). Twentieth Century Fox Video, DVD, 2006.

This Joint Is Jumpin. Screen Edge, DVD, 2009.

Warwick, Dionne

(Marie Dionne Warrwick, Dionne Warwicke) (1940–) *R & B singer*

A supreme vocal stylist for four decades, Dionne Warwick enjoyed a long collaboration with songwriters Burt Bacharach and Hal David, one of the most fruitful in the history of modern pop music.

She was born Marie Dionne Warrwick on December 12, 1940, in East Orange, New Jersey. Warrwick grew up with gospel music in her blood. Her father, Mancel, was a chef, and her mother, Lee, business manager for the leading gospel group, the Drinkard Singers. Marie sang in her church choir from the age of six. After high school, she attended Hartt College of Music in Hartford, Connecticut, as a music education major. To earn money for her tuition, Warwick who dropped the second "r" from her last name, sang in a gospel trio, the Gospelaires, with her sister Dee Dee Warwick and her aunt Cissy Houston, both of whom became successful rhythm and blues (R & B) artists. Cissy Houston is the mother of singer WHITNEY HOUSTON.

Warwick also worked part time as a backup singer in New York recording studios. This is how she met songwriter Burt Bacharach and his partner Hal David in 1962. They were impressed by her expressive voice and extraordinary range and helped her get a recording contract with Scepter Records. Warwick's first release on the label in late 1962 was the Bacharach-David song "Don't Make Me Over," one of the first pop songs to take a stand for female equality in a love relationship. Warwick's alternatively reflective and explosive interpretation of the intricate song sent it to number 21 on the pop charts. It was the beginning of a memorable string of hits for the singer and the songwriting team that would continue for nearly a decade. Among their many classic songs together are "Anyone Who Had a Heart" (1963), "Walk on By" (1964), "You'll Never Get to Heaven" (1964), "A Message to Michael" (1966), "Alfie" (1967), "I Say a Little Prayer" (1967), and "Do You Know the Way to San Jose" (1968). Ironically, Warwick's biggest success of the 1960s was "(The Theme from) *The Valley of the Dolls*" (1968), which was one of the few singles she recorded not written by Bacharach and David.

In 1968, the team wrote the score for the Broadway musical *Promises, Promises,* giving Warwick two more song hits, the musically challenging title song (1968) and the wistful ballad "I'll Never Fall in Love Again" (1969).

In 1971, Warwick left Scepter and signed with Warner Brothers Records. About the same time her long collaboration with Bacharach and David ended over creative differences. For the first time in a decade, her career began to flounder. A devoted follower of numerology, she added an "e" to her last name for a time for good luck. Whether it was luck or accident, she achieved her first number-one record in 1974 with "Then Came You," backed by the male soul group the Spinners, from Philadelphia. But the comeback did not last, and for the next five years Warwick's records barely made the pop charts.

Then, in 1979, she signed with Arista Records and again she experienced an impressive comeback. Her debut Arista album, *Dionne* (1979), with a million copies sold, went platinum and produced two hit singles, "I'll Never Love This Way Again" and "Déjà Vu." These two songs earned Warwick her first two Grammy Awards. She continued to record and tour successfully through the 1980s, singing hit duets with JOHNNY MATHIS, Luther Vandross, and Jeffrey Osborne. Her most ambitious collaborative effort was her second number-one hit, "That's What Friends Are For" (1986), which brought her together with Elton John, GLADYS KNIGHT, and STEVIE WONDER. The song was written by Burt Bacharach, who had finally reconciled with Warwick, and his new writing partner Carol Bayer Sager. It earned Warwick two more Grammys.

Dionne Warwick had her last hit record to date—her 55th—in 1987. In the 1990s, her passion for numerology led her to became an ardent spokesperson for the Psychic Friends Network, hosting many television infomercials for the organization and bewildering many of her old fans.

In 2006, Warwick released an album of duets with other artists, *My Friends and Me* (2006), pro-duced by her son Damon Elliott. Her sister Dee Dee Warwick, who died shortly after, sang with her on *Why We Sing* (2008), a gospel album. Warwick has been married twice to actor/drummer William Elliott, whom she divorced for the second time in 1975. Their other son, David Elliott, is a singer-songwriter.

Further Reading

Nathan, David. *The Soulful Divas: Personal Portraits of Over a Dozen Divine Divas from Nina Simone, Aretha Franklin, and Diana Ross, to Patti LaBelle, Whitney Houston and Janet Jackson.* New York: Watson-Guptil, 1999.

Ruhlmann, William. "Dionne Warwick." The Allmusic Web site. Available online. URL: http://allmusic.com/cg/amg.dll?p=amg&sq/=ll.aiftxqw5ldhe. Downloaded on February 11, 2009.

Warwick, Dionne. *My Point of View.* Mobile, Ala.: Lighthouse Press, 2004.

Further Listening

The Dionne Warwick Collection: Her All-Time Greatest Hits. Rhino, CD, 1989.

Dionne Warwick's Greatest Hits (1979–1990). Arista, CD, 1989.

Further Viewing

In Concert Classics. DPTV Media, DVD, 2005.

Washington, Denzel
(1954–) *actor*

The leading black actor in films today and the only black actor to win an Academy Award for both best actor and best supporting actor, Denzel Washington has everything it takes to make a movie star—good looks, charisma, intelligence, and finely honed acting skills.

He was born on December 28, 1954, in Mount Vernon, New York, the second of three children. His father, also Denzel, was a Pentecostal minister and his mother, Lennis, a beautician and former gospel singer. He attended Fordham University in New York to study medicine, then switched to journalism, and finally drama. He joined the American Conservatory Theater (ACT) in San Francisco, California, after graduating from college and played in a variety of both classic and modern plays. After a year at ACT, he left to look for television and film work. He was soon cast as Dr. Philip Chambers on the television medical drama *St. Elsewhere* (1982–88), where he stayed for the show's six-season run. Although he rarely was given the opportunity to shine on the series, it provided him with plenty of experience before the camera. In 1981, Washington made his film debut in the dubious comedy *Carbon Copy* with George Segal. He fared far better in *A Soldier's Story* (1984), about a racial murder on an army base during World War II. Washington had previously appeared in the original New York stage production of the play and won an Obie (Off-Broadway) Award for his small but pivotal role.

Like other serious black actors, Washington refused to accept stereotypical roles he was offered, and as a result he appeared mostly in quality pictures. He moved up to leading-man status when director Richard Attenborough cast him as South African political leader Stephen Biko in the drama *Cry Freedom* (1987). For this role Washington received an Academy Award nomination for best actor, the first of four acting nominations he has received to date. Two years later, he won the Oscar for best supporting actor as the runaway slave Tripp who joins a black regiment of soldiers during the Civil War in the stirring historical drama *Glory* (1989). With each subsequent role, Washington grew in stature and popularity. He was a Caribbean police chief on a murderer's trail in the thriller *The Mighty Quinn* (1989). He played a self-centered jazz musician in Spike Lee's *Mo' Better Blues* (1990) and a convincing romantic leading man in *Mississippi Masala* (1991).

In 1992, Washington took on his most challenging role to date playing Malcolm X in Spike Lee's biographical film about the black political

After more than two decades as a film actor, Denzel Washington stands at the top of his profession. *(Photofest)*

leader. In a towering performance, Washington captured Malcolm's many-sided personality as he progressed from pimp and petty criminal to committed Black Muslim to charismatic Muslim leader and finally a martyr to his cause. He was equally good as a black lawyer who reluctantly defends an AIDS-stricken attorney in *Philadelphia* (1993), the first major Hollywood film to deal directly with the AIDS epidemic. The same year he played an investigative reporter opposite Julia Roberts in the thriller *The Pelican Brief* (1993). He was an angel in a role originally played by Cary Grant in *The Preacher's Wife* (1996) with WHITNEY HOUSTON and the convict father of a basketball player in his third Spike Lee film, *He Got Game* (1998).

Now one of the hottest stars in Hollywood, Washington regularly earns $10 million and up per film. He was chosen by *People* magazine as one of the 50 Most Beautiful People in the World in

1990. To justify the money and publicity, he works hard on every role. To prepare for *The Hurricane* (2000), about the life of boxer Rubin "Hurricane" Carter who was falsely accused of robbery and murder, Washington worked out for a year with a boxing trainer. The role earned him another Academy Award nomination for best actor. Usually cast as heroes, idealists, and good guys, Washington took the risky role of a corrupt, villainous Los Angeles narcotics police detective in the thriller *Training Day* (2001) and gave a riveting performance. "He smiles, cajoles and threatens all in the same sentence," wrote *New York Times* film critic Elvis Mitchell, "and Mr. Washington can use even his smile as a weapon." The role earned Washington the best actor Oscar many fans felt was long overdue. The only previous black actor to win in the best actor category is SIDNEY POITIER, who, coincidentally, was awarded an honorary Oscar the same evening.

Denzel Washington made his directorial debut with the film *Antwone Fisher* (2002), in which he played a psychiatrist working with a troubled youth. He starred in the remake of the cold war thriller *The Manchurian Candidate* (2004) and played a hostage negotiator in the Spike Lee film *Inside Man* (2006). In his second directorial project, *The Great Debaters* (2007), Washington played real-life Melvin B. Tolson, team leader of the 1935 debating team at all-black Wiley College in Texas. He was nominated for a Golden Globe Award the same year for his portrayal of drug kingpin Frank Lucas in *American Gangster*. He returns to Broadway in August Wilson's *Fences* in April 2010.

Denzel Washington lives in Los Angeles with Pauletta Pearson, his wife of more than 25 years, and their four children, one of whom is named Malcolm in honor of Malcolm X, one of his favorite roles.

As director Ed Zwick, who worked with him on *Glory*, says of Washington, "Whatever that mysterious electrochemical process is that makes the camera love someone, he has more of it than any one person should."

Further Reading

Brode, Douglas. *Denzel Washington: His Films and Career.* Secaucus, N.J.: Carol Publishing Group, 1997.

Hill, Anne H. *Denzel Washington.* Black Americans of Achievement. New York: Chelsea House, 1998 (YA).

Nickson, Chris. *Denzel Washington.* New York: St. Martin's Paperbacks, 1996.

Parish, James Robert. *Denzel Washington: Actor.* New York: Ferguson Publishing, 2005 (YA).

Washington, Denzel. *A Hand to Guide Me.* Des Moines, Iowa: Meredith Books, 2006.

Further Viewing

Glory (1989). Sony Special Edition, 2 DVDs.

The Great Debaters (2007). Genius Products, DVD, 2008.

Training Day (2001). Warner Home Video, VHS/DVD, 2004.

Washington, Dinah
(Ruth Lee Jones, "Queen of the Blues")
(1924–1963) *blues, jazz, pop singer*

One of the most versatile and distinctive female black singers of the 1940s and 1950s, Dinah Washington was known for her crystal clear enunciation and her notorious life style.

She was born Ruth Lee Jones on August 29, 1924, in Tuscaloosa, Alabama. Her father Ollie Jones, was a professional gambler who was rarely home, leaving her mother, Alice, to support and raise four children. The family moved to Chicago when Ruth was four and she was soon playing piano and singing at St. Luke's Baptist Church with her mother. At 15, she won first prize in an amateur singing contest held at the Regal Theater. The following year gospel singer Sallie Martin hired her to sing and play piano for her group, the Sallie Martin Colored Ladies Quartet. During her two years with Martin she took the name "Dinah Washington" from a mystery novel.

Bandleader Lionel Hampton hired Washington in 1943 as a vocalist. As her fame grew, she left the band and became renowned as the best blues singer since BESSIE SMITH, earning the title "Queen of the Blues." She signed a long-term recording contract with Mercury Records in the late 1940s and through the 1950s had many hits on the rhythm and blues (R & B) charts. But she did not have a major pop hit until 1959 when "What a Difference a Day Makes" reached the top-10. Washington returned to the top 10 a year later with two classic duets with singer Brook Benton, "Baby (You've Got What It Takes)" and "A Rockin' Good Way (To Mess Around and Fall in Love)."

Washington herself fell in love frequently. Her affairs were legendary and she was married at least eight times, the last time to football player Dick (Night Train) Lane. Her rocky personal life was good material for the tabloid press. She carried a gun that she would use to threaten club owners who were slow in paying her. She was once arrested for holding her dress designer at gunpoint.

When her dramatic instincts were turned to her performing, the results were spectacular. According to QUINCY JONES, who produced some of her 1950s albums, she "could take the melody in her hand, hold it like an egg, crack it open, fry it, let it sizzle, reconstruct it, put the egg back in the box and back in the refrigerator, and you would've still understood every single syllable."

Dinah Washington died on December 14, 1963, at age 39 from an accidental overdose of pills and alcohol. She was inducted into the Rock and Roll Hall of Fame as an early influence in 1993. She was honored by a U.S. postage stamp that same year as part of the Legends of American Music Series.

Further Reading

Cohodas, Nadine. *Queen: The Life and Music of Dinah Washington*. New York: Billboard Books, 2006.
"Dinah Washington." The Alabama Music Hall of Fame Web site. Available online. URL: http:// www.alamhof.org/washingd.htm. Downloaded on April 26, 2001.
Haskins, James. *Queen of the Blues: A Biography of Dinah Washington*. New York: William Morrow, 1987.

Further Listening

The Best of Dinah Washington—20th Century Masters: Millennium Collection. Hip-O Records, CD, 2002.
Very Best of Dinah Washington. EMI Gold Imports, CD box set, 2006.

Further Viewing

Jazz on a Summer's Day. (1959). Indie Europe/Zoom/ DVD, 2009.
Swing Era, Dinah Washington & Friends. Music Video Distributors, DVD 2004.

Waters, Ethel
("Sweet Mama Stringbean")
(1896–1977)   *actress, singer*

The first black female performer to appeal widely to both white and black audiences, Ethel Waters was a uniquely gifted popular singer of the 1920s and 1930s who forged a second career in middle age as a dramatic actress of extraordinary depth and feeling.

She was born on Halloween, 1896, in Chester, Pennsylvania, although she often gave her birth year as 1900. "I was never a child," Waters wrote decades later in her autobiography. "I never was coddled, or liked, or understood by my family. I never felt I belonged." This is not surprising considering that her mother, Louisa Tar Anderson, was a 12-year-old rape victim when she gave birth to her, and two of Waters's aunts were alcoholics. Although raised by her grandmother, she largely grew up on the streets, the ringleader of a group of neighborhood children who stole food and ran errands for professional criminals. She may have ended up a criminal herself, if not for two years of Catholic school that gave her her moral bearings and a religious faith she would retain all her life.

Still in her early teens, Waters married, divorced, and found work as a chambermaid. Singing in a competition led to an offer to sing and dance on tour with a black vaudeville company when she was 17. Her singing style was unique among black vocalists of the day. She had crystal clear diction and treated every lyric with a keen intelligence and a strong dramatic sense. She could scat sing and imitate instruments and other singers in the best jazz tradition. "Besides being important in her own right," says jazz expert Dan Morgenstern, "she is the link between blues and jazz."

Waters was known as "Sweet Mama Stringbean" for her winning smile and her tall, thin body. But she was anything but sweet offstage. She

Ethel Waters brought a sincerity and spirituality to her stage and film roles that made her unforgettable. *(Photo courtesy of Showtime Archives, Toronto, and Pictorial Press)*

had the temper of a diva and throughout her long career made precious few friends in show business. Once, on a bill with blues singer BESSIE SMITH, she dared to sing a blues number and later got a dressing down from the Empress of the Blues. But by the early 1930s, Waters was herself a star of clubs, cabaret, and then the Broadway stage. Her classic recordings of such songs as "Dinah," "Stormy Weather," and "Am I Blue" became pop hits and she stormed Broadway in such musical revues as *Africana* (1927), *The Blackbirds of 1928*, and Irving Berlin's *As Thousands Cheer* (1933). In this last show she brought the house down each night singing "Heat Wave" in a tropical costume. She was the first African American to get star billing on the stage and the first to star in a coast-to-coast radio show with the Jimmy Dorsey Orchestra.

In 1938, Waters made an impressive dramatic debut in the play *Mamba's Daughters* and two years later starred in the all-black musical fantasy *Cabin in the Sky*. She later reprised her role as Petunia, the ever-faithful wife, in the Hollywood film version of *Cabin* with EDDIE ANDERSON and LENA HORNE. After that, she forsook her singing career to become exclusively a dramatic actress. But now middle-aged and overweight, film roles were few and far between for Waters. She finally found a role worthy of her talents in *Pinky* (1949), playing an old black woman devoted to her light-skinned granddaughter who is trying to pass for white. The performance earned her an Academy Award nomination for best supporting actress.

In the following year, Waters was cast as housekeeper Berenice Sadi Brown in the Broadway stage adaptation of southern author Carson McCullers's novel *A Member of the Wedding*. She positively shone as the mentor to a young girl coming to terms with the adult world and earned her second Academy Award nomination when she appeared in the film version in 1952.

Before that, she had played another maid in the television series *Beulah* (1951). She was the first black actor to star in her own television series, but Waters was attacked by many in the black community for taking such a traditionally stereotyped role. Waters countered that she had been a maid in real life and saw nothing wrong with it. As the Civil Rights movement gained steam in the 1950s, she was decidedly out of step with the times. "I'm not concerned with civil rights," she once said. "I'm only concerned with God-given rights, and they are available to everyone!"

In this spirit she joined evangelist Billy Graham's Crusade in 1957 and became one of his most stalwart supporters. Through Graham, she became good friends with Republican vice president and future president Richard Nixon, which further alienated her from the liberal black community.

A fiery individual to the last, Waters found little work in films and television through the 1950s and 1960s. Hounded by the Internal Revenue Service (IRS) for back taxes, she lived her final years close to poverty and in declining health in a tiny apartment in Pasadena, California. Ethel Waters died on September 1, 1977, a lonely and largely forgotten figure. Since then, her reputation as a song interpreter and actress has grown tremendously, placing her among the very greatest African-American performing artists of the 20th century.

Waters was honored with a U.S. postage stamp in 1994 as part of the Legends of American Music Series.

Further Reading
Bourne, Stephen. *Ethel Waters: Stormy Weather.* Lanham, Md.: The Scarecrow Press, 2007.

McCorkle, Susannah. "The Mother of Us All." *American Heritage* (February–March 1994): 60–73.

Waters, Ethel, with Charles Samuels. *His Eye Is on the Sparrow.* (reprint) New York: Da Capo Press, 1992.

Further Listening
The Incomparable Ethel Waters. Sony, CD, 2003.

Further Viewing
Cabin in the Sky (1943). Warner Home Video, DVD, 2006.

Stanley Kramer Film Collection, including *The Member of the Wedding* and five other films. Sony, DVD box set, 2008.

Waters, Muddy
(McKinley Morganfield)
(1915–1983) *blues singer, guitarist, songwriter*

A giant talent, Muddy Waters almost single-handedly brought Delta blues out of the Mississippi backwoods and into the big city, in the process transforming it into a contemporary art form, one that heavily influenced the beat of rock 'n' roll.

He was born McKinley Morganfield on April 4, 1915, in Rolling Forks, Mississippi. His father, Ollie, was a farmer. When his mother, Bertha, died when he was three, McKinley was raised by his maternal grandmother in Clarksdale. It was she who gave him the nickname "Muddy Waters" because of his fondness for splashing around in the rich Delta dirt after a rainstorm. He later made the nickname his professional name.

Waters's first instrument was the harmonica, and he didn't get a guitar until he was 17 and ordered one for $2.50 from the Sears, Roebuck catalog. The money came from his share of the sale of a family horse. He learned to play Delta blues guitar, modeling himself after blues greats ROBERT JOHNSON and Son House. He worked weekdays on a cotton plantation and on weekends turned his one-room log cabin into a meeting place for friends where he provided the drinks and the music.

Folklorist Alan Lomax recorded Waters's songs in 1941 while collecting authentic folk music for the Library of Congress. He encouraged Waters to pursue his music full time. Two years later he took this advice and moved to Chicago, where he began playing at parties and small clubs. Waters formed a small band and began to experiment with electric instruments and amplifications to appeal to a wider, urban audience. Waters's band developed a driving style with a strong backbeat that became the hallmark of what came to be called the "Chicago blues."

After a couple of missteps with record labels, Waters had a local hit on the Aristocrat label with "I Can't Be Satisfied" in 1948. He next reached the national rhythm and blues (R & B) charts with "Louisiana Blues" (1950), which featured the powerhouse sound of Little Walter's amplified harmonica. Among the other top musicians who played with Waters was bassist Willie Dixon, who was also a gifted songwriter. In 1954, Waters recorded three Dixon songs that would become among his most famous recordings—"Hoochie Coochie Man," "Just Make Love to Me" (also known as "I Just Wanna Make Love to You"), and "I'm Ready."

By the late 1950s, Waters was a national figure on the blues scene and played regularly at such leading venues as the Apollo Theater in Harlem, in New York City, and the Newport (Rhode Island) Folk and Jazz Festivals. Among the other talented blues musicians who played with him and later formed their own bands were Otis Spann, Buddy Guy, James Cotton, Junior Wells, and rock musician JIMI HENDRIX.

In the early 1960s, Waters's music had a profound effect on a new generation of British rock groups including the Yardbirds and the Rolling Stones, who took their name from Waters's song "Rollin' Stone." Folk singer Bob Dylan named his famous song "Like a Rolling Stone" in tribute to Waters.

As he grew older, Muddy Waters seemed to just get better. At 56, he won his first Grammy Award for best ethnic or traditional recording for the album *They Call Me Muddy Waters* (1971). The following year he won another Grammy in the same category for *The London Muddy Waters Sessions* (1972) on which he played with British musicians Steve Winwood and Mitch Mitchell, Jimi Hendrix's drummer.

Waters continued to record and tour until shortly before his death from a heart attack on April 30, 1983. Two years later the city of Chicago renamed East 43rd Street "Muddy Waters Drive" in honor of one of its most celebrated residents. Waters was inducted into the Rock and Roll Hall of Fame in 1987 and in 1992 posthumously received Grammy's Lifetime Achievement Award. He was honored with a U.S. postal stamp in 1994 as part of the blues and jazz singers series. Actor JEFFREY WRIGHT portrayed Waters on screen in *Cadillac Red* (2008).

Further Reading

Gordon, Robert. *Can't Be Satisfied: The Life and Times of Muddy Waters.* San Francisco, Calif.: Back Bay Books, 2003.

Rock and Roll Hall of Fame Inductees. "Muddy Waters." The Rock and Roll Hall of Fame and Museum Web site. Available online. URL: http://www.rockhall.com/inductee.muddy-waters. Downloaded on February 11, 2009.

Rooney, James. *Bossmen: Bill Monroe and Muddy Waters.* New York: Da Capo Press, 1991.

Further Listening

The Definitive Collection. Geffen Records, CD, 2006.

Further Viewing

Muddy Waters—Can't Be Satisfied. Winstar, DVD, 2003.

Muddy Waters—In Concert 1971. Grossman's Guitar Workshop, DVD, 2004.

Watts, André
(1946–   ) *classical pianist*

One of America's premier classical pianists, known for his bravura playing, André Watts burst on the musical scene at age 15 and has been breaking records with his concerts and recitals ever since.

He was born on June 24, 1946, in Nuremberg, Germany. His father, Herman, was a career U.S.

soldier, who met his mother, a displaced Hungarian, while stationed in Germany. Watts studied piano with his mother from the age of eight. A year later, his father was transferred back to the United States and the family settled in Philadelphia, Pennsylvania. That same year, Watts, age nine, competed for and won the opportunity to perform a Franz Joseph Haydn piano concerto with the Philadelphia Orchestra at a children's concert.

His parents separated when he was 13, and Watts lived with his mother, Maria Alexandra. His was a lonely childhood with no friends and long hours of practicing on an old, broken-down piano. But the hard work paid off when at 14 he was invited to play as soloist with the Philadelphia Orchestra in one of its regular subscription concerts. At 16, the young pianist auditioned for conductor Leonard Bernstein of the New York Philharmonic for his nationally televised Young People's Concerts series. Bernstein was amazed at Watts's technique and ability, and in January 1963 he invited him to appear on CBS-TV with the Philharmonic playing the Franz Liszt Piano Concerto No. 1. Two weeks later, pianist Glenn Gould was unable to appear with the Philharmonic, and Bernstein invited Watts to replace him. It was the first time since 1900 that a black male musician appeared as soloist with the world-famous orchestra in a regular concert.

Soon after, Watts signed a recording contract with Columbia Records and made two albums that earned him a Grammy Award as "the most promising classical artist of 1963." Watts made his European concert debut in June 1966, playing with the London Symphony Orchestra. A seven-week tour of Europe and Asia with the Los Angeles Philharmonic followed in 1967. By 1970, Watts had played with nearly every major orchestra in the world.

He performed a concert at Constitution Hall in Washington, D.C., at President Richard Nixon's inauguration. In November 1976 he became the first solo recitalist to be televised live nationally from New York's Avery Fisher Hall by the Public Broadcast Service (PBS).

Among the many honors André Watts has received is an honorary doctorate from Yale University in New Haven, Connecticut, in 1973. He was the youngest person in 200 years to receive this honor. In May, 2004, Watts was appointed to the Jack I. and Dora B. Hamlin Endowed Chair in Music at Indiana University.

Further Reading
"André Watts." CM Artists Web site. Available online. URL: http://www.cmartists.com/artists/andre_watts.htm. Downloaded on October 22, 2009.

Noyle, Linda J. *Pianists on Playing: Interviews with Twelve Concert Pianists.* Lanham, Md.: Scarecrow Press, 2000.

Further Listening
Beethoven: Piano Sonatas Nos. 13, 14 & 23. EMI Classics, CD, 2005.

Rachmaninoff: Piano Concertos Nos. 2 & 3. Sony, CD, 2003.

Further Viewing
André Watts in Concert (1985). Paramount Home Video, VHS, 1992.

Wayans, Damon
(1960–   ) *actor, comedian, writer, television and film producer*

A member of a talented family of actors, comics, writers, and directors, Damon Wayans possesses unique talents that have found greater success in the medium of television than in film.

He was born on September 4, 1960, in New York City with a misshapen foot. This deformity was later corrected by surgery. His father, Howell, was a supermarket manager and a devout Jehovah's Witness. His mother, Elvira, earned a college degree in social work after raising 10 children.

Wayans began his career as a stand-up comic at age 22. His success on the comedy club circuit eventually earned him a small role in the EDDIE

MURPHY film *Beverly Hills Cop* (1984). From there he was hired as a featured player on NBC-TV's late-night comedy show *Saturday Night Live* in 1985. He stayed on the show only for a season before appearing in small roles in a number of films, including the black satires *Hollywood Shuffle* (1987) and *I'm Gonna Git You Sucka* (1988), which was written and directed by his brother Keenan Ivory Wayans.

In 1990, Keenan created a half-hour comedy show, *In Living Color,* which he sold to the Fox Television Network. The program was a kind of *SNL* that poked fun at racial stereotypes and misconceptions. Keenan brought brother Damon and sister Kim on board as part of the talented ensemble cast, which also included the young white comic Jim Carrey. Damon Wayans quickly became one of the funniest and most popular cast members, as both performer and writer. He created such memorable characters on the show as Homey the Clown and Handi-Man, the first handicapped superhero.

As uneven and cruel as its humor could be, *In Living Color* soon proved popular with audiences and became one of Fox TV's first hit series. It won an Emmy Award in 1990 as the outstanding variety, musical or comedy series, and Wayans earned two Emmy nominations for his work on the show. It ran for five seasons.

Having succeeded as a television star, Wayans concentrated on film work. In *The Last Boy Scout* (1991), an action film, he had the thankless role of sidekick to Bruce Willis, a subservient role he would have gleefully spoofed on *In Living Color*. A more personal project was the comedy *Mo' Money* (1992), which he wrote, starred in, and produced. He was executive producer and star of *Blankman* (1994) about a goofy inventor who becomes a superhero, and *Major Payne* (1995), in which he portrayed a tough army officer who becomes head of a Junior Reserve Officer Training Corps (ROTC). None of these films rose to the level of his work on *In Living Color,* and in 1996 Wayans returned to television to produce the Saturday morning animated series *Waynehead,* which fea-

tured the voices of his sister Kim and younger brothers Shawn and Marlon.

In 1998, Wayans starred in and also produced his own situation comedy, *Damon,* on Fox TV. The series lasted only one season. A dramatic black series entitled *413 Hope Street,* for which he also served as executive producer, had even a shorter run on Fox. Soon after, Wayans announced "I'll never be on television again," criticizing network executives for a lack of support in both these projects. Wayans may have found the best role of his career to date in Spike Lee's controversial comedy *Bamboozled* (2000). He played a frustrated black television writer who created a program based on the old-fashioned minstrel show, featuring black actors in blackface. Unfortunately, this dark satire with something to offend everybody failed to find an audience. In 2001, Wayans, despite his earlier statement, returned on the ABC Network in the more traditional sitcom *My Wife and Kids,* playing a family man. Ironically, Wayans and his wife, Lisa Thorne, divorced the previous year. "The show has become my therapy," Wayans said in a 2001 interview. The sitcom ran until 2005. The following year, Wayans starred in *The Underground,* a sketch comedy series on Showtime, which Wayans has described as "*In Living Color* on steroids." He is currently working on a new sitcom for ABC, *Never Better,* based on a hit British series.

Further Reading

George, Nelson. *In Living Color: The Authorized Companion to the Fox TV Series.* New York: Warner Books, 1991.

Wayans, Damon. *Bootleg.* New York: Harper Paperbacks, 2000.

White, Katherine. *The Wayans Brothers.* Famous Families. New York: Rosen Publishing Group, 2005 (YA).

Further Viewing

Bamboozled (2000). New Line Video, VHS/DVD, 2001.

Damon Wayans: Still Standing. Fox Home Video, DVD, 2006.

In Living Color: Seasons 1–5. DVD box set, 2008.

Webb, Chick
(William Henry Webb)
(1902–1939) *jazz drummer, bandleader*

One of jazz's greatest drummers, Chick Webb overcame a debilitating disease to lead a celebrated swing band.

He was born William Henry Webb on February 10, 1902, in Baltimore, Maryland. Almost from birth he suffered from spinal tuberculosis, which stunted his growth, gave him a hunchback, and left his legs practically useless. The doctors suggested to his parents that drumming would help ease his stiff joints. Unable to afford a drum set, they let him bang on kitchen pots and pans. When he was older, Webb sold newspapers to earn enough money to buy a drum set.

Webb's energetic and flamboyant drumming style eventually got him a job playing with the Jazzola Orchestra. There he met musician John Trueheart, who invited Webb to go to New York City with him in 1924. In New York, Webb's reputation as a top drummer grew as he played with the band of DUKE ELLINGTON and others. Webb's playing was all the more impressive because he couldn't read music and had to memorize every piece he played.

In 1926, Webb formed his own band, the Harlem Stompers. The following year they got a job playing at the prestigious Savoy Ballroom in Harlem, the black section of New York City. Unable to stand in front of the band, Webb conducted from a raised platform in the center of the stage, where he played his drums. The band, which changed its name to the Chick Webb Orchestra, was so popular that it soon became the Savoy's permanent house band.

To draw even bigger crowds of listeners and dancers, Webb challenged any other swing band to compete for the audience's favor in what came to be called the "Battle of the Bands." Despite the fact that the band had no solo star players, it roundly defeated all comers, including such top jazz bands as those headed by COUNT BASIE, Benny Goodman, and Duke Ellington.

The band's immensely appealing swing technique, based on Webb's phenomenal drumming, set a new standard of excellence for other swing bands. Their signature song, "Stompin' at the Savoy," became a hit record and a jazz classic.

Among the great musicians who played at one time or another in the band were saxophonist Benny Carter and LOUIS JORDAN. However, the most famous artist to appear with Webb was a 17-year-old singer he hired in 1935, ELLA FITZGERALD. Over the next three years, she sang and recorded 60 songs with the band.

Beginning in 1938, Webb began to experience fainting spells after his shows. By early 1939, he was taken to Johns Hopkins Hospital in Baltimore, where his health deteriorated. To cheer him up, Fitzgerald wrote the novelty number "A-Tisket, A-Tasket," the song that would propel her to stardom.

Chick Webb lost his battle against the disease he fought all his life and died on June 16, 1939. His good friend Ella Fitzgerald took over his band for the next two years before striking out on her own as a soloist.

Although his career was relatively brief, Chick Webb remains a revered figure to jazz fans who remember his music and his long tenure at the Savoy Ballroom. His fluid, dynamic drumming was a major influence on many jazz drummers, including Gene Krupa.

Further Reading
"Chick Webb." Solid! Web site. Available online. URL: http://www.parabrisas.com/d_webbc.php. Downloaded on February 11, 2009.

Gourse, Leslie. *Time Keepers: The Great Jazz Drummers.* The Art of Jazz. Danbury, Conn.: Franklin Watts, 2000 (YA).

Further Listening

Ella Fitzgerald with Chick Webb. Swing Station Series. Vern, CD, 1998.

Stomping at the Savoy. Proper Box UK, CD box set, 2006.

Whitaker, Forest

(1961–   ) *actor, director, film producer*

The fourth African-American male to win an Oscar for best actor, Forest Whitaker is one of the few leading black actors to successfully make the transition to directing films.

He was born on July 15, 1961, in Longview, Texas, and raised in Los Angeles, California. His father was an insurance salesman and his mother a special-education teacher. He was a defense tackle on his high school football team, weighing in at 250 pounds. He also liked to sing, and his strong tenor voice earned him a classical music scholarship to the University of Southern California. But while there he switched to theater after seeing Robert De Niro's brilliant performance in

An actor who can play good and bad characters with conviction, Forest Whitaker won an Academy Award for his masterful portrayal of African dictator Idi Amin in *The Last King of Scotland. (AP Photo/Chitose Suzuki)*

the movie *Taxi Driver* (1976). Whitaker won another scholarship, this time to study drama in England, and then returned to California to pursue a film career.

His first movie role was as a high school student in the teen comedy *Fast Times at Ridgemont High* (1982). Although he lacked the good looks of a typical leading man, Whitaker quickly became a dependable character actor in such major films as *Platoon* (1986), *The Color of Money* (1986), and *Good Morning, Vietnam* (1987), in which he costarred with Robin Williams.

His first leading role was as jazz musician CHARLIE PARKER in *Bird* (1988), a biographical film directed by Clint Eastwood. Whitaker's performance won him the best actor trophy at the Cannes Film Festival in France and a Golden Globe nomination as best actor. Inspired by Eastwood's work on that film, he decided to try directing himself and helmed the Home Box Office (HBO) television movie *Strapped* (1989). He was named the best new director at the Toronto Film Festival for this film.

Strong acting roles followed in *A Rage in Harlem* (1991), where he also served as coproducer, and *The Crying Game* (1992), in which he played a British soldier kidnapped by the Irish Republican Army (IRA). Whitaker made his feature film directorial debut with the black women's film *Waiting to Exhale* (1995), which starred ANGELA BASSETT and WHITNEY HOUSTON. He has also directed the Sandra Bullock comedy *Hope Floats* and the television movie *Black Jaq,* both released in 1998.

Whitaker hosted a new version of television's *The Twilight Zone* in 2002 on the UPN Network. It lasted only one season. In 2006, he again played a historical character, the larger-than-life Ugandan dictator Idi Amin, in *The Last King of Scotland.* Whitaker's alternately empathetic and chilling portrayal earned him a best actor Academy Award. He returned to television to play a vengeful former patient of *ER*'s Dr. Kovach in six episodes during the medical drama's 2006–07 season. Whitaker portrayed the real-life Dr. James Farmer, Sr., president of Wiley College in Texas, in *The Great Debaters* (2007), directed by costar DENZEL WASHINGTON. More recently, he played real-life New Orleans high school basketball coach Al Collins, who assembled a winning team after Hurricane Katrina struck in *Hurricane Season* (2009).

An actor who likes to take risks, Whitaker is modest about his accomplishments. "I guess I've done so many movies I've achieved some visibility," he said in an interview. "But a star? I guess I still think of myself as kind of a worker ant."

Further Reading

"Forest Whitaker." The Internet Movie Database. Available online. URL: http://www.imdb.com/name/nm0001545/. Downloaded on February 11, 2009.

"Forest Whitaker—Biography." NetGlimse Web site. Available online. URL: http://www.netglimse.com/celebspages/Forest_whitaker/index.shtml. Downloaded on February 11, 2009.

Further Viewing

Bird (1988). Warner Home Video, VHS/DVD, 1992/2001.

The Great Debaters (2007). Genius Products, DVD, 2008.

The Last King of Scotland (2006). Fox Home Video, DVD, 2007.

White, Barry

("The Maestro," "The Guru of Love")
(1944–2003) *R & B singer, songwriter, record producer, conductor*

Rock's high priest of love for nearly a decade, Barry White had a sensuous baritone backed by a lush orchestra, which made him one of the 1970s' most consistent hit-makers.

He was born on September 12, 1944, in Galveston, Texas, and raised in Los Angeles, California.

His mother, Sadie Marie Carter, encouraged his love of music and by age eight he was singing in his church choir. At 11, he made his recording debut, playing piano on singer Jesse Belvin's hit rhythm and blues (R & B) ballad "Goodnight, My Love" (1956). White joined a Los Angeles R & B group, the Upfronts when he was 16. Two years later, on his 18th birthday, he quit high school and hitchhiked to Hollywood to pursue a career in music. Through the 1960s, he struggled as a musician and record producer. His biggest successes as a producer were two dance hits, "The Harlem Shuffle" (1964) by Bob and Earl and "The Duck" (1965) by Jackie Lee.

In 1970, White met three girl singers from San Pedro, California, and formed them into a group, Love Unlimited. He produced their first album, *Walking in the Rain* (1970), which became a huge hit. Later, White married Glodean James, a member of the group. In the recording studio, White began experimenting with spoken introductions to some of the new material he was writing for Love Unlimited. He intended to use another singer on the final recording but found his own deep voice was good enough. Soon the introductions spilled over into the whole song, making them into sexy-sounding monologues backed by his 40-piece Love Unlimited Orchestra. White's first solo release, "I'm Gonna Love You Just a Little Bit More, Baby," shot to number three on the pop charts. The song set a winning pattern for a string of best-selling singles and albums, including five number-one R & B chart hits, one of which, "Can't Get Enough of You, Babe" (1974), went to number one on the pop charts, too. White had a small music empire, with continuing hit releases from both the Love Unlimited group and the Love Unlimited Orchestra, which had the number-one hit "Love's Theme" (1973).

By the late 1970s, White's popularity faded. He emerged as a featured vocalist on QUINCY JONES's hit record "The Secret Garden" (1990) and began recording solo again for A & M Records. He had his first top-20 hit in 17 years, "Practice What You

Preach," in 1994. He experienced a bigger come-back in the late 1990s as his romantic music came back in fashion with pop listeners.

Barry White remained proud of his reputation as a supreme romantic mood setter for young couples. "A lot of babies have been named Barry," he commented in an interview with writer Joe Smith. "If there was a Barry born in '74, I was the one responsible for it." He died of kidney failure at age 58 on July 4, 2003.

Further Reading

"Barry White." The Allmusic Web site: Available online. URL: http://www.allmusic.com/cg/amg.dll?p=amg&sql=11.jifqxqr51dfe. Downloaded on February 11, 2009.

White, Barry, with Marc Eliot. *Love Unlimited: Insights on Life & Love.* London: Virgin Books, 2001.

Further Listening

Gold. Hip-O Records, 2 CDs, 2008.

Further Viewing

The Barry White Story: Let the Music Play. Eagle Rock Entertainment, DVD, 2007.

Williams, Bert

(Egbert Austin Williams)
(ca. 1876–1922) *comedian, singer, actor, songwriter*

Called "the funniest man I ever saw" by no less a comic talent than W. C. Fields, Bert Williams was the first black entertainer to become a Broadway star. But behind the stage buffoonery, Williams was a sophisticated intellectual who, because of the racist standards of his day, never achieved his ambition to become a serious actor.

He was born Egbert Austin Williams around 1876 on the island of Antigua in the West Indies. His family was well-to-do and he grew up on his grandfather's plantation. The family moved to New York City while he was still a child and then to California. Williams displayed a natural gift for mimicry and could play music by ear. In San Francisco, California, his father lost his fortune, and young Bert gave up his dream of becoming a civil engineer and went to work to help support the family. He worked for a time in mining and lumbering camps but was drawn to performing. He played minstrel songs on a banjo in San Francisco's seedy saloons and worked his way up to more sophisticated cafes.

When he was 19, Williams met another aspiring entertainer, George Walker, several years his junior. The two formed a vaudeville comedy team, calling themselves "Williams and Walker." Their snappy humor and original songs soon made them a top act in vaudeville, a kind of touring variety show. In their act, Walker was the brains of the team, always duping the slow-witted Williams with some scheme. After eight years in vaudeville, they starred in an all-black Broadway musical comedy, *In Dahomey* (1903), which became a smash hit. The show was so successful that they took it to England in 1904 and gave a command royal performance before the king and queen at Buckingham Palace. The team went on to appear in three more hit musicals—*Abyssinia* (1906), *Bandanna Land* (1908), and *Mr. Lode of Koal* (1909).

These shows portrayed blacks, as was common in that day, as lazy, shiftless, and funny. Williams played characters in these shows named Shylock Homestead, Jasmine Jenkins, and Skunkton Bowser. Although exaggerated and embarrassing by today's standards, Williams's characters were always grounded in reality. He based them on the poor blacks he knew growing up in New York. Unlike white writers of the day, he created black stage people who always had an underlying humanity.

George Walker became seriously ill in 1909, and Williams helped support him until his death later that year. Then a single act, Williams joined the celebrated annual Broadway musical extravaganza *The Ziegfeld Follies* in 1910. Dressed in his trademark top hat, tattered suit, and oversized shoes, Williams sang novelty songs, did pantomime, and delivered comic patter. Among the novelty songs he made famous were "I'm in the Right Church but the Wrong Pew" and "Come After Breakfast, Bring Along Your Lunch, and Leave Before Suppertime." The most famous of his songs and his signature number was "Nobody," a melancholic song that reflected the feelings of millions of African Americans living on the lowest rung of American society.

Williams remained with the *Follies* for 10 years. He became the show's highest-paid performer and the first black performer to receive star billing on Broadway. In 1920, he appeared in his own revue *Broadway Brevities*, which he followed with the revue *Under the Bamboo Tree* (1922). Exhausted and ill from overwork, he continued to perform the show on the road to prevent the show's promoter from losing money. On his return to New York he suffered a complete breakdown and died on March 4, 1922.

Nearly forgotten today, Bert Williams's great talent can only be glimpsed in the scratchy old recordings he made of his songs. "Bert Williams has done more for the [black] race than I have," confessed black educator and social leader Booker T. Washington. "He has smiled his way into people's hearts."

Further Reading

Chude-Sokei, Louis. *The Last 'Darky': Bert Williams Black-on-Black Minstrelsy and the African Diaspora.* Durham, N.C.: Duke University Press, 2006.

Forbes, Camille F. *Introducing Bert Williams: Burnt Cork, Broadway, and the Story of America's First Black Star.* New York: Basic Civitas Books, 2008.

Phillips, Caryl. *Dancing in the Dark.* New York: Vintage, 2006.

Further Listening

The Middle Years 1910–1918. Archeophone, CD, 2002.

Williams, Billy Dee
(William December Williams)
(1937–) *actor*

Perhaps the first African-American film actor to become a bona fide sex symbol, Billy Dee Williams spent years in obscurity before finally achieving stardom.

He was born in the Harlem section of New York City on April 6, 1937. His father, William December Williams was a black Texan and his mother, Loretta Anne, a West Indian. As a youngster he studied at the Actors Workshop with actor SIDNEY POITIER and made his stage debut at age seven in the Kurt Weill Broadway musical *Firebrand of Florence* (1945).

His first ambition, however, was to be a painter, not an actor. He attended New York's High School of Music and Art and later the National Academy of Fine Arts and Design. During this time, Williams saw acting as a way to pay for his art supplies. By 1959, he was committed to acting and appeared in his first film, *The Last Angry Man,* starring Paul Muni. The following year he appeared in the film adaptation of the British play *A Taste of Honey.*

A rocky personal life interrupted his career, and he entered a deep depression in 1964 following the breakup of his first two marriages. Williams was largely inactive for the rest of the 1960s but then landed the role of real-life football player Gale Ayers in the made-for-television drama, *Brian's Song* (1970). Williams was excellent as the best friend of Brian Piccolo, a fellow player dying of cancer, and the role earned him an Emmy nomination.

Berry Gordy, Jr., owner of Motown Records in Detroit, Michigan, was preparing to expand into film production and signed Williams to a seven-year contract. In 1972, Williams appeared opposite DIANA ROSS in *Lady Sings the Blues,* Gordy's biographical film about singer BILLIE HOLIDAY. As biography, the movie was highly fictional, but as old-fashioned entertainment, it was a great success. The romance that developed between Ross's and Williams's characters was a first of its kind in a Hollywood film. Unlike the action heroes of the blaxploitation films of the 1970s, who treated women like property, the handsome, debonair Williams was sensitive to a woman's needs and was an intensely romantic lover. Black audiences embraced this image of the black male he embodied. Three years later, Ross and Williams were teamed again in *Mahogany* (1975), directed by Berry Gordy. Ross played a super fashion model who must choose between her career and her lover, politician Williams.

After succeeding as a major star, Williams rarely got the opportunity to play such larger-than-life roles again. He was popular as the soldier of fortune Lando Carlrissian in two *Star Wars* sequels—*The Empire Strikes Back* (1980) and *Return of the Jedi* (1983). He was in fine form as a black baseball player in *The Bingo Long Travelling All-Stars and Motor Kings* (1976) and ragtime composer SCOTT JOPLIN in a made-for-TV biography. But most of his later films cast him in supporting roles where he was rarely able to shine. The only starring roles he had were usually in such exploitative crime films as *Fear City* (1985) and *Deadly Illusion* (1987). In 2007, he appeared on television as a cast member of the Scopnet series *General Hospital: Night Shift.*

Never abandoning his art, Williams's paintings are on permanent display in the National Gallery in Washington, D.C. He has also written several mystery thrillers with mystery writer Rob MacGregor. Billy Dee Williams was inducted into the Black Filmmaker's Hall of Fame in 1984.

Further Reading

"Billy Dee Williams." The Internet Movie Database. Available online. URL: http://imdb.com/name/nm0001850/. Downloaded on February 11, 2009.

Williams, Billy Dee, and Rob MacGregor. *Psi/Net* [a novel] New York: Forge Books, 2000.

Further Viewing

Brian's Song (1971). Sony, VHS/DVD, 1996/2000.

Lady Sings the Blues (1972). Paramount Home Video, VHS/DVD, 2005.

Williams, Mary Lou

(Mary Elfrieda Scruggs)
(1910–1981) *jazz pianist, composer, arranger, bandleader, record producer*

The first major female jazz performer who was not a singer, Mary Lou Williams left behind a body of work as musician and composer of extraordinary feeling and complexity.

She was born Mary Elfrieda Scruggs on May 8, 1910, in Atlanta, Georgia, and grew up in Pittsburgh, Pennsylvania. She was a child prodigy on the piano, exhibiting an extraordinary ability and perfect pitch by age four. She publicly performed in Pittsburgh homes and earned the name "The Little Piano Girl." At 12, she made her big band debut, playing piano in a traveling musical revue. Still in her teens, Scruggs played with such jazz greats as JELLY ROLL MORTON, FATS WALLER, and DUKE ELLINGTON, for whom she later wrote the jazz classic, "Trumpet No End" (1946).

Talking about her name, Williams once said, "I don't know where the Lou came from, but I got the Williams when I was married." She married bandleader and trumpeter John Williams, who left for Oklahoma to play with Andy Kirk and the Twelve Clouds of Joy in 1927. Williams took over leading his band, the Syncopaters. She joined Williams and the Clouds of Joy two years later and became their resident arranger and composer. Her work with this band brought her national recognition through such popular works as "Froggy Bottom" and "Walkin' and Swingin.'"

In 1942, she left the Clouds of Joy and moved to New York City. There, Williams played in clubs; formed an all women's jazz band, the Girl-Stars; and was mentor to young jazz musicians who were developing an exciting, new kind of jazz called bebop. Her apartment became a late-night gathering place for DIZZY GILLESPIE, CHARLIE PARKER, and other bebop musicians. She was especially close to pianists THELONIUS MONK and Bud Powell. Williams herself adapted to the fast-paced, free-form bebop style in such compositions as "In the Land of Oo-Blah-Dee." She also began to write larger, more ambitious works, much like her friend Duke Ellington. *Zodiac Suite* (1945), the first of these works, had 12 movements, one for each sign of the zodiac. She recorded many of her compositions on her own label, Mary Records, the first record company founded by a woman musician.

In the 1960s, the deeply religious Williams began writing liturgical jazz pieces, including *Mass for the Lenten Season* (1960) and *Mass for Peace* (1970). Her moving *Dirge Blues* (1963) commemorated the assassination of President John F. Kennedy.

Williams joined the faculty of the University of Massachusetts at Amherst in 1975. Two years later, she took a position as artist-in-residence at Duke University in Durham, North Carolina. She was still at Duke when she died on May 28, 1981, and the Mary Lou Williams Center for Black Culture was established at the university in her memory.

"Anything you are shows up in your music," she once said. "Jazz is whatever you are . . . playing yourself, being yourself."

Further Reading

Dahl, Linda. *Morning Glory: A Biography of Mary Lou Williams.* Berkeley: University of California Press, 2001.

———. *Stormy Weather: The Music and Lives of a Century of Jazzwomen.* New York: Limelight Editions, 1989.

Kernodle, Tammy. *Soul on Soul: The Life and Music of Mary Lou Williams.* Holliston, Mass.: Northeastern, 2004.

Further Listening

Mary Lou's Mass (1975). Smithsonian Folkways, CD, 2005.

My Mama Pinned a Rose on Me (1977). Pablo, CD, 2005.

Further Viewing

Norman Granz Jazz in Montreux Present, Mary Lou Williams '78. Eagle Rock Entertainment, DVD, 2004.

Williams, Vanessa
(Vanessa Lynn Williams)
(1963–   ) *actress, singer*

The first black Miss America, Vanessa Williams lost her title in a heated controversy, but has since gone on to success on stage, screen, and in the recording studio.

She was born Vanessa Lynn Williams on March 18, 1963, in the Bronx, New York, and grew up in Millwood, New York. Her parents, Milton and Helen Williams, are both music teachers, and early on she showed a talent for singing and acting. In 1981, Williams won a musical theater scholarship to Syracuse University in New York State. When her funding ended, she dropped out of college and entered the Miss America pageant in 1984. She won and was crowned Miss America, but her triumph was short-lived. Williams's crown was taken from her when nude pictures of her, taken several years earlier, appeared in *Penthouse* magazine. For a time, it looked like Vanessa Williams's time in the spotlight was over. But she persevered and turned the publicity from her resignation to her advantage.

In 1987, she had a small role in the film *The Pick-Up Artist,* which was soon followed by her debut record album, *The Right Stuff* (1988), the title song of which became a hit single. Williams began to find work on television, but projects such as the TV-movie *Full Exposure: The Sex Tapes Scandal* (1989), raised the question whether she was hired for her talent or her notoriety. With time, however, she proved herself to be a serious actress and a talented musical theater performer. Williams had a leading role in the television adaptation of the Broadway musical *Bye Bye Birdie* (1995) and appeared on Broadway in the lead role of another musical, *The Kiss of the Spider Woman* (1993).

Her recording career took off with the number-one hit "Save the Best for Last" (1992) and "Colors of the Winds" (1995) from the Disney animated film *Pocahontas.* In 1996, Williams costarred with Arnold Schwartzenegger in the action adventure

Eraser. The following year she won the National Association for the Advancement of Colored People's (NAACP) Image Award for outstanding leading actress in a motion picture for *Soul Food* (1997), which chronicled the lives and loves of three sisters. The movie spawned a television series (1999) on the cable network Showtime, in which the actress Vanessa A. Williams (no relation) stars.

Despite good notices in *Soul Food,* Williams has had better luck with roles on television than in the movies. She played the seductress Calypso in an excellent television adaptation of *The Odyssey* (1997) and portrayed the pioneering jazz musician HAZEL SCOTT in another TV movie, *The Adam Clayton Powell, Jr., Story* (2001). Williams starred in the short-lived series *South Beach* (2006), produced by actress Jennifer Lopez, and currently plays the character Wilhelmina Slater in the sitcom *Ugly Betty* (2006–), set in the offices of a New York City fashion magazine.

Williams's marriage to basketball player Rick Fox ended in 2005. She was the first black contestant to get to the "hot seat" on the popular television game show *Who Wants to Be a Millionaire.*

Further Reading

Freedman, Suzanne. *Vanessa Williams* (Black Americans of Achievement). New York: Chelsea House, 1999 (YA).

"Vanessa Williams." The Internet Movie Database. Available online. URL: http://www.imdb.com/name/nm0001853/. Downloaded on February 11, 2009.

Further Listening

Vanessa Williams—Greatest Hits: The First Ten Years (1993). Island/Mercury, CD, 2005.

Further Viewing

The Odyssey (1997). Lions Gate, DVD, 2001.

Soul Food (1997). Fox Home Entertainment, VHS/DVD, 2001.

Wilson, Dooley
(Arthur Wilson)
(1894–1953) *actor, singer, drummer*

Although he was a working black entertainer for more than four decades, Dooley Wilson will be forever remembered for sitting at a piano in Rick's Café in Casablanca, Morocco, and playing "As Time Goes By." The movie, of course, was *Casablanca* (1943), and the scene remains one of the most celebrated in movie history.

He was born Arthur Wilson on April 3, 1894, in Tyler, Texas. He first appeared on the stage with the Rabbit Fool Minstrels when he was 12. When Wilson was a little older, he moved to Chicago and joined a theatrical stock company. He next landed in New York City where he sang and performed comedy in vaudeville theaters. By the 1920s, Wilson had formed his own musical quintet, the Red Devils, in which he sang and played the drums. The group toured the nightclubs of Paris, France, and London, England. Wilson was so successful in Europe that he opened his own club in Paris, becoming the first black to receive a charter, or license, from the French government to do so.

He returned to the United States in 1930, dissolved the band, and pursued stage acting. Actor-director Orson Welles, head of the Federal Theater, cast him as the kindly Androcles in the play *Androcles and the Lion.* Wilson's biggest break, however, came in 1940, when he played opposite ETHEL WATERS in the all-black Broadway musical *Cabin in the Sky.*

Wilson made his film debut in the Bob Hope comedy *My Favorite Blonde* (1942). Four pictures later he appeared in his most famous role as Sam, the piano man, in *Casablanca,* although he almost didn't get the part. The producer Hal Wallis wanted to cast a woman in the role, but he was impressed enough with Wilson to use him instead. The scene in which he plays "As Time Goes By" to a love-sick Ingrid Bergman is one of the most memorable in any Hollywood film, although, contrary to legend neither Bergman nor her lover, portrayed by Humphrey Bogart, ever said, "Play it again, Sam." Furthermore, it was not Wilson who "played it"—he could not play the piano and the music was dubbed.

Wilson continued to appear in supporting roles in movies throughout the 1940s. His two best films after *Casablanca* were the black musical *Stormy Weather* (1943), in which he played BILL ROBINSON's best friend, and *Come to the Stable* (1949) where he helped a group of nuns build a hospital. He was also memorable as the slave Pompey in the Broadway musical *Bloomer Girl* (1945). Wilson was a member of the executive board of the Negro Actors' Guild of America, where he fought to end stereotypical roles for black actors and actresses.

His last role was as Beulah's boyfriend Bill Jackson in the television series *Beulah* (1951–53). Dooley Wilson died on May 30, 1953, in Los Angeles, California.

Further Reading
Hardman, Peggy. "Wilson, Arthur." The Handbook of Texas Online. Available online. URL: http://www.tsha.online.org/handbook/online/articles/WW/fwibk.html. Downloaded on February 11, 2009.

Parish, James Robert, and Lennard DeCarl. *Hollywood Players: The Forties.* New Rochelle, N.Y.: Arlington House, 1976.

Further Listening
Bloomer Girl (1944). Decca, CD, 2001.

Further Viewing
Casablanca (1943). Warner Home Video, VHS/DVD, 2001/2000.

Stormy Weather (1993). Fox Home Video, DVD, 2006.

Wilson, Flip
(Clerow Wilson)
(1933–1998) *comedian, TV variety show host*

The first black performer to host a successful television variety show, Flip Wilson created a memo-

Comedian Flip Wilson portrays Geraldine, the most popular character he created on his groundbreaking variety show. *(Photofest)*

rable gallery of comic characters whose ethnic humor endeared him to a generation of television viewers.

He was born Clerow Wilson in the poorest of circumstances in Jersey City, New Jersey, on December 8, 1933, one of 24 children, 18 of whom survived. His father was a janitor who drank too much, and Wilson spent most of his childhood in and out of foster homes with a stint in reform school. When he was 16, he joined the air force. During his four-year hitch, he earned the nickname "Flip," because he "flipped out" his friends with his funny, irreverent humor.

Returning to civilian life in 1954, Wilson spent the next 10 years struggling to make it as a stand-up comic in local clubs and bars, while holding down a variety of odd jobs to pay the rent. Life was tough and at times he had to sleep in bus stations. His luck changed when Monte Kay, DIAHANN CARROLL's husband, became his agent in 1963. Kay booked him into top nightclubs in New York City and San Francisco, California. This led to Wilson's first national television appearance on *The Tonight Show* in 1965. After that, he appeared frequently on all the top TV variety shows. Unlike BILL COSBY and some other African-American comics of the era, Wilson celebrated his blackness in his comedy, but he rarely used his characters to point up racism in American society. Wilson's characters were, above all, funny—to both black and white audiences. There was Sonny, the White House janitor; Freddy the Playboy; and the Reverend LeRoy of the Church of What's Happening Now, whom Wilson based on a preacher he had heard as a child. But his most popular creation was Geraldine, a sassy-mouthed, black woman with an eye for the men. Her favorite line, "The devil made me do it," quickly became a national catchphrase.

When a 1969 NBC television special starring Wilson got great reviews, the network cast him in his own weekly variety show. *The Flip Wilson Show* debuted in September 1970 and was an instant hit. It became the second-highest-rated program on television for its first two seasons. The show was unique among variety shows in that it featured no well-known regular supporting players, and it used a circular stage, which created an unusually intimate feeling for both the studio and home audience. Wilson's guests included such big-name stars as Bing Crosby, Bob Hope, and Lucille Ball.

Wilson saw himself as an entertainer and did not speak out on racial prejudice and other social issues. "It would be ridiculous for me to say anything negative regarding blacks having an equal opportunity on TV," he said in a 1971 interview.

"After all, I was number one in the ratings four times last year and twice this season. What could be more damn equal than that?" For all that, Wilson never hesitated to book black entertainers on his show, from Bill Cosby to ISAAC HAYES, giving them exposure they couldn't find elsewhere in prime time.

The show finally went off the air in June 1974, knocked out of the ratings by the immensely popular family drama *The Waltons*. Always an intensely private man, Wilson dropped out of sight, spending his time raising his four children, whose custody he had won in divorce proceedings with his second wife. A decade later, he returned to television to host a game show and then a sitcom, *Charlie and Company* (1985), that costarred singer GLADYS KNIGHT. Both shows had short runs. Wilson returned to private life, spending his time with his kids and flying in hot-air balloons. He died of liver cancer on November 26, 1998, in Malibu, California.

While he always considered himself an entertainer, Wilson took that job seriously. "With all the troubles black people have they try to forget on weekends," he once said. "You've got to be good to make them laugh." Flip Wilson was that good.

Further Reading

Bogle, Donald. *Prime Time Blues: African Americans on Network Television*. New York: Farrar, Straus & Giroux, 2002, pp. 175–183.

Sutherland, Meghan. *The Flip Wilson Show* (TV Milestone). Detroit, Mich.: Wayne State University Press, 2008.

Further Listening

Funny and Live at the Village Gate (1964). King Records, CD, 2005.

Further Viewing

The Best of the Flip Wilson Show (1970). Rhino Entertainment, DVD box set, 2007.

Wilson, Jackie
(Jack Leroy Wilson, "Mr. Excitement")
(1934–1984) *R & B singer*

One of the most riveting live performers in the history of rock 'n' roll, Jackie Wilson paved the way for superstars like MICHAEL JACKSON, although he himself never got the respect nor the fame he deserved while he was alive.

He was born Jack Leroy Wilson in Detroit, Michigan, on June 9, 1934. He sang in church gospel groups before becoming an amateur boxer. Wilson was good enough to get into the Golden Gloves division when he was 16, at which point his mother forced him to give up boxing. After finishing high school, Wilson sang with a group called the Royals, who later became better known as Hank Ballard and the Midnighters. In 1953, he replaced Clyde McPhatter, the popular lead singer of the doo-wop group the Dominoes. The Dominoes, however, were past their prime and even Wilson's soaring tenor couldn't produce more than one minor hit record in the three years he sang with them. In 1957, he went solo and signed with Brunswick Records, a label he would stay with for the rest of his recording career.

Wilson's first hit was a snappy novelty called "Reet Petite" (1957), written by his friend Berry Gordy, Jr., who a few years later would found Motown Records. Gordy cowrote five more hit songs for Wilson, including his best-known number, "Lonely Teardrops" (1958). Through the early 1960s, Wilson would enjoy an unbroken string of hit records, both infectious, upbeat songs such as "That's Why (I Love You So)" and "I'll Be Satisfied," as well as dramatic ballads such as "Night," and "My Empty Arms," some of which were derived from operatic and classical music themes. Much of his material was less than first-rate, and Brunswick's production values often left a lot to be desired. But when Wilson performed before a live audience, none of that mattered. He regularly worked the crowd into a feverish frenzy as he spun, split, and even did backflips with athletic grace, never missing a beat as he sang. His dazzling footwork quickly earned him the title "Mr. Excitement." Sometimes the excitement got out of hand, as in 1961 when a female fan shot the singer in a New York hotel, leaving him seriously injured.

After the top-10 dance hit *Baby Workout* (1963), Wilson's songs rarely reached the top 40, until producer Carl Davis revitalized his career with a more contemporary Motown-like sound. He had two more memorable hits—"Whispers (Getting Louder)" (1966) and "(Your Love Keeps Lifting Me) Higher and Higher" (1967), one of Wilson's finest recordings. After that, he tried many different styles to reclaim his popularity, even recording with COUNT BASIE's Orchestra, but all to little avail.

On the night of September 25, 1975, Wilson was performing as part of a Dick Clark "Oldies" Revue at the Latin Casino in Cherry Hill, New Jersey. In the middle of his act he suffered a major heart attack and was rushed to a hospital. For the next eight years, he drifted in and out of a coma, finally dying on January 20, 1984. Three years later he was inducted into the Rock and Roll Hall of Fame.

One of the greatest R & B performers, Jackie Wilson never received the fame and wealth of JAMES BROWN and other soul artists, but few of them could outsing or outmove "Mr. Excitement."

Further Reading
Carter, Dong. *The Black Elvis—Jackie Wilson.* Berkeley, Calif.: Heyday Books, 1998.
Douglas, Tony. *Jackie Wilson: Lonely Teardrops.* New York: Routledge, 2005.

Further Listening
The Ultimate Jackie Wilson. Brunswick Records, 2 CDs, 2006.

Further Viewing

Shindig Presents: Jackie Wilson (1965). Rhino Video, VHS, 1993.

Winfield, Paul
(1941–2004) *actor*

An outstanding actor of quiet strength and deep feeling, Paul Winfield found too few, worthy roles for his talents in movies but had far greater success on television.

He was born on May 22, 1941, in the Watts section of Los Angeles, California. After high school, he studied on scholarships at the University of Portland in Oregon, Stanford University, Los Angeles City College, and University of California at Los Angeles (UCLA). He gradually gave up his goal of teaching at a university to pursue acting. Winfield joined the Stanford Repertory Theater and later the Inner City Cultural Center Theater in Los Angeles. From television walk-ons, he landed a leading role as DIAHANN CARROLL's first boyfriend on the TV situation comedy *Julia* (1968–71), the first dramatic series to star an African-American actress since *Beulah* in the early 1950s.

A few years later, Winfield had one of the best roles of his career as a depression-era sharecropper in *Sounder* (1972). He was extraordinary as a poor black man, Nathan Lee Morgan, who is sentenced to a chain gang after stealing meat to feed his family. Both he and CICELY TYSON, who played his wife, were nominated for best acting Academy Awards.

Despite his appearance in one of the most praised movies of the decade, Winfield found few opportunities for acting in films thereafter. He was usually relegated to thankless supporting roles in such movies as *Hustle* (1975), *Star Trek II: The Wrath of Khan* (1982), *The Terminator* (1984), and *Presumed Innocent* (1990). An exception was *White Dog* (1982), in which he played an animal trainer who tries to "break" a dog trained to attack black people. Shelved for years by Paramount Pictures because of its controversial subject matter, few people saw *White Dog* when it was finally released.

Winfield fared far better on television, where he delivered a number of impressive performances in television movies and miniseries. He was fine as civil rights leader Martin Luther King, Jr., in the six-hour miniseries *King* (1978), which reunited him with Cicely Tyson as his wife, Coretta Scott King. He was nominated for an Emmy Award for best actor for the role and received a nomination for best supporting actor the same year for a part in *Roots II: The Next Generation*. Winfield finally won an Emmy in 1985 for outstanding guest actor as a judge in the dramatic television series *Picket Fences*.

He had regular roles in four television series from 1987 to 1997. The most unusual was the comic talking Mirror in the fairy-tale sitcom, *The Charmings* (1987). In 1999, he played Supreme Court Justice Thurgood Marshall in the television movie *Strange Justice*. Paul Winfield died of a heart attack on March 7, 2004.

Further Reading

Bogle, Donald. *Prime Time Blues: African Americans on Network Television*. New York: Farrar, Straus & Giroux, 2002, pp. 246, 247, 271, 310, 339, 347, 350, 351, 353, 360, 454, 455.

"Paul Winfield." The Internet Movie Database. Available online.URL: http://www.imdb.com/name/nm0934902/. Downloaded on February 11, 2009.

Further Viewing

King (1978). MGM Home Video, 2 DVDs, 2005.
Sounder (1972). Koch Vision, DVD, 2008.

Wonder, Stevie
(Steveland Morris, "Little Stevie Wonder")
(1950–   ) *R & B singer, songwriter, musician, record producer*

One of the best-selling recording artists of all time, Stevie Wonder began his musical career at

A giant of contemporary pop music, Stevie Wonder made his first record at the age of 12. *(AP Photo/Alex Brandon)*

age 12 as a boy wonder and grew up to become a versatile and immensely creative pop music performer and songwriter.

He was born Steveland Morris on May 13, 1950, in Saginaw, Michigan. His parents separated when he was a child and his mother, Lula Mae, moved the family to Detroit. At age five, despite being blind from birth, he began to play the piano and harmonica, the instrument he would be closely associated throughout his career. A friend, Gerald White, introduced Stevie to his older brother Ronnie White, a member of the Motown vocal group the Miracles. White was impressed by the youngster's talent and got him an audition with Berry Gordy, Jr., owner of Motown Records. Gordy immediately signed the 11-year-old to a recording contract and renamed him "Little Stevie Wonder."

Wonder's fourth single for Motown, "Fingertips—Part 2" (1963), a live, mostly instrumental, showcase for his talents, shot to number one on the charts as did the album it came from. Over the next two years, he had a handful of modest hits and even appeared in two teen films, *Bikini Beach* and *Muscle Beach Party* (both 1964). Wonder hit his stride in late 1965 with the driving rhythm and blues (R & B) number "Uptight (Everything's Alright)." Through the rest of the 1960s, Stevie Wonder—the "Little" was quickly dropped—scored more than a dozen hit singles in a wide range of styles from folk and message songs ("Blowin' in the Wind," "A Place in the Sun") to hard R & B ("I Was Made to Love Her") to appealing pop ("For Once in My Life," "My Cherie Amour"). Some of these songs were written by

Wonder, who in 1970 produced his first album by himself, *Signed, Sealed, and Delivered.*

In 1970, Wonder married singer Syreeta Wright. The marriage lasted only two years. He renegotiated his contract with Motown in 1971, gaining greater artistic freedom. At the same time he turned 21 and gained control of a $1 million trust fund Gordy had been holding for him. *Music of the Mind* (1972) revealed a new Stevie Wonder whose songs were concerned with social issues and a kind of mystical spirituality. He began using overdubbing on his records, allowing him to play all or most of the instruments by himself. His next album, *Talking Book* (1972), produced the hit "Superstition," Wonder's first number-one song since "Fingertips—Part 2." It was immediately followed by another number-one tune, "You Are the Sunshine of My Life," an upbeat ballad that quickly became a pop standard, recorded by dozens of singers, including Frank Sinatra. Both these songs won Grammy Awards and his next album, *Innervisions* (1973), won the Album of the Year Award. Amid all this success, near-tragedy struck. Wonder was traveling through North Carolina on a tour in August 1973 when the windshield of the car he was a passenger in was shattered by a log that fell off a truck. The log struck Wonder in the forehead, nearly killing him. He took months to recuperate and completely lost his sense of smell.

He came back strong in 1974 with another number-one song, "You Haven't Done Nothin'," with vocal backup by the Jackson 5. At Grammy time, Wonder took home five more awards. His next album, the four-sided *Songs in the Key of Life* (1976), debuted at number one on the charts, a rare feat for any recording artist. In 1982, he teamed up with former Beatle Paul McCartney on McCartney's song "Ebony and Ivory," a call for racial understanding.

Wonder's social concerns were not confined to his music. He lobbied the federal government to make civil rights leader Martin Luther King, Jr.'s birthday a national holiday. He performed at peace concerts, protested nuclear weapons, and wrote the song "Don't Drive Drunk" at the request of Mothers Against Drunk Driving (MADD).

In 1984, Wonder wrote his first film score for the Gene Wilder comedy *The Woman in Red* and produced his sixth number-one song, "I Just Called to Say I Love You." It also won the Academy Award for best original song. The album *In Square Circle* (1985) produced the top-10 hits "Part Time Lover" and "Go Home." Since, then his records have not sold as consistently well as his previous work, although his melodies and production work continues to be appealing. In 2005, Wonder released *A Time to Love*, his first new album in a decade. A single from it, "From the Bottom of My Heart," was a hit on the adult contemporary R & B charts and won him a Grammy for Best Male Pop Vocal Performance. He won his 22nd Grammy in 2006 for a duet of "For Once in My Life" with Tony Bennett. In August 2007, Wonder went on his first concert tour in years, "A Wonder Summer's Night." On January 20, 2009, Wonder performed at the Neighborhood Inaugural Ball for President Barack Obama in Washington, D.C. A month later, President Obama presented him with the Library of Congress's Gershwin Prize for pop music, making Wonder the award's second recipient.

After 45 years in the business, Stevie Wonder remains one of the most loved and respected of all recording artists. He was inducted into the Rock and Roll Hall of Fame in 1989 and received Grammy's Lifetime Achievement Award in 1996.

Further Reading

Davis, Sharon. *Stevie Wonders: Rhythms of Wonder.* London: Anova Books, 2006.

Lodder, Steve. *Stevie Wonder: A Musical Guide to the Classic Albums.* Milwaukee, Wisc.: Backbeat Books, 2008.

Werner, Craig. *Higher Ground: Stevie Wonder, Aretha Franklin, Curtis Mayfield, and the Rise and Fall of American Soul.* New York: Three Rivers Press, 2005.

Williams, Tenley, and James Scott Brady. *Stevie Wonder.* Overcoming Adversity. New York: Chelsea House, 2001 (YA).

Further Listening

Definitive Collection. Universal International, 2 CDs, 2002.

Further Viewing

Live at Last. Motown, DVD, 2009.

Woodard, Alfre

(1953–   ) *actress, social activist*

A gifted actress of unusual beauty, Alfre Woodard has been delivering fine performances on television, screen, and stage for more than 30 years but has only recently received the recognition she deserves.

She was born on November 8, 1953, in Tulsa, Oklahoma, the youngest of three children. She was given her unusual first name by her godmother who claimed to have seen it written in gold letters in a vision. Her father, Marion Woodard, was an interior decorator and her mother, Constance, a homemaker. In high school, she was a track star and cheerleader. She attended Boston University in Massachusetts where she studied acting. Woodard later moved to New York City where she appeared on Broadway in several plays and then headed for Los Angeles, California. She appeared in a production of the black drama *for colored girls who have considered suicide when the rainbow is enuf* and was seen by film director Robert Altman. He cast her in her first film *Remember My Name* (1978), which he produced, and then gave her a part as a hotel manager in *H.E.A.L.T.H.* (1979) a comedy-drama he directed about a health-food convention.

Woodard's breakthrough film was *Criss Cross* (1983), based on the life of Florida writer Marjorie Kinnan Rawlings in which she played Rawlings's servant and friend Geechee. The role earned her an Academy Award nomination for best supporting actress. Despite this honor, Woodard's film work through the 1980s was sparse and offered her few good roles. Like the actress CICELY TYSON,

to whom she is often compared, she found far more opportunities in television. She appeared in the Public Broadcasting Service's (PBS) television adaptation of James Baldwin's novel *Go Tell It on the Mountain* (1984) and won an Emmy Award the same year for outstanding guest performer in a drama series for her work on the police drama *Hill Street Blues.* Woodard was compelling as the mother of a young boy accidentally killed by a police officer when his toy gun is mistaken for a real one. She won a second Emmy as outstanding guest performer in a drama series in the same category on the legal drama series *L.A. Law* for portraying a rape victim who is dying of leukemia. She had a regular role in the medical drama *St. Elsewhere* (1985–87) as obstetrician-gynecologist Dr. Roxanne Tower.

Woodard was South African leader Nelson Mandela's wife Winnie, in the Home Box Office (HBO) television movie *Mandela* (1987), playing opposite her good friend DANNY GLOVER. In another HBO production, *Miss Evers' Boys* (1997), she played a nurse duped in an experiment that denied treatment to young black men with syphilis.

She was reunited with Glover in the film *Grand Canyon* (1991), about a group of diverse people living in Los Angeles. Woodard was excellent as a physical therapist to a soap opera star paralyzed in an auto accident in director John Sayles's *Passion Fish* (1993). In Spike Lee's *Crooklyn* (1994) she was a black mother raising a family in Brooklyn in the 1970s.

Woodard won her fourth Emmy in 2003 as outstanding guest actress in a dramatic series for her performance on an episode of *The Practice* (1997–2003). She played Betty Applewhite during the 2005–06 season of *Desperate Housewives* (2004–   ) and starred opposite Christian Slater on the short-lived crime series *My Own Worst Enemy* (2008).

A well-known political activist, Woodard cofounded with Glover the group Artists for a Free South Africa in 1989. In the 2000 presidential election, she campaigned for Democratic candidate Al Gore. Alfre Woodard lives in Santa Monica, California, with her husband, writer Roderick Spencer, and their two adopted children.

Further Reading

"Alfre Woodard." The Internet Movie Database. Available online. URL: http://www.imdb.com/name/nm0005569/. Downloaded on February 12, 2009.

Bogle, Donald. *Prime Time Blues: African American on Network Television.* New York: Farrar, Straus & Giroux, 2002, pp. 252, 265, 277, 278, 333–334, 351, 357, 440, 458.

Further Viewing

Miss Evers' Boys (1997). HBO Home Video, VHS/DVD, 2001/2002.
Passion Fish (1993). Sony, VHS/DVD, 1998/1999.
The Piano Lesson (1993). Hallmark, DVD, 2002.

Wright, Jeffrey
(1965–) *actor*

A consummate actor who has been likened to a chameleon for his ability to play any kind of part, Jeffrey Wright was a respected stage actor for years before making his mark in film.

He was born on December 7, 1965, in Washington, D.C., and attended private secondary school where he was one of only a handful of blacks. He graduated from Amherst College in Massachusetts in 1987 with a degree in political science. He decided to study film and was accepted into New York University's prestigious film program, then left after only two months to pursue stage acting.

Wright gradually worked his way up from small roles to big ones in such regional theaters as the Arena Stage in Washington and the Yale Repertory Theater in New Haven, Connecticut. His big break came when he played the nurse Belize who attends AIDS patients in the Broadway play *Angels in America* (1994). The play won the Tony Award for best play, and Wright won for best supporting actor in a play.

Although he had previously appeared in two movies, he now made the leap to starring roles. Wright won critical praise for his riveting portrayal of the gifted graffiti artist Jean Michel Basquiat who self-destructs on drugs in the film *Basquiat* (1996). For the next four years, he gave solid performances in a number of little-seen films, including *Critical Care* (1997) and *Ride with the Devil* (1999). His next big role was as the ruthless Dominican drug lord Peoples Hernandez opposite SAMUEL L. JACKSON in the remake of the 1970s blaxploitation classic *Shaft* (2000). The same year, Wright played the Gravedigger in the latest film version of Shakespeare's *Hamlet*.

In his first major television role, Wright was civil rights leader Martin Luther King, Jr., in the Home Box Office film *Boycott* (2001). The movie focused on the 13-month Montgomery, Alabama, bus boycott that first brought King to national attention. "I saw plenty of actors who could get up and do a pretty good impression of Martin," said the film's director Clark Johnson. "But Jeffrey was the one who actually got the essence of him."

In the summer of 2001, Wright returned to the Broadway stage with DON CHEADLE in the two-character Pulitzer Prize–winning play *Top Dog/Underdog*. He played a former con man who impersonated Abraham Lincoln in an arcade shooting booth. Wright, wrote *New York Times* critic Ben Brantley, "gives the kind of multidimensional performance that leaves you dizzy" and goes on to call him "one of the finest American stage actors of his generation."

In 2003, Wright won an Emmy for outstanding supporting actor in a miniseries or movie for the television adaptation of the play *Angels in America*. He was the first African American to play the part of Felix Leiter in an official James Bonds film in *Casino Royal* (2006) and *Quantum of Solace* (2008). Wright portrayed former secretary of state Colin Powell in *W* (2008), Oliver Stone's biopic of

George W. Bush, and bluesman MUDDY WATERS in *Cadillac Red* (2008).

Further Reading

"Jeffrey Wright." The Internet Movie Database. Available online. URL: http://www.imdb.com/name/nm0942482/. Downloaded on February 12, 2009.

Jeffrey Wright Web site. Available online. URL: http://www.jefferywright.20m.com/. Donwloaded on February 12, 2009.

Further Viewing

Angels in America (2003). HBO Home Video, 2 DVDs, 2004.

Basquiat (1996). Miramax Home Entertainment, DVD, 2002.

Boycott (2001). HBO Home Video, VHS/DVD, 2002.

Young, Andre   See DR. DRE.

Bibliography and Recommended Sources

Bekker, Peter O. E., Jr. *The Story of the Blues*. New York: Friedman/Fairfax, 1997.

Bogle, Donald. *Bright Boulevards Bold Dreams: The Story of Black Hollywood*. New York: One World/Ballantine, 2006.

———. *Brown Sugar: Over 100 Years of America's Black Female Superstars*. New York: Continuum, 2007.

———. *Prime Time Blues: African Americans on National Television*. New York: Farrar, Straus & Giroux, 2002.

———. *Toms, Coons, Mulattoes, Mammies & Bucks: An Interpretive History of Blacks in American Films*. New York: Continuum, 2001.

Brackett, Nathan. *(The New) Rolling Stone Album Guide*. New York: Simon & Schuster, 2008.

Cohen-Stratyner, Barbara Naomi. *Biographical Dictionary of Dance*. New York: Schirmer Books, 1982.

Craine, Debra, and Judith Mackrell. *The Oxford Dictionary of Dance*. New York: Oxford University Press USA, 2005.

Green, Stanley. *Encyclopedia of the Musical Theatre*. New York: Da Capo Press, 1980.

Haa, Erikka. *Soul*. New York: Friedman/Fairfax, 1995.

Hager, Andrew G. *Satin Dolls: The Women of Jazz*. New York: Friedman/Fairfax, 1997.

Henke, James, and Holly George-Warren. *The Rolling Stone Illustrated History of Rock & Roll*. New York: Random House, 2008.

Hughes, Langston, and Milton Meltzer. *Black Magic: A Pictorial History of the Negro in American Entertainment*. Englewood Cliffs, N.J.: Prentice Hall, 1968.

Katz, Ephraim, and Ronald Dean Nolen. *The Film Encyclopedia*, 6th ed. New York: HarperCollins, 2008.

Koerner, Julie. *Swing Kings*. New York: Friedman/Fairfax, 1997.

Kranz, Rachel, and Philip J. Koslow. *The Biographical Dictionary of African Americans*. New York: Facts On File, 1999 (YA).

Larkin, Colin. *The Guinness Encyclopedia of Popular Music*. Middlesex, England: Guinness World Records Limited, 1995.

Mapp, Edward. *African Americans and the Oscar: Seven Decade of Struggle and Achievement*. Lanham, Md.: The Scarecrow Press, 2004.

McNeil, Alex. *Total Television*. New York: Penguin Books, 1997.

Robertson, Allen, and Donald Hutera. *The Dance Handbook*. Boston: G. K. Hall, 1990.

Schipper, Henry. *Broken Record: The Inside Story of the Grammy Awards*. New York: Random House, 1994.

Smith, Joe. *Off the Record: An Oral History of Popular Music*. New York: Grand Central Publishing, 1989.

Stambler, Irwin. *The Encyclopedia of Pop, Rock and Soul*. New York: St. Martin's Press, 1989.

Whitburn, Joel. *Top Pop Singles 1955–2000*, 11th ed. Menomonee Falls, Wis.: Record Research, 2008.

Woodstra, Christopher. *All Music Guide Required Listening Series: Classic Rock*. Milwaukee, Wisc.: Backbeat Books, 2007.

BALLET DANCER
Mitchell, Arthur

BLUES SINGER AND MUSICIAN
Handy, W. C.
Hooker, John Lee
Johnson, Robert
King, B. B.
Leadbelly
Smith, Bessie
Terry, Sonny
Washington, Dinah
Waters, Muddy

CLASSICAL MUSICIAN AND CONDUCTOR
Lewis, Henry
Marsalis, Wynton
Watts, André

COMEDIAN
Cambridge, Godfrey
Cosby, Bill
Davis, Sammy, Jr.
Foxx, Jamie
Foxx, Redd
Goldberg, Whoopi
Gregory, Dick
Mabley, Moms
Morgan, Tracy
Murphy, Eddie

Pryor, Richard
Rock, Chris
Smith, Will
Wayons, Damon
Williams, Bert
Wilson, Flip

COUNTRY SINGER
Pride, Charley

FOLK SINGER
Belafonte, Harry
Chapman, Tracy
Havens, Richie
Leadbelly
Odetta
Simone, Nina

GOSPEL SINGER
Cooke, Sam
Green, Al
Jackson, Mahalia
Rawls, Lou
Reese, Della
Warwick, Dionne

FILM ACTOR
Allen, Debbie
Anderson, Eddie "Rochester"
Badur, Erykah
Bailey, Pearl

Baker, Josephine
Bassett, Angela
Belafonte, Harry
Berry, Halle
Blige, Mary J.
Braugher, Andre
Browne, Roscoe Lee
Calloway, Cab
Cambridge, Godfrey
Carroll, Diahann
Carter, Nell
Cheadle, Don
Cole, Nat King
Combs, Sean "Puffy"
Cosby, Bill
Dandridge, Dorothy
Davis, Ossie
Dee, Ruby
Dutton, Charles S.
Fetchit, Stepin
Fishburne, Laurence
Foxx, Jamie
Foxx, Redd
Freeman, Morgan
Glover, Danny
Goldberg, Whoopi
Gooding, Cuba, Jr.
Gossett, Louis, Jr.
Grier, Pam
Havens, Richie
Hayes, Isaac

Haysbert, Dennis
Hemsley, Sherman
Hines, Gregory
Holder, Geoffrey
Horne, Lena
Hudson, Jennifer
Ice Cube
Ice-T
Ingram, Rex
Jackson, Janet
Jackson, Samuel L.
Jones, James Earl
Kitt, Eartha
Knowles, Beyoncé
Lee, Canada
Little Richard
LL Cool J
Mabley, Moms
McDaniel, Hattie
McDonald, Audra
M. C. Hammer
McQueen, Butterfly
Morgan, Tracy
Mr. T
Murphy, Eddie
Nicholas, Fayard
Nicholas, Harold
Odetta
Phifer, Mekhi
Poitier, Sidney
Prince
Pryor, Richard
Queen Latifah
Rashad, Phylicia
Rhames, Ving
Robeson, Paul
Robinson, Bill
Rock, Chris
Ross, Diana
Roundtree, Richard
Scott, Hazel
Shakur, Tupac
Smith, Will
Snipes, Wesley

Snoop Dogg
Turner, Tina
Tyson, Cicely
Underwood, Blair
Usher
Vereen, Ben
Washington, Denzel
Waters, Ethel
Wayans, Damon
Whitaker, Forest
Williams, Billy Dee
Williams, Vanessa
Wilson, Dooley
Winfield, Paul
Woodard, Alfre
Wright, Jeffrey

JAZZ MUSICIAN AND SINGER
Armstrong, Louis
Basie, Count
Calloway, Cab
Cole, Nat King
Coltrane, John
Davis, Miles
Ellington, Duke
Fitzgerald, Ella
Gillespie, Dizzy
Holiday, Billie
Lewis, John
Marsalis, Wynton
McFerrin, Bobby
Mingus, Charles
Monk, Thelonius
Morton, Jelly Roll
Parker, Charlie
Peterson, Oscar
Scott, Hazel
Vaughan, Sarah
Waller, Fats
Washington, Dinah
Waters, Ethel
Webb, Chick
Williams, Mary Lou

MODERN DANCER
Ailey, Alvin
Allen, Debbie
Baker, Josephine
Dunham, Katherine
Holder, Geoffrey
Jamison, Judith
Jones, Bill T.
Primus, Pearl

OPERA AND CONCERT SINGER
Anderson, Marian
Burleigh, Henry T.
Hayes, Roland
McDonald, Audra
Norman, Jessye
Price, Leontyne
Robeson, Paul

POP SINGER
Bailey, Pearl
Carroll, Diahann
Cole, Nat King
Dandridge, Dorothy
Davis, Sammy, Jr.
Fitzgerald, Ella
Guillaume, Robert
Horne, Lena
Kitt, Eartha
Mathis, Johnny
McDonald, Audra
Rashad, Phylicia
Reese, Della
Ross, Diana
Short, Bobby
Uggams, Leslie
Vaughan, Sarah
Washington, Dinah
Williams, Bert

RAGTIME MUSICIAN
Blake, Eubie
Joplin, Scott

RAP SINGER
Combs, Sean "Puffy"
Dr. Dre
Ice Cube
Ice-T
LL Cool J
M. C. Hammer
Queen Latifah
Shakur, Tupac
Smith, Will
Snoop Dogg

ROCK SINGER
Berry, Chuck
Checker, Chubby
Diddley, Bo
Domino, Fats
Hendrix, Jimi
Little Richard
Prince

RHYTHM AND BLUES SINGER
Babyface
Badu, Erykah
Berry, Chuck
Blige, Mary J.
Brandy
Brown, James
Charles, Ray
Cooke, Sam
Diddley, Bo
Domino, Fats
Foxx, Jamie
Franklin, Aretha
Gaye, Marvin
Green, Al
Hayes, Isaac
Houston, Whitney
Hudson, Jennifer
Jackson, Janet
Jackson, Michael
Jean, Wyclef
Jones, Quincy
Jordan, Louis

Knight, Gladys
Knowles, Beyoncé
LaBelle, Patti
Little Richard
Lymon, Frankie
Mayfield, Curtis
Neville, Aaron
Pickett, Wilson
Rawls, Lou
Redding, Otis
Richie, Lionel
Robinson, Smokey
Ross, Diana
Summer, Donna
Turner, Tina
Usher
Warwick, Dionne
White, Barry
Williams, Vanessa
Wilson, Jackie
Wonder, Stevie

STAGE ACTOR
Aldridge, Ira
Allen, Debbie
Bailey, Pearl
Baker, Josephine
Bassett, Angela
Blige, Mary J.
Browne, Roscoe Lee
Calloway, Cab
Carroll, Diahann
Carter, Nell
Cheadle, Don
Combs, Sean "Puffy"
Davis, Ossie
Dee, Ruby
Dutton, Charles S.
Fishburne, Lawrence
Freeman, Morgan
Glover, Danny
Gossett, Louis, Jr.
Guillaume, Robert
Hines, Gregory

Ingram, Rex
Jackson, Samuel L.
Jones, James Earl
Lee, Canada
McDonald, Audra
Nicholas, Fayard
Nicholas, Harold
Poitier, Sidney
Rashad, Phylicia
Rhames, Ving
Robeson, Paul
Robinson, Bill
Rolle, Esther
Tyson, Cicely
Uggams, Leslie
Vereen, Ben
Waters, Ethel
Williams, Bert
Williams, Billy Dee
Williams, Vanessa
Wilson, Dooley
Woodard, Alfre
Wright, Jeffrey

TAP DANCER
Bates, Peg Leg
Glover, Savion
Hines, Gregory
Nicholas, Fayard
Nicholas, Harold
Robinson, Bill

TELEVISION ACTOR AND PERFORMER
Anderson, Eddie Rochester
Bassett, Angela
Blige, Mary J.
Brandy
Braugher, Andre
Browne, Roscoe Lee
Carroll, Diahann
Carter, Nell
Cole, Nat King
Combs, Sean "Puffy"

Cosby, Bill
Davis, Ossie
Dee, Ruby
Dutton, Charles S.
Fisher, Gail
Foxx, Jamie
Foxx, Redd
Guillaume, Robert
Gossett, Louis, Jr.
Haysbert, Dennis
Hemsley, Sherman
Hines, Gregory
Holder, Geoffrey
Hudson, Jennifer
Ingram, Rex
Jones, James Earl

Little Richard
McDonald, Audra
M. C. Hammer
McQueen, Butterfly
Morgan, Tracy
Mr. T
Odetta
Phifer, Mekhi
Poitier, Sidney
Queen Latifah
Rashad, Phylicia
Reese, Della
Rhames, Ving
Rolle, Esther
Roundtree, Richard
Scott, Hazel

Smith, Will
Snoop Dogg
Tyson, Cicely
Uggams, Leslie
Underwood, Blair
Usher
Vereen, Ben
Washington, Denzel
Waters, Ethel
Wayans, Damon
Williams, Billy Dee
Williams, Vanessa
Wilson, Dooley
Wilson, Flip
Woodard, Alfre

1800–1850
Aldridge, Ira

1850–1869
Burleigh, Henry T.
Joplin, Scott

1870–1879
Handy, W. C.
Robinson, Bill
Williams, Bert

1880–1889
Blake, Eubie
Hayes, Roland
Leadbelly

1890–1899
Ellington, Duke
Ingram, Rex
McDaniel, Hattie
Mabley, Moms
Morton, Jelly Roll
Robeson, Paul
Smith, Bessie
Waters, Ethel
Wilson, Dooley

1900–1909
Anderson, Eddie "Rochester"

Anderson, Marian
Armstrong, Louis
Baker, Josephine
Basie, Count
Bates, Peg Leg
Calloway, Cab
Fetchit, Stepin
Jordan, Louis
Lee, Canada
Waller, Fats
Webb, Chick

1910–1919
Bailey, Pearl
Cole, Nat King
Davis, Ossie
Dunham, Katherine
Fitzgerald, Ella
Gillespie, Dizzy
Holiday, Billie
Horne, Lena
Jackson, Mahalia
Johnson, Robert
McQueen, Butterfly
Monk, Thelonius
Nicholas, Fayard
Primus, Pearl
Terry, Sonny
Waters, Muddy
Williams, Mary Lou

1920–1929
Belafonte, Harry
Berry, Chuck
Brown, James
Browne, Roscoe Lee
Coltrane, John
Dandridge, Dorothy
Davis, Miles
Davis, Sammy, Jr.
Dee, Ruby
Diddley, Bo
Domino, Fats
Foxx, Redd
Guillaume, Robert
Hooker, John Lee
King, B. B.
Kitt, Eartha
Lewis, John
Mingus, Charles
Nicholas, Harold
Parker, Charlie
Peterson, Oscar
Poitier, Sidney
Price, Leontyne
Rolle, Esther
Scott, Hazel
Short, Bobby
Vaughan, Sarah
Washington, Dinah

1930–1939
Ailey, Alvin
Cambridge, Godfrey
Carroll, Diahann
Charles, Ray
Cooke, Sam
Cosby, Bill
Fisher, Gail
Freeman, Morgan
Gaye, Marvin
Gossett, Louis, Jr.
Gregory, Dick
Hemsley, Sherman
Holder, Geoffrey
Jones, James Earl
Jones, Quincy
Lewis, Henry
Little Richard
Mathis, Johnny
Mitchell, Arthur
Odetta
Pride, Charley
Rawls, Lou
Reese, Della
Simone, Nina
Turner, Tina
Tyson, Cicely
Williams, Billy Dee
Wilson, Flip
Wilson, Jackie

1940–1949
Carter, Nell
Checker, Chubby
Franklin, Aretha
Glover, Danny
Green, Al
Grier, Pam
Havens, Richie
Hayes, Isaac
Hendrix, Jimi
Hines, Gregory
Jackson, Samuel L.

Jamison, Judith
Knight, Gladys
LaBelle, Patti
Lymon, Frankie
Mayfield, Curtis
Neville, Aaron
Norman, Jessye
Pickett, Wilson
Pryor, Richard
Rashad, Phylicia
Redding, Otis
Richie, Lionel
Robinson, Smokey
Ross, Diana
Roundtree, Richard
Summer, Donna
Uggams, Leslie
Vereen, Ben
Warwick, Dionne
Watts, Andrew
White, Barry
Winfield, Paul

1950–1959
Allen, Debbie
Babyface
Bassett, Angela
Dutton, Charles S.
Goldberg, Whoopi
Haysbert, Dennis
Ice-T
Jackson, Michael
Jones, Bill T.
McFerrin, Bobby
Mr. T
Prince
Rhames, Ving
Washington, Denzel
Wonder, Stevie
Woodard, Alfre

1960–1969
Berry, Halle

Braugher, Andre
Chapman, Tracy
Cheadle, Don
Combs, Sean "Puffy"
Dr. Dre
Fishburne, Laurence
Foxx, Jamie
Gooding, Cuba, Jr.
Houston, Whitney
Ice Cube
Jackson, Janet
LL Cool J
Marsalis, Wynton
M. C. Hammer
Morgan, Tracy
Murphy, Eddie
Rock, Chris
Smith, Will
Snipes, Wesley
Underwood, Blair
Wayons, Damon
Whitaker, Forest
Williams, Vanessa
Wright, Jeffrey

1970–1979
Badu, Erykah
Blige, Mary J.
Brandy
Glover, Savion
Jean, Wyclef
McDonald, Audra
Phifer, Mekhi
Queen Latifah
Shakur, Tupac
Snoop Dogg
Usher

1980–1989
Hudson, Jennifer
Knowles, Beyoncé

Boldface locators indicate main entries. *Italic* locators indicate photographs. For a full list of references, see the main entry for the individual concerned.